Studies in *HISTORICAL ARCHAEOLOGY*

ROY S. DICKENS, JR., (Ed.) *Archaeology of Urban America: The Search for Pattern and Process*

ROBERT PAYNTER *Models of Spatial Inequality: Settlement Patterns in Historical Archeology*

JOAN H. GEISMAR *The Archaeology of Social Disintegration in Skunk Hollow: A Nineteenth-Century Rural Black Community*

KATHLEEN DEAGAN *Spanish St. Augustine: The Archaeology of a Colonial Creole Community*

KENNETH E. LEWIS *The American Frontier: An Archaeological Study of Settlement Pattern and Process*

JOHN SOLOMON OTTO *Cannon's Point Plantation, 1794–1860: Living Conditions and Status Patterns in the Old South*

WILLIAM M. KELSO *Kingsmill Plantations, 1619–1800: Archaeology of Country Life in Colonial Virginia*

THERESA A. SINGLETON *The Archaeology of Slavery and Plantation Life*

In Preparation

SARAH PEABODY TURNBAUGH *Domestic Pottery of the Northeastern United States, 1625–1850*

Contents

Contributors

Numbers in parentheses indicate the pages on which the authors' contributions begin.

WILLIAM H. ADAMS (309), Department of Anthropology, University of Florida, Gainesville, Florida 32611

DOUGLAS ARMSTRONG (261), Museum of Cultural History, University of California at Los Angeles, Los Angeles, California 90024

SHAWN BONATH CARLSON (97), Department of Anthropology, Texas A&M University, College Station, Texas 77843

AMY FRIEDLANDER (215), Louis Berger and Associates, Inc., Washington, D.C. 20036

PATRICK GARROW (239), Garrow & Associates, Inc., Atlanta, Georgia 30341

TYSON GIBBS (163), The Gerontology Center, Meharry Medical College, Nashville, Tennessee 37208

JEROME HANDLER (15), Department of Anthropology, Southern Illinois University at Carbondale, Carbondale, Illinois 62901

STEVEN L. JONES (195), American Civilization Department, University of Pennsylvania, Philadelphia, Pennsylvania 19104

FREDERICK LANGE (15, 97), Museum, University of Colorado, Boulder, Colorado 80309

KENNETH E. LEWIS (35), Department of Anthropology, Michigan State University, East Lansing, Michigan 48824

LYNNE G. LEWIS (121), National Trust for Historic Preservation, Washington, D.C. 20036

SUE M. MOORE (141), Department of Sociology and Anthropology, Georgia Southern College, Statesboro, Georgia 30460

ANNETTE M. NEKOLA (67), Institute of Labor and Industrial Relations, University of Illinois, Champaign, Illinois 61820

CHARLES E. ORSER, JR. (67), Department of Geography and Anthropology, Louisiana State University, Baton Rouge, Louisiana 70803

TED RATHBUN (163), Department of Anthropology, University of South Carolina, Columbia, South Carolina 29208

ELIZABETH REITZ (163), Department of Anthropology, University of Georgia, Athens, Georgia 30602

THERESA A. SINGLETON (1, 291), South Carolina State Museum, Columbia, South Carolina 29211

STEVEN D. SMITH (309), Louisiana Division of Archaeology, Baton Rouge, Louisiana 70804

THOMAS WHEATON (239), Garrow & Associates Inc., Atlanta, Georgia 30341

Preface

The idea of preparing this book developed as I worked on my dissertation on slave archaeology. It became increasingly apparent to me as I did my own work that most of the research which was being done by others on the subject was being published in serials of very limited distribution, seriously inhibiting the disclosure of findings, especially to students and scholars in related fields. What was desperately needed, I realized, was a volume surveying the exciting new research being done throughout the American South and the Caribbean. More important, however, than simply making the literature available, the book should examine the nature and variety of the empirical data derived from this research, synthesize work contributed by investigators of diverse backgrounds and areal specializations, and raise questions for future investigation.

This is the result, the first collection of essays on plantation archaeology. It is intended to guide advanced students and professional archaeologists, but will be of interest to all students of the plantation system who seek to understand the by-products associated with plantation settlement.

Acknowledgments

Every major undertaking is always the product of numerous individuals. This volume is no exception. It has been realized through the efforts of my colleagues whose research is included within it. They are to be congratulated for making it a success. A special thanks goes to each of them for permitting me, a novice to publication, the opportunity to bring together our shared interests, ideas, and goals.

There are several individuals who have contributed to my personal knowledge of plantation systems. Paramount among these is the late Charles H. Fairbanks, who introduced me to plantation archaeology close to 10 years ago. Several specialists in the history of coastal South Carolina and Georgia have been very inspirational, including Peter Wood, George Terry, George Armstrong, Julie Saville, Nan Woodruff, Mary Bullard, and Leland Ferguson.

I am deeply indebted to Lewis Larson, State Archaeologist of Georgia, who is responsible for my involvement in plantation site investigations in Georgia, and to Craig Sheldon and Karl Steinen for inviting me to supervise the excavations at Colonel's Island. I am very grateful to Mark Barnes, Mary Bullard, George Terry, and the advisors of this publication series for Academic Press for their review comments, and to Stanley South for his enthusiasm for this project from the beginning and for his constant encouragement. Acknowledgment is due to Beverly Littlejohn, Darlene Montgomery, Joan McBride, and Sherry LeTempt of the South Carolina State Museum for their assistance in the preparation of the manuscript for publication.

Introduction

Theresa Singleton

New World plantations became the focus of archaeological research with the inception of slave site excavations by Charles H. Fairbanks in the late 1960s. From this preliminary testing, "plantation archaeology" emerged as the investigation of sites located on former plantations. A growing number of professionals and students have been attracted to this special area of interest which has resulted in numerous survey and excavation projects in the American Southeast and Caribbean (see Figure 1.1). Yet, in spite of the enthusiasm for plantation archaeology, the formulation of its objectives, parameters, and research requirements have not been adequately addressed and its accomplishments have not been evaluated. Increased archaeological activity at plantation sites dictate that beginning efforts be directed toward the development of trajectories. It is precisely for this development that this volume has been prepared.

The purpose of this book is to present in one place the substantive results of plantation archaeology in an attempt to offer an incipient research design for future studies. In the following chapters, the special goals, data, methods, models, techniques, and theory necessary for undertaking this research are examined within the broad scope of historical archaeology. Several subjects are considered and preliminary syntheses are offered. This anthology elevates plantation archaeology from its too frequent particularistic orientation to the exploration of trends characteristic of all New World plantation systems.

A fundamental omission apparent in much of the plantation archaeology literature has been the failure to define the plantation as it pertains to archaeological concerns, as distinct from other forms of settlement. Generally, a *plantation* refers to an agricultural enterprise in which a number of workers of a subordinate class work together to produce a crop for someone else to be sold in a market, usually an international one (Degler 1979:11). The origins of New World plantations (the only concern herein) are rooted in slaveholding although indentured labor sometimes preceded it and free labor supplanted it. Plantations are sharply and historically

ISBN 0-12-646480-4

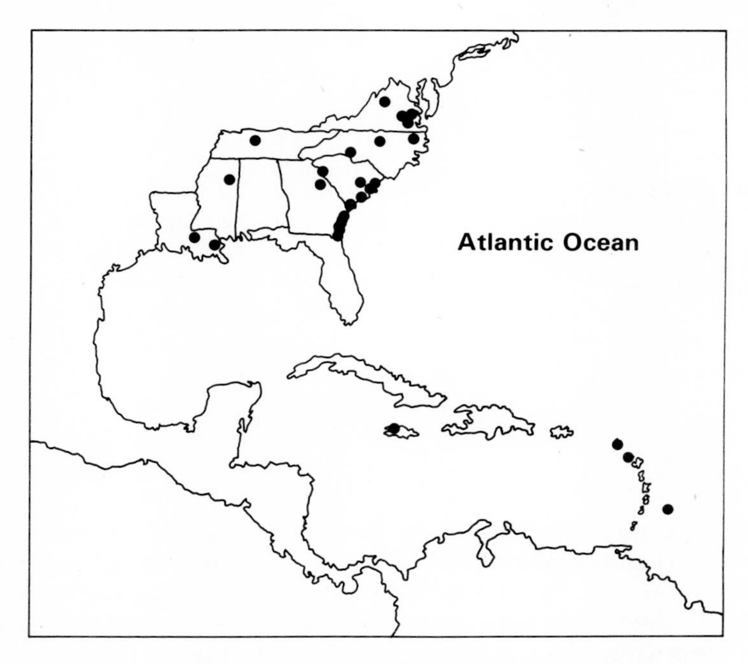

Figure 1.1 Approximate extent of plantation site investigations.

distinguished from farms. A *farm* is a settlement for which a family supplies most of the labor with little help from the outside and where goods are produced for subsistence and domestic consumption (Thompson 1975:18–19). Occasionally, large farms did develop into plantations. This process occurred in portions of the upland South with the rapid spread of the short staple cotton culture during the early nineteenth century. An archaeological example of this overlap between farm and plantation has been reported at the Hermitage in Nashville, Tennessee, by Samuel Smith (1976).

The concept *plantation system* forms the basis of this book because plantations are at "once ecosystems, agricultural systems, economic systems, social and cultural systems, and at times even political systems" (Courtenay 1980:10). A plantation system embraces all the connecting and supporting institutions associated with plantation settlement. Only within this purview is it possible to understand any one aspect of plantation history, culture, or society. The archaeological study of plantation systems seeks to explain plantation history and culture process from behavorial by-products.

Early archaeological investigations of plantations were designed to recover artifact and architectural data associated with plantation structures for the interpretation and preservation of planter lifestyles (Caywood 1955; Ford 1937; Noël Hume 1962, 1966). Interest shifted from planter sites to slaves sites as the outcome of a movement led by historians to direct attention to the history of ordinary or "inarticulate" people who left few records. This emphasis upon social history, spurred by political changes of the 1960s in American society, inspired new approaches to Afro-American history. In plantation history, slavery, the main force behind the plantation system, became the primary focus.

The aim of plantation archaeology today is to understand behavioral patterns within and between the three different groups of plantation residents (owners, managers, and laborers) that are derived from artifacts, food remains, and human skeletal remains. Excavations of slave sites supplies details for the ways in which transplanted Africans adapted to New World situations. The displacement, modification, and survival of an African heritage was the initial goal and remains a major research objective. John Otto's pioneering study (1975) of social class on the plantation through the analysis of planter, overseer, and slave sites placed the archaeological study of slavery within the wholistic framework of plantation social structure. His work not only establish an index for the recognition of status differences frequently employed in other areas of interest within historical archaeology, but it continues to influence all subsequent plantation archaeology.

The essays within this collection address these concerns; however, they reflect several methodological departures from previous efforts. These are evident in interdisciplinary approaches, regional models, innovative applications of analytical techniques, and diachronic perspectives. Together, these themes provide a framework into which each study is woven to form a method tied to anthropological theory for the archaeological study of plantations.

Interdisciplinary approaches are essential to understanding the complex nature of plantation systems. Because of their complexity, plantations are of interest to a wide range of specialists from the social and natural sciences (Courtenay 1980:10). If archaeology is to make a contribution to the broad field of plantation scholarship, archaeologists must be informed of the significant studies pursued in other disciplines and their implications for archaeological problems. Although most of the authors of this volume are archaeologists, the studies from which the following chapters are abstracted either involved the participation of specialists from related disciplines or extensively utilized resources from other fields in the formulation of research strategies and in the interpretation of results. From the authors who are not archaeologists, valuable perspectives are offered that are often absent in archaeological literature but that are vital to archaeological concerns.

The unit of socioeconomic analysis for a plantation system is the *region,* and the single plantation must be viewed within this context. Plantation regions are maximally designated by criteria such as one or more of the following: political and/or cultural entities (Brazil, Jamaica, United States), agricultural belts—areas where the production of a specific cash crop prevails (cotton, rice, sugar, tobacco); and geographic variables (upland, tidewater). Archaeological testing has been undertaken in several former plantation regions (see Figure 1.1). The coastal southeastern United States, particularly in South Carolina and Georgia, has been subjected to the most intensive activity of anthropological archaeology and is therefore emphasized here. Historically, this region is related to the British Caribbean and studies undertaken in

Jamaica and Barbados are included here to provide a rare opportunity for systematic cross-regional analysis.

The earliest settlers in South Carolina were planters and slaves from Barbados and other English colonies of the Caribbean. Historians have long considered the coastal strip from Charleston, South Carolina, to the St. Johns River in northern Florida to be the northernmost extension of the West Indies (Phillips 1907). More recently, the structural similarities linking these plantation societies have been identified in terms of wealth, land ownership, patterns of racial demography, and intensive use of labor (Dunn 1976; Julie Saville, personal communication, 1982; Wood 1974). Comparison of archaeological manifestations reveal several striking relationships. Notable among them is the similar position occupied by ceramics, presumably made by slaves, and used in slave households in coastal South Carolina and Jamaica (see Chapters 11 and 12). Although the wares differ in the two places, both apparently suggest an African or an Afro-American heritage.

Perhaps no one thing has revolutionized historic site archaeology more than the analytical techniques proposed by Stanley South (1977). In every archaeological case study presented here, some aspect of these techniques are employed. At times, modifications to South's original formulas are proposed that appear to be more relevant to plantation studies. Of paramount importance is artifact pattern recognition, a procedure in which artifacts are quantified into functional categories (kitchen, architecture, furniture, arms, clothing, personal, tobacco, activities). Its application here goes beyond the mere academic exercise of ordering descriptive data. Rather every case reveals behavioral patterns in which social class, site function, cultural change, and temporal and regional distinctions are delineated.

Archaeologists have traditionally studied diachronic processes; however, synchronic processes have been overemphasized in plantation archaeology. While synchronic studies are important and several are included here, this focus alone ignores the dramatic changes the plantation regime underwent from its colonial inception with forced labor to its more recent reconstitution with free labor at the end of the nineteenth century. Unfortunately, it is often difficult to document culture change at historic sites because of the inherent problems of isolating closely dated proveniences of a few years. This is particularly true at nineteenth-century sites where the characteristics of certain artifacts remained unchanged throughout that century. Despite the archaeological bias favoring synchronic interpretation, several studies here consider two processes of culture change: slave acculturation and the transformation from slavery to free labor.

The following 13 chapters reflect the current state of the art in plantation archaeology. They are subdivided into six parts entitled Research Strategies, Settlement, Artifact Patterns, Foodways, Afro-American Traditions, and Transformation. In the remainder of this essay, each chapter is discussed as it relates to the previously stated objectives.

Part I: Research Strategies. The development of research strategies for plantation archaeology is still in the formative stages. This introductory chapter reviews current approaches to the archaeological study of plantations, evaluates the findings, and offers directions for the future.

The formulation of a research design for the study of plantation slavery is the subject of Frederick Lange and Jerome Handler's essay (Chapter 2). In historic site archaeology, research designs must rely upon some aspect of written, oral, or ethnographic resources. Written records are most frequently used in plantation archaeology. These documents, though vital to the identification and interpretation of sites, often yield little specific information for artifact analysis. Archaeology on the other hand can only address a limited set of questions concerning past lifeways. Lange and Handler discuss the problems presented by both data sets in the study of slavery. They examine several categories of archaeological patterns indicative of slavery: settlement, region, site, intrasite, subsistence, material cutlure, and mortuary practices. They offer a research strategy that integrates archaeology and history and that can be compared with cultural patterns derived for other sites and regions.

Part II: Settlement. The study of settlement patterns has played a vital role in the interpretation of prehistoric archaeology for over 30 years. Its application to problems in historical archaeology is steadily increasing, and a recent model proposed for discerning social stratification at historical settlements offers implications for prehistory (Paynter 1982). In these essays, the relationship between the physical structure of a plantation and its economic purpose and social order are explored.

Kenneth Lewis (Chapter 3) presents a model capable of discerning plantation composition, layout, and organization from archaeological resources. Two eighteenth-century rice plantations in coastal South Carolina were investigated using a sample derived from a stratified, systematic unaligned sampling technique. Analysis revealed structural layouts and artifact patternings of several categories (domestic, specialized, high status, low status) observed through a Synagraphic Computer Mapping Program (SYMAP) capable of graphically depicting quantitative and qualitative variables. Results not only confirmed conclusions drawn from documentary sources but also supplied additional information on the form and composition of plantation settlement. Lewis's study demonstrates the ability of archaeology to recognize the relationship between plantation function in the colonial world enconomy and its organization on the basis of material culture.

In contrast to K. Lewis's synchronic emphasis upon colonial settlement in the South Carolina tidewater, Charles Orser and Annette Nekola (Chapter 4) examine settlement dyanmics at the Millwood Plantation located in the South Carolina piedmont. They designate three periods of spatial organization for the use of archaeological, historical, and oral data: the nucleated settlement of the antebellum period (1832–1865) characterized by linearly arranged slave dwellings located near the houses of the planter and overseer and surrounded by agricultural fields; a somewhat elusive configuration of hamlet communities associated with the squad labor system of the immediate postwar period (1865–1875); and the fragmented settlement of the postbellum era (1875–1930) in which tenant farmers established their own plots on rented lands. To better understand the distribution of these house sites,

17 variables were selected for further study and subjected to statistical tests. Although their findings generally supported models proposed by historical geographers for settlement dynamics in the plantation South, they were able to add refinements to these models based upon their Millwood data.

Part III: Artifact Patterns. In these chapters, analytical techniques are applied specifically to evaluate intrasite and intersite patterns in which status differences, site function, temporal distinctions, and regional models are considered.

Frederick Lange and Shawn Carlson (Chapter 5) identify significant parallels in the ceramic assemblages of Barbados and those of the southeastern United States. Limited to only horizontal distribution of artifacts, they establish chronological control over their collection through the application of an adapted version of the Mean Ceramic Date formula (MCD) that appears to be more appropriate for the Caribbean. Chi-square tests are used to determine similarities and differences between and among six Barbadian plantations. Test results coincide with historical documentation in which slave sites and special use sites (mills, hospitals, agricultural fields) are distinguished. Artifact changes from pre- to postemancipation are also indicated.

Lynne Lewis (Chapter 6) addresses the questions: Is socioeconomic status reflected in the archaeological record. What artifact classes, functional groups, or types best indicate status differences? Focusing upon the planter class, she applies Otto's criteria (1975) for the recognition of social class to evaluate data recovered from Drayton Hall, the plantation of a very wealthy South Carolina family occupied continuously by them from 1743 to 1860. Drayton Hall is then compared to other planter sites nearby—Middleton Place and Hampton Plantation both in South Carolina (see Chapter 3) and Cannon's Point (Otto 1975) in Georgia. These planter assemblages are contrasted with those of three slave/low-status sites: Yaughan and Curriboo (see Chapter 11) and Spiers Landing (Drucker 1981).

L. Lewis's analysis suggests that artifact classes and types provide only subtle differences in the recognition of social class. A more fruitful approach is found in the examination of specific attributes within each artifact class or the variety of types and forms rather than the mere presence or absence of a particular type or class of artifacts. Functional groups, on the other hand, appear to indicate social class, particularly in the frequency of architecture group artifacts. Significantly higher percentages of architectural artifacts were recovered at the planter sites than at slave sites. This finding is interpreted to have been the result of extensive repairs, alterations, and rehabilitation to large, substantial dwellings which would naturally produce more architectural debris.

Sue Moore (Chapter 7) also examines plantation social structure, but she considers an additional dimension absent in previous discussions—the economic position of the planter determined by the size of his slaveholdings. Several nineteenth-century plantations located primarily on St. Simons Island, Georgia, are ranked into three categories according to the number of slaves: more than 100 slaves, 20–100 slaves, fewer than 20 slaves. Functional artifact categories provide the analytical tools for delineating social class and economic status. Significant differences in the material lives of plantation occupants are seen between those who lived on large plantations and these who lived on small plantations. For example, the assemblage of an overseer at a large plantation is found to be quite similar to that of a small planter. From analogous observations Moore concludes that the wealth of the planter affected the nature of material conditions for all plantation residents.

Working with different sets of data primarily within the confines of state boundaries, L. Lewis and Moore identify totally opposite relationships between architecture and kitchen group artifacts. In South Carolina, L. Lewis finds high percentages of architecture group artifacts and low percentages of kitchen group artifacts at planter sites, and low percentages of architecture and high percentages of kitchen artifacts at slave sites. Conversely, Moore finds Georgian plantations to be characterized by low percentages of architecture and high percentages of kitchen artifacts at planter sites, and slaves sites by very high percentages of architecture and low percentages of kitchen group artifacts. I have suggested that dwellings are the major material aspect of slavery viewed from archaeological resources (Singleton 1980: 217). This interpretation, based upon the study of late antebellum slave sites in coastal Georgia, has historical support. The greater availability of machine-manufactured building hardware and improvements in the construction and size of slave housing (Genovese 1974:525) are conditions of the nineteenth century that should result in higher frequencies of architectural artifacts at nineteenth-century slave sites than those of an earlier period. While the differences between the Georgian and South Carolinian slave and planter assemblages need to be systematically studied, this temporal distinction in slave housing does provide a tentative clue. All the South Carolinian sites used in these comparisons have a major eighteenth-century component, while most of the Georgian sites date from the mid-nineteenth-century. A recent excavation of a late antebellum slave occupation in South Carolina with a possible freedmen component produced an artifact profile quite similar to the sites in Georgia (Zierden and Calhoun 1983:32, 36). These studies of slavery and plantation social structure demonstrate that artifact pattern recognition is indeed a very useful tool in discerning social class, temporal differences, and regional patterns.

Part IV: Foodways. Slave diet and nutrition is a very controversial topic among students of slavery. A few scholars maintain that slave diet was nutritious and suggest that caloric intakes often exceeded modern recommended levels of chief nutrients (Fogel and Engerman 1974:109–115). The more accepted view is that slave diet was inadequate and malnutrition was a frequent problem evinced in high child mortality (Kiple and Kiple 1977) and in prevalence of diseases resulting from nutritional deficiencies (Sutch 1976). Archaeologists attracted to this problem have been successful in documenting some portions of slave diet from food remains, subsistence gear, and human skeletal remains.

Elizabeth Reitz, a zooarchaeologist, Tyson Gibbs, a medical anthropologist, and Ted Rathbun, a physical anthropologist (Chapter 8) combine their varied approaches in a thorough evaluation of the data, techniques, and interpretation derived from the archaeological resources of plantation foodways. Emphasizing zooarchaeological resources, they examine data from 19 coastal and interior plantations in which the technique Minimum Number of Individuals (MNI) is used for the purpose of quantification. Although MNI does not provide information for the relative percentage a good resource contributes to slave diet, it does indicate an approximate number of a particular species consumed at the site. Evidence of exploitation of nondomestic foodstuffs is indicated to some extent at all sites, particularly at coastal sites where slaves could possibly forage during the spare time available through the task labor system. This labor system—used throughout the lower Southeast in the production of tidewater staples—was a vital element in the development of slavery and perhaps in postbellum labor reorganizations (see Chapter 13). The presence of nondomestic food confirms their thesis that slave diet was only made nutritious through the slaves' efforts to supplement plantation rations. Additionally, the potential contribution of human skeletal remains to the study of plantation life in terms of health, disease, and nutritional adequacy is discussed.

Part V: Afro-American Traditions. The anthropological study of Afro-American life initiated under the pioneering efforts of Melville Herskovits (1958) attempted to isolate cultural forms and patterns that were directly traced to African origins from those presumably developed in the New World. He referred to the retention of African forms as "Africanisms" and to those that resulted from amalgamations of one cultural tradition with another as "syncretisms." Slave archaeology has sought to identify artifact patterns suggestive of an African heritage. After more than 10 years of slave site investigations, however, only a few suggestions of an African past have been uncovered. Moreover, it appears that the archaeological record tends to preserve the assimilative quality of Afro-American life, that is, the use of Euro-American artifacts. Such artifacts are more often made from durable materials (clay, glass, metal) than the perishable materials (plant and animal fiber, hide, wood) commonly used to fashion African-styled objects. In spite of this archaeological problem, these studies demonstrate that material culture unique to the African presence in the New World is "visible" within the archaeological record.

Steven Jones (Chapter 9), a student of vernacular architecture, employs an interdisciplinary approach to investigate "above-ground" manifestations of Afro-American architectural traditions. He identifies African elements in the plans, spatial distribution, building materials, and design found in a variety of contexts: slave, free, rural, urban. From his own fieldwork in Africa, Jones is able to point to specific African proveniences for many New World forms while his careful use of archaeological, folkloristic, and documentary resources provides tentative answers to how and when these architectural traditions emerged.

Amy Friedlander (Chapter 10) and Thomas Wheaton and Patrick Garrow (Chapter 11) collectively present a model that documents slave acculturation at two eighteenth-century plantations (Yaughan and Curriboo) in the South Carolina tidewater. Friedlander's study establishes the historical basis for the underlying archaeological assumption that the slave community that produced African-influenced artifacts (colonowares and architectural patterns) was culturally stable. In other words, changes in the artifacts over time was the consequence of culture change within the same community, not the infusion of new slaves into the population. She traces the structure of the black population at the two plantations from 1740 to 1820 through the careful use of census, probate, and provisioning records. The development of the slave community at Yaughan and Curriboo is consistent with trends found in adjacent plantations and parishes.

During the colonial period, an extremely high ratio of blacks to whites fostered demographic conditions conducive to black autonomy and the perpetuation of African customs. This pattern was further reinforced by inheritance and sale practices that minimized the dislocation of slaves. By the end of the eighteenth century, however, the demography of the region changed with a decrease in the ratio of blacks to whites. Thus, the isolation from the white community that slaves previously experienced began to dissipate, which ushered in a period of accelerated acculturation.

Wheaton and Garrow examine the archaeological correlates from this process of culture change with data derived from three separate slave quarters. Several shifts in the artifact assemblages dating from the mid-eighteenth to the early nineteenth century are suggested to be indicators of acculturation: African-styled mud-wall huts are replaced by European-styled framed dwellings; the frequency of colonoware decreases; proportions of kitchen group to architecture group artifacts take on a more Euro-American appearance; subsistence changes from a vegetal-based diet to one with increased amounts of animal protein.

Douglas Armstrong (Chapter 12) searches for material evidence of the African past in Jamaica through an examination of archaeological resources at the Drax Hall plantation. The cultural dynamics of Afro-Jamaican society are investigated from features that correspond to three periods in the historical development of this cultural system: slavery, the transition from slavery to freedom, and free labor. Through hypothesis testing in which artifact pattern recognition and functional analysis of ceramic vessel shapes are employed, he finds that Afro-American society to be characterized by elements of *continuity* within a system of *change*. African continuity is implied in the presence of locally manufactured Afro-Jamaican wares reminiscent of West African potting techniques and communal foodways. These wares occur throughout the three periods and increase with emancipation. Change is evident within the broad scope of ceramic usage reflective of European patterns in North America that are partially related to worldwide patterns of ceramic availability. Armstrong also discusses analogies in artifact group proportions with those of South Carolina.

Part VI: Transformation. Some plantation systems survived the demise of slavery. In many places, they were reconstituted with laborers that were often "bound by repressive contracts and miserably paid" (Mintz 1974:66, 133). Consequently, the material lives of free plantation laborers was similar to, if not worse than, those of slaves. These chapters consider lifeways associated with this transformation.

In Chapter 13, I review archaeological evidence recovered from a site reflective of the transitional period (1865–1880) from slavery to free labor at Colonel's Island, Georgia. During and immediately after the Civil War, the coastal region from Charleston, South Carolina, to Jacksonville, Florida, became a haven for recently emancipated slaves who frequently settled at former slave villages. The Colonel's Island site appears to represent this form of settlement. References to ex-slave occupation at the site are suggested from historical records; however, the basis for the archaeological interpretation was derived from an 1867 construction date for one of the excavated structures, the makeshift and temporary quality of the occupation, and from qualitative and quantitative artifact differences between this site and the established slave artifact pattern for the area. Colonel's Island not only provided discernible features of the immediate postwar period but also implications for the material effects of emancipation upon former bondsmen.

William Adams and Steven Smith (Chapter 14) examine black tenant farmer material culture through an innovative use of archival and archaeological data. Functional categories of purchased household items are inferred from a general store ledger and are compared against archaeological artifact categories. The result is an interpretation of material life that surpasses one obtained solely from archaeology because it embraces items that actually entered the tenant farmer cultural system as well as those preserved in residue. The ledger categories also supply information for the discussion of a differential pricing structure, the comparison of purchases made by tenants, landowners, and storekeepers, and the effects of seasonality upon purchases. The combined insights gained from both forms of data permit the authors to conclude that tenant farmers had little and therefore left little in the archaeological record.

The essays that follow illustrate that there is indeed a place for archaeology in the multidisciplinary study of plantation systems. At present, this role is limited to a specific range of questions concerning the ways in which plantation residents lived, the relationships of these living conditions to other places, and how these changed through time. These few words summarize the orientation of this volume and provide the basis for a paradigm of plantation archaeology.

Readers may find that many questions are raised but few are answered. They are reminded that this anthology serves only as the first step toward the development of a research design for plantation archaeology. Hopefully, it will generate discussion and inspire new avenues to broaden the scope of what promises to be an exciting and challenging area of research.

REFERENCES

Caywood, Louis R.
1955 *Green Spring Plantation: Archaeological Report.* Yorktown, Virginia: Colonial National Historical Park.

Courtenay, P. P.
1980 *Plantation Agriculture.* Revised edition. London: Bell E. Hyman.

Degler, Carl
1979 Plantation society: old and new perspective on hemisphere society. *Plantation Society in the Americas* 1 (February):9–14.

Drucker, Leslie M.
1981 Socio-economic patterning at an undocumented late 18th century low country site: Spiers Landing, South Carolina. *Historical Archaeology* 12(2):58–69.

Dunn, Richard
1976 The English Islands and the founding of South Carolina. In *Shaping Southern Society: The Colonial Experience.* T. H. Breen, ed. New York: Oxford University Press. Pp. 48–58.

Fogel, Robert W. and Stanley L. Engerman
1974 *Time on the Cross: The Economics of American Negro Slavery, Vol. I.* Boston: Little, Brown, and Company.

Ford, James A.
1937 An archaeological report on the Elizafield ruins. In *Georgia's Disputed Ruins.* E. Merton Coulter, ed. Chapel Hill: University of North Carolina Press. Pp. 193–205.

Genovese, Eugene
1974 *Roll Jordan Roll: The World the Slave Made.* New York:Pantheon Books.

Herskovits, Melville
1958 *The Myth of the Negro Past.* Boston: Beacon Press.

Kiple, Kenneth F., and Virginia H. Kiple
1977 Slave child mortality: some nutritional answers to a perennial puzzle. *Journal of Social History* 10:294–309.

Mintz, Sidney
1974 *Caribbean Transformations.* Chicago: Aldine.

Noël Hume, Ivor
1962 Excavations at Rosewell in Gloucester County, Virginia, 1957–1958. *United States National Museum Bulletin 225, Contributions from the Museum of History and Technology, Paper 18.* Washington, D.C.: Smithsonian Institution.
1966 Excavations at Tutter's Neck in James City County, Virginia, 1960–1961. *United States National Museum Bulletin 249, Contributions from the Museum of History and Technology, Paper 53.* Washington, D.C.: Smithsonian Institution.

Otto, John
1975 Status differences and the archaeological record—a comparison of planter, overseer, and slave sites from Cannon's Point Plantation (1794–1861), St. Simons Island, Georgia. Ph.D. dissertation, Department of Anthropology, University of Florida, Gainesville.

Paynter, Michael
1982 *Models of Spatial Inequality: Settlement Patterns in Historical Archaeology.* New York: Academic Press.

Phillips, Ulrich B.
1907 The slave labor problem in the Charleston district. *Political Science Quarterly* 22 (September):416–439.

Singleton, Theresa A.
1980 The archaeology of Afro-American slavery in coastal Georgia: a regional perception of slave household and community patterns. Ph.D. dissertation, Department of Anthropology, University of Florida, Gainesville.

Smith, Samuel, ed.
1976 An archaeological and historical assessment of the first Hermitage. Research Series 2, Division of Archaeology, Tennessee Department of Conservation.

South, Stanley
1977 *Method and Theory in Historical Archaeology.* New York: Academic Press.

Sutch, Richard
1976 The care and feeding of slaves. In *Reckoning with Slavery: A Critical Study in the Quanitative History of American Negro Slavery.* Paul A. David, ed. New York: Oxford University Press. Pp. 231–301.

Thompson, Edgar T.
1975 *Plantation Societies, Race Relations, and the South: The Regimentation of Populations*. Durham, N.C.: Duke University.

Wood, Peter
1974 *Black Majority: Negroes in Colonial South Carolina from 1670 through the Stono Rebellion*. New York: W. W. Norton.

Zierden, Martha, and Jean Calhoun
1983 *An archaeological assessment of the Greenfield Borrow Pit, Georgetown Country*. Charleston, S.C.: The Charleston Museum.

PART I

Research Strategies

2

The Ethnohistorical Approach to Slavery

Frederick W. Lange

Jerome S. Handler

INTRODUCTION

The concept of plantation slavery as used in this chapter is limited to the form of social control and economic exploitation of non-European workers characteristic of the British Caribbean and American South during the seventeenth to nineteenth centuries. The development and longevity of plantation slavery differed in the British Caribbean and the American South, but the common origins of the slave populations, patterns of development, and communality of material culture are sufficient to allow comparative analyses. The ideas expressed here draw heavily from our research in Barbados (Handler and Lange 1978), as well as other studies of plantation contexts in the British Caribbean and North America (e.g., Armstrong 1982; Drucker 1979; Fairbanks 1974; Lees 1980; Mathewson 1973; Otto 1975; Pulsipher and Goodwin 1982; Singleton 1980).

Prior to 1970, historical documents generated most of our data regarding slavery and in our previous reports on the Barbados research (Handler 1972; Handler and Lange 1978, 1979; Lange 1972), we concluded that slavery cannot be identified through archaeological efforts alone. We reiterate this premise about the "archaeology of slavery" at the outset. Within the ethnohistoric approach we review how research during the past decade has demonstrated the potential for the study of

ISBN 0-12-646480-4

slavery and how the archaeology of known slave sites has begun to produce patterns that may also be applied to sites with less or no documentation. Fairbanks (1984) and Orser (1984) have presented similar summaries focusing on southeastern North American data.

Following the ethnohistoric approach advocated by Baerreis (1961), the Barbados research combined documentary and archaeological data and demonstrated that relative social/economic status or rank can be defined archaeologically, but that at the present time legal or imposed status cannot. This position has been corroborated by reports of a lack of clearly defined separation between slave and overseer remains (cf. Otto 1977). Lewis and Haskell stated (1980:2, our emphasis) "despite cultural differences which *should* be evident in the archaeological record, the living standards of white overseers were not much above those of their African charges," and this view has been echoed by Fairbanks (1984:11). Status can change quickly and definitively, as with emancipation in 1834–1838 (in the British Empire), with no directly correlated changes in archaeological patterns or remains.

The combination of archaeological and documentary data continues to provide the most fruitful approach to the study of slavery. On Barbados, the documentary resources usually yield locational, descriptive, and economic data about the institution of slavery from the viewpoint of Europeans and their New World descendants, but little about the actual daily lives of the slaves. While continuing to rely on documentary sources for locational data, the archaeological approach provides a chance to examine cultural remains left by the slaves themselves, and sometimes their skeletal remains. Archaeology also provides some level of verification or amplification of the white-produced documentary sources. The most important step is to introduce a feedback or interplay relationship between the archaeology and the documentation, but in the final analysis only documentation can irrefutably establish the presence of slavery.

Archaeology provides details on slave life in particular locations: settlement pattern, material culture, and subsistence and nutritional data have been most frequently recovered. Excavated data form patterns which, in sufficient repetition, can suggest a high probability of slave status in nondocumented situations (cf. Drucker 1979). The accumulation of data upon which such patterns can be established, and the increasingly numerous situations in which archaeological and documentary data can be compared mark the principal progress in the archaeology of plantation slavery in the past decade. Otto (1977:91–92) has remarked on the method usually employed: to short-cut the pattern development process by excavating at the site of documented slave activity. The clear implication is that archaeological patterns resulting from slave behavior are not sufficiently well defined to be used independently. Excavations in such settings have also indicated a confusion of patterns in which there is an overlap between planter, white overseer, black slave overseer, free white, free black, and Amerindian archaeological patterns. Further refinement of these patterns is clearly dependent upon increased interplay between documentary and archaeological resources.

Cross-Evaluating Documentary and Archaeological Data

In historic sites archaeology we utilize three categories of data: (1) material culture objects described in documents, but not found archaeologically; (2) material culture (and patterns) found archaeologically, but not mentioned in documents; and (3) material culture and patterns found archaeologically and mentioned in documents. For interpretive purposes, we consider category 3 to be of the most utility, category 2 to be of somewhat less utility, and category 1 to be of questionable utility. This hierarchy of data utility is applied to some of the examples incorporated in this chapter.

THE IDENTIFICATION OF ARCHAEOLOGICAL PATTERNS INDICATING SLAVERY

Settlement Patterns

Sites of plantation slavery have particular spatial distributions and patterns of organization, as do other archaeological sites. However, they represent a forced pattern in which the slaves had only very limited options, if any. Thus, some of the ecological/locational interaction seen in other settlement pattern studies (such as location near the most reliable water sources or intersections of transportation routes) is not necessarily present in slave sites. We also find that plantation settlement patterns changed rapidly in postemancipation times. Price (1982) has recently confirmed the importance of settlement research in cultural–economic interpretations. The three-tiered hierarchy of regional, local, and microsite study outlined by Trigger (1967) and Parsons (1972) for prehistoric sites also seems appropriate for studies of plantation slavery.

Regional Patterns

Broad patterns of plantation slavery existed on regional, island, or statewide bases relative to political, geographical, and environmental limitations. Plantations generally occupied extensive areas of relatively level ground although, as Pulsipher and Goodwin (1982) described for the Galways Plantation location on Montserrat, they also can be found on rough, uneven terrain. However, the location of Galways appears to have reflected conflicts between the local Irish and English populations, rather than free choice of settlement. In the American South there seems to have been little difference in general patterns regardless of whether the plantations were dedicated to rice, sugar, or cotton.

No archaeological attempts at an intensive regional approach similar to that advocated by Struever (1971) in prehistoric archaeology have been applied to problems of plantation slavery, although much of the documentary research on slavery has been at this level. Some regional archaeological syntheses based on accumulated data have been attempted (Gibbs *et al.* 1980; Singleton 1980). Fairbanks [1984:6–7] has contrasted the nature of wet rice and cotton cultivation; the two systems of cultivation required utilization of different niches in the coastal environment. Such differences in the plantation system were not present on Barbados. In this sense there is an imperfect fit between the available literature on plantation slavery and the archaeology.

Local Site Patterns

On the individual plantation level, studies have begun to deal with the spatial organization of plantations and the variables imposed by considerations of size and location. Most studies have dealt with the location of slave work and living areas relative to the main house and the industrial areas of the plantation. Approaches have varied from the analysis of the entire plantation to investigating only those parts to be impacted by some construction project. In most of these cases, documentary investigations of the plantation as a whole have been more thorough than the limited archaeological investigations.

The Plantation Pattern. Based on both British Caribbean (Handler and Lange 1978:46; Pulsipher and Goodwin 1982:38) and North American data (K. Lewis 1979:64), a general pattern seems to have emerged that places the main house in a central location to the industrial complex and the slave village in a peripheral but proxemic position to the main complex. A major variable in local settlement pattern seems to have been whether the slaves built their own housing from materials either provided by the plantation or scavenged from the natural settings, or lived in houses built and maintained by the plantation. The former seems to have been more common in the British Caribbean, especially in the earlier periods of slavery, and the latter in North America, and this may affect quality and permanancy of construction and hence the archaeologist's ability to locate domestic remains (Handler and Lange 1978:51–54).

In Barbados a significant shift in settlement pattern occurred after emancipation when the former slaves were moved to villages on the peripheries of plantation lands at some distance from the central complex. L. Lewis (1978:36) described a similar shift for ante- and postbellum settlement patterns on Hampton Plantation in South Carolina. Fairbanks (1984:11) has pointed out the need for additional research on immediately postbellum sites and patterns.

Micropatterns

On individual plantations detailed investigations of living or activity areas provide in depth information on patterns of living and adaptation. Colonoware (Ferguson 1980), which is only very superficially described in the documents, is the artifact most often utilized as a means of distinguishing between planter and slave remains.

However, as Lees (1980:136) pointed out, much better distributional data are required before this assumption about colonoware can be generally applied.

Planter Remains. Studies at the Drayton Hall (L. Lewis 1978:62–65, 178), Cannon's Point (Otto 1977), and Limerick plantations (Lees 1980:135) have shown that in addition to ceramic wares associated only with the planter class, the planter class contexts (main houses, kitchens, and refuse) also show the presence of colonoware and other data generally thought to have been associated with the lower classes.

Slave Remains. Studies such as Ascher and Fairbanks (1971), Fairbanks (1974), McFarlane (1975), Kelso (1976), Otto (1975, 1977), and Singleton (1980) are examples of the microlevel of research and have focused on slave cabins or refuse deposit areas. Among the more interesting results of these researches have been the consistent finding of firearms and writing materials (both of which were generally considered to be against the law) and a richer amount of material culture than anticipated; surprisingly, however, no derivatives from African material culture have been found. Again, once documents established slave locations, numerous artifacts and patterns were revealed that complemented the historical data. In the Barbados research in particular, a Ghanaian (Gold Coast) pipe and metal bracelets suggest imported indications of the African heritage. However, this heritage does not seem to have been reflected in locally adapted patterns and traditions.

Subsistence Patterns

At both the regional and microlevels, subsistence patterns reflecting the means by which slaves were able to obtain, process, and distribute foodstuffs are also of importance. Documentary sources have described, and archaeological research is beginning to confirm, a wide variety of practices. Of general importance are questions of whether or not sufficient foodstuffs were grown by the plantation or whether imports were necessary, as well as questions concerning basic patterns of food storage, preparation, distribution, and consumption. Artifacts have yielded some subsistence information such as processing tools and storage vessels, while other data have been derived from faunal and floral remains and from analysis of slave skeletal remains.

Food production was a critical factor for most plantations. Any foods that were not grown locally had to be imported and represented significant economic outlays to the plantation management. In the American South, where transportation networks were more widespread, this presented less of a problem. In island settings such as Barbados, however, the increased cost of transportation and uncertainty as to arrival of supplies made provisions a much more critical issue. Natural factors were also significant on Barbados and in the Southeast; for example, hurricanes, droughts, and insects destroyed crops and either necessitated increased levels of food imports or caused starvation. Fluctuations in plantation agricultural production also affected the slave diet.

In many areas a good deal of the slaves' diet was provided from rations distributed by the plantation. Where most food was supplied by the plantation the storage facilities would have been at the institutional rather than the consuming level. To the extent that storage and cooking facilities are two of the most commonly identified features on domestic sites, their presence or absence is critical to archaeological interpretation. Other foodstuffs that slaves grew or obtained for themselves through gardening, hunting, fishing, and collecting were most likely consumed almost immediately and not stored. Establishing plantation control over the distribution of basic foodstuffs would have been a very effective means of social control. To this extent, slave patterning would not always reflect more traditional or normal domestic patterns of kitchen, storage, and eating areas. Fairbank's summary (1984) of southeastern United States data suggests most cooking in this area was done by domestic units and not communally.

Within activity areas specific artifacts will also provide insights into subsistence activities. There are documentary references to milling stones having been utilized in Barbados, but none were found during fieldwork (Handler and Lange 1978:54, 73). This is an example of document-based material culture whose archaeological presence, and therefore interpretive validity, has yet to be demonstrated.

Vessel form is very closely related to function and the styles and the variety of vessels present also indicate subsistence activities. South (1972:79) advanced the idea that shapes rather than types might be "more sensitive indicator(s) of function and possible socioeconomic level." At Hampton, Lewis and Haskell (1980:77) observed that colono bowls outnumbered definite serving vessels and noted that Otto (1977:98) and Booth (1971:33) both consider that slaves principally ate from bowls. In another setting, Lees (1980:137) observed that the remains of colonoware were so fragmentary that vessel forms could not be reconstructed. In general, the absence or low frequency of storage jars in domestic areas would tend to reinforce interpretations of centralized distributions and consumptions, while their frequent occurrence would support interpretations of household activities.

Increasing attention is also being paid to faunal remains from plantation sites, not only because they can help reconstruct subsistence patterns, but also because they may indicate social status and food distribution patterns. Lewis and Haskell (1980:-78) pointed out that assumptions about culturally preferred types and cuts of meat are not at all as clear-cut as they had seemed previously. Planter–overseer–slave distinctions cannot be made purely on the basis of which animal or which bones are present.

The skeletal remains of the slaves themselves can also provide information regarding subsistence and nutrition. Studies focusing on the dentition of skeletons from Barbados's Newton cemetery (Corruccini *et al.* 1982, in press; Handler and Corruccini 1983) have shown, for example, very severe growth arrest lines (hypoplasia) indicative of extreme dietary deficiency or starvation; various types of malocclusion also reflect conditions of malnutrition.

The Newton skeletal sample, representing 104 individuals (Corruccini *et al.* in press), constitutes the largest group of African and African-descended slaves yet excavated from any archaeological context in a New World site; it is also the earliest such group, spanning an interment period from about 1660 to 1820. Thus, this skeletal collection is at present a unique population and cannot in and of itself be considered a "pattern." However, the remains suggest the types of data that can be expanded into patterns with broader sampling to reconstruct regional patterns of nutritional well-being.

The Barbados skeletal material showed little evidence of pathologies or traumas indicative of overt physical abuse. The dental data indicated that the abuse was much more subtle. Corruccini *et al.* (1982:456) concluded "that the Barbadian skeletal population would be among the most metabolically insulted on record" (cf. Dirks 1978). Based on a study of the Newton dentition, Handler and Corruccini (1983) noted that the Barbados slave skeletal remains indicate extreme nutritional conditions, with individuals literally being on the edge of starvation for substantial periods between much longer periods of more adequate caloric nutrition.

Gibbs *et al.* (1980), Fairbanks (1984), Dirks (1978), and Handler and Corruccini (1983) have all commented on the importance of nutritional considerations in the management and success of the plantation system. Fairbanks suggested that roughly 50% (3000/6000) of the required calories for the average field hand in the southeastern United States were provided by the plantation, and there seems to be general agreement that similar figures would apply as well to the British Caribbean. The remainder of the diet was either provided through hunting, fishing, and gardening, or resulted in dietary shortfall and nutritional stress. Dirks (1978:142–143) concluded for the British Caribbean that food allowances were clearly inadequate and protein rations marginal at best. Handler and Corruccini (1983) concur in extending these observations to the specific Barbados context. The data for Newton Plantation suggest numerous cases of stress rather than supplement. As Fairbanks suggests, dietary adequacy would be one factor in the success of a particular plantation or in the system as a whole.

Analyses of bone collagen being conducted on prehistoric skeletal remains (Bender 1968, 1971; Bender *et al.* 1981; Norr 1980) can also be useful in historic analyses, although apparently none have been done so far. Bone collagen study shows promise for describing the composition of the diet. While still in its early stages, this technique shows the ability to evaluate levels of maize and meat consumption and to indicate the presence or absence of other foodstuffs. Such a technique would permit the checking of documentary (and white Creole or European self-serving) statements about the quality and quantity of diet supplied to or consumed by the slaves. It would also provide some indication of the level of grain consumption, even in the absence of grinding stones or other artifact data. Analyses might be somewhat more complicated than those for prehistoric peoples because of a "shadow effect" of the native African diets in persons brought across the Atlantic. Slaves born in the New World would be expected to show much more consistent patterns.

Within the mound and nonmound burial groups excavated in Barbados, selective burial practices were clearly demonstrated (Handler and Lange 1978) and possible extended family plots were suggested (Corruccini *et al.* 1982; Handler and Corruccini 1983). Bone collagen analysis also would permit an evaluation of dietary favoritism and/or deprivation relative to rank and status within the plantation social structure.

Early developments of subsistence systems were often based on pre-Columbian techniques. Arawaks were brought to Barbados in the first year of colonization in 1627 to help with subsistence techniques (Handler 1969, 1970), and Amerindian influences on African slave cultivation practices were also evident in the early development of Montserrat (Pulsipher and Goodwin 1982:99). The overlap between the Indians and the African slaves may in many cases have helped the slaves develop patterns that were locally adaptive and guaranteed their survival in the face of uncertain food supplies on the early plantations.

Material Culture

South (1977) has documented initial attempts to develop artifact patterns for colonial America. None of these patterns are directly derived from plantation slavery contexts and therefore there is no "plantation slave pattern"; however, the patterns are socioeconomically based and therefore can be used as a point of departure for defining and differentiating planter class and worker class patterns in the plantation context.

The distribution of material culture within the slave plantation must be considered as part of the distribution of goods in society at large. The pyramid of white society, with the planter at the top and the white overseer at the bottom, was to some extent mirrored within the slave society, perhaps most specifically in the role of the black overseer. While the social position or privileges of a lower-class white and a higher-rank slave would never have been confused, slaves at the top of the slave pyramid had more privileges than did most of their lower-ranking fellows.

The sources of the material culture found with slave remains come from a multitude of nonexclusive sources. There are three principal categories: (1) brought from Africa, (2) commercial European, or (3) handmade in the New World. Within the first category, African goods may either have been brought by the person or persons ultimately responsible for their archaeological deposition, or they may be far removed from their original New World context. The general assumption that slaves brought very little in the way of personal goods on the transatlantic journey is probably correct in the vast majority of cases. However, the burial remains of carnelian beads from India, Indo-Pacific Ocean cowries, and a Ghanaian smoking pipe on Barbados (Handler 1983a; Handler and Lange 1978, 1979; Handler *et al.* 1979) demonstrate that such transfers did take place. The rarity of such items may reflect either random retention of African source items, or specialized retention by persons who held high rank within the slave community.

The second category (European goods) is perhaps the largest associated with slave remains to date and the most difficult to deal with archaeologically. These goods were often possessed by persons of both African and European heritage, to say nothing of the occasional Amerindian. As with the African-derived goods, some of the European goods represent direct acquisitions by persons responsible for their ultimate archaeological deposition, while others represent recycling or redistribution of these goods.

European-produced (principally British) ceramics were certainly one of the most important artifact classes in both North America and the British Caribbean. South (1977:173) suggested that the presence of colonoware largely represents eighteenth-century gaps in ceramic needs that were filled from local sources when imports were either unavailable or too expensive. Lees (1980:137) concurs and cites colonoware as another example of "local initiative for the successful subversion of colonial policy." When English industrial development flooded the market with cheap and easy to obtain earthenwares at all levels of society, Otto (1977:100) concluded that the Cannon's Point Plantation bought cheap imported earthenwares to distribute to the slaves (and overseers) and colonoware quickly lost its traditional consumers.

Lange and Carlson's analysis of European earthenwares from Barbados (Chapter 5, this volume) shows that in broad categories the ceramic assemblage and ceramic patterns from Barbados are very similar to that from the southeastern United States (Otto 1977:105–106) and Montserrat (Pulsipher and Goodwin 1982:86) indicating similar trade networks and levels of socioeconomic utilization of the earthenwares. Handler and Lange (1978:135–136) did not fully recognize the level of slave access to earthenware on Barbados (their assumptions having been based largely on documentary sources). Lewis and Haskell (1980:76), Carrillo (1980:57), and Otto (1977:100), in the southeastern United States, concluded that slave access to European earthenwares, through a variety of means, was not as restricted as is generally assumed. Otto (1977:97) explicitly rejected the notion that planters at Cannon's Point customarily or frequently passed along broken or discarded household dishes to either the slaves or the overseers. Implicit in Otto's view is also the conclusion that slaves and overseers did not obtain such discards on their own initiative, either through theft or rummaging in trash.

The third category of goods (hand-manufactured in the New World) could be most expected to demonstrate vestiges of the African heritage.Colonoware ceramics, the crude soft ceramic already mentioned as a consideration in settlement pattern research and early colonial ceramic assemblages, has often been cited as the most widespread indicator of slave presence. There is little documentary evidence regarding either its manufacture or distribution, although Fairbanks (1984:21) cited the presence of a similar ceramic in historic Venezuela.Colonoware has been found in slave/Amerindian contexts (Ferguson 1980:15–20) and is still manufactured in some varieties by modern-day Catawba Indian potters (Lewis and Haskell 1980:64). It has been found in distinctly slave contexts, but also in planter-class settings, with Lewis and Haskell (1980:73) noting that even wealthy whites utilized colonoware on the frontier. As with many other artifacts from the slave milieu, colonoware is not an absolute indicator of slave status, but one component in an archaeological/documentary based pattern through which slave presence can be inferred.

On Barbados the unique burial mentioned previously that yielded cowry shells, a carnelian bead, and an African pipe also contained handmade copper and copper alloy bracelets/armlets and finger rings (Handler and Lange 1978:125–132, 1979). Such artifacts could have been made in Africa and brought to the New World, or have been produced in Barbados by African techniques. While written sources indicate that skilled craftsmen were among the slaves brought to the New World, they are silent on any particular cases involving these artifacts from Barbados.

Expectations that slave sites would contain a significant proportion of material goods reflecting the African heritage have been demonstrated in Jamaica. Mathewson (1972a, 1972b) defined a large ceramic complex derived from African traditions, but this has not been the usual experience in plantation settings. In his research elsewhere on Jamaica, Armstrong (1982) had substantial difficulty, as we had on Barbados (Handler and Lange 1978:224–225), and as did Fairbanks (1974) in Florida in identifying material remains with any overtones of African origin. The Ghanaian pipe and various jewelry found in Barbados were from mortuary contexts. Although there are few comparative data, this might suggest that such goods were restricted to special functions. As Fairbanks (1984:8) noted, the Barbados cemetery sample is unique and there are difficulties with gathering comparable data for North American slavery. However, the contrast between the absence of African materials in domestic contexts in the southeastern United States and their presence in mortuary contexts on Barbados (and then limited to one interment) merits emphasis.

Perhaps in the majority of cases we are still dealing with small samples and nonperishable remains. We may also be erring on the side of individual artifacts and "trait diffusion" evidence, rather than addressing patterns. Published examples of slave settings have depended less on the presence or absence of particular artifact types, and more on the documentation of the slave context. As Lees (1980:135) suggested, when material culture can blur the lines between planters, overseers, and slaves, plantationwide distribution patterns are required in order to have any chance of delineating socioeconomic or ethnic differences. Most often it has been the occurrence of particular artifact classes together with settlement-pattern and activity area data from written sources that has allowed us to relate material culture to slave behavior. So far, mortuary patterns (discussed later) seem to offer the strongest potential for indicating African heritage.

In addition to the diversity of geographical areas from which the slaves obtained material goods, they also obtained them by a diversity of means. On Barbados material items could be bought or stolen from a variety of sources, recycled through discard, or be acquired through the internal marketing system (Handler and Lange 1978:30–32)

Cultural Practices

Handler and Corruccini (1983; also Handler *et al.* 1982; Corruccini *et al.* 1982, in press) devote considerable detail to interpreting historical and archaeologically derived physical anthropological data to delineate such cultural practices as dental mutilation, dentistry, pipe smoking, weaning, and the use of family burial plots. On the other hand, in Barbados cultural practices that were related to musical traditions and dance (fundamental dimensions of slave life in the New World) are represented exclusively by documentary data (Handler and Frisbee 1972).

Mortuary Patterns, Demographic Data, and Osteological Analyses

Mortuary patterns at Newton Plantation indicated the use of burial mounds and seem to offer strong connections to African burial customs (Handler and Lange 1978:208–215). At least two levels of mortuary behavior affected slaves on the plantation: the social structure as managed by the planters and the structure of the slave community itself. Status in either the slave community or the planters' scheme might determine burial within the slave cemetery and the conditions under which one was buried (with or without coffin, in a mound or not, and with or without African or European grave goods).

Few slave burial areas (formal or informal) have been studied to date (Angel 1977; Burnston 1980a, 1980b; Dailey 1974; Handler and Lange 1977, 1978; and Hudgins 1977). Pulsipher and Goodwin (1982:84) noted a well-preserved possible slave cemetery (also employing mounds) on Montserrat, but research has not yet been done there. Excavation in such burial grounds may be very difficult to arrange under most circumstances (cf. Fairbanks 1984:8). This is unfortunate since the Newton excavation results strongly suggest that through their physical remains will the former slaves speak most clearly to modern scholars. However, in the cumulative information from wide- ranging reports on slave skeletal remains, we are beginning to derive some suggestions of patterned behavior.

First, not all slaves were buried in formal cemeteries, such as on Newton Plantation where there certainly was selection by age and possibly by rank and status as well. Infants and young persons are consistently underrepresented in all skeletal series, not just slave series. There is some suggestion of at least some family groupings in the Newton cemetery (Corruccini *et al.* 1982:446; Handler and Corruccini 1983). Deetz (1977) has noted that changes from communal to individual burials in English and colonial North American society paralleled changes from communal to individual table service and eating patterns. Chronological control is not sufficient for the Newton cemetery to detect similar shifts there with any certainty. Even should such shifts be detected, it would be impossible on the basis of current data to conclude whether changes were due to shifts in English patterns or more localized plantation changes. On Barbados all slave burials have shown an increased use of coffins through time (no white cemeteries from the same time period have been excavated to compare the frequency of coffin use or to compare the types of coffins used). Documentary records from Barbados suggest (Handler and Lange 1978:80–81) that plantation managements prepared coffins only for selected slaves, probably as part of a reward-incentive system. The mismatched handles and other hardware found with the Barbados coffins suggest that they were made with whatever was available at the time. Very few grave goods were encountered at Newton; these occurred with only 33% of the interments and principally consisted of glass beads and European clay pipes.

The greatest concentration of grave goods came from the interment of an old man who had been buried without a coffin and relatively early in the slave period (Handler and Lange 1978:125–132; 1979). He had been interred in a location where at least three earlier individuals of the same approximate age and the same sex had been buried. The grave goods found with him, with the exception of a metal knife, could be considered exotic to the extent they had either been brought from extra-island sources or had been made on the island according to traditional African practices. This concentration of non-European goods with a single individual is in stark contrast to the rest of the pattern at Newton and suggests that the deceased was someone who held a special status within the slave community.

While the documents from Barbados are very extensive (Handler 1971, 1980, 1981, 1982, 1983b, 1985) and speak to general levels of material culture and behavior, the archaeological data provide more specific information. Patterns of pipe smoking and the symbolism of the reward-incentive system (via plantation pipe and tobacco allocations, the selective giving of coffins, and the extensive dietary and nutritional information) are significant examples. The skeletal data, in short, provide an independent data source and expansion or verification of narrative or literary sources.

The assessment of demographic data from the Newton cemetery (Corruccini *et al.* 1982) again emphasizes the utility of integrating historical and archaeological data. Documents have provided the most reliable population statistics and age profiles. The archaeological and historical data agree on a balanced sexual division in the population, while the documents illuminated an underrepresentation of infants in the archaeological sample and analysis.

Osteological and pathological conditions not addressed in the documents have been observed on skeletal material from Newton and elsewhere. The genetic marker data from skeletons at Newton have, as already indicated, suggested the possibility of family burial plots. Since interment in the cemetery was apparently selective and only a portion of the slaves known to have died on the plantation are thought to be present, we assume these related genetic traits mirror families who were important as families above and beyond whatever individual significance they held. Also, the dental evidence for pipewear correlated with the documentary mention of the slaves' fondness for smoking and the presence of pipes (many of them pristine and unused) in some graves. Interestingly, many of the individuals accompanied by pipes did not show definite signs of dental pipewear. This suggests the pipes may have had symbolic as well as functional value.

Corruccini *et al.* (1982:447, in press) interpreted a significant amount of data from the Newton cemetery dental material and in doing so supplemented a very nonspecific documentary data base. Most important were the findings of high percentages of hypercementosis (60%–80%) and enamel hypoplasia (55%–75%).

Hudgins (1977:65) noted syphilitic inflammation in one individual from College

Landing (Virginia), a general lack of arthritic conditions, and skeletal evidence of dedication to craft activities. Comparison with other data from the continental colonies indicated that the College Landing skeletal series (dating from the early nineteenth century) was slightly taller than the average group and was of normal longevity for the colonial period (36 years for adults). These individuals had all been buried in coffins, which matches well with the placement of coffin use later in the period of slavery on Barbados (Handler and Lange 1978:164).

The physical remains of the slaves themselves clearly demonstrate their African heritage and the mortuary patterns reflect African traditions. However, it has taken a concerted effort at integrating documentary and archaeological data to partially reconstruct some knowledge of mortuary patterns. It seems likely that the traditions were preserved in the behavior preceding and associated with the interment, while the location of burial grounds were influenced by plantation policies. These details are in fact gray areas, as existing documentation is silent on many dimensions of the mortuary customs of plantation slaves. In a detailed assessment of the documentary and archaeological data for slave mortuary practices on Barbados, Handler and Lange (1977:35–36) concluded that:

> Despite the extensive data on Newton interments, the archaeological data could not deal, for example, with mortuary activities away from the burial sites, or a variety of behaviours and ideological patterns at the sites themselves; moreover, it is important to note the archaeological data *per se* did not establish that the persons interred were slaves.

CONCLUSIONS

This discussion argued in favor of a combined documentary/archaeological (ethnohistorical) approach to the study of plantation slavery. It is clear that any patterns ascertained as being indicative of slavery have been established in the documented sites studied. Almost every study of plantation slavery has made a gesture at giving equal attention to both archaeological and documentary data, but it requires constant and concerted effort to derive the most productive results from the method.

Documentary sources have identified loci of slave activity which in turn have been excavated to yield material culture patterns that can be sought in other places without adequate documentation. For example, artifact remains within the identified areas have shown what the domestic kits of plantation slaves consisted of, while the documentary record has indicated they either ate in nuclear units or communal settings. Remains of cooking and eating dishes, food-processing equipment, and faunal and floral remains have provided some hard data on what the slaves ate; in one case (Newton) the physical remains of the slaves themselves attest to severe dietary stress, a point that was ambiguous in the documentation.

Documentary sources have been generally vague on slave material culture, and the discovery of basically European assemblages has not been what many scholars anticipated. There is very little of the African heritage in the material remains, but much that is identical to what European overseers and planters were using.

Present conclusions about mortuary behavior are similar to those for material culture. However, so few slaves burials have been excavated, and only in one case in sizeable numbers, that it is premature to generalize.

The mortuary data also provide perhaps the best example of the value of interplay between the documentary and archaeological sources. Fairbanks followed this same procedure in reconstructing nutritional information in Georgia, stating that "These questions suggest another look [at] plantation records specifically seeking observations on this point. Until the question is raised, no systematic documentary search could have been undertaken" (1984:19).

Slave settlement locations were dictated by the planter on all plantations and are usually described in documents at least in general terms, although details of distribution and microspatial organization are usually ignored. Material culture is very unevenly reported in most documents, and mortuary behavior and detailed dietary data are referenced even less frequently. Research to date suggests the almost inevitable possibility of blurring between slave and overseer contexts and categories in material culture. However, so few overseer sites have been excavated, and specifically none in the British Caribbean, that one must be cautious not to overgeneralize. When comparing North American and British Caribbean data, patterns of material culture distribution, especially within the context of settlement pattern analyses, have reached a relatively reliable degree of comparability. In the archaeological sense, domestic, nutritional, and mortuary data and their related behavioral implications so far seem to have been the most productive in yielding data on slave life. Unfortunately, these data will probably be the most difficult to develop on a broad-scale comparative basis because of social and ethical constraints.

In much of the data gathered so far there is also a strong hint that the ethnohistorical approach needs to deemphasize strictly racial–ethnic divisions in plantation research. Much of the data suggests that the basic division was between the planters and their overseers and slaves, rather than a three-level separation of status and privilege. Thus, we need to revise our thinking of "the slaves" as an ethnic–racial unit and also focus on plantation slavery at the level of socioeconomic separation.

There is a much higher probability than there was 10 years ago that slavery can be defined from purely archaeological data. The relative presence and absence or percentage of occurrence of isolated traits will not provide the answers, however, and both British Caribbean and North American data acquired to date indicate comparative patterns are more likely to engender success. Historic sites archaeology—using an ethnohistoric methodology emphasizing an interplay between the documentary and archaeological data bases—offers the potential to develop quantifiable patterns for slave-period and postemancipation slave remains similar to those developed by Stanley South (1972, 1977) for other cultural patterns. The delineation of patterns with a high probability of indicating plantation slavery conditions will allow us to search for these patterns in undocumented historic sites or, by extension, to search for evidence of slavery in preliterate sites as well.

ACKNOWLEDGMENTS

We are grateful to Robert Dirks and Robert Corruccini for their comments on earlier drafts on this essay. Research on Barbados was generously supported by grants from the National Science Foundation and the Wenner–Gren Foundation for Anthropological Research.

REFERENCES

Angel, J. L.
1977 Appendix II-1. In Historical archaeology and salvage archaeological excavationa at College Landing, Hudgins, C. F., ed. Unpublished manuscript.

Armstrong, D.
1982 A progress report on the "Old Village" at Drax Hall, St. Ann's Bay, Jamaica. *Archaeology at UCLA,* 2(7). Institute of Archaeology, UCLA.

Ascher, R., and C. Fairbanks
1971 Excavation of a slave cabin: Georgia, U.S.A. *Historical Archaeology* 5:3–17.

Baerreis, D.
1961 The ethnohistoric approach and archaeology. *Ethnohistory* 8:49–77.

Bender, M.
1968 Mass spectrometric studies of C(13) variations in corn and other grasses. *Radiocarbon* 10:468–472.
1971 Variations in (13)C/(12)C ratio of plants in relation to the pathway of photosynthetic carbon dioxide. *Phytochemistry* 10:1239–1244.

Bender, M., D. Baerreis, and R. Steventon
1981 Further light on carbonisotopes and Hopewell agriculture. *American Antiquity* 46:346–353.

Booth, S.
1971 *Hung, Strung, and Potted: A History of Eating in Colonial America.* New York: Clarkson N. Potter.

Burnston, S.
1980a Archaeological Investigations at an Unmarked Cemetery, Catoctin Furnace, Maryland (Check #6). In *1980 Archaeological Investigations at Catoctin Furnace, Frederick County, Maryland.* R. A. Thomas *et al.*, eds. Newark, Delaware: Mid-Atlantic Archaeological Research, Inc. Unpublished manuscript.
1980b *1980 Archaeological Investigations at Catoctin Furnace (Check #6), Frederick County, Maryland.* Newark, Delaware: Mid-Atlantic Archaeological Research, Inc. Unpublished manuscript.

Carrillo, R.
1980 Green Grove Plantation: archaeological and historical research at the Kinlock site (38Ch109), Charleston County. Columbia, South Carolina: Department of Highways and Public Transportation.

Corruccini, R., J. Handler, R. Mutaw, and F. Lange
1982 Osteology of a slave burial population from Barbados, West Indies. *American Journal of Physical Anthropology* 59:443–459.

Corruccini, R., J. Handler, and K. Jacobi
in press Chronological distribution of enamel hypoplasias and weaning in a Caribbean slave population. *Human Biology.*

Dailey, R. C.
1974 Osteological analysis of human skeletal remains from the Virgin Islands. Tallahassee: Florida State University. Unpublished manuscript.

Deetz, J.
1977 *In Small Things Forgotten.* New York: Doubleday.
Dirks, R.
1978 Resource fluctuations and competitive transformations in West Indian slave societies. In *Extinction and Survival in Human Populations.* C. D. Laughlin and I. Brady, eds. New York: Columbia University Press. Pp. 122–180.
Drucker, L.
1979 Spier's Landing site: an archaeological investigation in Berkeley County, South Carolina. Columbia, S.C.: Carolina Archaeological Services.
Fairbanks, C.
1974 The Kingsley slave cabins in Duval County, Florida, 1968. *The Conference on Historic Site Archaeology Papers 1972* 7:62–93.
1984 Plantation archaeology of the southeastern coast. *Historical Archaeology* 18:1–14.
Ferguson, L.
1980 Looking for the "Afro" in colono-Indian pottery. In *Archaeological Perspectives on Ethnicity in America.* R. L. Schuyler, ed. New York: Baywood Press. Pp. 14–28.
Gibbs, T., C. Cargill, L. Lieberman, and E. Reitz
1980 Nutrition in a slave population: an anthropological examination. *Medical Anthropology* 4:175–262.
Handler, J.S.
1969 The Amerindian slave population of Barbados in the 17th and early 18th centuries. *Caribbean Studies* 8:38–64.
1970 Aspects of Amerindian ethnography in seventeenth-century Barbados. *Caribbean Studies* 9:50–72.
1971 *A Guide to Source Materials for the Study of Barbados History, 1627–1834.* Carbondale: Southern Illinois University Press.
1972 An archaeological investigation of the domestic life of slaves in Barbados. *Journal of the Barbados Museum and Historical Society* 34:64–72.
1980 Addenda to "A guide to source materials for the study of Barbados history, 1627–1834: Part I." *Journal of the Barbados Museum and Historical Society* 36:172–177.
1981 Addenda to "A guide to source materials for the study of Barbados history, 1627–1834: Part II." *Journal of the Barbados Museum and Historical Society* 36:279–285.
1982 Addenda to "A guide to source materials for the study of Barbados history, 1627–1834: Part III." *Journal of the Barbados Museum and Historical Society* 36:385–397.
1983a An African pipe from a slave cemetery in Barbados, West Indies. In *The Archaeology of the Clay Tobacco Pipe,* Vol. III: America. P. Davey, ed. British Archaeological Reports, International Series 175:245–254.
1983b Addenda to "A guide to source materials for the study of Barbados history, 1627–1835: Part IV." *Journal of the Barbados Museum and Historical Society* 37:82–92.
1985 Addenda to "A guide to source materials for the study of Barbados history, 1627–1834: Part V." *Journal of the Barbados Museum and Historical Society* 37:296–307.
Handler, J., R. Corruccini, and R. Mutaw
1982 Tooth mutilation in the Caribbean: evidence from a slave burial population in Barbados. *Journal of Human Evolution* 11:297–313.
Handler, J., and R. Corruccini
1983 Plantation slave life in Barbados: a physical anthropological analysis. *Journal of Interdisciplinary History* 14:65–90.
Handler, J., and C. Frisbee
1972 Aspects of slave life in Barbados: music and its cultural context. *Caribbean Studies* 11:5–46.
Handler, J., and F. Lange
1977 Mortuary patterns of plantation slaves in Barbados. Paper presented at the Ninth conference of the Association of Caribbean Historians, Cave Hill, Barbados.

1978 *Plantation Slavery in Barbados: An Archaeological and Historical Investigation.* Cambridge: Harvard University Press.
1979 Plantation slavery on Barbados, West Indies. *Archaeology* 32:45–52.

Handler, J., F. Lange, and C. Orser, Jr.
1979 Carnelian beads in necklaces from a slave cemetery in Barbados, West Indies. *Ornament* 4:15–18.

Hudgins, C. L.
1977 Historical archaeology and salvage archaeological excavations at College Landing, an interim report. Virginia Research Center for Archaeology. Unpublished manuscript.

Kelso, W.
1976 The colonial silent majority: tenant, servant, and slave settlement sites at Kingsmill, Virginia. Paper delivered at the Seventy-fifth annual meeting, American Anthropological Association, Washington, D.C.

Lange, F.
1972 An archaeological investigation of the domestic life of plantation slaves in Barbados, West Indies. Paper presented at the Thirty-seventh annual meeting, Society for American Archaeology, Miami Beach.
1976 Slave mortuary practices, Barbados, West Indies. In *Actas,* XLI Congreso Internacional de Americanistas (Mexico) 2:477–483.

Lees, W. B.
1980 Limerick: old and in the way. Archeological Investigations at Limerick Plantation, Anthropological Studies No. 5, Occasional Papers of the Institute of Archeology and Anthropology. Columbia: The University of South Carolina.

Lewis, K. E.
1979 Hampton, initial archeological investigations at an eighteenth-century rice plantation in the Santee Delta, South Carolina. Research Manuscript Series No. 151, Institute of Archeology and Anthropology. Columbia: University of South Carolina.

Lewis, K., and H. Haskell
1980 Hampton II: further archeological investigations at a Santee River rice plantation. Research Manuscript Series No. 161, Institute of Archeology and Anthropology. Columbia: University of South Carolina.

Lewis, L. G.
1978 *Drayton Hall: Preliminary Archaeological Investigations at a Low County Plantation.* Charlottesville: University of Virginia Press.

McFarlane, S.
1975 The ethnohistory of a slave community: the Couper Plantation site. Master's thesis, Department of Anthropology, University of Florida, Gainesville.

Mathewson, R. D.
1972a History from the earth: archaeological excavations at Old King's House. *Jamaica Journal* 6:3–11.
1972b Jamaican ceramics: an introduction to the 18th century folk pottery in West African tradition. *Jamaica Journal* 6:54–56.
1973 Archaeological analysis of material culture as a reflection of sub-cultural differentiation in 18th century Jamaica. *Jamaica Journal* 7:25–29.

Norr, L.
1980 Prehistoric diet and bone chemistry: initial results from Costa Rica. Paper presented at Forty-fifth annual meeting, Society for American Archaeology, Philadelphia.

Orser, C. E., Jr.
1984 The past ten years of plantation archaeology in the southeastern United States. *Southeastern Archaeology* 3:1–12.

Otto, J. S.
1975 Status differences and the archaeological record: a comparison of planters, overseers, and

slave Sites from Cannon's Point Plantation (1794–1861), St. Simon's Island, Georgia. Ph.D. dissertation, Department of Anthropology, University of Florida, Gainesville. Ann Arbor: University Microfilms.

1977 Artifacts and status differences: a comparison of ceramics from planter, overseer, and slave Sites on an antebellum plantation. In *Research Strategies in Historical Archaeology*. S. South, ed. New York: Academic Press. Pp. 91–118.

Parsons, J.
1972 Archaeological settlement patterns. *Annual Review of Anthropology* (1972). Pp. 127–150.

Price, B. J.
1982 Cultural materialism: a theoretical review. *American Antiquity* 47:709–741.

Pulsipher, L. M., and C. M. Goodwin
1982 Galways: a Caribbean sugar plantation. A report on the 1981 field season. Department of Geography, University of Tennessee.

Singleton, T.
1980 The archaeology of Afro-American slavery in coastal Georgia: a regional perception of slave household and community patterns. Ph.D. dissertation, Department of Anthropology, University of Florida, Gainesville. Ann Arbor: University Microfilms.

South, S.
1972 Evolution and horizon as revealed in ceramic analysis in historical archaeology. *The Conference on Historic Site Archaeology Papers 1971* 6:71–106.

1977 *Method and Theory in Historical Archaeology*. New York: Academic Press.

Struever, S.
1971 Comments on archaeological data requirements and research strategy. *American Antiquity* 36:9–19.

Trigger, B.
1967 Settlement archaeology: its goals and promise. *American Antiquity* 32:149–60.

PART II

Settlement

3

Plantation Layout and Function in the South Carolina Lowcountry

Kenneth E. Lewis

INTRODUCTION

The role played by individual settlements in a larger socioeconomic system is reflected in their physical structure. A basic element of structure is the overall arrangement, or patterning, of structures and activities at a habitation site and their differential use through time. Archaeologists have long recognized that patterns of settlement are sensitive indicators of economic, social, and political organization (Chang 1967; Trigger 1967; Willey 1953), and are capable of revealing continuity as well as change in adapting societies. Consequently, the observation of settlement patterning should be useful in identifying both traditional settlements and those evolving to meet changing conditions. This essay is concerned with a particular colonial settlement type and the relationship between function and the general layout of its activities.

In the American Southeast, a number of settlement types emerged during the colonial period. They reflect not only the traditional roles of particular settlements, but also the position of the region in the expanding European economy. One of the most prominent settlement types in British North America is the plantation, which arose in the seventeenth century and has persisted, albeit in drastically altered form, until the present (Prunty 1955). Plantations, like other settlement types, developed in response to particular social and economic needs, and their form and content are expected to reflect behavioral adaptations required to accomplish certain tasks.

This essay explores the plantation's role in the colonial world and develops a model relating settlement pattern to socioeconomic function. The model will be employed in an examination of settlement patterning at two plantations in South Carolina using both documentary and archaeological data pertaining to these settle-

ISBN 0-12-646480-4

ments. The results should help determine the applicability of the model to the region. Moreover, they will permit a detailed comparative look at structure and activity patterning and provide a comprehensive picture of the social and economic structure of this settlement type in a particular geographical area.

THE PLANTATION'S ROLE IN THE EXPANSION OF EUROPE

The World Economy of the Expansion

In order to examine the plantation as a settlement type, it is necessary to understand the economic role it played in the colonization of the New World. Plantations developed as an integral part of the world economy created by the expansion of Europe after the fifteenth century. Wallerstein (1974:7) has suggested the term *world economy* to characterize the system in which the European nations of the postmedieval period participated because of the particular nature of the system's organization. In this system individual nation-states were tied together by a web of mutual interdependence. The self-contained development of this world economy resembled an empire, but its capitalistic economic mode prevented domination by a single nation because these economic factors operated within an area larger than any political entity could completely control. This situation gave capitalistic entrepreneurs a structurally based freedom of movement and allowed a continual expansion of the world economy (Wallerstein 1974:348). The role of commercial forces in the initiation of British colonization is Scotland, Ireland, and America is well known. The flexibility of privately organized, economically oriented ventures proved the key to the successful establishment of many early sustained British colonial settlements (Cheyney 1961; MacLeod 1928; Rowse 1957).

Of particular significance to a discussion of British colonial North America is the nature of the relationship between an expanding world system and those areas outside its boundaries. Because of the system's economic orientation this relationship was largely one of exchange. This exchange consisted of two types: (1) that involving trade with external areas dominated by other world systems, and (2) that with areas on the system's own periphery.

In the latter type, production was limited to low-ranking goods (those whose labor was less well rewarded), yet remained an integral part of the overall division of labor because the commodities involved were essential for daily use (Wallerstein 1974:302). Exchange between the periphery and the "core" states at the center of the system tended to have a "vertical specialization" involving the movement of raw materials from the former to the latter and the movement of manufactured goods and services in the opposite direction (Gould 1972:235–236). Such was the case in much of colonial North America, especially in the agricultural South (Sellers 1934:302).

The Plantation in the World Economy

The *plantation* is a settlement type designed to efficiently and cheaply produce staples on a large scale for a substantial nondomestic market (Wagley and Harris 1955:435). The competition of agricultural staples for suitable land, labor supplies, and market favors the location of plantations so as to minimize cost while maximizing access to markets. These conditions would be found in frontier regions on the periphery of a world economic system where native resources could be cheaply exploited to obtain raw commodities that could then be shipped directly from a colonial entrepot to markets in the parent state (J. Smith 1973:2; Thompson 1959:29–30).

A plantation may be seen as "a capitalistic type of agricultural organization in which a number of unfree laborers are employed under unified direction and control in the production of a staple crop" (Mintz 1959:43). The organization of a plantation is marked by (1) a relatively large population and territorial size, (2) an emphasis on the production of specialized cash crops, (3) a use of labor beyond the owner-family, and (4) a dependence upon the authority principle as the basis for collective action (Pan American Union 1959:190). To these may be added (5) a centralized control of cultivating power, (6) a relatively large input of cultivating power per unit of area, and (7) the necessity of producing subsistence crops to support, at least in part, the plantation population (Prunty 1955:460). These characteristics reflect the manner in which agricultural activities are organized to facilitate production. The plantation not only provides a setting for these activities, but also an arrangement to facilitate carrying them out. This arrangement constitutes the form of the plantation settlement.

PLANTATION SETTLEMENT PATTERNS: A MODEL OF FORM AND FUNCTION

The layout of structures and activities on plantation was related to the basic economic role of these settlements—the labor-intensive production of staple crops. The management of a large labor force engaged in specialized agricultural work requires that the control of cultivating power and its manner of employment be centralized. This was accomplished most efficiently by organizing plantation activities in a compact settlement centered around the owner's residence. Prunty (1955:465–466) described the typical North American plantation settlement as a nucleated village consisting of a cluster of service buildings and slave quarters grouped compactly on roads arranged in a square or rectangle around or near the main house.

Although the plantation itself might be large, its settlement was compact. The actual layout of buildings varied but seems generally to followed a common pattern. Waterman and Barrows (1969:xiv) noted that eighteenth-century English plantations in the American Southeast centered around a main house and its dependencies.

Throughout the eighteenth century these structures exhibited a basic Georgian symmetry in their arrangement (Waterman 1945:17), with the house and its forecourt flanked by the dependencies which were sometimes attached by passages to the main house (Kimball 1922:79). In the last quarter of the century the dependencies shifted from a position on either side of the forecourt to one in line with the orientation of the house. Dependencies apparently did not possess definite functions on every plantation and served variously as kitchens, offices, overseers' quarters, libraries, and servants' quarters, as well housing for other support activities related to the main house (Waterman 1945:61, 259, 341).

Farm and service buildings (consisting of shelters for work stock and plantation tools) were situated in a cluster apart from but near to the main house complex. They were generally placed in a linear or geometric arrangement (Phillips 1929:332; Waterman and Barrows 1969). The proximity of these structures to the main house complex, which also placed them close to croplands, pasture, and the laborers' quarters, insured that cultivating power was centrally located within the area to which it was applied and among the human elements on whose effective employment it depended (Prunty 1955:466).

The slave quarters were generally situated near the agricultural buildings to one side of the main house. They were commonly arranged in rows facing a cleared square at one end of which the main house and its dependencies stood. Quarters varied in size and method of construction from one-room huts to larger buildings of log, frame, or brick (Rawick 1972:70–71, 77). Often its relative proximity to the main house reflected the status of the structure's occupants in the social structure of the plantation (Anthony 1976:13).

In general the entire plantation settlement was not situated directly on a main road linking the region's other settlements. Rather, it was usually placed at the end of a branch road leading from the main road into the plantation lands (Phillips 1929:335). The settlement complex was usually adjacent to the earliest cultivated land. The exhaustive cropping of many crops, especially cotton, and generally increasing production required a continual clearing of new land for planting (Dodd 1921:25), resulting in a constant expansion of cultivated lands accompanied by a general movement away from the site of the main plantation settlement (Olmsted 1957:53).

An example of typical eighteenth century plantation settlement patterning is provided by Mt. Vernon in Fairfax County, Virginia (Architects' Emergency Committee 1933:70–73). The geometric layout of the structures is clearly discernible (Figure 3.1), with the main house and dependencies situated at the center of a U-shaped plan. Service buildings are arranged in rows stretching to either side of the forecourt. The slave quarters form a block oriented at a right angle to the service buildings. The positions of entrance roads, paths, walls, and ornamental and vegetable garden plots further define the U-shape of the layout.

The plantation may be seen to have arisen as a settlement type developed for a specific purpose deriving from its function in the world economy. An organization of activities necessary for plantation production is reflected in their spatial distribution on the plantation site. The layout of activities characteristic of plantation settlement

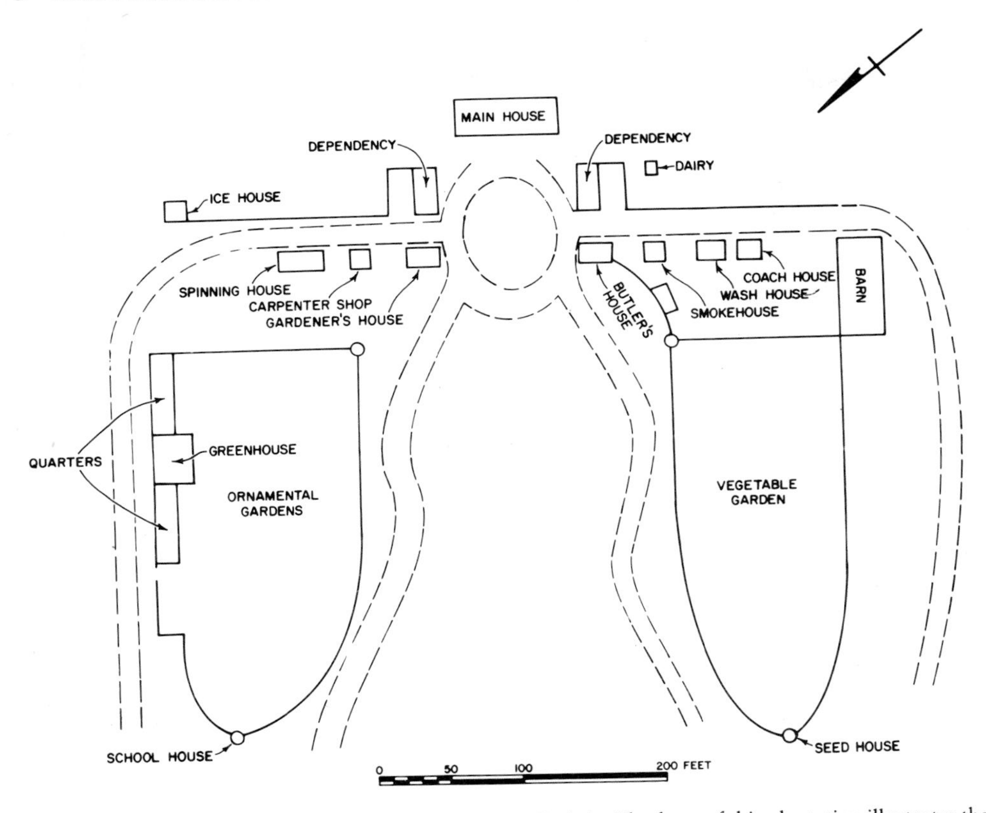

Figure 3.1 Plan of Mt. Vernon in Fairfax County, Virginia. The form of this plantation illustrates the layout typical of eighteenth century plantations in the America Southeast. (Source: Architects' Emergency Committee 1933:70–71.)

appears to exhibit a uniform pattern that should be recognizable at the site of the two South Carolina settlements examined here.

THE SOUTH CAROLINA PLANTATION ECONOMY

The British colonization of South Carolina began in 1670 with the establishment of a permanent settlement on the Ashley River. This area formed the nucleus for coastal expansion—a movement that characterized the early period of the colony's growth. Initial coastal settlement was confined to the area between the Santee and Edisto rivers and was centered on the developing port of Charleston (Figure 3.2). Early land allotments were made along the rivers and tidal inlets, for these watercourses offered the easiest means of trade and communications as well as some protection against potential Indian attack (Petty 1943:20). The development of Charleston as South Carolina's principal port, or entrepot, provided the colony with

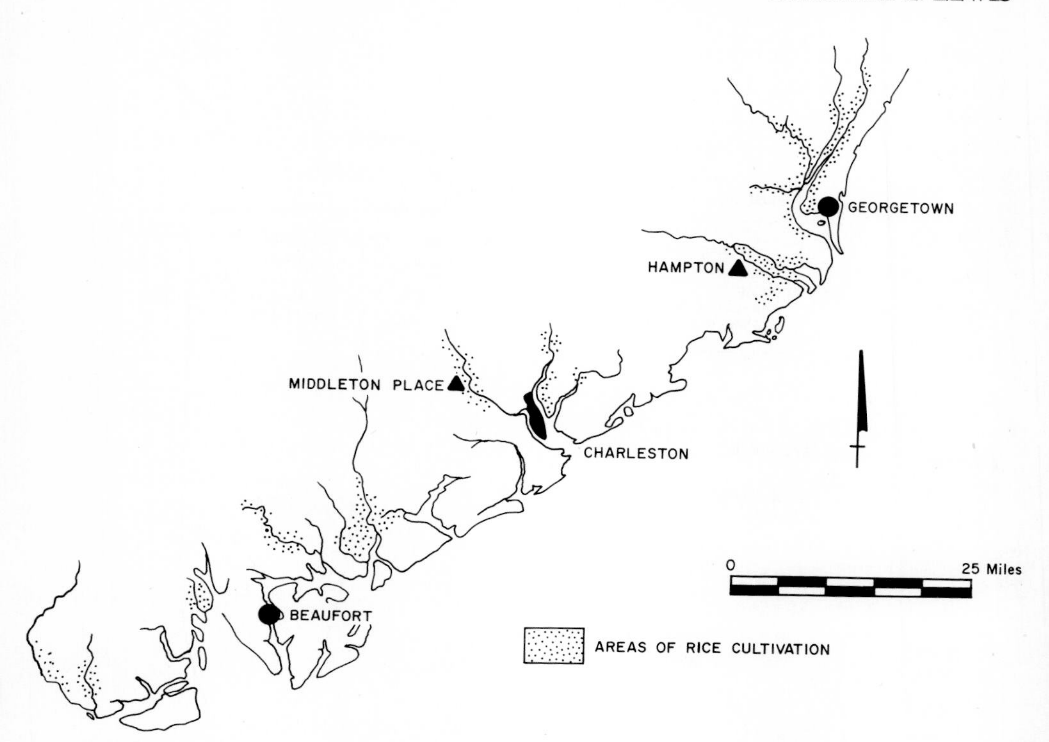

Figure 3.2 Major rice-growing areas in the eighteenth century South Carolina Lowcountry. Middleton Place and Hampton may be seen to lie in the areas adjacent to Charleston and Georgetown, respectively. (Source: Hilliard 1975:63.)

a direct trading link to Great Britain as well as to English colonial ports in the New World. Its location at the mouth of the Cooper River greatly facilitated the emergence of a plantation economy on the Lower Coastal Plain and it served as a collecting point for colonial export commodities and a redistribution center for imported commercial goods and plantation slaves (Sellers 1934:5). In addition to supplying its own inland settlements, Charleston developed as a re-export center for the West Indies (Earle and Hoffman 1976:17). Not only was Charleston the focus of the coastal plantation economy but it also served as the terminus of the British–Indian trade in the Southeast (Crane 1929:108). In addition to Charleston the two subsidiary ports of Beaufort and Georgetown arose in the early years of the eighteenth century. Each served a relatively restricted hinterland and remained largely collection points for agricultural commodities shipped to Charleston (Grayson 1960:14).

Settlement in the coastal region of South Carolina, or lowcountry, centered largely around the production of rice. Following a period of experimentation in which a variety of crops were tried (Clowse 1971:8; Gray 1933:50), rice had emerged as the dominant staple commodity (Salley 1936:51). Encouraged by an increasing demand in Europe and by loose trade restrictions, rice production rose dramatically after 1719 (Gray 1933:286).

The requirements of commerical rice-growing were ideally suited to the development of plantation agriculture in this region. First, it required a complex agricultural technology that was to evolve throughout the colonial period. A need for continuous and precise irrigation led to the increasingly efficient use of hydraulic resources. Initially inland fields fed by freshwater streams were used and later inland swamps were cleared to permit the impoundment of water. By the latter part of the eighteenth century rice cultivation had shifted to the tidal portions of the major coastal rivers where it employed an elaborate irrigation system utilizing the tidal flow of fresh water (Hilliard 1975:58). Second, rice cultivation was an extremely labor-intensive activity, requiring continual labor inputs throughout the year (Doar 1936:8). As such, it facilitated the introduction of a slave labor force. Slave plantation agriculture had proven immensely successful in the British West Indies in the seventeenth century (Handler and Lange 1978:16–17), and its introduction here was probably influenced strongly by the West Indian experience as well as by the availability of West African slaves already knowledgeable in the cultivation of this crop (Wood 1974).

The profitability of rice agriculture and its adaptiveness to the coastal environment of South Carolina restricted its geographical spread and allowed plantation farming to maintain a competitive advantage over other forms of agricultural production after the close of the colonial period (Hilliard 1978:114; Petty 1943:56). The retention of an economic structure originating in the colonial period retarded the development of complex institutions in favor of maintaining direct economic linkages between plantation and port. As the economic organization of the area stabilized, so did the patterns of settlement arising from it. Coastal South Carolina remained a plantation region with a relatively low overall population density. Its economy, dominated by the production of rice, required few urban centers apart from the rice ports (Sellers 1934:88) and the plantation became established as the dominant settlement type in the region.

TWO RICE PLANTATIONS: A HISTORICAL OVERVIEW

The production of rice in the South Carolina lowcountry was concentrated in the vicinity of Georgetown, Charleston, and Beaufort (Figure 3.2). Each port served as the collection and processing center for the crops produced in its area (Hilliard 1975:62). Plantations were abundant in all of these areas and the sites of several have been examined archaeologically. The results of investigations at two plantations are presented in this chapter.

Middleton Place

Middleton Place is situated on the west bank of the Ashley River northwest of Charleston (Figure 3.2). This area was settled soon after the founding of the colony as agricultural settlement spread up the coastal rivers (H. Smith 1919). The site of

Middleton Place was granted in 1675 (South Carolina, Records of the Secretary of State, 38:9) and passed into the Middleton family through marriage in 1741 (H. Smith 1919:118).

A wealthy planter with numerous estates, Henry Middleton made his new acquisition the principal family residence, a role it fulfilled until its destruction in 1865. Few descriptions of Middleton Place exist and it is unclear whether the structures were built by Middleton or were inherited from a previous owner. A 1753 "poetical essay" mentions only that the estate "would make a good figure in England" (*Gentleman's Magazine* 1753:337). Henry Middleton is known to have begun the extensive landscaping of the area adjacent to the main house complex, creating the terraces and formal gardens that were expanded by his successors (Redfield 1978:-104). An Italian nobleman, Luigi Castiglione, who visited Middleton Place in 1786 described only the main house complex as a three-storied castle with symmetrical wings. He also mentioned the presence of tidal rice fields, the remains of which are still clearly discernible (Castiglione 1790:233–234). A 1798 description by the Duke de la Rochefoucault-Liancourt adds little to our knowledge of the eighteenth century plantation, except to reveal that the dependencies accommodated a kitchen, workroom, and offices (H. Smith 1919:119).

The best description of Middleton Place dates from the 1840s and consists of a sketch made by Paolina Bentivoglio Middleton. The drawing shows the main house and its two symmetrically placed dependencies as well as a group of out-buildings, including an arcaded stable set among trees to the right of this complex (Figure 3.3). The main house is a relatively small, three-storied structure with an entrance tower centered on its front facade. Its Jacobian style (Waterman 1945:4) is similar to that employed in Ashley Hall and Medway, two late seventeenth century plantation houses in South Carolina (National Register File), and suggests that it was constructed prior to the Middleton family's acquisiton of the property. In contrast, the Georgian sytle of the two dependencies, with their pedimented, hipped roofs and central cupolas, implies that they were a later addition, perhaps constructed during the early Middleton occupancy of the plantation. A spring house, rice mill, and privy are also believed to date from this period. By this time the ornamental gardens occupied the area to the left of the main house complex and the space between it and the river had been transformed into a series of terraces and artificial ponds (Middleton 1929:153) (Figure 3.4).

In February 1865 Federal troops looted the plantation and burned the main house, its dependencies, the stable, the barn, and some slave houses (Drayton 1865). Following the Civil War the southern dependency was rebuilt as a family residence and was occupied at least part-time until about 1900 and again after 1925. Several out-buildings to house servants and equipment were constructed during this time in the area just south of the main house and were replaced in the 1930s by a brick stable yard and guesthouse which still stand (*News and Courier* 1937). In 1970 the plantation became the Middleton Place Registered National Historic Landmark, Inc. The Middleton Place Foundation was created in 1975 to oversee the restoration of the residence and conduct research pertaining to past lifeways at Middleton Place.

Figure 3.3 Middleton Place in the 1840s; sketch by Paolina Bentivoglio Middleton. (Photograph courtesy Middleton Place Foundation.)

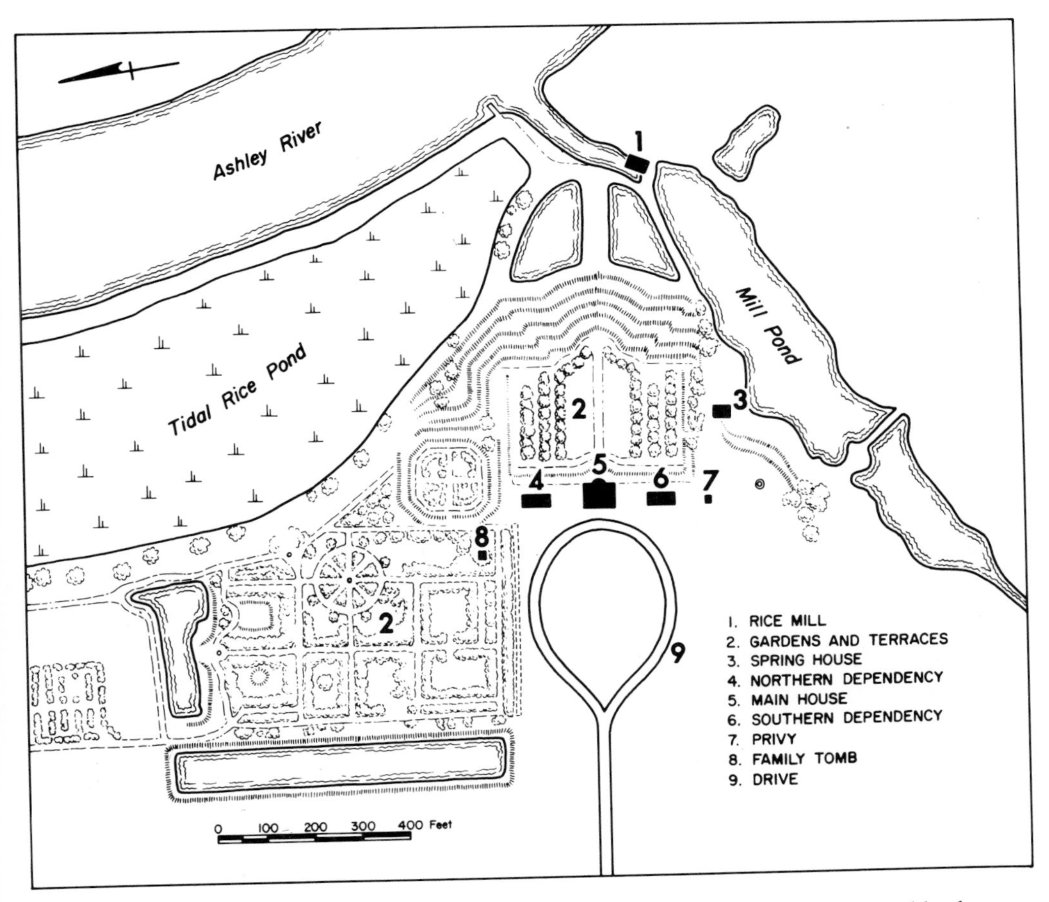

Figure 3.4 Plan of Middleton Place showing surviving eighteenth century structures and landscape features.

Hampton

Hampton Plantation is situated on the southern bank of the South Santee River at its confluence with Wambaw Creek. It lies at the edge of the vast Santee Delta, formerly an area of extensive rice production southwest of Georgetown. The early ownership of the Hampton property is uncertain, however, in the 1730s Daniel Horry acquired a number of tracts in the area of Wambaw Creek that are likely to have included these lands (Lewis 1979:11). The earliest mention of Horry's plantation appears on William DeBrahm's map of 1757 which places it in the approximate location of Hampton. Although established in the eighteenth century, most accounts of Hampton plantation postdate this period. The main house is believed to have been built about 1750 (Rutledge/Hampton Plantation Folder) and was enlarged in several stages to its present form by 1790 (Foley 1979:30–31). The relatively large size of this frame structure, together with its hipped roof and large pedimented portico supported by columns, clearly identify the present structure as a high-status residence of this period (Figure 3.5). Portions of a smaller frame building located to one side of the main house are also believed to represent a contemporaneous kitchen structure (Foley 1979:63).

An 1809 plan of Hampton Plantation (Diamond 1809) provides our only documentary clue to the layout of the early settlement (Figure 3.6). In addition to showing both impounded and tidal rice fields, the plan illustrates the main house and kitchen as well as a number of regularly arranged structures of varying size lying to the west of this complex. All but one of the buildings are unidentified but are likely

Figure 3.5 The main house at Hampton as it appeared in the early twentieth century. (Photograph courtesy South Carolina Department of Parks, Recreation, and Tourism.)

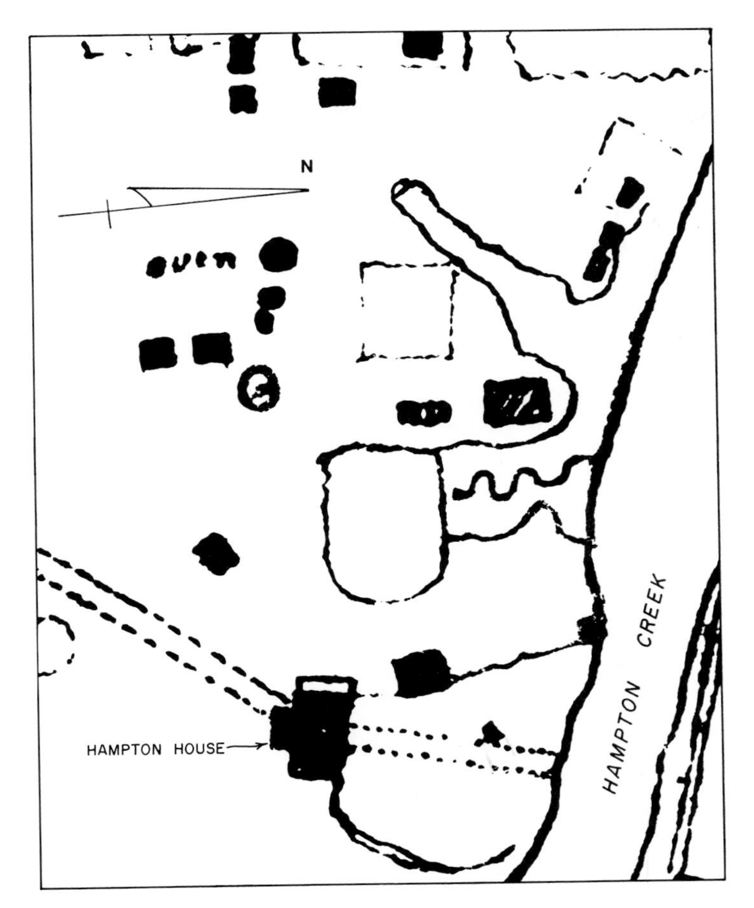

Figure 3.6 A portion of the 1809 Diamond plan of Hampton showing the layout of the plantation settlement.

to represent those associated with plantation production. The presence of agricultural processing and small-scale industrial activities at Hampton was noted by an 1804 visitor (Mason 1885:24) and the "oven" shown on the 1809 plan provides further evidence of the occurrence of these activities.

Unlike Middleton Place, Hampton survived the Civil War undamaged. Economic misfortunes prior to the war had greatly reduced the size of the original property (Lewis 1979:17), and the postbellum decline of the rice industry (Doar 1936:42) brought an end to commercial agricultural production at Hampton by the close of the nineteenth century (Rutledge 1937:34). Hampton served as a family residence and home to several tenant families until 1971, when the house and the surrounding land was purchased by the State of South Carolina for development as a historical park (Owens 1974:4).

AN ARCHAEOLOGICAL EXAMINATION OF MIDDLETON PLACE AND HAMPTON

Documentary data and surviving architecture have provided evidence that both Middleton Place and Hampton conformed to the general layout of plantation settlement described in the model. These data have indicated that each settlement contained a central complex composed of a mansion with one or more dependencies and that structures devoted to other plantation activities were placed to the side of this complex in a geometric arrangement reflecting a degree of overall site planning. These sources also reveal that the large-scale commercial production of rice took place at both settlements during the eighteenth century leaving little doubt as to function of these plantations.

The archaeological record is also capable of identifying settlement function by revealing information about layout and activity composition. Archaeological data can be employed to identify overall settlement function on the basis of such patterning even in the absence of other types of evidence. At Middleton Place and Hampton an analysis of archaeological data can play an important role in defining plantation settlement patterns by supplying new information as well as confirming conclusions drawn on the basis of other types of evidence. In order to explore settlement patterning here, it is necessary to employ a methodology that will permit us to examine the characteristics set forth in the plantation model.

Archaeological Methodology for the Study of Plantation Patterning

The model of plantation settlement emphasizes two aspects of site patterning, layout and content. In order to examine both archaeologically, it is necessary to employ a method designed to explore extensive areas while at the same time gathering data capable of revealing particular site elements. The investigations at Middleton Place and Hampton were aimed at discovering evidence of such patterning in the archaeological record. Because they represent the initial examination of these sites, the patterning they have revealed is of a broad nature. Consequently, questions asked at this point must deal with phenomena that relate to general behavioral variables rather than to specific aspects of the past settlements.

The discovery phase of investigations required the use of an exploration technique designed to gather a representative sample of the archaeological materials distributed over the areas to be surveyed. In order to achieve a maximum dispersal of the sample units within this area, a stratified systematic unaligned sampling technique was chosen (Haggett 1966:196–198). Redman and Watson (1970:281–282) have suggested that this technique is the best for revealing overall artifact patterning because it prevents the clustering of sample units and assures that no parts of the survey area are left unsampled. It is capable of discovering patterning in the archaeological record occurring both at regular and irregular intervals. It accomplishes this by dividing the area to be sampled into a series of square units (strata) based upon the coordinates of the site grid and then sampling a smaller unit within each stratum. The positions of the smaller units are determined by the intersection of coordinates selected along both axes of the grid from a random numbers table. The relative sizes of the units involved determine the percentage of the site area samples. Naturally the greater the size of the sample, the more reliable will be the results; however, the difficulty of enlarging the sample increases in direct proportion to the size of the site.

The sample excavations at Middleton Place and Hampton were intended to explore those areas likely to contain evidence of the plantation settlements. At the former the archaeological work examined the areas to the south and west of the main house complex. Because the formal gardens occupied the area to the other side of this complex, the sampled area was considered most likely to yield evidence of the service buildings shown in the 1840 drawing as well as those of an earlier period. A total of 1% of an area encompassing 137,500 square feet was sampled in these excavations (Figure 3.7).

At Hampton the sample area lay largely to the west of the main house. It was designed to explore a zone likely to have been occupied by at least a portion of the settlement indicated on the 1809 plan. Excavations were also extended to include the area around the main house to search for other earlier structures not shown on this map. These excavations sampled 1% of an area encompassing 150,000 square feet (Figure 3.8).

Using this sampling methodology it is possible to examine both the layout of settlement at each site as well as the contents of individual site elements. These two aspects of plantation settlement are explored by analyzing the nature and distribution of critical artifact variables at the two sites under consideration.

Settlement Layout

Documentary sources have revealed that Middleton Place and Hampton Plantations contained numerous out-buildings. Their geometric arrangement to one side of the main house complex conforms to the expectation of the plantation model and indicates that both these settlements exhibited the anticipated spatial layout. Although in these cases it is not necessary to rely on archaeological evidence to establish this aspect of settlement pattern, the material record can help isolate the exact locations of structures. Because these are likely to mark the sites of the most intensive activity and the most concentrated deposition from such activities, the structure-based activity areas defined here should also provide the basis for identifying intrasite variation, a task primarily dependent upon an analysis of the material data.

In order to ascertain the form of past settlement, it is necessary to examine the distribution of those artifacts most likely to reveal the spatial layout of activities associated with the plantation settlement. Because of the largely intact condition of the two sites, it is assumed that material remains generated by past activities there have remained concentrated in those areas where they were discarded, lost, or abandoned. This pattern of accumulation in the vicinity of use is typical of English medieval and postmedieval living sites (Hurst 1971:116) as well as those in British

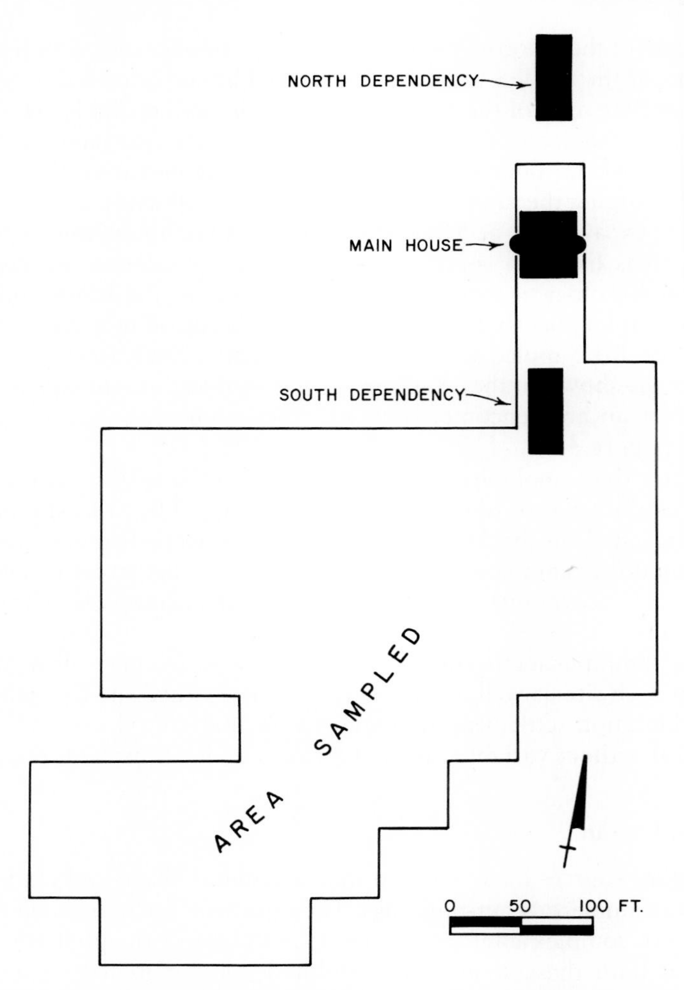

Figure 3.7 Plan of the area sampled archaeologically at Middleton Place.

colonial North America, including those areas occupied by slaves of African descent (Otto 1977:92; South 1977:47).

In order to observe the occurrence of settlement and activity patterning at the site of a settlement, it is helpful to display the frequencies of the archaeological evidence of such patterns on a map. A Synagraphic Computer Mapping Program (SYMAP) was employed in the analysis of the plantation data because this program has the ability to graphically depict dispersed quantitative variables (in this case artifact classes) by weight or count, and qualitative variables such as the presence or absence of particular classes. SYMAP accomplishes this by taking the assigned values for the coordinate locations of data points (here positions of the archaeological test units) and interpolating a continuous surface in the regions where there are no data points, basing these interpolated values on the distances to and the values of the neighboring data points (Dougenik and Sheehan 1976/I:1). The result is a contour map of the intensity of a particular archaeological variable's occurrence over the area of the site. It is important to remember, however, that the patterns produced by the SYMAP are not pictures based on the entire contents of the site, but rather projections based on the sample gathered. Although some distortions may be present, it is emphasized that the patterns displayed on the SYMAP are true reflections of actual patterns in the archaeological record.

The layout of structures is the key to defining plantation settlement pattern and may be ascertained by observing the distribution of those classes of artifacts most likely to represent the archaeological by-products of architectural activities. The distributions of architecturally related artifacts at Middleton Place and Hampton are shown in SYMAPs of these materials.

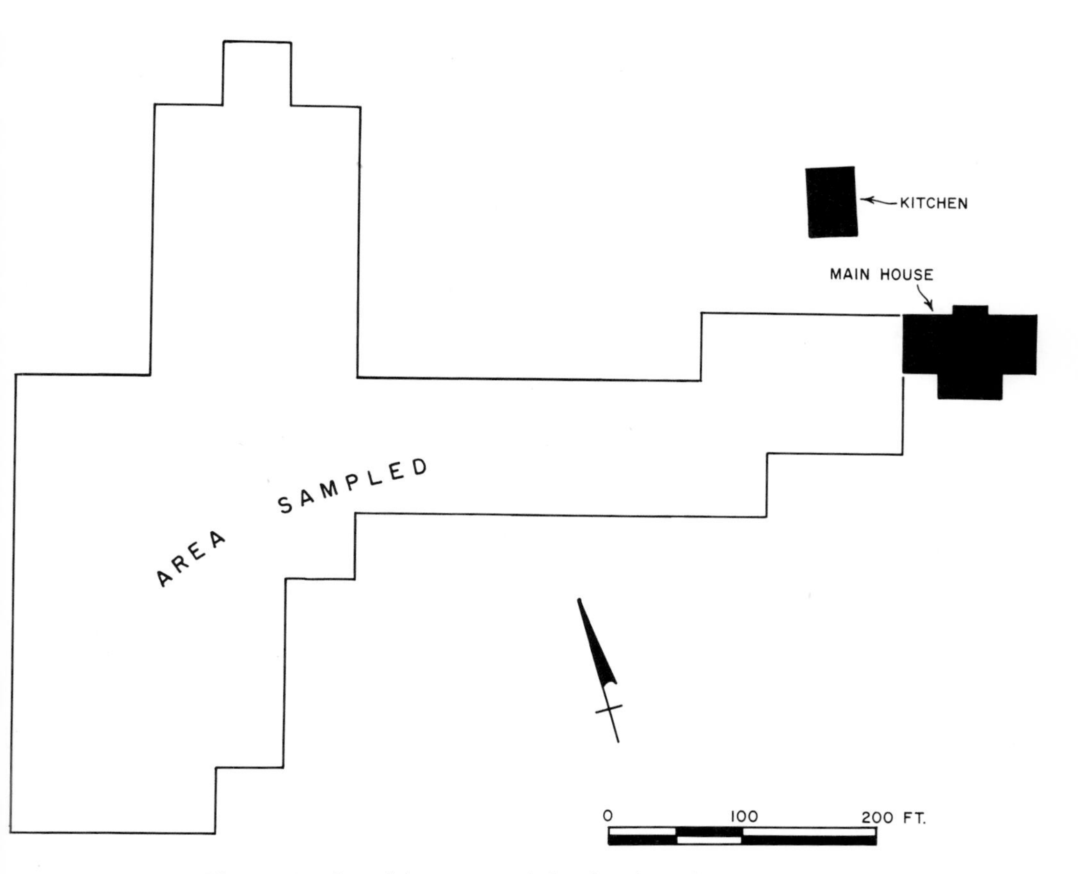

Figure 3.8 Plan of the area sampled archaeologically at Hampton.

The SYMAP of Middleton Place (Figure 3.9) reveals the locations of the two destroyed buildings of the main house complex. A third building, the southern dependency, is still standing and has produced a lesser amount of structural debris. Four other clusters of architectural debris mark the locations of at least eight buildings arranged in a manner suggested by the 1840 sketch (Lewis and Hardesty 1979:36).

At Hampton the distribution of structural remains has permitted us to define the locations of nine structural concentrations (Figure 3.10), including three that comprise the main house complex. Their layout corresponds roughly to the distribution of structures shown on the 1809 map and shows a geometric arrangement of buildings to the side of the main house complex. Additional archaeological investigations revealed the presence of a dependency to the east of the main house, creating a

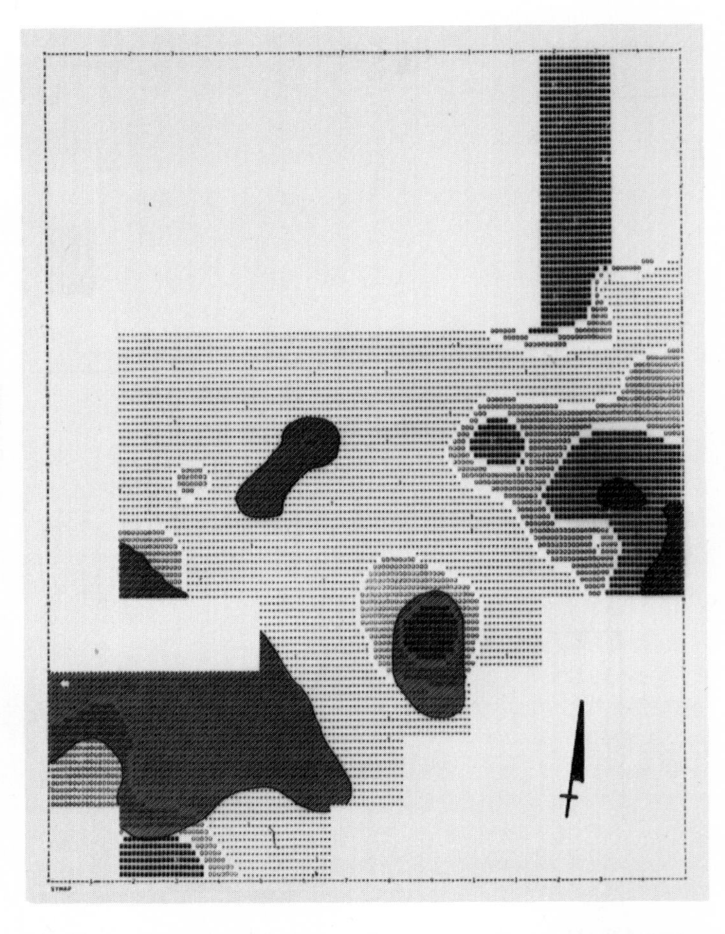

Figure 3.9 SYMAP showing the distribution of structural materials at Middleton Place.

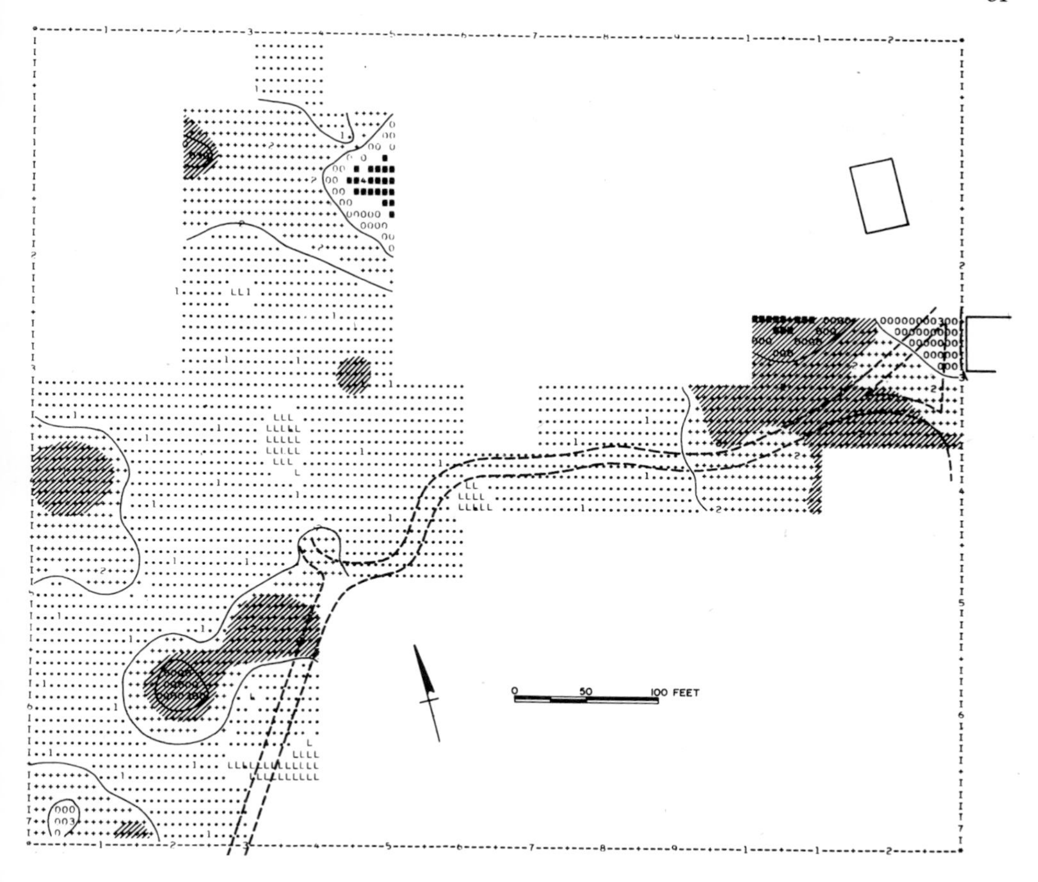

Figure 3.10 SYMAP showing the distribution of structural materials at Hampton.

symmetrical arrangement of these structures to either side of the mansion (Lewis and Haskell 1980:31, 46).

The concentrations of structural materials at each site may be assumed to represent loci of structure-based activity areas. These areas are shown in Figures 3.11 and 3.12 and will constitute the units upon which a comparison of archaeological materials will be based in the following discussion of intrasite activity patterning.

Activity Patterning

As plantations, Middleton Place and Hampton would have been the sites of similar types of activities. The composition of these settlements was described in the plantation model. Based on the characteristics of the model and the layout of the two plantations, we may expect that the settlements would be composed of a main house area and a group of structures devoted to other plantation activities. The main house

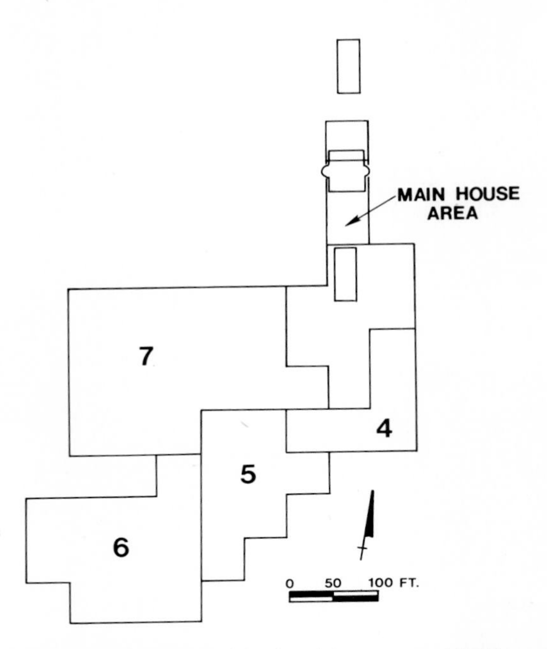

Figure 3.11 Map of structure-based activity areas at Middleton Place.

complexes should be identifiable as multifunction areas, reflecting their role as a center for high-status as well as specialized domestic activities. Buildings and activity areas situated to the side of these complexes, on the other hand, should reflect their function of workers' living areas and the sites of other specialized plantation activities.

Plantation activities may be identified by observing variation in the occurrence of functionally significant artifact classes among the structure-based activity areas defined earlier. On the basis of this comparison, it should be possible to distinguish patterning in the archaeological record that is related to the types of activities postulated to have taken place at Middleton Place and Hampton. Variation in this patterning should permit us to observe the arrangement of these activities on each site. Because the spatial extent of the archaeological sampling was not unlimited, only a portion of the total occupied area at each site and the activities they contained is identifiable at this time. The sampled areas are likely, however, to be large enough to have encompassed loci of those activities previously described, and evidence of these should be discernible in the archaeological record.

The structure-based activity areas at Middleton Place and Hampton may be identified archaeologically by analyzing their contents with respect to various functionally significant classes of artifacts. Variation in artifact class occurrence is likely to be related to the presence of different types of activities, and the association of patterns of activity class variation with particular areas should permit the identification of each areas's function.

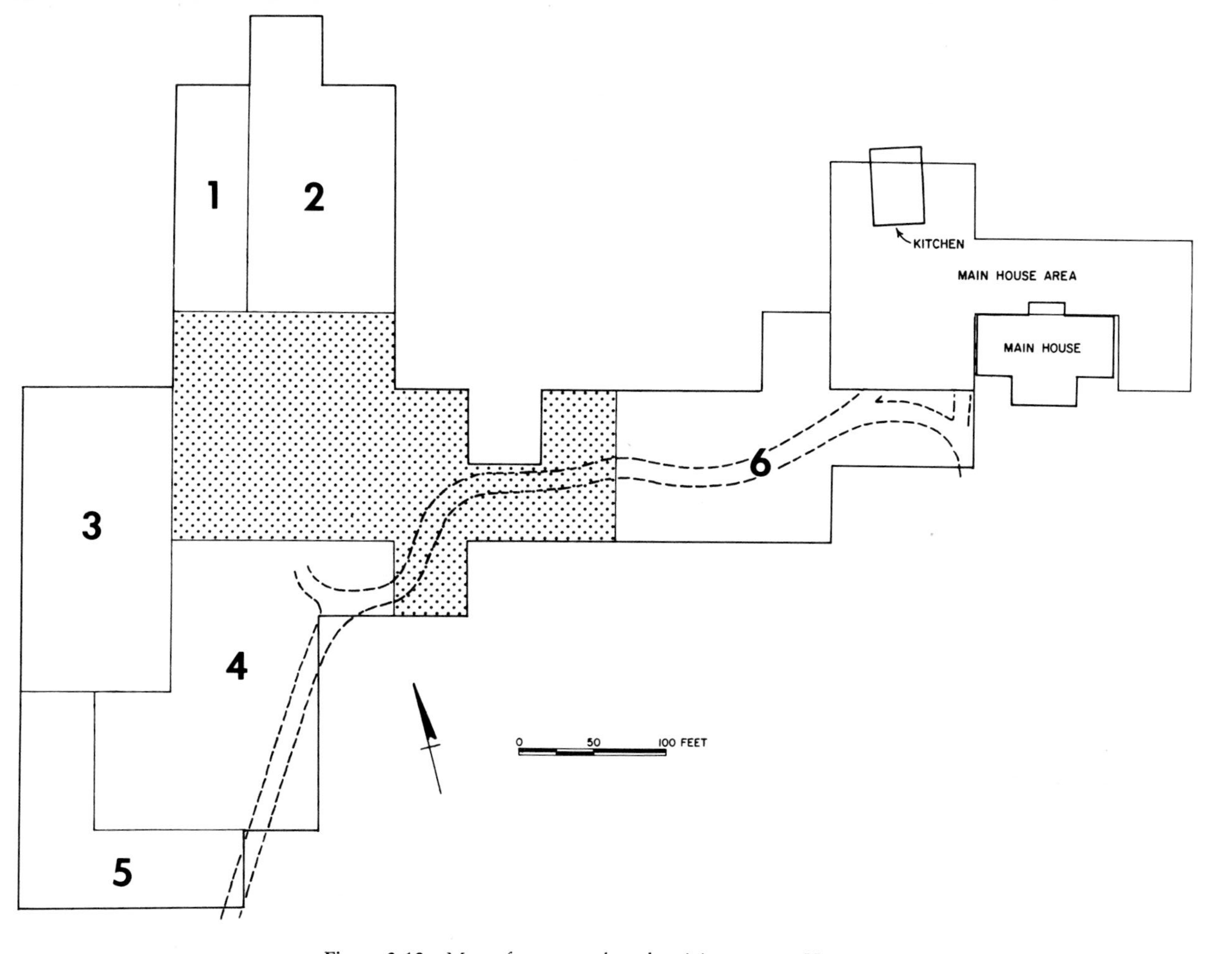

Figure 3.12 Map of structure-based activity areas at Hampton.

Table 3.1
SUBSISTENCE ACTIVITY CATEGORIES AND ASSOCIATED ARTIFACT CLASSES

Activity category	Artifact class
Subsistence	Food storage containers Food processing tools Cooking and eating utensils Floral and faunal remains Fishing and hunting equipment
Subsistence–Technological	Architectural artifacts Personal artifacts
Technological	Tools Processing equipment Storage containers

Domestic versus Specialized Activity Occurrence

Several basic distinctions between activities have been described. These are domestic versus specialized activities and the high versus low status of an area's occupants. The first group of activities may be distinguished by employing categories designed to identify the degree to which domestic activity is likely to have produced the total archaeological output of a particular activity area. Three activity categories may be examined: (1) Subsistence activities that are likely to occur in the context of a living area; (2) Subsistence–Technological activities that may occur in areas that supported both a domestic and nondomestic occupation; and (3) Technological activities that would have taken place only in a nondomestic, specialized activity context (Lewis 1976:119–120). The artifact classes associated with these activity categories are summarized in Table 3.1.

A tabulation of the Middleton Place and Hampton data according to these categories was made on the basis of the relative size of the first two categories. It is assumed that the accumulation of artifacts associated with the Subsistence–Technological category would remain relatively constant regardless of the nature of the activity performed in a given area or structure where they were deposited. The size of the Subsistence activity artifact component, however, should vary with the role of subsistence activities performed there. Thus, those areas containing the largest relative frequencies of Subsistence activity artifacts should be domestic activity areas, while those with lower frequencies are more likely to represent—at least in part—the sites of other types of activities. Because specialized areas are often characterized by a low rate of by-product discard and a high rate of associated artifacts, their recognition in the archaeological record is uncertain, especially in the case of small samples such as those obtained from Middleton Place and Hampton. Consequently, the occurrence of specialized activities at these sites may be measured by the relative frequencies of

Table 3.2

COMPARISON OF PERCENTAGE FREQUENCIES OF ACTIVITY CATEGORY ARTIFACTS BY STRUCTURE-BASED ACTIVITY AREA AT MIDDLETON PLACE AND HAMPTON

	Area							
Activity category	1	2	3	4	5	6	7	Main house
				MIDDLETON PLACE				
Subsistence	—	—	—	71.2	44.7	71.4	74.1	58.2
Subsistence–Technological	—	—	—	28.5	29.6	28.4	25.5	41.2
Technological	—	—	—	0.3	25.7	0.2	0.4	0.6
				HAMPTON				
Subsistence	65.0	56.7	63.4	69.2	72.9	65.8	—	56.2
Subsistence–Technological	35.0	43.2	36.1	30.7	27.0	34.1	—	43.6
Technological	0	0.1	0.1	0.1	0.1	0.1	—	0.2

Sources: Lewis (1979); Lewis and Hardesty (1979); Lewis and Haskell (1980).

artifacts falling within the Subsistence and Subsistence–Technological activity categories.

The percentage frequencies of artifacts in the three activity categories at Middleton Place and Hampton are presented in Table 3.2. An examination of the frequenies in Table 3.2 reveals a wide variation in the two larger categories and a consistently low frequency of Technological activity artifacts except in Area 5 at Middleton Place. When compared graphically (Figure 3.13), the percentage frequencies of the Subsistence and Subsistence–Technological activity artifacts fall into several clusters. The highest frequencies of Subsistence activity artifacts occurs in Areas 4 and 5 at Hampton and Areas 4, 6, and 7 at Middleton Place. Areas 1, 3, and 6 at Hampton cluster slightly below this group. A third cluster contains the Main House areas at both plantations and Area 2 at Hampton. Area 5 at Middleton Place is unique in that it is characterized by a substantial amount of refuse from a Technological activity, dramatically reducing the frequency of its Subsistence activity artifact component.

If we assume that the relative occurrence of Subsistence activity artifacts reflects the intensity of an area's domestic occupation, then the first cluster would appear to represent living areas. The next cluster is likely to include areas of mixed domestic and specialized activity that left no substantial by-product. The presence of such combined activity loci were not uncommon on plantations. Although most slaves are reported to have lived in separate structures (Fogel and Engerman 1974:115), house servants and those associated with industries and crafts were often housed in or adjacent to structures devoted to these activities (Anthony 1976:13–14). If the cluster of structures at Hampton represents a settlement where such activities were carried out, the occurrence of an archaeological assemblage reflecting a mixed domestic-specialized activity occupation would not be unexpected.

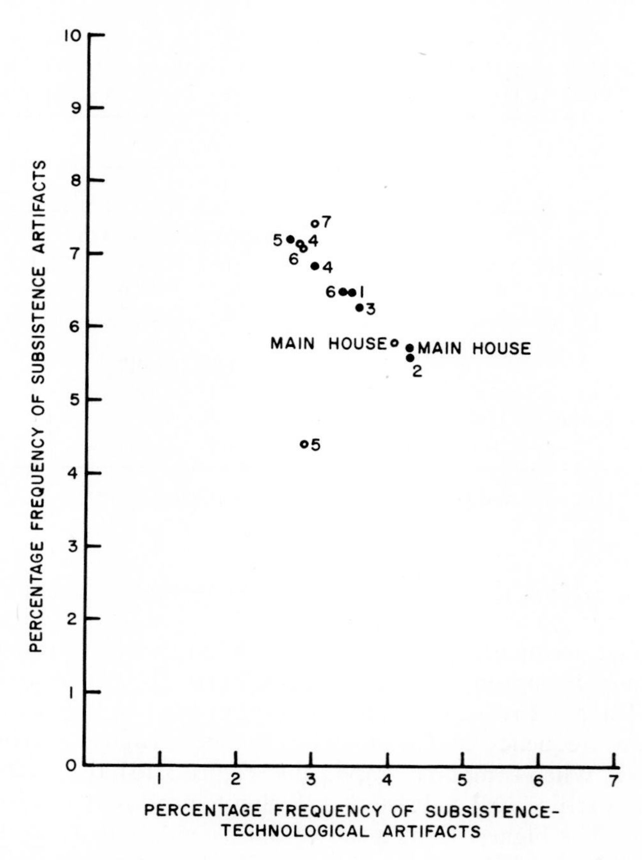

Figure 3.13 Relative percentage frequencies of Subsistence and Subsistence–Technological activity artifacts at (●) Middleton Place and (○) Hampton.

Area 5 at Middleton Place contains a great deal of slag produced as a by-product of a Technological activity, probably smithing. As a consequence, the other two activity artifact frequencies are lower than would be the case if no such by-product had been produced. If the Technological activity artifact component is subtracted, the relative frequencies of the other two activity classes are similar to those found in the three areas at Hampton constituting the second cluster previously discussed (Figure 3.13).

As anticipated, the main house areas at Middleton Place and Hampton also exhibit a lower relative frequency of Subsistence activity artifacts. This reflects each area's combined use as both a residence and the site of administrative and other specialized activities. Additionally, because the main house was the central element of a plantation and a focal point for the display of wealth, discard activities that normally would have taken place near living areas are less likely to have been carried out here. If we are sure that Subsistence activity artifact discard is primarily redeposited refuse and Subsistence–Technological activity artifacts accumulate generally as a result of abandonment, loss, or other modes of unintentional disposal, then it is probable that such refuse would have been removed from areas intentionally kept free of debris. This could well preclude the deposition of this refuse in the vicinity of a main house settlement. Subsistence–Technological remains, on the other hand, are less likely to have been redeposited elsewhere. Consequently, the size of this artifact component should be relatively larger at the site of a main house settlement (kept clean of Subsistence activity refuse) than at the sites of other living areas where no social prohibitions against the adjacent accumulation of redeposited refuse existed.

Area 2 at Hampton also exhibits a relatively high frequency of Subsistence–Technological artifacts. Its location away from the main house complex and the absence of high-status architecture here implies that its archaeological contents are not a result of the processes discussed earlier. Rather, it is likely to represent a specialized activity area at which a much lesser amount of domestic activity took place.

On the basis of material evidence, it has been possible to generally classify activity areas at the two plantations into those of domestic and specialized activities. This classification marks the major division of the plantation settlement into residence and production areas. Plantations were also characterized by a fixed-status hierarchy that clearly differentiated between the managers and workers involved in the production process. This social and economic inequality should be discernible archaeologically and is discussed next.

High- versus Low-Status Occupations

The presence of the standing main house structure at Hampton and its visible ruins at Middleton Place clearly mark the areas of the sites occupied by high-status individuals, the plantation owners. The remaining areas in each of these sites—because of their location in the settlements—are assured to have been areas lived in and used by persons of much lower status, the plantation laborers or their supervisors. Their lower status relative to the owner's should be reflected in a differential use of material culture items (Otto 1977) and the subsequent appearance of these artifacts in the archaeological record.

An obvious indicator of status within a site is the differential distribution of wealth goods—access to which would be restricted to persons of high social and economic status. The appearance of such items in the archaeological record, however, is complicated by the fact that they are often, in themselves, highly valued objects that are subject to a high rate of retention. For this reason, their occurrence is usually not as much a result of discard and abandonment, as is the case with less valuable artifacts, rather, their appearance is nearly always considered a consequence of loss.

An examination of the archaeological records at Middleton Place and Hampton reveals that at both sites high-status artifacts were confined to the main house areas alone. These artifacts included portable items such as lead-glass drinking glass fragments, wine glass fragments, an abalone button, and a silver-stringed instrument tuning knob. Architectural artifacts consisting of marble veneer and purple delft tile fragments were also recovered (Lewis and Hardesty 1979:47; Lewis and Haskell 1980:52).

Another artifact that is likely to be linked to status within the colonial plantation context is oriental procelain, an important ware that gained increasingly in popularity during the eighteenth century. Its use was particularly associated with the tea ceremony, an English social custom in which people of both sexes gathered to exchange information, engage in conversation, and court while consuming the beverage (Roth 1961:70). The tea ceremony and its required use of porcelain had become commonplace in British colonial North America in the second half of the century, making the archaeological occurrence of this ceramic unreliable as a status marker in most colonial settlements.

In a plantation settlement, however, only a small portion of the population was English (its owners and managerial staff) and the occurrence of the tea ceremony is likely to have been restricted to the areas they occupied. The remainder of the plantation population consisted of slaves. They were not ethnically British nor are they believed to have participated extensively in this ceremony in their living areas. Consequently, the use of porcelain by these two groups may be expected to have been dramatically different. In addition, with the exception of locally made earthen wares, or colonowares (Ferguson 1980), most ceramics used on the plantation were obtained and distributed by the owner or manager. This centralized acquisition of ceramics is likely to have further systemized the kinds of ceramics used and served particularly to restrict the flow of porcelain to those individuals of higher status. Plantation slaves, particularly household servants whose work regularly placed them in close proximity to the behavior of high-status persons, may be expected to have become acculturated to the use of porcelain and have begun to acquire it in small quantities by the close of the colonial period (Otto 1977:106).

Archaeologically it is predicted that porcelain will occur in deposits associated with the living areas of both manager and worker. However, differences in the use patterns make it very likely that a great deal of disparity will exist in the occurrence of porcelain between these two areas. For this reason the areas within and adjacent to the main house complex should exhibit a higher frequency of procelain than other areas at Hampton and Middleton Place.

Table 3.3 shows the percentage frequencies of occurrence of porcelain at Middleton Place and Hampton. The main house areas at both sites and adjacent Area 4 at Middleton Place exhibit markedly higher frequencies of porcelain than do all of the other areas. The consistency of this frequency suggests a similarity in the use rate of this artifact at both plantation settlements. This concentration of porcelain use in the main house area is reflected not only by the low frequencies of its occurrence elsewhere on the plantations, but also by the fact that its use appears to have increased with proximity to the main house where it may have accumulated as either redeposited refuse discarded at the periphery of this area, or as refuse produced as a

Table 3.3
FREQUENCIES OF OCCURRENCE OF PORCELAIN BY STRUCTURE-BASED ACTIVITY AREA AT MIDDLETON PLACE AND HAMPTON[a]

Area	Total European ceramics (%)
Middleton Place	
Main house[b]	18
4[b]	20
5	10
6[b]	9
7[b]	7
Hampton	
Main house[b]	20
1	1
2	2
3	4
4[b]	7
5[b]	4
6	12

[a]Sources: Lewis and Hardesty (1979:48); Lewis and Haskell (1980:54).
[b]Denotes domestic activity area.

result of recycling it to house servants or other living close to the main house (cf. Otto 1977:97).

The distribution of status-sensitive artifacts reflects the pattern of high- and low-status occupation indicated by architectural remains and supports the differential use of plantation areas described in the plantation model. Functional variation with regard to domestic versus specialized activity also has been examined using archaeological data and has permitted us to distinguish basic functional differences within the two plantation settlements.

The results of these two analyses reveal that, as expected, each settlement contained living areas as well as areas of production. The presence of a substantial Subsistence activity artifact component in nearly all areas, however, suggests that most areas contained a domestic component as well, perhaps indicating the housing of laborers near their places of work. Main house areas at both sites, although built around an owner's residence, were primarily sites of administrative and specialized activities, a function that is reflected in the relatively smaller Subsistence activity artifact component recovered. The archaeological record also clearly reveals the high status of its occupants in contrast to those who lived and worked elsewhere on the two settlements.

By observing the differential occurrence of functionally significant artifacts, it has been possible to identify and observe the spatial layout of activities at Middleton Place and Hampton. The results of the archaeological analyses not only substantiate conclusions drawn from documentary sources regarding the two eighteenth century plantations, but also have provided additional information about the form and composition of these settlements. The study of material evidence has shown that both settlements shared a functional pattern associated with eighteenth century plantations. By doing so it has demonstrated not only the utility of archaeological methodology, but also the usefulness of employing the plantation model as an interpretive tool in the investigation of colonial settlement in South Carolina.

CONCLUSIONS

In this chapter a general model of plantation settlement patterning has been developed and examined at the sites of two eighteenth century plantations in the South Carolina lowcountry. Within the context of the model, plantations are viewed as agricultural "factories" engaged in the large-scale production of staple crops and organized to permit centralized control to be exercised over a variety of activities associated with this task. Plantation organization was manifested in a settlement pattern characterized by an orderly layout of activities and structures concentrated in the vicinity of the main house complex from which production was directed. Middleton Place and Hampton both exhibit this settlement pattern. The distribution of structures and the nature of activities at each reflect both the social and economic complexity of plantation settlements as well as the systematic arrangement of their components in space. On the basis of settlement patterns, these settlements clearly conform to the model.

The results of this study have several important implications regarding our ability to discern functionally meaningful settlement patterning. First, they demonstrate the utility of employing archaeological methodology to discern patterning capable of revealing past activities and their organization in space. Although documentary evidence relating to settlement layout at both sites is available, the nature and actual locations of structures and activities can only be ascertained through an analysis of the material evidence. In the absence of written records, an analysis of archaeological data should accomplish this task with equal certainty. The usefulness of material data in exploring functional patterning by no means negates the importance of documentary sources in the study of this phenomenon—each is a separate form of data resulting from a different process of transmission. Consequently, the information obtained from one source may not mirror that revealed by the other and each reflects different aspects of a past social system. The roles of these two sources will vary depending on the questions asked and the availability of each type of data. Each, however, may be employed to investigate processual aspects independently and thus also has the potential of verifying as well as supplementing conclusions drawn from the other.

Second, in order to distinguish the elements crucial to the recognition of plantation settlement pattern, it has been necessary to identify artifact patterning linked to the occurrence of particular categories of activity. Two broad activity categories have been employed to discern domestic activity areas from those where specialized activities were carried out. Each included a series of artifact classes, the relative occurrence of which is likely to vary with the nature of the activity that produced a particular archaeological assemblage. By measuring the relative frequencies of occurrence of these artifact classes between areas at both sites, it has been possible to distinguish archaeological patterns that appear to be linked to the presence of certain activities at these sites. Archaeological patterning linked to status differentiation has also been observed. The delineation of these functional artifact patterns implies the existence of others related to different aspects of past activity. The importance of discovering and employing such patterns should not be underestimated.

Finally, the archaeology at Middleton Place and Hampton involved the use of sampling, a technique by which only a small portion of either site was examined. The archaeological patterns obtained from sample data, while representative of the site as a whole, are broad and are not intended to discern the material variation observable through the use of more intrusive investigations. As such, these patterns are likely to represent only the "tip of the iceberg" of data contained in plantation and other relevant sites. The usefulness of the material record in the study of functional patterning is only beginning to be explored in historic sites archaeology. Its potential, though as yet unrealized, is especially great with regard to those settlements and groups about which little documentation exists. Plantations, because of their social and organizational complexity, offer an excellent opportunity to study a variety of behaviors through the investigation of patterning in the archaeological record.

ACKNOWLEDGMENTS

I wish to thank several individuals and organizations for their help in carrying out the research upon which this essay is based. Donald L. Hardesty worked with me at Middleton Place and coauthored the initial report of the findings. On the two projects at Hampton plantation I was assisted by James B. Scurry and Helen Haskell, the latter of whom collaborated in the report of the second season's work. Stanley South read the manuscript of this paper and offered many helpful suggestions. Darby Erd prepared several of the illustrations appearing here and Azalee Swindle typed several drafts of the manuscript. I also wish to acknowledge the support of the Institute of Archaeology and Anthropology of the University of South Carolina under whose auspices the archaeological work discussed here was carried out. The Middleton Place Foundation kindly allowed the reproduction of the 1840 sketch of Middleton Place.

REFERENCES

Anthony, Carl
1976 The big house and the slave quarters, part 1: prelude to New World architecture. *Landscape* 21(1):8–19.

Architects' Emergency Committee
1933 *Great Georgian Houses of America,* Vol. 1. New York: Kalkhoff Press. Reprint edition, New York: Dover, 1970.

Castiglione, Luigi Conte
1790 *Viaggio negli Stati Uniti dell' America Settentrionale, fatto negli anni, 1785, 1786, e 1787.* 3 vols. Milano: Stamperia di G. Marelli.
Chang, Kwang-Chih
1967 *Rethinking Archaeology.* New York: Random House.
Cheyney, Edward Potts
1961 *European Background of American History: 1300–1600.* New York: Collier Books.
Clowse, Converse D.
1971 *Economic Beginnings in Colonial South Carolina.* Columbia: University of South Carolina Press.
Crane, Verner W.
1929 *The Southern Frontier, 1670–1732.* Ann Arbor: University of Michigan Press. Reprint ed., Ann Arbor Paperbacks, 1956.
Diamond, John
1809 The plat of a body of lands on Santee in the state of South Carolina in three plantations contiguous known by three different names of Hampton, Wambaw, & Jack's Bluff, containing in the whole five thousand three hundred and eighty-five acres, belonging to C. L. Pinckney Horry Esqr. from a survey made in June 1809. Map 96 × 76 cm., no scale given. Charleston County, Records of the Register of Mesne Conveyance, McCrady Plats #4329 and 4330. Charleston, S.C.
Doar, David
1936 Rice and rice planting in the South Carolina Lowcountry. *Contributions from the Charleston Museum* 8:7–42.
Dodd, William E.
1921 *The Cotton Kingdom, a Chronicle of the Old South.* New Haven: Yale University Press.
Dougenik, James A., and David E. Sheehan
1976 *SYMAP user's reference manual.* Cambridge, Massachusetts: Harvard University, Laboratory for Computer Graphics and Spatial Analysis.
Drayton, John
1865 Letter to Williams Middleton, June 2, 1865. Middleton Family Papers/7-2. Middleton Place Foundation, Charleston.
Earle, Carville, and Ronald Hoffman
1976 Staple crops and urban development in the eighteenth century South. *Perspectives in American History* 10:7–80.
Ferguson, Leland G.
1980 Looking for the "Afro" in Colono-Indian Pottery. In *Archaeological Perspectives on Ethnicity in America.* Rober L. Schuyler, ed. New York: Baywood Press. Pp. 14–28.
Fogel, Robert William, and Stanley L. Engerman
1974 *Time on the Cross, the Economics of American Negro Slavery.* Boston: Little, Brown.
Foley, David Michael, ed.
1976 *A Master Plan for Hampton Plantation State Park.* Columbia: South Carolina Department of Parks, Recreation, and Tourism, Division of State Parks.
Gentleman's Magazine
1753 Poetical essay from C. W. in Carolina to E. J. at Gosport. 23:337–338.
Gould, J. D.
1972 *Economic Growth in History, Survey and Analysis.* London: Methuen & Co., Ltd.
Gray, Lewis Cecil
1933 *History of Agriculture in the Southern United States to 1860.* 2 vols. Washington, D.C.: Carnegie Institute of Washington. Reprint ed., Gloucester, Massachusetts: Peter Smith, 1958.
Grayson, William John
1960 Recollections of an island boyhood. In *Port Royal Under Six Flags.* Katherine M. Jones, ed. New York: Bobbs-Merrill Company. Pp. 144–151.

Haggett, Peter
1966 *Locational Analysis in Human Geography*. New York: St. Martin's Press.
Handler, Jerome, and Frederick Lange
1978 *Plantation Slavery in Barbados: An Archaeological and Historical Investigation*. Cambridge, Massachusetts: Harvard University Press.
Hilliard, Sam Bowers
1975 The Tidewater rice plantation: an indigenous adaptation to nature, *Geoscience and Man* 12:57–66.
1978 Antebellum tidewater rice culture in South Carolina and Georgia. In *European Settlement and Development in North America: Essays on Geographical Change in Honor and Memory of Andrew Hill Clark*. James R. Gibson, ed. Toronto: University of Toronto Press. Pp. 91–115.
Hurst, John G.
1971 A review of archaeological research. In *Deserted Medieval Villages*. Maurice Beresford and John G. Hurst, eds. London: Butterworth Press. Pp. 76–144.
Kimball, Fiske
1922 *Domestic Architecture of the American Colonies and of the Early Republic*. New York: Charles Scribner's Sons. Reprint ed., New York: Dover Publications, 1966.
Lewis, Kenneth E.
1976 Camden, a frontier town in eighteenth century South Carolina. *University of South Carolina, Institute of Archeology and Anthropology, Anthropological Studies*, Vol. 2.
1979 Hampton, initial archeological investigations at an eighteenth century rice plantation in the Santee Delta, South Carolina. *University of South Carolina, Institute of Archeology and Anthropology, Research Manuscript Series*, Vol. 151.
Lewis, Kenneth E., and Donald L. Hardesty
1979 Middleton Place: initial archeological investigations at an Ashley River rice plantation. *University of South Carolina, Institute of Archeology and Anthropology, Research Manuscript Series*, Vol. 148.
Lewis, Kenneth E., and Helen Haskell
1980 Hampton II: further archeological investigations at a Santee River rice plantation. *University of South Carolina, Institute of Archeology and Anthropology, Research Manuscript Series*, Vol. 161.
MacLeod, William Christie
1928 *The American Indian Frontier*. New York: Knopf.
Mason, Jonathan
1885 Extracts from travel diary (1804). *Proceedings of the Massachusetts Historical Society*, 2nd Series, 2:23–25.
Middleton, Nathaniel R., Jr.
1929 Record. In *Life in Carolina and New England During the Nineteenth Century*. N. R. Middleton, ed. Bristol, R.I.: privately printed. Pp. 138–182.
Mintz, Sidney, W.
1959 The plantation as a socio-cultural type. In *Plantation Systems of the New World*. Pan American Union, Social Science Monographs 7:42–49.
National Register File
South Carolina Department of Archives and History, Columbia.
News and Courier (Charleston, S.C.)
1937 New guest house and stable constructed at famous estate harmonize in tone with residence on the Ashley River. *News and Courier*, April 12, 1937.
Olmsted, Frederick Law
1957 A tobacco plantation in Virginia. In *The Plantation South*. Kathrine M. Jones, ed. Indianapolis: Bobbs-Merrill. Pp. 49–55.

Otto, John Solomon
1977 Artifacts and status differences—a comparison of ceramic differences from planter, overseer, and slave sites on an antebellum plantation. In *Research Strategies in Historical Archaeology*. Stanley South, ed. New York: Academic Press. Pp. 91–118.
Owens, Loulie Latimer
1974 Guide to the Archibald Hamilton Rutledge papers, 1860–1970. South Caroliniana Library, University of South Carolina, Columbia.
Pan American Union
1959 Appendix: summaries of workshops. In *Plantation Systems of the New World*. Social Science Monographs 7:188–196.
Petty, Julian J.
1943 *The Growth and Distribution of Population in South Carolina*. Columbia: South Carolina State Planning Board, Bulletin 11. Reprint ed., Spartanburg, S.C.: The Reprint Company, 1975.
Phillips, Ulrich Bonnell
1929 *Life and Labor in the Old South*. Boston: Little, Brown and Co.
Prunty, Merle, Jr.
1955 The renaissance of the southern plantation. *The Geographical Review* 45(4):459–491.
Rawick, George P.
1972 *The American Slave: a Composite Autobiography*. Vol. 1:*From Sundown to Sunup, the Making of the Black Community*. Westport, Connecticut: Greenwood Publishing Co.
Redfield, Margaret
1978 Historic houses: Middleton Place annals. *Architectural Digest* 35(9):104–111.
Redman, Charles L., and Patty Jo Watson
1970 Systematic intensive surface collection. *American Antiquity* 35(3):279–291.
Roth, Rodris
1961 Tea drinking in eighteenth century America: its etiquette and equipage. *United States National Museum,* Bulletin 225.
Rowse, A. L.
1957 Tudor expansion: the transition from medieval to modern history. *William and Mary College Quarterly,* Series 3, 14(3):309–316.
Rutledge, Archibald
1937 *My Colonel and His Lady*. Indianapolis: Bobbs-Merrill.
Rutledge, Lise
Untitled manuscript in Hampton Plantation folder. South Carolina Historical Society, Charleston.
Salley, A. S., Jr.
1936 The true story of how the Madagascar gold seed rice was introduced into South Carolina. *Contributions of the Charleston Museum*. 8:51–53.
Sellers, Leila
1934 *Charleston Business on the Eve of the American Revolution*. Chapel Hill: University of North Carolina Press.
Smith, Henry A. M.
1919 The Ashley River: its seats and settlements. *South Carolina Historical and Geneological Magazine* 20(1):3–51 and (2):75–122.
Smith, Julia Floyd
1973 *Slavery and Plantation Growth in Antebellum Florida, 1821–1860*. Gainesville: University of Florida Press.
South, Stanley
1977 *Method and Theory in Historical Archeology*. New York: Academic Press.
South Carolina Records of the Secretary of State
Land Grants, Colonial Series, 1694–1776, 43 vols. South Carolina Archives, Columbia.

Thompson, Edgar T.
1959 The plantation as a social system. In *Plantation Systems of the New World.* Pan American Union, Social Science Monographs 7:26–37.
Trigger, Bruce G.
1967 Settlement archaeology—its goals and promise. *American Antiquity* 32(2):149–160.
Wagley, Charles, and Marvin Harris
1955 A typology of Latin American subcultures. *American Anthropologist* 57(3):428–451.
Wallerstein, Immanuel
1974 *The Modern World System, Capitalist Agriculture and the Origins of the European World Economy in the Sixteenth Century.* New York: Academic Press.
Waterman, Thomas Tileston
1945 *The Mansions of Virginia, 1706–1776.* Chapel Hill: University of North Carolina Press.
Waterman, Thomas Tileston, and John A. Barrows
1969 *Domestic Colonial Architecture of Tidewater Virginia.* New York: Dover Publications.
Willey, Gordon R.
1953 Prehistoric settlement patterns in the Viru Valley, Peru. *Bureau of American Ethnology,* Bulletin 155.
Wood, Peter
1974 *Black Majority: Negroes in Colonial South Carolina from 1670 through the Stono Rebellion.* New York: Norton.

4

Plantation Settlement from Slavery to Tenancy: An Example from a Piedmont Plantation in South Carolina

Charles E. Orser, Jr.

Annette M. Nekola

INTRODUCTION

Archaeologists have understood the value of studying the spatial arrangement of settlement locales since the nineteenth century, but it has only been within the last three decades that archaeologists have begun to view the study of past settlement systems as a respectable and fruitful area of research (Chang 1972:1; Clarke 1977:3). Since the 1950s archaeologists in North America and Europe have sought to understand settlement systems better and have adopted a number of geographical and statistical techniques for use with their archaeological data sets (Hodder 1977; Hodder and Orton 1976; Zimmerman 1978). While many different types of spatial analyses have been conducted by archaeologists, perhaps the greatest potential is in the area of settlement dynamics (Crumley 1979). It is in this area of study that plantation archaeology can make the greatest contribution to our knowledge of past settlement practices.

Although the development of a slave-based system of plantation agriculture in the American South has received considerable attention, less notice has been paid to the

ISBN 0-12-646480-4

plantation as a physical entity. The plantation, because of its special economic purpose and social configuration, had a particular spatial organization that was designed to maximize its economic profitability. Even the social relationships that developed at plantations had clear spatial correlates (Blassingame 1979:223; Thompson 1975:32; Wolf 1959:136–137). With the Civil War and emancipation, the settlement system of the plantation underwent a radical change as the social relationships and economic composition of the plantation was altered. The purpose of this chapter is to present a model of plantation spatial organization in the North American Southeast and to evaluate how the spatial organization of one nineteenth-century South Carolina piedmont plantation conforms to the model.

MODELING PLANTATION SETTLEMENT SYSTEMS

While it is true that there has not been a concentrated effort to study the spatial organization of southern plantations, there have been at least two notable exceptions. These studies, by David Crenshaw Barrow and Merle Prunty, Jr., provide the basis for the following model of plantation settlement organization and change.

In 1881 David C. Barrow published an article in *Scribner's Monthly* in which he attempted to explain to skeptical Southerners—who could remember the Civil War and who believed that southern agriculture would come to total ruin once slavery was abolished—that the "labor-relations of the two races are adjusting themselves and working out a solution of the dreaded 'negro problem' in a practical way" (Barrow 1881:830). Even though a subtle strain of racism runs through the article, Barrow makes a number of interesting observations on the social life of the postwar plantation and his comments on plantation spatial organization are particularly interesting.

Speaking of antebellum plantation settlement, Barrow (1881:831–832) noted that the houses of the planter and overseer were located near the linearly arranged slave dwellings, or "quarters," in order to provide the maximum in slave control and surveillance. With formal emancipation this spatial pattern changed as the houses of the former slaves, now small farmers, became dispersed throughout the plantation lands as the freedmen attempted to acquire "more elbow-room." According to Barrow, "the transformation has been so gradual that almost imperceptibly a radical change has been effected" (1881:831).

The settlement pattern shift observed by Barrow was later expanded upon by geographer Merle Prunty, Jr. who used the works of Barrow and others in conjunction with his own empirical data to define what he termed the "Ante Bellum Plantation Occupance Form" and the "Post Bellum 'Fragmented' Occupance Form" (Prunty 1955). (Prunty also identified a third form, the "Neoplantation Occupance Form" which was developing at the time of his study. This third settlement form is not considered here because it is characterized by the agricultural mechanization of the 1950s.) The postbellum form evolved, not through the destruction of the antebellum form, but rather through its modification. For Prunty (1955:460) the plantation continued to exist after 1865 as a discrete physical unit with a distinctive spatial form.

Prunty (1955:465) observed, as had Barrow earlier, that the antebellum plantation settlement pattern was distinctive in that the owner's house was usually "situated near a cluster of service buildings and slave quarters" which were "grouped compactly in rows along short roads." The agricultural fields were arranged on the lands surrounding the buildings in ways that would permit the slaves quick access to the fields with a minimal loss of work time.

Prunty reinforced Barrow's observation that after 1865 the clustered settlement pattern was abandoned in favor of a more dispersed system. Within this fragmented form, Prunty distinguished between the "cropper type" and the "tenant-renter type" based on the arrangement each small farmer had made with the plantation owner and landlord. In the cropper type, the owner supplied everything used in production except the labor and one-half of the seed and fertilizer, while in the tenant-renter type, the tenant supplied everything necessary for cultivation including two-thirds of the seed and fertilizer costs (Prunty 1955:474–475). According to Prunty (1955:467), the cropper type was the most common form of postbellum settlement with approximately 60% of all southern plantations organized in this manner in 1936. There is no compelling evidence to suggest that the type of tenancy practiced had any racial basis (Higgs 1974).

For the purposes of this discussion, the differences between Prunty's fragmented settlement subtypes are of minor importance because the dispersed settlement pattern after 1865 is characteristic of both systems. The only significant spatial differences between the settlement subtypes do not concern the actual dwellings themselves, but rather the out-buildings associated with the dwellings. Barns and sheds tended to be more centralized in the cropper subtype because they belonged to the plantation owner who was responsible for their maintenance. On the other hand, each tenant-renter was required to maintain his own barns and sheds, which in turn were located on his land. In a tenant-renter system, then, there were many more outbuildings associated with each dwelling rather than more dwellings. The differences exhibited between the cropper and tenant-renter subtypes are important only if a between-structure, or micro, settlement analysis (after Clarke 1977:11–14) is conducted; such differences are not important when studying the general shift in settlement patterns from the antebellum to postbellum periods on the macro, or between-site, level. In this discussion, the settlement change from slavery to tenancy noted by Prunty can be considered, in Chang's (1968:3) terms, "significant and meaningful" because the configuration and structure of the plantation community was altered to such a degree that a new spatial organization resulted.

The observations of both Barrow and Prunty are consistent in that two distinct forms of plantation spatial organization, according to the time of occupancy, were recognized. On antebellum plantations, the racial basis of slavery was reflected in living arrangements, in that whites lived separately from blacks. In reality, however, division of labor actually determined settlement location; it was just that all slaves were black. The spatial separation between blacks and whites was largely a function of the size of the plantation. Spatial divisions in housing were clear on large plantations, but on smaller plantations it was not uncommon for the owner to labor alongside his slaves (Stampp 1956:35). In some cases, slaves on larger plantations resided in the owner's house in order to render special services such as tending the fire or emptying the chamber pot at night (Genovese 1974:327–441). Field slaves generally resided in the "quarters" located perhaps as much as several hundred yards from the owner's home, or as one contemporary writer observed, "neither too near nor too far from the [owner's] house" (Durr n.d.). Owners did not want to be too close to the slave quarters for fear of contracting the terrible diseases which were rampant in the quarters (Savitt 1978:57).

Spatial Organization Based on the Division of Labor

The idea that antebellum plantation settlement was organized around divisions of labor rather than strict divisions of race must be reinforced. The groups formed by this organization produced what Wolf (1959:136) has termed the "class structure" of a plantation. Important qualifications exist to demonstrate that plantation groups were not necessarily spatially organized strictly on the basis of race. First of all, there were those slaves mentioned previously who performed special tasks within the planter's home, and who often resided in or very near this structure. Secondly, there were also white overseers who lived in spatial proximity to the slave quarters. While many overseers were sons or relatives of planters, the largest number of overseers came from the semiprofessional class of itinerant overseers who expected to oversee until they had enough money to buy their own land (Bonner 1944:677; Genovese 1974:12–13). These simple qualifications suggest that the spatial organization of the plantation was one based on the division of labor rather than one based strictly and solely on race. However, because all slaves were black, racial characteristics did seem to determine plantation settlement to some observers.

Even though exceptions and qualifications to this simple view of antebellum plantation settlement do exist, the antebellum plantation was usually characterized by a fairly nucleated settlement pattern that contained a cluster of dwellings and service buildings surrounded by agricultural fields. This nucleation is the distinctive element of antebellum plantation settlement.

Barrow's (1881:831) observation that the change in plantation spatial organization was a subtle one must be reiterated. Confronted with emancipation, blacks and whites faced a host of problems, none more severe than those involving agriculture. Labor shortages were common as black women and children withdrew from the labor pool and as black families migrated out of the rural South (Ransom and Sutch 1977:44–47). Immediately after the Civil War and often until the end of Reconstruction, planters employed wage laborers as field hands. Except for the receipt of wages in return for labor, this system did not result in the significant spatial reorganization of most plantations (Wright 1978:161). Under the wage labor system, blacks continued to labor in groups under the supervision of either white or black foremen (Shlomowitz 1979a,b). The wage system did not cause the complete break-

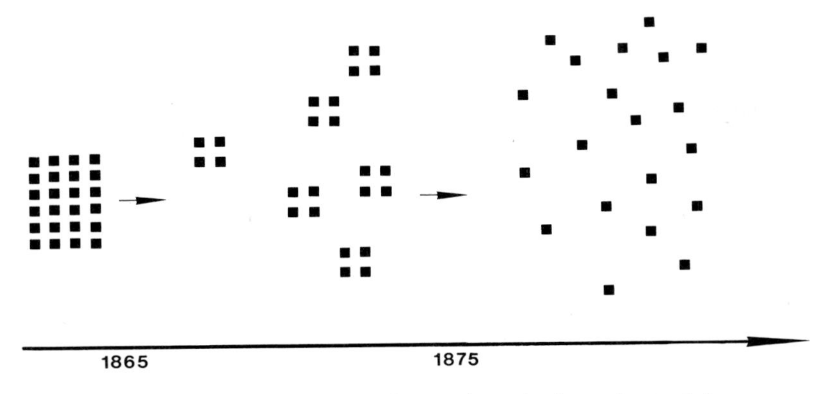

Figure 4.1 Idealized model of plantation settlement dynamics from clustered slave quarters to dispersed tenant farmer and sharecropper homes with a "squad" arrangement intermediary.

up of the nucleated plantation settlement system because the planter continued to own and house the agricultural tools and animals necessary for cultivation. The development of the "squad system" of agriculture after 1865, however, did cause some modification in the plantation settlement system as former slaves and wage laborers were divided into semiautonomous groups of peer workers. According to Shlomowitz (1979b:571, 1982), each squad was composed of an extended family core and usually contained from 2 to 10 workers. Each group would conceivably occupy its own settlement cluster close to its fields. The nucleated settlement form disappeared gradually as freedmen acquired freedom from constant supervision and the control of agricultural lands and animals (Prunty 1955:470). During the 1880s and 1890s, the owner's home was no longer "the center of a busy life revolving around a great social and economic establishment" (Coulter 1929:159).

In summary, a general shift in settlement form from nucleation during antebellum times to full dispersion during postbellum times occurred at some plantations (Figure 4.1). Such a shift has been observed both by contemporary writers (Barrow 1881) and by modern scholars (Prunty 1955). What is not known is how widespread this settlement shift was or whether it can be used as a general model that has recognizable archaeological correlates. The applicability of this simple model of settlement dynamics, however, can be evaluated with empirical archaeological and historical data from Millwood Plantation in Abbeville County, South Carolina, and Elbert County, Georgia.

DATA SET

Millwood Plantation, located on both sides of the Savannah River in northwestern South Carolina and northeastern Georgia, was owned and inhabited by James Edward Calhoun from 1832 until his death in 1889. Calhoun was the brother-in-law and cousin of the famous southern statesman, John C. Calhoun. James Edward was a well-educated gentleman who had served as the "young astronomer" with the Stephen H. Long Expedition of 1823 through Minnesota (Blegen 1963:111; Kane and Holmquist 1978). Even though Millwood was located in a rugged portion of the piedmont region, by 1860 Calhoun had transformed the plantation into a large enterprise that included 194 slaves and over 15,000 acres (United States Census 1850, 1860a,b). Calhoun was an eccentric man who left a lasting impression on the Abbeville area long after his death, and his Millwood Plantation is still remembered by local residents (Dundas 1949; Perrin 1933).

The site of Millwood Plantation (38AB9) was excavated in 1980 and 1981 under the direction of Charles E. Orser, Jr. (Orser *et al.* 1981, 1982). The site was located within the floodpool of the future Richard B. Russell Reservoir and contained 33 building foundation ruins within the main site area and many others at smaller sites throughout the estate lands. Two of these small sites (38AB12 and 9EB253) and 28 of the foundations at the main site (38AB9) were archaeologically tested. A number of the yard areas, which were devoid of archaeological remains, were also tested. The extensive research was funded by the U.S. Army Corps of Engineers, Savannah District, and was monitored and administered by the Southeast Office of the Archaeological Services Division of the National Park Service. This research effort provided the data for this chapter.

DOCUMENTING SETTLEMENT PATTERN DYNAMICS AT MILLWOOD PLANTATION

The Antebellum Period (1832–1865)

The site of Millwood Plantation was occupied until the 1930s, and much of the evidence for the antebellum plantation has been removed or drastically altered by natural forces such as severe erosion (see, for example, Bennett 1943:164–167 and Trimble 1974), and by cultural processes such as yard sweeping (see Bonner 1977:3). As a result, much of our archaeological perception of Millwood's antebellum spatial form stems from historical information and inferences based on the present condition of the site.

Even though the majority of the material culture collected from the Millwood foundations was clearly of postbellum age (Orser *et al.* 1982:674–736), the spatial characteristics of the foundations conformed to the antebellum settlement model proposed by Prunty (1955). While the entire Calhoun estate included over 15,000 acres, the main plantation area was located within only 32 acres (Figure 4.2). Spatial clusters are apparent within the complex of structural remains that comprise the Millwood archaeological site. The first of these clusters contains nine foundations (Figure 4.3). This cluster includes Calhoun's home (Structure 1), a brick smokehouse (Structure 9), three possible storage sheds (Structures 3, 4, and 5), the home of Calhoun's long-time black servant, Caroline Calhoun Walker (Structure 2), two

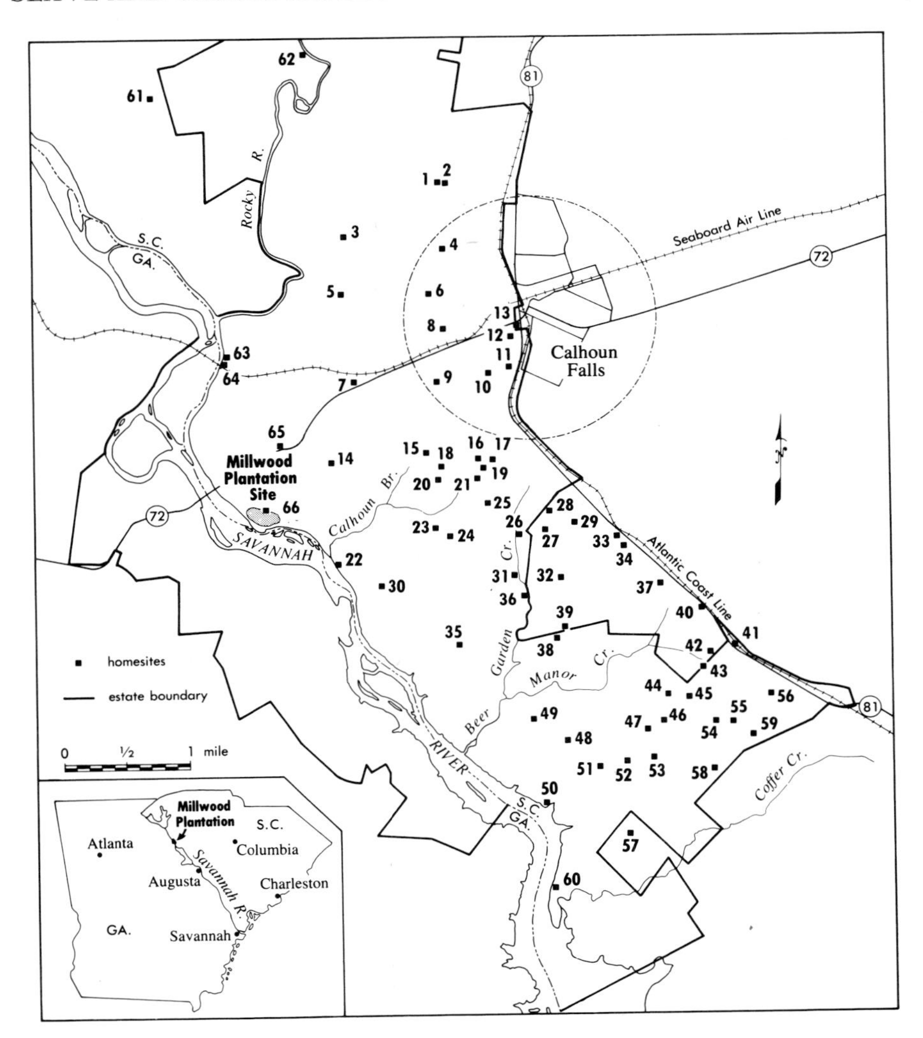

Figure 4.2 The James Edward Calhoun estate, showing the location of Millwood Plantation (38AB9), the estate boundaries, and the location of houses according to the 1932 soil survey.

other probable dwellings (Structures 6 and 7), the home of an overseer/manager (Structure 8), and a well.

At a distance of about 350 feet east of Structure 1 is a small complex of structures in physical proximity to the millrace. Three structures are located within this cluster. One of them is identified as a dwelling and the possible home of the plantation's millwright (Structure 27), one as an unidentified dwelling (Structure 25), and the third was probably the main millhouse (Structure 26).

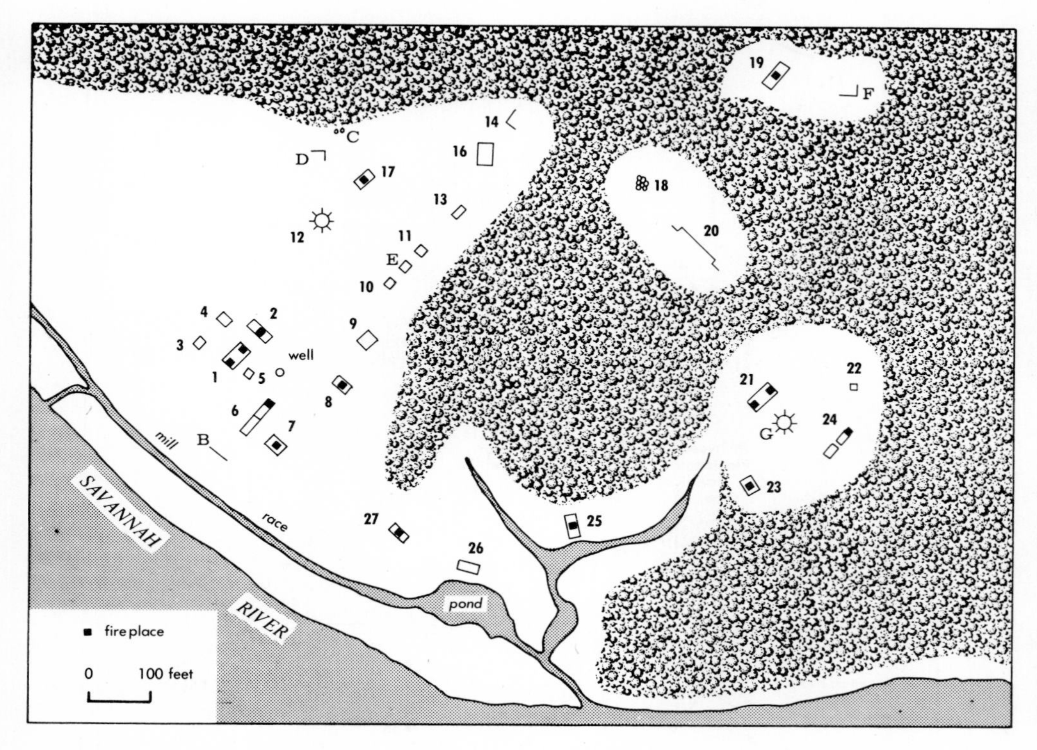

Figure 4.3 Simplified plan of Millwood Plantation showing the location of the various foundation ruins.

The third distinct spatial cluster of structures contains four structural ruins, three of which were probably residential (Structures 21, 23, and 24); the fourth was a dependent, nonresidential out-building (Structure 22). One possible structure was designated Structure G. There are eight more structures immediately north of the first cluster. This area includes five small structures which are identified as dwellings because they contain fireplace hearths (Structures 10, 11, 13, 17, and E). Two dependent out-buildings (Structures 12 and 15), and a sorghum processing structure (Structure 16) occur within this complex (Orser 1985). Two possible structures of unknown function were designated Structures C and D. Another cluster of foundations on the far northeastern side of the main plantation area contains one dwelling (Structure 19), one possible support structure (Structure 20), and two possible structures (Structures 18 and F) (Fig. 4.3). The main residential portion of the site occurs within the first and fourth clusters.

The available historical documentation states that by 1834 Calhoun occupied an overseer's house at Millwood while awaiting the time when he could build something better (Calhoun 1834). This evidence is unclear and confusing with regard to the number, location, and nature of the homes Calhoun eventually occupied at

Millwood, but it is certain that with his marriage to Maria Simpkins in 1839 he started the construction of a better house. However, local legend claims that Calhoun abandoned this new house upon the death of Mrs. Calhoun in childbirth in 1844, moved back to the overseer's cabin, and allowed the new house to fall into disuse and ruin (Dundas 1949; Perrin 1933).

While the actual design of Calhoun's antebellum home is not known, the large, grand homes often associated with southern plantations were infrequent in the rural South (Bonner 1945), and he probably lived in a simple home. Those classic homes that did occur on plantations evolved slowly from simple "dog-trot" log cabins that contained only two rooms and a central open breezeway (Eaton 1961:121–122). These breezeways were later developed into the great central hallways in many plantation "big houses" (Bonner 1945:388). Nonetheless, planters' homes, while often not grand, did frequently contain porches and special use areas, and were constructed from durable materials (Otto 1975:123). Even though the exact appearance of Calhoun's antebellum home is a mystery, one description of his house as it looked in 1879 may provide some clues about its antebellum form:

> [it was] a long and very comfortable one story building. At the west end were two rooms, one used as a living room and an office, and one as a bedroom. Extending east was a long hall, with shelves on each side and filled with a very valuable collection of books. . . . At the east end of the hall was the dining room. (Dundas 1949:7)

Both the archaeological remains located at Structure 1 and the historical documentation for Calhoun's Millwood residence strongly support the contention that Structure 1 was indeed Calhoun's home (Orser *et al.* 1982:140–172). Having established this spatial reference point, it was next necessary to establish the location of the slave quarters. As noted earlier, slave houses were commonly located in tight clusters near the planter's home. In Calhoun's case, however, this arrangement may have presented problems. As a common practice, planters wanted their slaves housed within easy walking distance of the agricultural fields to which they were assigned in order to minimize their transportation time. If all of Calhoun's slaves were housed near his residence, some would have had to travel at least 4 miles to reach the northernmost fields. Some would have even had to cross the Savannah River to reach those fields in Georgia. As a result, some of Calhoun's slaves probably lived away from his home area outside the nucleated settlement. In addition, Calhoun also operated a number of mills along the Savannah, and he probably had slave millwrights housed in these locales. For economic reasons, then, Calhoun probably had slave quarters located throughout his sprawling estate. It is equally likely that he also retained a resident overseer at each locale as was common practice (Stampp 1956:292).

Even though it is possible and even quite likely that in 1860 Calhoun housed his 194 slaves at various locations around the plantation, it is also possible that some field slaves lived near Calhoun in order to work those fields around the plantation nucleus. The small structures that appeared in a row north of Structure 1 (Structures 10, E, 11, and 13) may represent the remains of slave quarters that were inhabited by

Table 4.1
AVAILABLE LIVING SPACE PER DWELLING

Structure/resident	Family size	Square feet	Square feet per person
1 (planter/owner)	1.0	773.0	773.0
8 (overseer)	4.0	539.0	134.7
11 (slave)	5.2[a]	224.0	43.1
11 (slave)	5.7[b]	224.0	39.3

[a]Mean size of slave family as suggested by Fogel and Engerman (1974:115–116).
[b]Mean size of slave family at Millwood Plantation at suggested by the 1860 slave schedule (United States Census 1860b).

some of Calhoun's field slaves. These are small structures of simple construction with simple fireplace hearths. It is also quite possible, as the local oral tradition suggests, that Calhoun's slaves lived at the base of a hill north of Structure 1. At least two informants questioned stated that slaves had lived in this area; another knowledgeable and reliable informant stated that slaves lived on the other side of a slough that ran north of Calhoun's house in the approximate area of the hill (Orser *et al.* 1982:559, 563, 570–571). The location of this slough has been identified by Clemson University botanist, Dr. John E. Fairey III, during his survey north of Structure 1 (Orser *et al.* 1982:585–610).

If it can be assumed that Structure 1 was the planter's home and that the slaves were housed north of this structure, either around the base of a hill or in Structures 10, 11, 13, and E, Structure 8, which is intermediate between the two, may have been an overseer's house. Structure 8 contained at least two rooms and a central brick chimney and included a small porch on its northwest side and probably a small shed or addition on its northeast side. Based on this design, the inhabitants of Structure 8 enjoyed at least some specialized space and probably a separation between living and sleeping areas.

An analysis of the living space available in the structures attributed to the planter, overseer, and slaves supports the conclusion that such groups inhabited these structures. Since the historical data states that Calhoun lived alone throughout most of his life, it is assumed that he had all of the 773 square feet in Structure 1 available to him (Table 4.1). In the absence of knowing the exact composition of the Millwood overseer's household, an arbitrary figure of four persons has been adopted. Using this number, almost 135 square feet of living space per person is obtained for Structure 8. The size and simple construction of the structures north of Structure 1 suggest that they were probably intended for slave use, with Structure 11 being representative of them. With interior dimensions of 13 by 17 feet, the size of Structure 11 is consistent with the size of slave cabins reported at other archaeologically investigated plantations. For example, the slave cabins at the Stafford Plantation on Cumberland Island, Georgia, were found to measure 18 by 18 feet (Ascher and

Table 4.2
PRESENCE OF STRUCTURAL ITEMS AT STRUCTURES

	Architectural		Furnishings		Total	
Structure/resident	No.	%	No.	%	No.	%
1 (planter/owner)	8387	86.6	104	81.9	8491	86.5
8 (overseer)	1147	11.8	18	14.2	1165	11.9
11 (slave)	153	1.6	5	3.9	158	1.6
	9687	100.0	127	100.0	9814	100.0

Fairbanks 1971:8) and 16 by 21 feet (Ehrenhard and Bullard 1981:33), while those at the Kingsley Plantation in northeastern Florida ranged in size from 5 by 7 feet to 18.6 by 24.5 feet (Fairbanks 1974:67, 76). Using the figure of 5.2 slaves per dwelling, as suggested by Fogel and Engerman (1974:115–116), the available space per person for Structure 11 was 43 square feet. These figures correlate well with the findings at Cannon's Point Plantation where between 45.3 and 53.3 square feet per slave was the living space norm (Otto 1975:134).

An 1860 listing of the 194 Millwood slaves suggests that they were housed according to family groupings in 29 dwellings (United States Census 1860b). Adult males and females appear first in these lists followed by a series of minors. A figure of 5.7 persons per dwelling was obtained by averaging the number of people contained in each of these "families." This figure is within the range of from 3.7 to 8.8 slaves per dwelling noted at other plantations (Blassingame 1979:254–255). A figure of 39.3 square feet results when 5.7 persons per dwelling is used to compute the available living space in Structure 11.

Similarly, an analysis of the structural elements present at Structures 1, 8, and 11 also supports their association with the antebellum planter, overseer, and slave if it is assumed that planters and overseers were accorded more elaborate living spaces than slaves. Structure 1, the largest and most massively constructed building, contained the most architecturally related items (nails, flat glass, tile, brick, slate, and mortar) and the most furnishings (hinges, screws, latches, hooks, stove parts, furniture fittings, fireplace hardware, and decorative fasteners). Structure 8 contained less such materials, and Structure 11 even less (Table 4.2). While these simple frequencies are undoubtedly affected by sample size and excavation strategy, the differences between the structures and their contents appear striking.

In summary, all of the available evidence—archaeological, historical, oral, and comparative—supports the conclusion that during the antebellum period Millwood Plantation conformed to the antebellum nucleated settlement pattern identified by Prunty (1955). The planter's home was located near the center of the plantation, at least some of the slave force was housed north of the planter's home within the plantation nucleus, and at least one overseer was probably housed between the two.

The Immediate Postwar Period (1865–1875)

After emancipation, Calhoun, like all southern planters, was forced to confront new social and economic conditions (Gallman and Anderson 1977:41–42; Roark 1977). While some planters in the Abbeville District adopted a modified wage system to conduct their agricultural businesses (see, for example, Freedman's Bureau 1867a), Calhoun organized around another system. On January 1, 1867, Calhoun entered into an agreement with seven freedmen (three of whom had the last name Calhoun, suggesting that they were former slaves) who were to "cultivate carefully and industriously" on seven different large field plots. Each of the seven was required to pay Calhoun a rent of one-half of their total production (Freedmen's Bureau 1867b). So, rather than organizing a unified plantation on the basis of either cash or share wages, Calhoun subdivided his estate into seven parts and organized around a share tenancy system.

This system, however, was not the simple family sharecropping system that later became prevalent throughout the South. In the Millwood case, each of the seven freedmen was required to hire a crew of laborers to cultivate their fields. In effect, these freedmen were subcontractors who were responsible not only for the labor but also for the behavior of their employees. The distribution of this system within Abbeville District is uncertain, but this system was popular elsewhere in South Carolina. This system, called the "squad system," has been identified as an important stage in the transition from slave to tenant agriculture (Shlomowitz 1979a,b).

The spatial ramifications of the squad system, as represented in Figure 4.1, are that the slave quarters were disassembled in favor of a number of small "hamlets" of agricultural squad laborers. In Calhoun's case, these squads may have been composed of the various slave populations that were undoubtedly dispersed throughout the 15,000-acre plantation during the antebellum period. If such an organization did occur, then it is possible that the squad labor arrangement would not have clear spatial correlates at Millwood Plantation because of the possible location of different slave quarters throughout the estate (Orser 1983, 1984).

The Postbellum Period (1875–1930s)

Both the available historical evidence and the oral data gathered from local informants indicate that by the 1880s Millwood Plantation had evolved into a full tenant system that included both share and cash renting (Orser 1981). In 1880 Millwood Plantation housed 33 tenants, one-third of whom rented their land on shares while the remainder paid fixed rents (United States Census 1880). By 1890 the estate had 94 tenants, and as late as 1928 Millwood supported 98 tenants (Abbeville County Court of Probate 1890; Orser *et al.* 1982:771). Just how many of these tenants rented for set crop amounts, shares of their produce (called "working on halves" by the informants), or variations of the two, is unclear. Of the eight informants who discussed tenant farming arrangements, five reported both "standing" crop rentals and sharecropping, four reported sharecropping exclusively, and one renting exclusively. It is possible, therefore, that many variations in rent arrangements existed at Millwood as they did at other southern plantations (Orser and Holland 1984). Nonetheless, the ramifications of the development of a tenancy system, regardless of form, are obvious in terms of settlement. The dispersed settlement system, or the "fragmented occupance form" of Prunty (1955), was adopted as the tenants began to farm their own plots of rented land at a ratio of about 1 to every 30 or 40 acres (The History Group 1981:187).

While the informants questioned stated that there were many tenants spread throughout the Calhoun estate in the early twentieth century, the only evidence for the actual house locations derives from a 1932 map of Abbeville County soils. In addition to showing the distribution of soil types within the county, this map also shows many house sites. This map was used to provide the data for the postbellum settlement pattern of Millwood Plantation under the assumptions that this map shows the locations of all standing structures on the estate in 1932, that all structures shown are located accurately, and that all of the structures represent tenant or sharecropper home sites (Figure 4.2).

An examination of Figure 4.2 shows the degree to which the plantation settlement pattern was altered after the antebellum period. The site of the main complex of Millwood Plantation occurs at house location 66 near the left center of the map. The other 65 houses are distributed throughout the estate in what can clearly be considered a "fragmented" form of occupation.

ANALYZING THE DATA

In order to understand the distribution of these house sites in more detail, 17 variables were selected for further study. These variables were: soil association (SOILASSC), agricultural, pasturage, and woodland potential of the land (AGPOTEN, PASPOTEN, and WDPOTEN), current vegetation (CURRVEG), elevation above mean sea level (ELEV), direction or aspect of land slope (SLOPEASP), distance to Savannah River (DISSAVR), distance and direction to nearest stream (DISNRST and DIRNRST), rank order and type of nearest stream (STORDER and STRTYPE), proximity to confluence of nearest stream (STPROX), and distance to the nearest road, railroad, neighbor, and Calhoun Falls—the closest town (DISROAD, DISRROAD, DISNEIG, and DISCFALS). Distance measurements, slope aspect, current vegetation, elevation, and stream order data were gathered from modern (1964) topographic maps, while the environmental data were taken from the 1980 Abbeville County soil survey (Herron 1980). The environmental variables were selected for study because of the suspected importance of environmental factors to small farmers, and the distance variables were included in order to account for cultural choice in settlement location. We hoped that the combined study of both types of variables would yield the most information about the choice of house locales for tenants and sharecroppers. The raw data appear in the Appendix.

Once values for each variable were collected for each of the 66 sites in the sample, descriptive statistics were generated using the SPSS (Statistical Package for the Social

Table 4.3
FREQUENCIES AND PERCENTAGES OF ENVIRONMENTAL VARIABLES

Variable/label	No.	%	Variable/label	No.	%
SOILASSC			WDPOTEN		
Cataula SL B	15	22.7	Low	4	6.1
Cataula SL C	6	9.1	Medium	59	89.4
Cataula SCL	4	6.1	High	3	4.5
Cecil SL B	10	15.2	CURRVEG		
Cecil SL C	3	4.5	Open	22	33.3
Cecil SL D	2	3.0	Forested	44	66.7
Cecil SCL	2	3.0	ELEV		
Chewacla L	1	1.5	Above 475 ft	14	21.2
Davidson L B	6	9.1	Below 475 ft	52	78.8
Davidson L C	1	1.5	SLOPEASP		
Enon SL	1	1.5	North	6	9.1
Madison SL	1	1.5	Northeast	7	10.6
Mecklenburg SL	1	1.5	East	4	6.1
Pacolet SL	7	10.6	Southeast	10	15.2
Pacolet CL	1	1.5	South	8	12.1
Toccoa SL	2	3.0	Southwest	11	16.7
Wilkes SL	3	4.5	West	11	16.7
AGPOTEN			Northwest	9	13.6
Low	19	28.8	DIRNRST		
Medium	30	45.5	North	10	12.5
High	17	25.8	Northeast	5	7.6
PASPOTEN			East	10	15.2
Low	11	16.7	Southeast	12	18.2
Medium	9	13.6	South	8	12.1
High	45	69.7	Southwest	7	10.6
			West	8	12.1
			Northwest	6	9.1
			STORDER		
			First	6	9.1
			Second	1	1.5
			Third	4	6.1
			Fourth	55	83.3
			STRTYPE		
			Intermittent	56	84.8
			Permanent	10	15.2

Sciences) subprogram entitled FREQUENCIES (Nie *et al.* 1975:181–202). The frequencies for the environmental variables appear in Table 4.3, and the frequencies for the distance variables appear in Table 4.4. Using these data as a guide, a profile of the "typical" Millwood Plantation tenant/sharecropper farm was compiled.

The typical farm was located above 475 feet mean sea level on Cataula sandy loam B horizon soil. The land of this idealized farm presently has medium agricultural and woodland potential, a high pasture potential, and is forested. This farm was located near a slope that faced either southwest, west, or southeast, $1\frac{1}{2}$ miles

Table 4.4
FREQUENCIES AND PERCENTAGES OF DISTANCE VARIABLES

	Distance (in miles)					
	<0.30		0.30–0.50		>0.50	
Variable	No.	%	No.	%	No.	%
DISNRST	65	98.5	1	1.5	0	0.0
DISNNEIG	37	56.1	13	19.7	16	24.2
	<0.50		0.50–1.50		>1.50	
	No.	%	No.	%	No.	%
DISSAVR	9	13.6	33	50.0	24	36.3
STPROX	45	68.2	20	30.0	1	1.5
DISROAD	22	33.3	34	51.5	10	15.2
DISRROAD	26	39.4	31	47.0	9	13.6
DISCFALS	2	3.0	7	10.6	57	86.4

from the Savannah River with the nearest stream being a fourth-order, intermittent stream located less than $\frac{3}{10}$ mile in a southeastern direction. The proximity of the stream confluence was less than $\frac{1}{2}$ mile away. This farm was also from $\frac{1}{2}$ to $1\frac{1}{2}$ miles from the nearest road and railroad, less than $\frac{3}{10}$ mile from its nearest neighbor, and over $1\frac{1}{2}$ miles from Calhoun Falls. Information gathered from local informants supports the picture of Millwood's tenant homes as "dilapidated, unpainted, weatherbeaten frame cabin[s] leaning out of plumb on rock or brick pilings" (Tindall 1967:411). (For similar comments on tenant housing, see Agee and Evans 1941:127–253; Hagood 1977:93–99; Vance 1936).

In order to determine whether there are significant interrelationships between the variables, pairs of variables were statistically compared. The nominal-level (environmental) variables compared by employing the SPSS subprogram CROSSTABS, while the ratio-level (distance) variables were compared using the SPSS subprogram SCATTERGRAM (Nie *et al.* 1975:218–248, 293–300).

Once the contingency tables were generated by the CROSSTABS subprogram, the nominal-level variables were compared using the symmetric uncertainty coefficient (U). The derived coefficients appear in Table 4.5. The uncertainty coefficient is a measure of association between two nominal-level variables that computes the amount of certainty for predicting the dependent variable once the independent variable is known (Nie *et al.* 1975:226–227). The symmetric version of this statistic measures the proportional reduction of uncertainty that is gained by knowing the joint distribution of cases rather than by knowing the combined uncertainty of the row and column totals as in the asymmetric version. A value of 1.000 denotes the complete reduction of uncertainty, while a value of 0.000 indicates that there has been no improvement in predictive power.

Table 4.5

SYMMETRIC UNCERTAINTY COEFFICIENTS FOR ENVIRONMENTAL VARIABLES

	PHYZONE	SOILASSC	AGPOTEN	PASPOTEN	WDPOTEN	CURRVEG	SLOPEASP	DIRNRST	STORDER	STRTYPE
PHYZONE	1.000									
SOILASSC	0.236	1.000								
AGPOTEN	0.066	0.607	1.000							
PASPOTEN	0.078	0.503	0.434	1.000						
WDPOTEN	0.274	0.287	0.145	0.242	1.000					
CURRVEG	0.040	0.126	0.025	0.057	0.007	1.000				
SLOPEASP	0.081	0.359	0.094	0.093	0.110	0.048	1.000			
DIRNRST	0.116	0.310	0.043	0.043	0.087	0.011	0.267	1.000		
STORDER	0.273	0.271	0.135	0.100	0.267	0.091	0.126	0.125	1.000	
STRTYPE	0.188	0.164	0.054	0.016	0.239	0.014	0.043	0.045	0.761	1.000

An examination of Table 4.5 reveals that the vast majority of environmental variables are not strongly associated or, in terms of the uncertainty coefficient, that our ability to predict one value from knowledge of the other is not great. The largest coefficients occur where they would be expected. For example, the coefficient of 0.607 between soil association and agricultural potential is one that is reasonable because there is a known relationship between a soil type and its agricultural potential. Similarly, the strong association between stream order and stream type (U = 0.761) is to be expected because such variables are known to be interrelated; first- and second-order streams are permanent, while third- and fourth-order streams are intermittent. The low values throughout the remainder of the matrix suggest that little covariation exists between the variables.

The distance variables were compared using the Pearson product-moment correlation coefficient (r). This statistic is a widely used measure that is employed to assess the relationship between two variables. Values of 1.000, −1.000, and 0.000 denote a perfect positive linear relationship, a perfect negative linear relationship, and no relationship between the variables respectively (Roscoe 1975:97–99). The Pearson coefficients generated for the distance variables appear in Table 4.6.

It will be observed that stronger correlations occur between the distance variables than among the environmental variables. Some of these correlations are predictable. For example, the relatively high correlation between elevation and distance to the Savannah River (r = 0.641) is understandable because the elevation of the land increases naturally as the distance from the Savannah increases. Nonetheless, meaningful correlations do occur within this data set.

The highest correlation occurs between the distance to nearest road and distance to nearest railroad variables (r = 0.794). This high correlation is perhaps partially due to the fact that the two railroads in the area, the Atlantic Coast Line and the Seaboard Air Line, parallel South Carolina highways 81 and 72, respectively. However, this explanation does not account for all of the association between the variables because the original measurements for this study were made to the nearest road regardless of size. The network of minor two-track roads throughout the Calhoun estate, on which many of the sites were situated, serves to lessen the effect of the physical correlation between the railroads and the current major highways near the estate.

These analyses suggest that little real correlation exists within the environmental variables and the distance variables for the 66 suspected tenant sites located within the boundaries of the Calhoun estate. Even though the sites appear roughly clustered when inspected visually, it would seem that no standard criteria of settlement were selected by the tenant or sharecropper who first settled there. The apparent site randomness, of course, is only related to the variables selected for study here. It remains possible that the locations were not at all random in terms of social, familial, economic, and political factors which were not measured by the variables chosen for analysis.

In order to make the determination of site clustering in an unbiased manner, the nearest-neighbor statistic was used. Many strengths and weaknesses are inherent in

Table 4.6

PEARSON PRODUCT-MOMENT CORRELATION COEFFICIENTS FOR DISTANCE VARIABLES

	ELEV	DISSAVR	DISNRST	STPROX	DISROAD	DISRROAD	DISNNEIG	DISCFALS
ELEV	1.000							
DISSAVR	0.641	1.000						
DISNRST	0.448	0.089	1.000					
STPROX	0.588	0.492	0.591	1.000				
DISROAD	−0.490	−0.581	−0.098	−0.267	1.000			
DISRROAD	−0.436	−0.564	−0.061	−0.194	0.794	1.000		
DISNNEIG	−0.436	−0.299	0.001	−0.196	0.553	0.578	1.000	
DISCFALS	−0.199	−0.374	−0.103	−0.479	0.483	0.562	0.254	1.000

this statistical method. Perhaps the most serious limitation is the problem faced when determining the universe boundaries and the dangers of excluding sites that were within the network under study but outside the created boundaries. Others have demonstrated that the presence of artificial boundaries has a marked effect on the results of nearest-neighbor analysis (Hodder and Orton 1976:41–42), and the boundaries used in this study are those of the original Calhoun estate.

Those sites that were closer to the Calhoun estate boundary than to a neighbor were dropped from the sample in order to reduce and hopefully eliminate the edge effect in the data set. This process resulted in the exclusion of 13 sites. Another 3 sites were dropped from the sample because they were located within Calhoun Falls, and their nearest neighbors could not be accurately calculated. The total sample for the nearest-neighbor sample consisted of 50 sites.

The computation of the nearest-neighbor statistic demonstrated that the sites were indeed clustered ($R = 0.76$, where $R = 1.000$ represents a random distribution). These clusters may be the remnants of the squad spatial arrangement that occurred in the 1865–1875 period. In this case, the "randomness" of the tenant locations probably relates to this earlier squad system. This clustering may also be a function of location near poor roads that have since disappeared. A fairly even distribution of tenant houses along poor roads was common in the rural South during the 1920s (Hart 1980:518–519; Hart and Chestang 1978:454).

The lack of association between the different environmental variables may merely represent the problem of using environmental data from 1964 and 1980 in conjunction with locational data from 1932. This over 48-year difference may be too great given the destructive nature of severe soil erosion in the Piedmont region. Nonetheless, it would seem that meaningful correlations in the distance variables should have occurred if the house locations were chosen along similar distance criteria.

CONCLUSIONS

Based on the preceding analysis, Millwood Plantation can be considered to have developed along the lines consistent with the model presented by Prunty (1955). The nucleated antebellum settlement that once existed at the center of the plantation largely disintegrated as the plantation labor burden shifted from slaves to tenant farmers and sharecroppers. The study of the spatial organization of Millwood Plantation, however, suggests the following qualifications to Prunty's model:

1. While the general models of settlement nucleation during the antebellum period and settlement fragmentation during the postbellum period appear valid, Prunty failed to recognize the apparent continued use of the settlement nucleus following emancipation. For example, at Millwood Plantation the late nineteenth-century mean dates derived from the artifact samples (Orser *et al.* 1982:736) imply a continued use of most of the structures within the nucleus until at least 1900. After 1865 a resident manager probably occupied Structure 8 and wage hands probably lived in Structures 10, 11, 13, and E. These houses probably served as overseer and slave

residences, respectively, before 1865. Structure 1 was inhabited by Calhoun until his death and may have been inhabited by someone else thereafter. The spatial proximity of wage laborers' and employers' homes has been documented in the postbellum rural South (Woofter *et al.* 1936), and the presence of resident managers at Millwood has been affirmed by local informants, including the wife of one such manager (Orser *et al.* 1982: 559–584). It would appear, then, that the plantation nucleus retained its form, if not its function, throught time.

2. The plantation nucleus itself has meaningful internal spatial divisions which appear on the microlevel (or between structures). These divisions are functional ones that relate to the maintenance of plantation production. Internal spatial organization is characterized by task-specific structures, but moreover by the orientation of dwellings to specific site areas. Certain elements of this organization should be common to all plantations, varying only with plantation size, prosperity, and economic diversification.

3. The spatial separation of living quarters of different ethnic groups on the plantation is primarily a function of the division of labor rather than race. The physical separation of resident plantation groups is racial only insofar as one's role in plantation production is racially ascribed. In addition, the dwellings inhabited by each resident group will be recognizable by their structural elements and associated artifacts (Otto 1975, 1977, 1984).

4. The possible presence of the squad labor arrangement as an intermediate step between slave and tenant settlement must be considered. Such labor arrangements have a particular settlement organization that may affect the settlement pattern of the full tenancy system.

The archaeological and historical record for Millwood Plantation is sufficient in revealing the general settlement pattern change that occurred throughout the nineteenth-century and early twentieth-century plantation South. Millwood Plantation continued to exist as an entity after 1865 and generally developed along the lines suggested by Barrow (1881) and Prunty (1955). The settlement nucleus, however, was not abandoned but was only functionally reorganized. Nonetheless, it must be kept in mind that the spatial evolution of Millwood Plantation may be particular only to this one Piedmont plantation. While this possibility does not seem too likely, the settlement dynamics observed at Millwood deserve further study at other plantation sites.

APPENDIX: RAW DATA FOR POSTBELLUM ANALYSIS

Column number	Variable name	Value	Label
1	Site number	—	—
2	United States Geological Survey quadrangle map	1	Calhoun Falls
		2	Heardmont
3	Universal Transverse Mercator northing	—	—
4	Universal Transverse Mercator easting	—	—
5	Soil association	01	Cataula sandy loam B
		02	Cataula sandy loam C
		03	Cataula sandy clay loam
		04	Cecil sandy loam B
		05	Cecil sandy loam C
		06	Cecil sandy loam D
		07	Cecil sandy clay loam
		08	Chewacla loam
		09	Davidson loam B
		10	Davidson loam C
		11	Enon sandy loam
		12	Madison sandy loam
		13	Mecklenburg sandy loam
		14	Pacolet sandy loam
		15	Pacolet clay loam
		16	Toccoa sandy loam
		17	Wilkes sandy loam
6	Agricultural potential	1	High
		2	Medium
		3	Low
7	Pasture potential	1	High
		2	Medium
		3	Low
8	Woodland potential	1	High
		2	Medium
		3	Low
9	Current vegetation	1	Forested
		2	Open
10	Elevation above sea level*	—	—
11	Slope aspect	1	North
		2	Northeast
		3	East
		4	Southeast
		5	South
		6	Southwest
		7	West
		8	Northwest
12	Distance to Savannah River	—	—
13	Distance to nearest stream	—	—

(*continued*)

APPENDIX: RAW DATA FOR POSTBELLUM ANALYSIS

Column number	Variable name	Value	Label
14	Direction to nearest stream	1	North
		2	Northeast
		3	East
		4	Southeast
		5	South
		6	Southwest
		7	West
		8	Northwest
15	Stream rank order	1	First
		2	Second
		3	Third
		4	Fourth
16	Stream type	1	Intermittent
		2	Permanent
17	Proximity to stream confluence	—	—
18	Distance to nearest road	—	—
19	Distance to nearest railroad	—	—
20	Distance to nearest neighbor	—	—
21	Distance to Calhoun Falls	—	—

*All distance measurements are in meters.

Table of raw data begins on facing page.

1	2	3	4	5	6	7	8	9	10	11	12	13	14	15	16	17	18	19	20	21
01	1	3775050	351550	14	1	1	2	1	530	1	3450	100	1	4	1	0750	0975	0875	0100	2615
02	1	3775050	351675	14	1	1	2	1	530	1	3540	090	1	4	1	0780	0875	0775	0100	2515
03	1	3774300	350350	17	1	1	2	1	535	3	1950	080	3	4	1	0300	2575	0880	0750	3725
04	1	3774120	351720	03	1	2	1	2	500	5	1900	130	4	4	1	0150	1250	0700	0600	4020
05	1	3773550	351300	06	1	2	2	2	440	4	1600	140	4	3	2	0170	3080	1000	0750	3270
06	1	3773550	351440	03	1	2	1	1	500	6	2700	030	7	4	1	0830	1095	0800	0300	1500
07	1	3772380	350450	02	2	3	2	1	460	5	1850	150	5	3	2	0400	0075	0100	1050	1355
08	1	3773050	351620	15	1	1	2	2	515	4	2850	250	5	4	1	0750	1370	0200	0500	1850
09	1	3772350	351540	14	1	1	2	1	500	6	2900	140	5	4	1	0340	0375	0400	0650	1675
10	1	3772460	352180	05	2	3	2	1	530	1	3600	040	6	4	1	0880	0400	0380	0275	1300
11	1	3772540	352440	01	2	3	2	2	570	8	3850	230	6	4	1	1110	0160	0140	0275	1050
12	1	3772960	352490	01	2	3	2	2	560	7	3700	400	7	4	1	2100	0150	0200	0175	0250
13	1	3773100	352550	01	2	3	2	2	555	1	3800	400	3	4	1	2540	0020	0130	0175	0050
14	1	3771280	350150	10	2	3	2	2	555	5	1000	200	2	4	1	0900	0750	1200	1100	3000
15	1	3771420	351375	14	1	1	2	1	490	5	1900	000	8	4	1	0800	1650	1200	0250	1400
16	1	3771340	352040	05	2	3	2	2	560	8	2300	350	2	4	1	1300	1100	0700	0150	2700
17	1	3771320	352240	04	3	3	2	2	570	8	2450	350	1	4	1	1460	1050	0580	0150	2650
18	1	3771210	351560	07	2	2	2	2	555	2	1850	300	8	4	1	1075	1200	1140	0175	2800
19	1	3771200	352110	04	3	3	2	2	585	7	2300	480	1	4	1	1430	0950	0720	0150	2550
20	1	3771060	351510	07	2	2	2	2	565	5	1700	300	6	4	1	0720	1400	1275	0150	3000
21	1	3771040	352015	04	3	3	2	1	570	6	2150	275	6	4	1	1180	0900	0875	0175	2500
22	1	3769910	350200	17	1	1	2	1	375	6	0050	175	8	1	2	0600	2500	2500	0600	4100
23	1	3770380	351480	09	3	3	2	1	550	6	1400	200	1	4	1	0680	1880	1750	0200	3480
24	1	3770275	351660	09	3	3	2	2	525	4	1450	130	3	4	1	1410	2030	1660	0200	3630
25	1	3770720	352160	09	3	3	2	1	560	5	2100	350	4	4	1	1150	1000	1100	0400•	3450
26	1	3770300	352520	02	2	3	2	2	485	7	2200	050	7	4	1	0600	1150	1200	0350	2800
27	1	3770340	352900	01	2	3	2	2	530	4	2700	100	4	4	1	0600	0800	0900	0250	3800
28	1	3770605	352940	02	2	3	2	2	530	6	2700	250	4	4	1	1000	0500	0650	0250	3550
29	1	3770450	353280	02	2	3	2	1	535	7	3000	100	1	4	1	0850	0300	0450	0350	2750
30	1	3769630	350780	11	2	2	2	1	445	7	0350	250	1	3	1	0400	0300	3100	0650	3900
31	1	3769750	352500	14	1	1	2	1	465	2	1900	050	3	4	1	0100	1400	1450	0300	3350
32	1	3769050	353120	12	2	3	2	1	495	7	2350	150	6	4	1	0350	1000	1100	0500	3450

(*continued*)

1	2	3	4	5	6	7	8	9.	10	11	12	13	14	15	16	17	18	19	20	21
33	1	3770250	353780	01	2	3	2	2	570	6	3200	450	5	4	1	1200	0050	0100	0150	3100
34	1	3770130	353875	01	2	3	2	2	570	6	3250	350	5	4	1	1200	0100	0150	0150	3250
35	1	3768840	351780	09	3	3	2	1	450	6	0750	500	8	4	1	0700	2600	0650	1050	4350
36	1	3769750	352600	02	2	3	2	1	450	3	1800	050	3	4	1	0200	1450	1500	0300	3650
37	1	3769640	354340	09	3	3	2	2	565	4	3450	200	8	4	1	0850	0150	0200	0400	3900
38	1	3768900	352030	01	2	3	2	1	510	4	1900	100	4	4	1	0500	1600	1650	0200	4250
39	1	3769040	352115	01	2	3	2	1	535	8	2050	150	4	4	1	0650	1400	1450	0200	4100
40	1	3769320	354860	09	3	3	2	2	570	4	3800	300	4	4	1	0850	0050	0075	0200	4450
41	1	3768800	355250	01	2	3	2	1	565	1	3250	150	2	4	1	1100	0050	0050	0100	5100
42	1	3768710	354970	04	3	3	2	1	555	6	2800	200	6	4	1	0800	0300	0350	0250	5000
43	1	3768510	354880	01	2	3	2	1	560	1	2550	100	1	4	1	0750	0500	0550	0200	5150
44	1	3768140	354620	04	3	3	2	1	555	8	2000	200	4	4	1	0700	1000	1100	0250	5300
45	1	3768100	354700	04	3	3	2	1	550	6	2200	200	3	4	1	0700	0850	0900	0250	5400
46	1	3767800	354350	04	3	3	2	1	530	4	1750	150	3	4	1	0400	1300	1350	0200	5600
47	1	3767680	354170	03	1	2	1	2	520	5	1500	300	3	4	1	0400	1550	1600	0200	5650
48	1	3767540	353115	01	2	3	2	1	515	8	1000	350	4	4	1	0700	2400	2500	0500	5600
49	1	3767820	352725	01	2	3	2	1	500	8	0950	300	1	3	2	0450	2600	2650	0500	5300
50	1	3766710	352870	17	1	1	2	1	350	4	0050	050	4	1	2	0100	3150	3200	0850	6400
51	1	3767200	353520	02	2	3	2	1	470	4	0750	050	4	4	1	0500	2300	2350	0350	5950
52	1	3767250	353550	01	2	3	2	1	510	8	1050	100	8	4	1	0800	2000	2050	0350	6000
53	1	3767315	354225	01	2	3	2	1	540	7	1450	250	3	4	1	0300	1750	1850	0350	6000
54	1	3767790	355030	04	3	3	2	1	540	8	2400	200	7	4	1	0600	1950	2000	0200	5900
55	1	3767780	355280	04	3	3	2	1	530	2	2600	200	6	4	1	0350	0800	0850	0200	6000
56	1	3768125	355740	01	2	3	2	1	520	2	3250	100	7	4	1	0450	0250	0300	0650	5950
57	1	3766300	353910	05	2	3	2	1	490	2	0900	300	5	4	1	0750	2850	2900	0950	6900
58	1	3767140	355010	04	3	3	2	1	545	5	2000	200	2	4	1	0550	1450	1500	0650	6400
59	1	3767590	355520	06	1	2	2	1	545	3	2800	150	2	4	1	0150	0850	0900	0300	6250
60	1	3765610	352940	14	1	1	2	1	420	7	0050	050	7	1	2	0250	4000	4100	1200	7500
61	2	3776210	347820	14	1	1	2	1	530	2	1350	400	1	4	1	1550	4800	4750	2000	5750
62	2	3776740	349840	08	2	3	3	2	415	2	3350	050	3	2	2	0350	2850	2825	2000	4500
63	2	3772750	348760	16	1	3	3	1	420	7	0050	050	7	1	2	0250	1400	1050	0100	3750
64	2	3772660	348700	16	1	3	3	1	400	7	0050	050	7	1	2	0150	1400	0050	0100	3800
65	2	3771540	349610	03	1	2	1	1	530	3	1000	250	5	4	1	0800	0050	0950	0750	3450
66	2	3770670	349200	13	3	3	2	1	425	7	0250	250	5	1	2	0200	0600	1800	0850	4100

ACKNOWLEDGMENTS

We would like to acknowledge the great assistance given us by our valued colleague and fine Southern historian, James L. Roark, who conducted the original historical research for our bigger research effort at Millwood Plantation. We are also grateful to Edwin A. Hession of the National Park Service, Atlanta, who showed great professional and personal interest in the Millwood project, and to Janice L. Orser who read, commented upon, and typed this essay. We also wish to acknowledge Dr. Milton Newton and the cartography laboratory of the Department of Geography and Anthropology Louisiana State University, who prepared the maps.

REFERENCES

Abbeville County Court of Probate
1890 Return on estate of James Edward Calhoun, deceased. Abbeville County Courthouse, Abbeville, South Carolina.
Agee, James, and Walker Evans
1941 *Let Us Now Praise Famous Men: Three Tenant Families.* Boston: Houghton, Mifflin.
Ascher, Robert, and Charles H. Fairbanks
1971 Excavation of a slave cabin: Georgia, U.S.A. *Historical Archaeology* 5:3–17.
Barrow, David Crenshaw
1881 A Georgia plantation. *Scribner's Monthly* 21:830–836.
Bennett, H. H.
1943 Adjustment of agriculture to its environment. *Annals of the Association of American Geographers* 33:163–198.
Blassingame, John W.
1979 *The Slave Community: Plantation Life in the Antebellum South.* Revised and enlarged ed. New York: Oxford University Press.
Blegen, Theodore C.
1963 *Minnesota: A History of the State.* Minneapolis: University of Minnesota Press.
Bonner, James C.
1944 Profile of a late ante-bellum community. *The American Historical Review* 49:663–680.
1945 Plantation architecture of the lower south on the eve of the Civil War. *Journal of Southern History* 11:370–388.
1977 House and landscape design in the antebellum south. *Landscape* 21(Spring–Summer):2–8.
Calhoun, James Edward
1834 Diary entry, March 13. John Ewing Calhoun Papers, Southern Historical Collections, University of North Carolina, Chapel Hill.
Chang, K. C.
1968 Toward a science of prehistoric society. In *Settlement Archaeology.* K. C. Chang, ed. Palo Alto, California: National Press. Pp. 1–9.
1972 *Settlement Patterns in Archaeology.* Addison-Wesley Module in Anthropology 24. Reading, Massachusetts: Addison-Wesley.
Clarke, David L.
1977 Spatial information in archaeology. In *Spatial Archaeology.* David L. Clarke, ed. London: Academic Press. Pp. 1–32.
Coulter, E. Merton
1929 A century of a Georgia plantation. *Agricultural History* 3:147–159.
Crumley, Carole L.
1979 Three locational models: an epistemological assessment for anthropology and archaeology. In *Advances in Archaeological Method and Theory.* Michael B. Schiffer, ed. 2:141–173.
Dundas, Francis de Sales
1949 *The Calhoun Settlement District of Abbeville, South Carolina.* Stauton, Virginia: Francis de Sales Dundas.

Durr, Lucy Judkins
n.d. Brazilian recollections. Judkins-Durr Papers, Alabama Department of Archives and History, Montgomery.
Eaton, Clement
1961 *The Growth of Southern Civilization, 1790–1860.* New York: Harper & Row.
Ehrenhard, John E., and Mary R. Bullard
1981 *Stafford Plantation, Cumberland Island National Seashore, Georgia: Archaeological Investigations of a Slave Cabin.* Southeast Archaeological Center, National Park Service, Tallahassee.
Fairbanks, Charles H.
1974 The Kingsley slave cabins in Duval County, Florida, 1968. *The Conference on Historic Site Archaeology Papers 1972,* 7:62–93.
Fogel, Robert W., and Stanley L. Engerman
1974 *Time on the Cross: The Economics of American Negro Slavery.* New York: Little, Brown, and Company.
Freedmen's Bureau
1867a Contract between W. V. Clinkscales and freedmen, January 1. Bureau of Refugees, Freedmen, and Abandoned Lands, National Archives, Washington, D.C.
1867b Contract between James Edward Calhoun and freedmen, February 5. Bureau of Refugees, Freedmen, and Abandoned Lands, National Archives, Washington, D.C.
Gallman, Robert E., and Ralph V. Anderson
1977 Slaves as fixed capital: slave labor and southern economic development. *The Journal of American History* 64:24–46.
Genovese, Eugene D.
1974 *Roll, Jordan, Roll: The World the Slaves Made.* New York: Pantheon.
Hagood, Margaret Jarman
1977 *Mothers of the South: Portraiture of the White Tenant Farm Woman.* New York: Norton. Originally published in 1939.
Hart, John Fraser
1980 Land use change in a Piedmont county. *Annals of the Association of American Geographers* 70:492–527.
Hart, John Fraser, and Ennis L. Chestang
1978 Rural revolution in east Carolina. *Geographical Review* 68:435–458.
Herron, Edward C., comp.
1980 *Soil Survey of Abbeville County, South Carolina.* Soil Conservation Service, United States Department of Agriculture, Washington, D.C.
Higgs, Robert
1974 Patterns of farm rental in the Georgia cotton belt, 1880–1900. *Journal of Economic History* 34:468–482.
History Group, The
1981 *Historical Investigations of the Richard B. Russell Multiple Resource Area.* Report submitted to the Interagency Archaeological Services, Southeast Regional Office, Atlanta.
Hodder, Ian
1977 Some new directions in the spatial analysis of archaeological data at the regional scale. In *Spatial Archaeology.* David L. Clarke, ed. London: Academic Press. Pp. 223–351.
Hodder, Ian, and Clive Orton
1976 *Spatial Analysis in Archaeology.* Cambridge: Cambridge University Press.
Kane, Lucile M., and June D. Holmquist, eds.
1978 *The Northern Expedition of Stephen H. Long: The Journals of 1817 and 1823 and Related Documents.* Minneapolis: Minnesota Historical Society.
Nie, Norman H., C. Hadlai Hull, Jean G. Jenkins, Karin Steinbrenner, and Dale H. Bent
1975 *Statistical Package for the Social Sciences.* 2nd. ed. New York: McGraw-Hill.
Orser, Charles E., Jr.
1981 Uniting public history and historical archaeology. *The Public Historian* 3:75–83.

1983 The spatial organization of a postbellum plantation. Paper presented at the 40th Southeastern Archaeological Conference, Columbia, South Carolina.
1984 The archaeology of the squad system of labor on southern cotton plantations. Unpublished manuscript in possession of the senior author.
1985 The sorghum processing industry of a nineteenth-century cotton plantation in South Carolina. To appear in *Historical Archaeology* 19(1).

Orser, Charles E., Jr., and Claudia C. Holland
1984 Let us praise famous men, accurately: toward a more complete understanding of postbellum southern agricultural practices. To appear in *Southeastern Archaeology* 3(2).

Orser, Charles E., Jr., Annette M. Nekola, and James L. Roark
1981 *Summary Report of Phase I Testing and Evaluation at Millwood Plantation (38AB9), Abbeville County, South Carolina.* Report submitted to the Interagency Archaeological Services, Southeast Regional Office, Atlanta.
1982 *Exploring the Rustic Life: Multidisciplinary Research at Millwood Plantation, A Large Piedmont Plantation in Abbeville County, South Carolina, and Elbert County, Georgia.* Draft report submitted to the Archaeological Services Division, National Park Service, Southeast Regional Office, Atlanta.

Otto, John Solomon
1975 Status differences and the archaeological record: a comparison of planter, overseer, and slave sites from Cannon's Point Plantation (1794–1861), St. Simon's Island, Georgia. Ph.D. dissertation, Department of anthropology, University of Florida. Ann Arbor: University Microfilms.
1977 Artifact and status differences: a comparison of ceramics from planter, overseer, and slave sites on an antebellum plantation. In *Research Strategies in Historical Archaeology.* Stanley South, ed. New York: Academic Press. Pp. 91–118.
1984 *Cannon's Point Plantation, 1794–1860: Living Conditions and Status Patterns in the Old South.* Orlando: Academic Press.

Perrin, Lewis
1933 The hermit of Millwood: an account of the life of Mr. James Edward Calhoun. *The Press and Banner and Abbeville Medium,* June 29. Abbeville, South Carolina.

Prunty, Merle, Jr.
1955 The renaissance of the southern plantation. *The Geographical Review* 45:459–491.

Ransom, Roger L., and Richard Sutch
1977 *One Kind of Freedom: The Economic Consequences of Emancipation.* Cambridge: Cambridge University Press.

Roark, James L.
1977 *Masters Without Slaves: Southern Planters in the Civil War and Reconstruction.* New York: Norton.

Roscoe, John T.
1975 *Fundamental Research Statistics for the Behavioral Sciences.* 2nd ed. New York: Holt, Rinehart, and Winston.

Savitt, Todd L.
1978 *Medicine and Slavery: The Diseases and Health Care of Blacks in Antebellum Virginia.* Urbana: University of Illinois Press.

Shlomowitz, Ralph
1979a The transition from slave to freedman labor arrangements in southern agriculture, 1865–1870. Ph.D. dissertation, Department of Economics, University of Chicago.
1979b The origins of southern sharecropping. *Agricultural History* 53:557–575.
1982 The squad system on postbellum cotton plantations. In *Toward a New South? Studies in Post–Civil War Southern Communities.* Orville Vernon Burton and Robert C. McMath, Jr., eds. Westport, Connecticut: Greenwood. Pp. 265–280.

Stampp, Kenneth M.
1956 *The Peculiar Institution: Slavery in the Ante-Bellum South.* New York: Random House.

Thompson, Edgar T.
1975 *Plantation Societies, Race Relations, and the South: The Regimentation of Populations.* Durham: Duke University Press.
Tindall, George Brown
1967 The emergence of the new South, 1913–1945. In *A History of the South*. Vol. 10. Wendell Holmes Stephenson and E. Merton Coulter, eds. Baton Rouge: Louisiana State University Press.
Trimble, Stanley W.
1974 *Man-Induced Soil Erosion on the Southern Piedmont, 1700–1970*. Ankeny, Iowa: Soil Conservation Society of America.
United States Census
1850 Agricultural schedule for Abbeville district, South Carolina. South Carolina Department of Archives and History, Columbia.
1860a Agricultural schedule for Abbeville district, South Carolina. South Carolina Department of Archives and History, Columbia.
1860b Slave schedule for Abbeville district, South Carolina. South Carolina Department of Archives and History, Columbia.
1880 Agricultural schedule for Abbeville county, South Carolina. South Carolina Department of Archives and History, Columbia.
Vance, Rupert B.
1936 *How the Other Half is Housed: A Pictoral Record of Sub-Minimum Farm Housing in the South*. Southern Policy Paper 4. Chapel Hill: The University of North Carolina Press.
Wolf, Eric
1959 Specific aspects of plantation systems in the New World: community sub-cultures and social class. In *Plantation Systems of the New World*. Vera Rubin, ed. Washington, D.C.: Pan American Union. Pp. 136–146.
Woofter, Thomas J., Jr., Gordon Blackwell, Harold Hoffsommer, James G. Maddox, Jean M. Massell, B. O. Williams, and Waller Wynne, Jr.
1936 *Landlord and Tenant on the Cotton Plantation*. Works Progress Administration, Washington, D.C.
Wright, Gavin
1978 *The Political Economy of the Cotton South: Households, Markets, and Wealth in the Nineteenth Century*. New York: Norton.
Zimmerman, Larry J.
1978 Simulating prehistoric locational behavior. In *Simulation Studies in Archaeology*. Ian Hodder, ed. Cambridge: Cambridge University Press. Pp. 27–37.

PART III

Artifact Patterns

5

Distributions of European Earthenwares on Plantations on Barbados, West Indies

Frederick W. Lange

Shawn Bonath Carlson

INTRODUCTION

This chapter analyzes the horizontal distribution of European-made earthenwares recovered from six plantations investigated in Barbados during 1971–1973 (Figure 5.1) (Handler and Lange 1978) and demonstrates that the archaeological patterns observed are similar to those in slave and nonslave contexts on North American sites. Such data contribute to an understanding of the extent to which North American and British Caribbean archaeological patterns of material culture from the period of plantation slavery may be either interchangeable or restricted for interpretive purposes.

Fourteen plantations were initially surveyed on the basis of strong documentary backgrounds. These 14 plantations were also selected because of their spatial distribution on the 166-square-mile island. It was hoped this would reveal micro-geographical variables.

Horizontal control was maintained at each plantation by collecting from fields of known historic use, as established by documentary and cartographic records. Most of the plantations surveyed had fields designated for the slave village, ponds, and mill area. Some also retained the names of former garden areas. Because field names are used even today for crop recording and management, there has been very strong

ISBN 0-12-646480-4

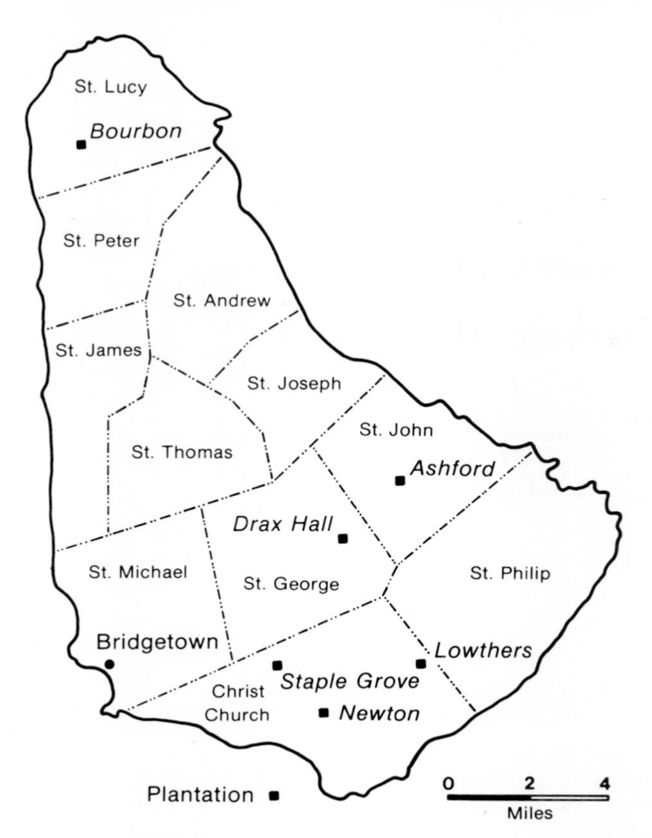

Figure 5.1 Map of Barbados, showing locations of study plantations.

conservatism of the preemancipation names (Chandler 1968; Handler and Lange 1978:44–45). Both Jerome Handler (1983) and Ronald Hughes (personal communication, 1983) agree that modern designations of Negro Yard Fields approximately denote the location, but not always the full extent, of the area dedicated to the slave village in preemancipation times. With this knowledge of each plantation, and approximately known manufacturing dates for the ceramics recovered from them, several research possibilities became apparent:

1. The applicability of South's Mean Ceramic Date (MCD) formula (1972, 1977a,b) to the Caribbean area could be evaluated (Lange and Handler 1980). Because there was no vertical control over the data, chronologically relevant patterns established through the use of Mean Ceramic Date formula would be critical. Previous studies in Antigua (Nicholson 1979:52) have shown that the MCD formula is accurate to within 5 years from surface collections for sites of known historic

dates, while studies by Turnbaugh and Turnbaugh (1977) have shown that irregularities in the MCD results can isolate significant cultural variables.

As a British colony subject to several seventeenth-century navigation acts that limited trade with other countries (Handler and Lange 1978:19–20), Barbados traded almost exclusively with Britain and the British Colonies throughout the slave period. Trade with the North American colonies was also very important, although it was interrupted temporarily during the revolutionary war. Spargo (1926:54–57) raised the possibility that white stoneware was exported from near Burlington, New Jersey, to Jamaica and Barbados during the late seventeenth century.

There was clearly the potential for variability in historic patterns of trade between the American colonies and the Caribbean colonies (and specifically Barbados). Irregularities in the MCD formula might detect differences in the composition of consumer populations in the two geographical areas, or differences between the settlement patterns of North American versus Barbadian plantation populations. Thus, it became necessary to examine whether or not South's formula, derived entirely from North American sites, could, in its original format or in some adaptation, provide adequate chronological control over the use of individual fields at each plantation.

2. Additionally, an improved ceramic dating program (Carlson 1983) derived from South's original formula was applied to the ceramic data to graphically present the range of occupation or use of each field and to pinpoint the period of maximum use (or fluctuations in the maximum use) of each field. These ranges of use were based on combined ceramic assemblages, rather than on individual types.

3. Chi-square tests could be used to measure the statistical significance of similarities or differences (1) between individual fields on each plantation, (2) between fields of similar use at different plantations, and (3) between the combined assemblages from each plantation.

4. Most importantly, these data manipulations could be the basis for further interpretation of slave activity and for supplementing Handler and Lange's original investigations. We anticipated that the data would once again demonstrate the advantage of a strong ethnohistoric approach to the study of slavery in order to obtain the most complete results.

In preparing and interpreting these data, it was fully recognized that the European earthenwares formed only one element in the total archaeological assemblage. However, they were among the most dominant materials surface-collected from the plantation fields during the surveys. Locally produced wheel-made redware ceramics were also recovered in quantity, but are omitted from this analysis pending further field research (Hayward 1972). Reassessment of these data, in conjunction with the present study, suggests the possibility that redwares were not only made for plantation industrial use, but also were made for domestic use. In this sense they may have filled a chronological and functional niche similar to that of colonoware in the southeastern United States. There, Lees (1980:137) and others have suggested that colonoware was essential in meeting the needs of both planters and slaves prior to the beginning of a large-scale importation of cheap earthenwares from England.

There is little reason to suspect that ceramic needs were significantly different on Barbados.

A definite time gap exists between the establishment of most Barbadian plantations (and related slave villages) and the initial appearance of inexpensive European earthenwares (Figure 5.2). Local redwares were presumably manufactured prior to the introduction of European wares, as well as afterwards. These locally produced redwares were, however, of extremely high quality relative to published general descriptions of colonoware (cf. Ferguson 1978).

Colonoware seems to have had part of its roots in native American ceramics and was a nonwheel product. This was not the case with the Barbadian redwares. While these ceramics were made by slave potters for the use of the plantations, the documentary record is unclear as to what extent these same artisans may have produced other wares for domestic use (Handler 1963a; Handler and Lange 1978:142–144). Handler and Lange (1978:136) observed that: "The glazed earthenwares or "redwares" are similar to materials being manufactured in Barbados today [Handler 1963b]. . . . Glaze colors range from dark green through light green and from yellow to brown, depending on the glaze and the temperature at firing." The paste of the redwares is either dark red or gray and has small white inclusions of limestone temper (Riordan 1972).

In contrast to Jamaica (Mathewson 1972a,b, 1973) and the southeastern United States (Ferguson 1980; Lees 1980), only three sherds were found during the Barbados research that suggested historic Indian manufacture or the continuity of African ceramic traditions within the plantation slavery context. Stratigraphic evidence is needed before a complete parallel between the southeastern United States and Barbados patterns can be fully assumed. However inferential, the distributional data are supportive of such an interpretation, as are the Newton cemetery data (Handler and Lange 1978:135–139). At Newton, redware ceramics were incorporated into grave fill contexts which clearly antedate the 1760s and the increased importation of earthenwares from Britain.

A BRIEF HISTORY OF SLAVERY ON BARBADOS

The archaeology of slavery on Barbados must be examined within the historical context of slavery (Handler 1971, 1974; Handler and Lange 1978). Barbados's first English settlers arrived in 1627 with a handful of Africans; large-scale importation did not start until the 1640s. The plantation slave system was well established by the 1650s, with the transformation of the island's economy from the small-scale farming of tobacco, cotton, and indigo (largely using white indentured servant labor) to the large-scale cultivation of sugar under the plantation system dependent on slave labor. All three of the plantations discussed in this chapter are from the part of the island settled relatively early. The slave trade reached its zenith from 1769 to 1773

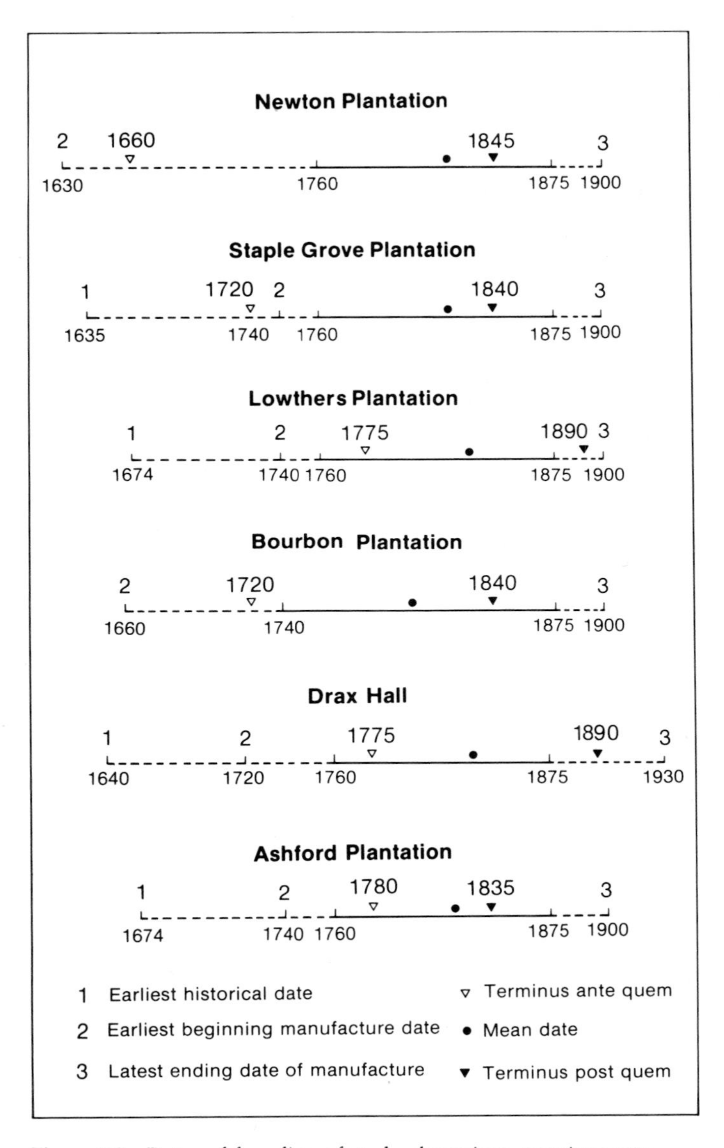

Figure 5.2 Dates of founding of study plantations, *terminus ante quem* dates, mean dates, and *terminus post quem* dates.

(Handler and Lange 1978) and declined rapidly thereafter, ending with Britain's Abolition Act in 1807.

Slaves were emancipated throughout the British Empire in 1834. While the slaves' legal status changed, their social status did not. There were shifts in settlement patterns (see Lange and Handler, 1980, Chapter 3), but economic patterns remained much as before. Artifact distribution patterns and the presence and absence of specific types will span slave and nonslave contexts and may show if the impact of emancipation was rapid, or much more gradual.

METHODS OF DATA RECOVERY

One of the problems of data recovery was the extreme impact of historic land use on the terrain, especially agricultural practices, since World War II. Barbados is quite small, relatively flat, and very little land was left untouched, even during the slave period. Since World War II, intensive deep plowing and disking, leveling, and filling have further altered the surface: in many places tractors have churned up the limestone bedrock. Handler and Lange had partially anticipated the impact of agriculture, but found it to be much more pervasive than they had suspected (1978:49–50).

In most fields, surface collecting was constrained by the dense growth of sugar cane, while cultivation of food crops affected other fields. In some places former slave villages or other use areas were in mature cane fields and could not be collected. Fields of young cane could be collected with little difficulty, as could fields with most other agricultural crops. Field conditions at the time of collection are noted later.

Each field was surveyed in a series of transects by four to six persons spaced 2 m apart. They walked systematically from one end of the field to the other, picking up any cultural materials. Observations were also made on the relative distribution of materials in each field. Piles of rock, which had been cleared from the fields, were checked for old foundation stones or grinding/milling stones (such stones had been anticipated, based on general historical literature [Handler and Lange 1978:54] but none were encountered.)

The principal survey efforts during 1972–1973 were devoted to fields historically associated with specific domestic activities, the Negro Yards, or former slave villages. However, all plantation fields were the sites of slave activities and any field might be expected to yield refuse representing slave behavior. While the documentary resources suggested fairly specific locations of historic behavior, it was not certain that the modern field boundaries exactly paralleled those from the eighteenth and nineteenth centuries. For this reason, fields adjacent to designated Negro Yard Fields were examined. Also, some plantations had multiple Negro Yard Fields (Newton had four; Figure 5.7), and in such cases all were collected if accessible. Another concern was the extent to which postemancipation dumping might have affected the density and content of cultural assemblage in slave utilized areas. Collections from fields distant from the village areas were expected to provide a good comparative data base.

SUMMARY OF DATA ANALYSIS

As Handler and Lange reported (1978:58) various considerations led to focusing on Newton plantation; the other 13 received only limited surface or testing treatment. The ceramic data from all plantations were analyzed originally by A. Zipris (1972) and reanalyzed by S. Carlson for this chapter (Table 5.1). Preliminary distributional data were summarized by Accola (1972). Eight of the collections are very limited, and only six were selected for discussion. Data and space limitations ultimately conspired to restrict discussion to Newton, Staple Grove, and Lowthers plantations. Comparative data from Bourbon, Drax Hall, and Ashford plantations are summarized, but are not discussed in detail (Figure 5.3A,B). They did, however, generally reflect the same patterns described here.

As noted previously, the analysis was limited to horizontal distributions. Only ceramics of known dates of manufacture are discussed in terms of how slave behavior might be reflected in the archaeological record. The analyses were also carried out within the methodological limits of the original project, which did not address any of the plantations as total entities, but concentrated only on the slave dimension.

A ceramic dating program (D. Carlson 1983) was developed which weighted ceramics with shorter ranges of manufacture more heavily than it did ceramics with longer ranges of manufacture. This program had previously been tested using the same 15 sites utilized by South (1977b:260) and was found to more accurately predict the mean date of site occupation. By combining the frequency of dated ceramic types with their manufacture dates (Table 5.1), not only was a mean date of occupation produced for each provenience, but also charts showing a uniform distribution of the ceramics through time (Figures 5.4, 5.5, and 5.6). This method uses the same principles as South's line graphs which show ceramic manufacture date ranges, and Salwen's and Bridges's (1977) bar graphs which account for both manufacture date range *and* frequency of individual ceramic type. However, Carlson's system incorporated this information into a uniform distribution which graphically reflects an *area* that corresponds to the frequency of the ceramic types through time.

Chi-square tests, using a confidence level of 0.05, were employed to evaluate the observed differences or similarities between and among the ceramic assemblages from the different plantations. Chi-square tests of ceramic types and their frequencies have been shown to reflect status differences in the archaeological record (Drucker 1981; Otto 1975, 1977) that correspond well with the cost differences in ceramics suggested by Miller (1980). Attempts at comparative observations were planned for the Barbadian data which could also be applied to other British colonial or American plantations that employed Barbadian sugar production techniques, such as the Sutherland Plantation in Jackson County, Texas (Freeman and Fawcett 1980).

Table 5.1
ANALYSIS OF HISTORIC CERAMICS

Ceramic type	Begin	End	Midpoint	References
1. Buckley	1720	1775	1747.5	(Miller & Stone 1970:51; Noël Hume 1970:132–133; South 1972)
2. Metropolitan slipware	1630	1660	1645.0	(Noël Hume 1970; South 1972)
3. Delftware, plain white	1640	1802	1721.0	(Noël Hume 1970:109, 105–111; South 1972)
4. Delftware, decorated	1570	1802	1686.0	(Noël Hume 1970:105–111; South 1972)
5. Delftware, English	1620	1720	1670.0	(Noël Hume 1970:108–109; South 1972)
6. Sgrafitto slipware	1670	1795	1732.5	(Noël Hume 1970:99, 134; South 1972)
7. Creamware	1760	1820	1790.0	(Noël Hume 1970:125–126; South 1972; Towner 1957)
8. Wheildonware	1740	1780	1760.0	(Godden 1965:xvi; Noël Hume 1970:123–124)
9. Pearlware, plain	1780	1830	1805.0	(Noël Hume 1970:128; South 1972)
10. Pearlware, annular	1790	1739	1810.0	(Lofstrom 1976; Noël Hume 1970:131; South 1972)
11. Pearlware, mocha	1799	1830	1814.5	(Noël Hume 1970:131; Price 1979:31)
12. Pearlware, blue shell-edged	1780	1830	1805.0	(Lofstrom 1976; Noël Hume 1970:129–131; Price 1979:31; South 1972)
13. Pearlware, green shell-edged	1800	1830	1815.0	(Lofstrom 1976; Noël Hume 1970:129: Price 1979:31)
14. Pearlware, hand-painted fineline polychrome	1780	1835	1807.5	(Lofstrom 1976; Noël Hume 1970:129; Price 1979:31)
15. Pearlware, hand-painted monochrome blue	1780	1830	1805.0	(Lofstrom 1976; Noël Hume 1970:125; Price 1979:31; South 1972)
16. Pearlware, transfer-printed	1787	1830	1808.5	(Godden 1963:113; Hughes and Hughes 1968:150; Noël Hume 1970:128; South 1972; Towner 1957:47)
17. Whiteware, plain	1820	1900	1860.0	(Lofstrom 1976; Noël Hume 1970:130–131; Price 1979:31; South 1972)
18. Whiteware, annular	1830	1875	1852.5	(Lofstrom 1976; Noël Hume 1970:131; Price 1979:31)
19. Whiteware, mocha	1830	1875	1852.5	(Price 1979:31)
20. Whiteware, gilded edged-decoration	1890	1930	1910.0	(Hughes & Hughes 1968:83)
21. Whiteware, blue shell-edged	1830	1860	1845.0	(Lofstrom 1976; Noël Hume 1970:129–131; Price 1979:31)

22. Whiteware, molded (embossed)	1845	1885	1865.0	(Fairbanks 1974:77; Price 1979:31; South 1974:247–248; Wetherbee 1980:18)
23. Whiteware, hand-painted fineline and broad-line polychrome	1825	1860	1842.5	(Lofstrom 1976; Price 1979:31)
24. Whiteware, hand-painted monochrome blue	1830	1860	1845.0	(Price 1979:31)
25. Whiteware, spatterware/sponged	1830	1865	1847.5	(Collard 1967; Greaser & Greaser 1973:101–110; Keyes 1930:333; Lofstrom 1976; Price 1979:3; Towner 1957:56)
26. Whiteware, stamped/cut sponge	1840	1870	1855.0	(Godden 1963:111–112; Lofstrom 1976; Price 1979:31)
27. Whiteware, blue transfer-print	1830	1865	1847.5	(Price 1979:31)
28. Whiteware, flow blue transfer-print	1835	1870	1852.5	(Collard 1967; Lofstrom 1976; Mankowitz & Hagger 1975:90; Price 1979)
29. Whiteware, other transfer-prints	1825	1875	1850.0	(Price 1979:31)
30. Yellowware	1830	1940	1885.0	(Hughes & Hughes 1968:113; Noël Hume 1970:131)
31. Agate Sgrafitto	1740	1775	1757.5	(Noël Hume 1970:132; South 1972)
32. Ironstone	1805	1900	1852.5	(Fairbanks 1974:77; Hughes & Hughes 1968:108; South 1972)
33. Brown stoneware bottles	1820	1900	1860.0	(Noël Hume 1970:78–79; South 1972)
34. Rhenish stoneware, blue/manganese painting with cordoning	1635	1765	1700.0	(Noël Hume 1970:280; South 1972)
35. Bellarmine	1550	1699	1624.5	(Hughes & Hughes 1968:17; Noël Hume 1970:55; South 1972)
36. Black basaltes	1750	1820	1785.0	(Godden 1965:xix; Hughes & Hughes 1968:15; Noël Hume 1970:121; South 1972)
37. Scratch blue	1740	1775	1757.5	(Noël Hume 1970:117; South 1972)
38. Debased scratch blue	1723	1775	1749.0	(Noël Hume 1970:118; South 1972)
39. White salt-glazed stoneware, thin	1744	1775	1759.5	(Noël Hume 1970:115; South 1972)
40. White salt-glazed stoneware, thick	1765	1795	1780.0	(Noël Hume 1970:115)
41. Porcelain, underglaze blue Chinese	1660	1800	1730.0	(Noël Hume 1970:263; South 1972)
42. Porcelain, underglaze blue English	1745	1795	1770.0	(Noël Hume 1970:137; South 1972)
43. Porcelain, Chinese export	1660	1800	1730.0	(Noël Hume 1970:258: South 1972)
44. Porcelain, Canton	1800	1835	1867.5	(Noël Hume 1970:262; South 1972)
45. Porcelain, parian	1840	1895	1867.5	(Godden 1965:xxv; Hughes & Hughes 1968)

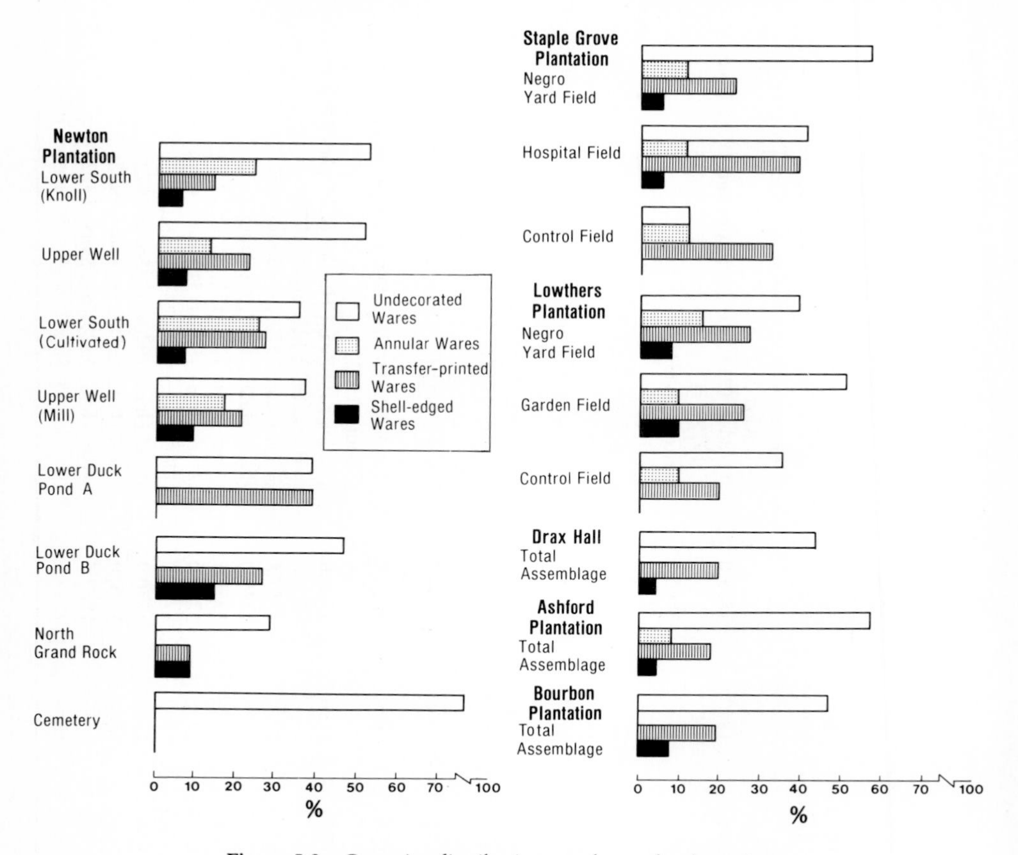

Figure 5.3 Ceramics distributions at the study plantations.

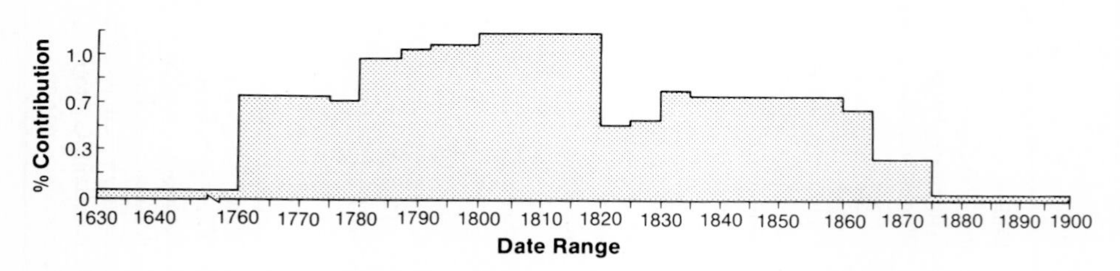

Figure 5.4 Uniform distribution of ceramics from Newton Plantation.

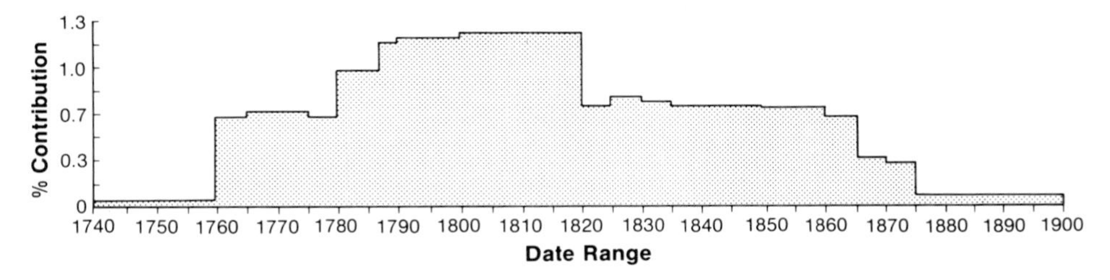

Figure 5.5 Uniform distribution of ceramics from Staple Grove Plantation.

NEWTON PLANTATION

Newton Plantation was a typical larger-sized Barbadian plantation in terms of historical development, land size, slave population size, and agricultural practices. The plantation was well established by 1675 and covered approximately 450 acres. The owner's home, sugar factory, and other industrial buildings defined the central complex at the plantation (Figure 5.7). The slave village was usually located nearby where it could be supervised and the agricultural fields extended beyond (Handler and Lange (1978:60–62). This general pattern is typical of Barbadian plantations and is also reported for the southeastern United States (Lewis 1979).

Surface collections at Newton were made from eight fields of known historic use. These fields, which included the Upper North Negro Yard Field, Lower North Negro Yard Field, Upper South Negro Yard Field, Lower South Negro Yard Field, North Grand Rock Field, Upper Well Field, Lower Duck Pond Field, and the slave cemetery area were associated with specifically documented slave activity (habitation or work) and yielded 67% of the total 1105 dateable European earthenwares collected. Four major ceramic groups were recovered from these fields: undecorated wares, annular wares, transfer-printed wares, and shell-edged wares (Figure 5.3).

Lower South Negro Yard Field (Knoll Section)

At the time of survey, the Knoll section (Fig. 5.7) was partially in low grass, with some bedrock exposed and visibility of about 50%. A *terminus ante quem* of 1803

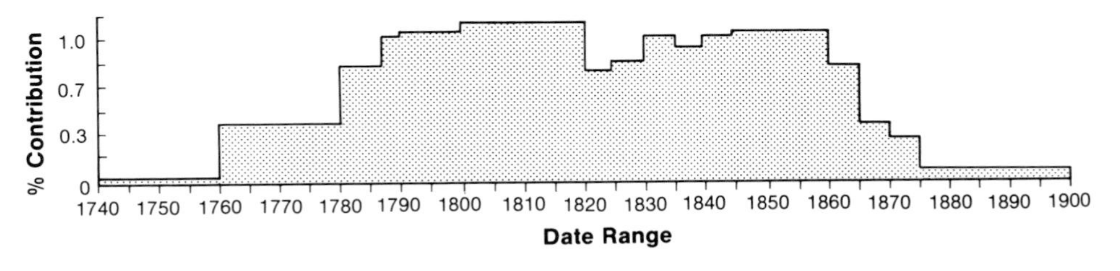

Figure 5.6 Uniform distribution of ceramics from Lowthers Plantation.

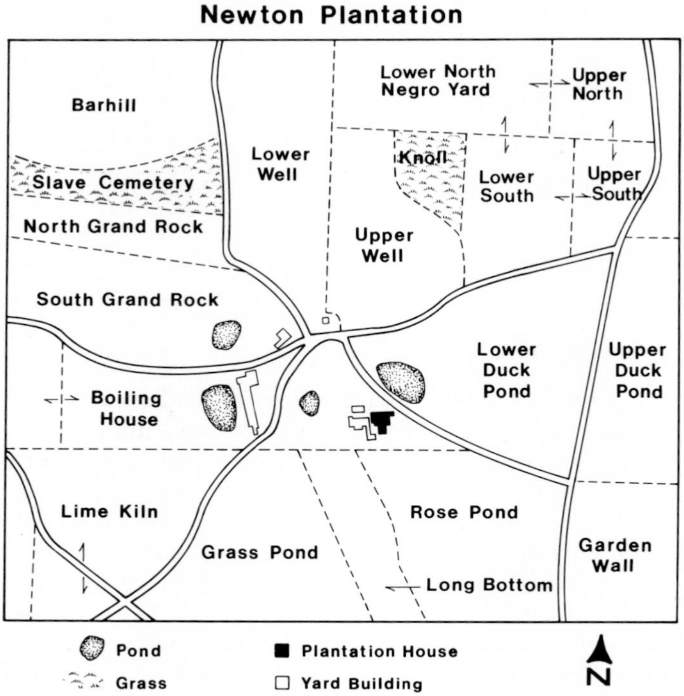

Figure 5.7 Fields at Newton Plantation.

was established by the presence of Buckley earthenware (Lange and Handler 1980) while a *terminus post quem* of 1830 was established from the decorated whitewares present, particularly annular wares and transfer-printed wares. However, the largest group of ceramics consisted of the undecorated wares, totaling 50.2% (Figure 5.3). Some of these may represent the plain parts of decorated specimens, largely blue feather-edged (Fairbanks 1962:13). Both South's and Carlson's formulas produced a mean occupation date of 1822.5. A uniform distribution of the data (Figure 5.4) suggests an occupation from 1760 to 1875, with the greatest number of ceramics found having been manufactured between 1787 and 1820.

Lower North and Lower South Negro Yard Fields (Cultivated Section)

These lower yard fields were adjacent to the knoll (Figure 5.7) and had fewer ceramics. The Lower North Field was in mature cane and the Lower South Field was in yams when they were collected. Visibility was about 10% in the former and 60% in the latter. A *terminus ante quem* of 1795 (debased scratch-blue stoneware) and a *terminus post quem* of 1840 (cut sponged ware) were established, with a mean site date of 1835.7. The range of occupation or use of this field, indicated by a uniform distribution, was the same as in the two preceding fields. However, in this case, a bimodal distribution indicated fewer ceramics manufactured between 1780 and 1820 than those manufactured from 1830 to 1860. This later use is reflected in the proportions of ceramic types recovered from this field; while the undecorated wares still represent the largest category, the annular wares and transfer-printed wares increased in number (Figure 5.4).

Upper Well Field

The Upper Well Field (Figure 5.7) was in young cane at the time it was collected and visibility was about 60%. A uniform distribution produced from the data from this field was almost identical to that representing the Lower South Negro Yard Field, suggesting the same range of occupation and the distinct possibility that the slave village may have extended into this area. Buckley earthenware and decorated whitewares were again used to establish a *terminus ante quem* (1803) and a *terminus post quem* (1830), with a calculated mean site date of 1824.6.

Upper Well Field (Old Mill Section).

The Upper Well Field was adjacent to the overseer's house and only slightly farther from the main house (Figure 5.7). The highest density of cultural material was encountered in the immediate area of the old mill. A wide variety of ceramics was collected from this area and an early *terminus ante quem* of 1699 (a Bellarmine medallion) suggests a long period of use. A *terminus post quem* of 1830 was established by the decorated whitewares and the calculated mean site date was 1826.7. An increased number of hand-painted wares (5.8%) was also noted. The uniform distribution of these data indicated that the greatest number of ceramics found were manufactured between the years 1800 and 1820. A gap occurred between 1820 and 1830, with another dense concentration from 1830 to 1860. The proportions of ceramics recovered were more similar to those recovered from the cultivated portion of the Lower South Negro Yard Field (Figure 5.4).

Other Fields

Upper North and Upper South Negro Yard Fields, as well as Lower Duck Pond Field and North Grand Rock Field show very low densities of ceramics (Figure 5.3) suggesting that these areas lay outside the main limits of slave habitation activities. Excavations in the slave cemetery have been described in detail (Handler and Lange 1978, Chapter 5) but yielded very few earthenware ceramics.

Summary

The ceramic assemblage from Newton Plantation was largely composed of undecorated wares (54.5%), annular wares (12.3%), transfer-printed wares (14.8%), and shell-edged wares (6.5%). Metropolitan slipwares established the *terminus ante quem* for the plantation as 1660, while molded whiteware provided a *terminus post quem* of 1845. The mean date of occupation calculated for the whole plantation was 1819.9, with the greatest number of analyzed ceramics having been manufactured between 1760 and 1875. A bimodal distribution shows that the densest concentration of ceramics was for those dating from 1800 to 1820, with a lesser concentration from 1830 to 1860.

Comparative analysis of the ceramic assemblages from the different fields revealed a number of similarities:

1. In each of the eight fields, undecorated wares were always most common and shell-edged wares the least common, with percentages of annular wares and transfer-printed wares in between (Figure 5.3).

Table 5.2
COMPUTED CHI-SQUARE VALUES COMPARING MAJOR CERAMIC GROUPS[a]

	1	2	3
Newton Plantation			
1. Negro Yard Field			
2. Upper Well Field	7.1011		
3. Upper Well Field (Mill portion)	15.7759[b]	10.2088[b]	
4. Lower South Negro Yard Field (cultivated section)	14.2647[b]	11.1682[b]	4.5553
Staple Grove Plantation			
1. Negro Yard Field			
2. Hospital Field	7.6876		
Lowthers Plantation			
1. Negro Yard Field			
2. Field adjacent to Negro Yard Field	12.9364[b]		
3. Control Field	9.4581	22.8526[b]	
Negro Yard Fields			
1. Newton			
2. Lowthers	21.7637[b]		
3. Staple Grove	8.3190	7.9683	
Habitation versus special use			
1. Lower South Negro Yard Field (Newton)			
2. Hospital Field (Staple Grove)	12.3204[b]		

	1	2	3	4	5
Combined proveniences					
1. Newton					
2. Staple Grove	15.6993[b]				
3. Lowthers	82.7377[b]	68.6899[b]			
4. Bourbon	13.6932[b]	16.0840[b]	23.2640[b]		
5. Drax Hall	17.1853[b]	14.7487[b]	39.1179[b]	3.4786	
6. Ashford	7.8269	.6495	37.0999[b]	11.7585[b]	11.8515[b]

[a]Numbers at heads of columns correspond to numbered entries in the left column.
[b]Significantly different at the .05 level.

2. From the fields in the general area of the former slave village, the quantities of undecorated wares were highest; the old mill area had demonstrably lower percentages of undecorated wares (Figure 5.3). A chi-square test verified the *similarities* observed between the fields defined as habitation areas; the chi-square test also supported the *differences* between the living and old mill areas (Table 5.2).

3. The quantities of decorated wares collected from the fields at Newton Plantation did not seem to change as dramatically in number from field to field as did the undecorated wares. However, a bimodal distribution was represented by the data from the old mill area, suggesting longer use. This was apparent in the slightly higher number of decorated wares in the ceramic assemblage. The remaining fields at Newton yielded fewer ceramics, although in the same general proportions (Figure 5.3).

4. Finally, in examining the total dated ceramics from Newton, similar ranges of occupation or use were evident, generally falling within the period from 1760 to 1875 (Figure 5.4). The fields representing slave habitation had mean dates ranging from 1822.5 to 1824.6, while the mill area had a mean date ranging from 1821.4 to 1835.7, again suggesting a slightly longer period of use. This conforms to the expected pattern since habitations changed location after emancipation, but common fields remained constant. The most frequently occurring *terminus ante quem* was 1803, while the most frequently occurring *terminus post quem* was 1830. Combined these data suggest that the most intensive occupation of the site occurred between 1760 and the beginning of emancipation in 1834. These data also mirror a significant increase in the slave population between 1750 and 1776 (Handler and Lange 1978, Table 6), as well as an increase in the production of earthenwares in Great Britain and their export to the colonies (Miller 1980). An influx of numerous decorated whitewares being manufactured circa 1830 to 1860, combined with a dense island population, make it impossible to pinpoint the historical moment of emancipation in the ceramic analyses. While some shift in settlement pattern occurred after emancipation, this cannot be demonstrated from the available ceramic distribution data.

STAPLE GROVE PLANTATION

Five fields at Staple Grove were surface-collected, including a Negro Yard Field, Hospital Field, a field adjacent to Hospital Field (Ch-8-0), a control field across the road from the plantation house (Ch-7-0), and a control field (Ch-6-0) located at a distance from the main house (Figure 5.8). Eighteen test units were also excavated in Negro Yard Field; all encountered plowed strata and are treated here as part of the surface collection. The Negro Yard Field was in mature cane and visibility ranged from almost 0% in some areas to almost 100% in areas where the cane had wilted due to excess moisture or other problems; the Hospital Field and the two control fields were in young cane and visibility was approximately 90%. The same four major groups of ceramics were recovered in similar proportions to those recovered from Newton Plantation (Figure 5.3).

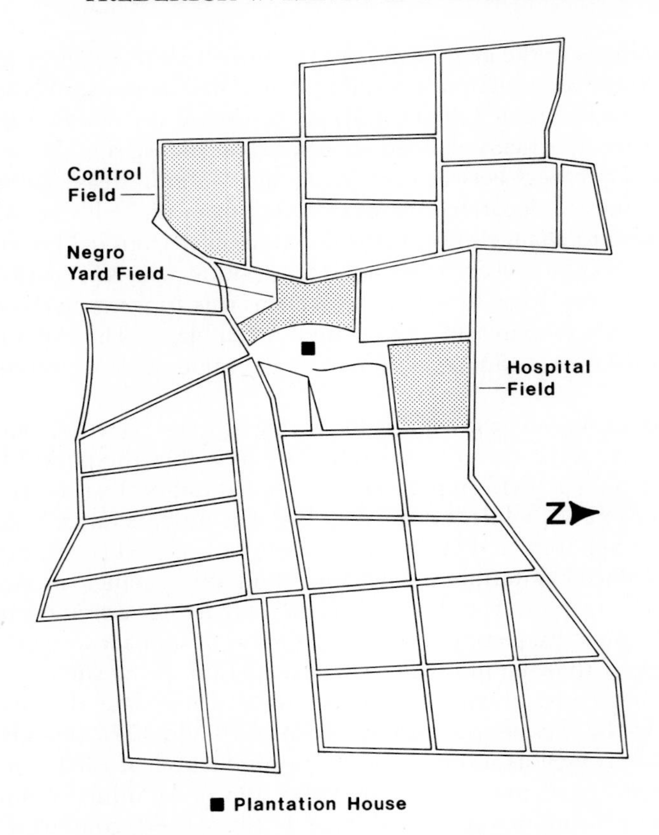

Figure 5.8 Fields at Staple Grove Plantation.

Negro Yard Field

Ceramics from the Negro Yard Field yielded a calculated mean site date of 1820.1, with a *terminus ante quem* of 1820 and a *terminus post quem* of 1830 established by plain creamware and a number of decorated whitewares. A uniform rectangular distribution of the data suggest the range from 1800 to 1820 as the period of manufacture for most of the ceramics present. A chi-square test between the Negro Yard Fields at Newton and Staple Grove Plantations indicated no statistically significant differences (Table 5.2). However, comparisons of the total ceramic assemblage from each plantation did suggest significant differences, perhaps due to the functional differences inherent in the Hospital Field at Staple Grove.

Hospital Field

Ceramics from the Hospital Field produced a calculated mean date of 1826.5, with a *terminus ante quem* of 1775 (white salt-glazed stoneware) and a *terminus post quem* of 1840 (cut sponged ware). The range of ceramic manufacture suggested by the uniform distribution of the data was from 1760 to 1900. The greatest number of ceramics present were manufactured between 1800 and 1820; however, a strong cluster of ceramics dating from 1825 to 1865 reflected the large numbers of transfer-printed whitewares recovered in this field. A chi-square test comparing the Hospital Field at Staple Grove with the habitation patterns at both Newton and Staple Grove did indicate a statistically significant difference, probably due to the higher quantities of transfer-printed wares (Table 5.2). Transfer-printed wares would be more likely to have come from the main house and would suggest that slaves in the hospital may have received some food directly from the planter's kitchen. This would have been in accord with the planter's efforts to limit loss of productive time due to sickness, whether feigned or real, or to supplement the diets of mothers with young infants.

Control Field (Ch-7-0)

This field yielded a high density of material in the area closest to the plantation house. Slave settlement may be reflected in this area of the plantation as well as in the designated Negro Yard Field. It may also represent dumping.

Control Field (Ch-6-0)

The last field discussed for Staple Grove was a control field at some distance from the main house (Figure 5.8), with no indication of use other than for general agricultural purposes. It yielded few artifacts, with the recovered ceramics representing a mean use date of 1846, a *terminus ante quem* of 1830 (plain pearlware) and a *terminus post quem* of 1835 (flow blue transfer-printed whiteware). A uniform distribution of the data suggested a use range from 1780 to 1940, with the period of most intensive use falling between 1830 and 1860.

Summary

The dateable ceramic assemblage from Staple Grove Plantation appeared to be very similar to that from Newton Plantation. The *terminus ante quem* was 1775 (white salt-glazed stoneware) and the *terminus post quem* was 1840 (cut sponged ware). A common time range of approximately 1760 to 1875 was established for the bulk of the ceramics by a uniform distribution of the data from Staple Grove (Figure 5.5). A mean site date ranged from 1820.1 to 1826.5 in the central areas to a mean site date of 1846 in the control field.

At both Newton and Staple Grove the same four major groups of ceramics occurred most frequently. Undecorated wares accounted for at least 50% of the ceramics recovered from the slave village areas of each plantation, while at least 35% undecorated wares were recovered from other areas (Figure 5.3). At Staple Grove the large quantities of undecorated wares were related to the intensity of use/occupation noted during the period 1760 to 1830, while the much less intense use/occupation from 1825 to 1860 was associated with quantities of decorated wares.

LOWTHERS PLANTATION

Three fields were surface-collected at Lowthers: the Negro Yard Field, Garden Field, and a control field (CH-5-OB) some distance from the main house (Figure 5.9). All three fields were in young cane and visibility ranged from 50% to 90%. Again, the same four major groups of ceramics were collected, but the frequency of undecorated wares recovered from living and working areas was different from the previously discussed plantations.

Negro Yard Field

Ceramics recovered from the Negro Yard Field (Figure 5.9) spanned the years from 1760 to 1900, with a mean date of 1830.2. Buckley earthenware established a *terminus ante quem* (1803) and gilded-edge-decorated whiteware the *terminus post*

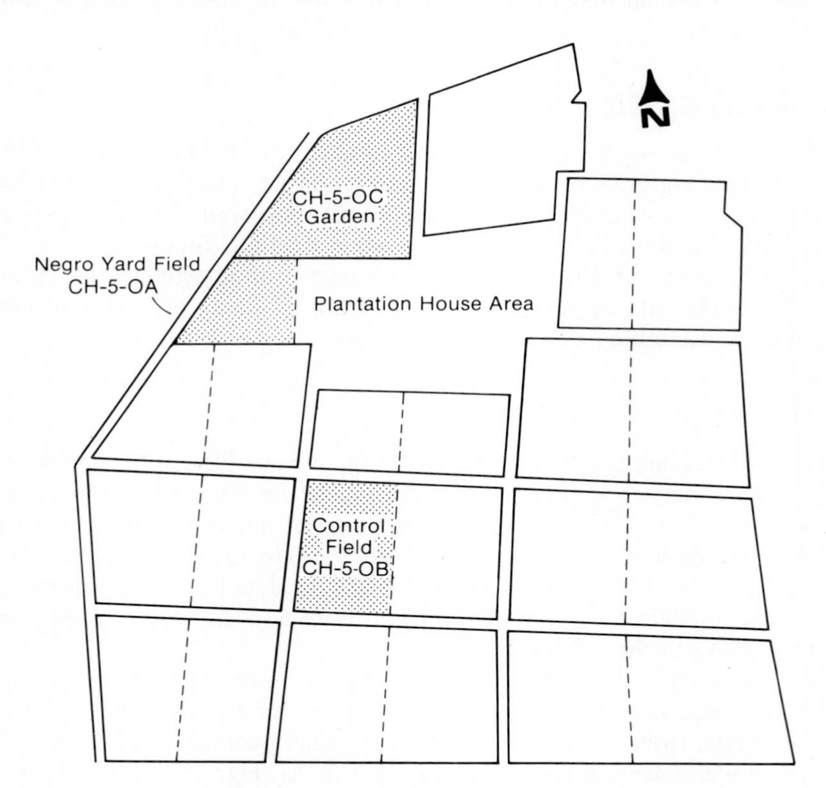

Figure 5.9 Fields at Lowthers Plantation.

quem (1890). A bimodal distribution, suggesting two ranges (1790 to 1820 and 1840 to 1860) of manufacture for the most common ceramics, was generated.

Garden Field

The ceramics from the Garden Field produced a *terminus ante quem* of 1820 (plain creamware) and a *terminus post quem* of 1840 (cut sponged ware). The range of use reflected by the rectangular distribution was from 1760 to 1875 with the period of most intense use between 1800 and 1820. A less intense use of the field was noted from 1840 to 1860. These bimodal distributions are very similar to those for the Negro Yard Field and may indicate an extension of the Negro Yard Field into this area.

Control Field

The last field collected at Lowthers was a control field that produced a *terminus ante quem* of 1820 and a *terminus post quem* of 1830, represented by plain creamware and annular and transfer-printed whitewares. The calculated mean date was 1837.9, possibly reflecting a tenantry. The range of ceramic manufacture suggested by the uniform distribution of the data was from 1760 to 1940, with the most intense concentration from 1830 to 1865.

Summary

The ceramics from Lowthers represent a period of manufacture from 1760 to 1875 (Figure 5.6) with a mean date of 1828. In Negro Yard Field, a *terminus ante quem* of 1775 and a *terminus post quem* of 1890 were established, while the adjacent garden field and more distant control field had a much later *terminus ante quem* of 1820 and an earlier *terminus post quem* of 1830 to 1840 (Figure 5.2). The most intense periods of manufacture are from between 1800 and 1820, with strong but fluctuating periods of manufacture represented from 1820 to 1865 (Figure 5.6).

At Lowthers, undecorated wares accounted for 38% of the ceramics collected in the Negro Yard Field as compared to 50.2% at Newton Plantation and 55% at Staple Grove Plantation (Figure 5.3). In the Garden Field, 50.6% undecorated wares were recovered from Lowthers as compared to 30.6% from Newton and 39.1% from Staple Grove.

A chi-square test (Table 5.2) indicated no statistically significant differences between Lowthers's Negro Yard Field and the Staple Grove's Negro Yard Field, but did indicate differences with Newton's Negro Yard Field. This may be due to the large amount of annular ware recovered from Newton, while Lowthers and Staple Grove both had higher percentages of transfer-printed wares than annular wares. Economic differences may be reflected by both the transfer-printed wares, which were the most expensive, and the annular wares, which were cheap and usually produced in utilitarian bowl forms and mugs. Otto (1977:107) concluded that slaves ate mostly from bowls, and this observation seems to have been confirmed by Lewis and Haskell (1980:77) and by Booth (1971:33). A similarity suggested by the chi-square test (Table 5.2) between Lowthers's Negro Yard Field and the control field may have little significance because of the small number of sherds (24) recovered from the latter.

CONCLUSIONS

The major conclusions that can be derived from this study are: (1) four major ceramic groups (undecorated wares, annular wares, transfer-printed wares, and shell-edged wares) occurred most frequently at the six plantations; (2) this pattern correlates well with ceramic assemblages from the American South and other Caribbean sites; (3) chi-square tests have supported the historical documentation by distinguishing differences between slave-village and nonslave village areas (a mill area, a hospital area, and a generally agricultural area), largely by indicating differences in the quantities of undecorated wares that were present; (4) the field defined as a mill area showed a longer period of use, reflecting both pre- and postemancipation activities; this was demonstrated by the increased quantities of decorated wares that were present; and (5) postemancipation distributions at two of the plantations may reflect changes in settlement patterns from central villages to peripheral tenantries. While the data suggest broad similar patterns when comparing North American and British Caribbean remains, we should bear in mind that deviations from these generalizations (cf. Turnbaugh and Turnbaugh 1977) may be indicators of the most significant areas for interpretation.

The four groups of ceramics accounted for 87.2% of the combined total ceramic assemblages, with undecorated wares accounting for an average of 52.4% of the total, transfer-printed wares for 18%, annular wares for 11.6%, and shell-edged wares for 5.2%. Undecorated wares were always the most common and they varied in frequency from 35% to 55% on each plantation, probably reflecting the types of ceramics purchased for and utilized by the slaves and perhaps overseers as well. Transfer-printed wares and annular wares fluctuated in their frequencies but were always the second and third most common wares; where transfer-printed ceramics dominate, dumping activity from the main house may be represented, whereas the dominance of annular wares might reflect a slave or overseer context. Likewise, shell-edged wares varied in frequency but were always the fourth most common ceramic.

Although no collections were made in the immediate vicinity of the plantation owners' or overseers' houses, the materials collected may represent the remains of slave domestic and working behavior. Historically, all fields that were surface-collected were generally defined as slave village areas, gardens fields, or mill areas or, in the case of the control fields, lands that had been devoted exclusively to agriculture.

The results of this analysis compare favorably with those of Cannon's Point

Plantation in Georgia where Otto (1975, 1977:98) found 29% undecorated wares, 25% annular wares, 21% transfer-printed wares, and 12% shell-edged wares associated with a slave cabin site. In contrast, the planter's kitchen site at Cannon's Point yielded 77% transfer-printed wares. Otto concluded that "the differences in type frequencies were statistically significant, and the classifications (status and ceramic types) were statistically associated" (1977:105). Pulsipher and Conrad (1982) reported similar ceramic assemblages from Montserrat. Differences in the percentages of the four ceramic groups do differ from area to area and this may reflect variations in imported quantities, may be a further reflection of differing manufacturing and trade patterns, or may reflect the economic status or management policies of individual plantation owners.

While the present study lacked comparative data associated with the planter's home, George Miller's study (1980) of economic scaling of ceramics (combined with the historical documentation) supports the date presented here as being representative of lower-class occupation. Miller noted that undecorated wares were the most inexpensive of all ceramics, with shell-edged wares and annular wares being the least expensive decorated wares available during the nineteenth century (1980:34). The further conclusion that slave behavior is reflected is supported by correlations between documentary data and archaeological distribution patterns.

A high correlation existed between the documentary record and the archaeological evidence. The frequency of ceramics recovered from fields documented as living sites shows that slave habitation occurred over a wider area than that incorporated in the Negro Yard Fields. The statistical significance of these results suggests that it may be possible to identify undocumented slave village areas on Barbados and in other British Caribbean settings.

Finally, at Newton the bimodal distributions of data from the mill area, with a second period of intense acquisition of manufactured ceramics between 1830 and 1865, reflects the historical fact that sugar production areas continued to be used after the slave villages had been relocated to the tenantries after 1834.

The bimodal distribution of ceramics defined for many fields discussed here may be attributed to population increase and postemancipation use. By the early 1820s the number of slaves per plantation averaged 229 (Handler and Lange 1978:34) with the greatest population increases having occurred between 1750 and 1780. Many decorated whitewares were available by 1830, just prior to emancipation, and it is suggested that their presence in the archaeological record (24.6% of the total assemblage as opposed to 10.2% decorated pearlwares) reflects a larger slave population. Few ceramics were recovered with beginning manufacturing dates later than 1830, indicating that the 1830-to-1860-use ranges generated by the uniform distribution of this data represent either postemancipation activities or an increased population prior to 1834.

The suggested use of locally produced redwares prior to the mass production of cheap earthenwares in England further demonstrates a general unity of the evolution of patterns of ceramic utilization in the Caribbean as well as the American South.

ACKNOWLEDGMENTS

David Carlson developed the analytical program that enhanced the research summarized in this chapter. Jerome S. Handler was of immeasurable assistance in reviewing an early draft and in sharpening the focus and correcting data regarding the historical background of the island. Dr. Ronald Hughes of the University of the West Indies responded quickly and generously to a request for information about the historical starting dates of the six plantations. Robert V. Riordan codirected the fieldwork with Lange in 1972 and Richard M. Accola, Arthur Zipris, and Michele Hayward wrote student papers that formed the basis for many of our initial ideas regarding artifact distributions. Figures were prepared by Roger Coleman (Texas A&M University).

REFERENCES

Accola, R.
1972 Artifact association study on Barbados. Department of Anthropology, Southern Illinois University. Unpublished manuscript.

Booth, S.
1971 *Hung, Strung, and Potted: A History of Eating in Colonial America.* New York: Clarkson N. Potter.

Carlson, D.
1983 Computer analysis of dated ceramics: estimating dates and occupational ranges. Southeastern Archaeology 2(1):8–20.

Chandler, Sir J.
1968 Plantation field names in Barbados. *Journal of the Barbados Museum and Historical Society* 32:133–143.

Collard, E.
1967 *Nineteenth-Century Pottery and Porcelain in Canada.* Montreal: McGill University Press.

Drucker, L.
1981 Socioeconomic patterning at an undocumented late 18th century lowcountry site: Spiers Landing, South Carolina. *Historical Archaeology* 15:58–68.

Fairbanks, C.
1962 European ceramics from the Cherokee capital of New Echota. Papers presented at the First and Second Conferences on Historic Sites Archaeology *SEAC Newsletter* 9:10–16.
1974 The Kingsley slave cabins in Duval County, Florida; 1968. *The Conference on Historic Site Archeology Papers, 1972* 7:62–93.

Ferguson, L.
1980 Looking for the "Afro" in colono-Indian pottery. In *Archaeological Perspectives on Ethnicity in America.* R. L. Schuyler, ed. New York: Baywood Press. Pp. 14–28.

Freeman, M., and W. Fawcett, Jr.
1980 The antebellum period in the Stephen F. Austin Colony: historical and archeological research in the Palmetto Bend reservoir area, Jackson County, Texas. Research Report No. 70, Palmetto Bend Reservoir Series, Vol. 5, Texas Archaeological Survey. Austin: University of Texas.

Godden, G.
1963 *British Pottery and Porcelain 1780–1850.* New York: A. S. Barnes.
1965 *An Illustrated Encyclopedia of British Pottery and Porcelain.* New York: Crown Publishers.

Greaser, A., and Paul Greaser
1973 *Homespun Ceramics.* Des Moines, Iowa: Wallace-Homestead Book Co.

Handler, J.
1963a A historical sketch of pottery manufacture in Barbados. *Journal of the Barbados Museum and Historical Society* 30:1–24.
1963b Pottery making in rural Barbados. *Southwestern Journal of Anthropology* 19:314–334.

1971 *A Guide to Source Materials for the Study of Barbados History, 1627–1834.* Carbondale: Southern Illinois University Press.

1974 *The Unappropriated People: Freedmen in the Slave Society of Barbados.* Baltimore: Johns Hopkins University Press.

Handler, J., and F. Lange

1978 *Plantation Slavery in Barbados: An Archaeological and Historical Investigation.* Cambridge: Harvard University Press.

Hayward, M.

1972 Redware from Barbados. Department of Anthropology, Southern Illinois University. Unpublished manuscript.

Hughes, G., and T. Hughes

1968 *The Collector's Encyclopedia of English Ceramics.* London: Abbey Library.

Keyes, H.

1930 Spatter. *Antiques* 17:332–337.

Lange, F., and J. Handler

1980 Application of the South ceramic formula on Barbados, West Indies. Paper presented at 13th annual meeting, Society for Historical Archaeology, Albuquerque.

Lees, W.

1980 Limerick, old and in the way: archaeological investigations at Limerick Plantation. Occasional Papers of the Institute of Archeology and Anthropology, Anthropological Studies No. 5., University of South Carolina, Columbia.

Lewis, K.

1979 Hampton, initial archeological investigations at an eighteenth century rice plantation in the Santee Delta, South Carolina. Research Manuscript Series No. 151, Institute of Archeology and Anthropology, University of South Carolina, Columbia.

Lewis, K., and H. Haskell

1980 Hampton II: further archeological investigations at a Santee River rice plantation. Research Manuscript Series 161, Institute of Archeology and Anthropology, University of South Carolina, Columbia.

Lofstrom, E.

1976 An analysis of temporal change in a nineteenth century ceramic assemblage from Fort Snelling, Minnesota. *The Minnesota Archaeologist* 35:16–47.

Mankowitz, W., and R. Hagger

1975 The Concise Encyclopedia of English Pottery and Porcelain. New York: Hawthorn Books, Inc.

Mathewson, R.

1972a History from the earth: archaeological excavations at Old King's House. *Jamaica Journal* 6:3–11.

1972b Jamaican ceramics: an introduction to 18th century folk pottery in West African tradition. *Jamaica Journal* 6:54–56.

1973 Archaeological analysis of material culture as a reflection of sub-cultural differentiation in 18th century Jamaica. *Jamaica Journal* 7:25–29.

Miller, G.

1980 Classification and economic scaling of 19th century ceramics. *Historical Archaeology* 14:1–40.

Miller, J., and L. Stone

1970 Eighteenth century ceramics from Fort Michilimackinac: a case study in historical archaeology. Smithsonian Studies in History and Technology No. 4, Smithsonian Institution Press, Washington, D.C.

Nicholson, D.

1979 The dating of West Indian historic sites by the analysis of ceramic sherds. *Journal of the Virgin Islands Archaeological Society* 7:52–74.

Noël Hume, I.
1970 *A Guide to the Artifacts of Colonial America.* New York: Alfred A. Knopf.
Otto, J.
1975 Status differences and the archaeological record—a comparison of planter, overseer, and slave sites from Cannon's Point Plantation (1794–1861), St. Simon's Island, Georgia. Ph.D. dissertation, University of Florida, Gainesville. Ann Arbor: University Microfilms.
1977 Artifacts and status differences—a comparison of ceramics from planter, overseer, and slave sites on an antebellum plantation. in *Research Strategies in Historical Archeology.* S. South, ed. New York: Academic Press. Pp. 91–118.
Price, C.
1979 *19th Century Ceramics in the Eastern Ozark Border Region.* Monograph Series No. 1, Center for Archaeological Research, Southwest Missouri State University, Springfield, Missouri.
Pulsipher, L., and C. M. Goodwin
1982 Galways Plantation—1981 Field Report. Earthwatch, Inc., Ms.
Riordan, R.
1972 Notes on redware ceramics. Notes on file, Department of Anthropology, Southern Illinois University.
Salwen, B., and S. Bridges
1977 Cultural differences and the interpretation of archeological evidence: problems with dates. *Researches and Transactions of the New York State Archeological Association* 17:165–173.
South, S.
1972 Evolution and horizon as revealed in ceramic analysis in historical archaeology. *The Conference on Historic Sites Archaeology Papers, 1971* 6:165–173.
1974 Palmetto parapets. Anthropological Studies 1, Institute of Archeology and Anthropology, University of South Carolina, Columbia.
1977a Evolution and horizon as revealed in ceramic analysis in historical archaeology. In *Historical Archaeology: A Guide to Substantive and Theoretical Contributions.* R. Schuyler, ed. New York: Baywood Publishing Company. Pp. 68–82.
1977b *Method and Theory in Historical Archeology.* New York: Academic Press.
Spargo, J.
1926 *Early American Pottery and China.* New York: Garden City Publishing Co.
Towner, D.
1957 *English Cream Colored Earthenware.* London: Faber and Faber.
Turnbaugh, W., and S. Turnbaugh
1977 Alternate applications of the mean ceramic date concept for interpreting human behavior. *Historical Archaeology* 11:90–104.
Wetherbee, J.
1980 *A Look at White Ironstone.* Des Moines, Iowa: Wallace-Homestead Book Co.
Zipris, A.
1972 Analysis of earthenware and stoneware. Department of Anthropology, Southern Illinois University. Unpublished manuscript.

6

The Planter Class: The Archaeological Record at Drayton Hall

Lynne G. Lewis

INTRODUCTION

Over the years many archaeologists have endeavored to determine if and how socioeconomic status is reflected by the archaeological record. That this determination is considered possible is most succinctly stated by Deetz (1973:20): "Depending on an individual's place within the socioeconomic scale, the artifacts with which he furnishes his household will vary in quantity and quality." The ability, however, to determine socioeconomic status from an archaeological site is complicated by a number of factors. The major one is that the artifacts most likely to be considered an indication of high status do not enter the archaeological record as frequently or in the same manner as other objects (Lewis and Hardesty 1979:47). Some, such as furniture or fabrics, are rarely recovered from a site, while others, such as silver and jewelry, tend to enter through accidental loss.

Another factor is that the way in which the wealth of a site's owner is expended may differ according to class. While an overseer might invest in material goods to reflect his status, the planter may do likewise only to a certain point and then invest in land, labor, and crops. An observation of this nature was made in Bonner's (1945) study of plantation architecture in the South where travelers observed that wealthy planters invested in labor, land, and crops, often to the detriment of their physical surroundings. "Travelers who visited the South were frequently astounded at the great number of wealthy men they found living in miserable dwellings" (Bonner 1945:371). Although his study was confined to the Deep South during the nineteenth century, it is possible that the results can be applied to plantations in other areas of the South during both the eighteenth and nineteenth centuries.

ISBN 0-12-646480-4

The study of socioeconomic status has been approached from many angles, most commonly by the direct method of analyzing the range of artifacts from a given site (best exemplified by Otto's [1975] study and comparison of a planter's, overseer's and slave's site on St. Simon's Island, Georgia) or a particular class of artifacts such as ceramics (G. Miller 1974; Stone *et al.* 1973) or faunal remains (H. Miller 1979). Another direction has been the use of inventories, with an emphasis on the study of ceramics (Herman *et al.* 1975; Stone 1970). A few have taken other approaches, most particularly George Miller (1980) by using economics directly in his study of the price scaling of ceramics.

Despite the attempts to define socioeconomic indicators, no one artifact or class of artifacts has emerged that serves this function. The question of socioeconomic status as reflected by the archaeological record continues to be a vexing one and, in an attempt to address it once again, the archaeological record from the main house area of Drayton Hall will be considered and compared in the following essay.

DRAYTON HALL

In 1738 John Drayton purchased 350 acres of land on the west bank of the Ashley River, about 12 miles northwest of Charleston, South Carolina (CCC 1738:30).[1] This purchase was to form the core of a plantation system that at its zenith encompassed at least 20 other homes and working plantations (Ruth P. Reeves, personal communication, 1982) and was to be the site of one of the finest Georgian villas in the United States—Drayton Hall (Cornforth 1974:n.p.). Construction was begun shortly after John's purchase of the land and was completed by 1742 when his son William Henry Drayton was born there (SCHS 1817:43).

Drayton Hall is a three-story brick building with a raised English basement, a first and second floor and an unfinished attic. It is 52 by 70 feet (3640 square feet per floor) with the land and river facades finished as formal entrances (Figure 6.1). The size of Drayton Hall compares favorably with other "mansions" of coastal plantations (e.g., Middleton Place, 2100 square feet per floor [Lewis and Hardesty 1979:47]; Hampton, 3168 square feet, first floor [Lewis and Haskell 1980:52]; and the Couper house at Cannon's Point, estimated 4837 square feet [Otto 1975:153]).

The first and second floors consist of five rooms each (a large central room with four rooms off each corner) and a stair hall. Each room is fully paneled from floor to ceiling with bald cypress. Wooden cornices, ranging from simple dentil patterns to elaborate egg-and-dart work adorn each room. All the rooms once had plaster ceilings (most probably molded) although today only two molded ones, on the first floor, remain intact.

[1]CCC—Charleston County Courthouse, Charleston, South Carolina; CLS—Charleston Library Society, Charleston, South Carolina; HCF—Historic Charleston Foundation, Charleston, South Carolina; MPF—Middleton Place Foundation, Charleston, South Carolina; SCHS—South Carolina Historical Society, Charleston, South Carolina; SCSA—South Carolina State Archives, Columbia, South Carolina; WHL—Waring Historical Library, Medical University of South Carolina, Charleston, South Carolina.

Figure 6.1 Drayton Hall west (land-side) façade. (Courtesy of the National Trust for Historic Preservation.)

Although the architect is unknown, it is clear that he was aware of the most current architectural trends and built for John Drayton what then and today is considered an architectural gem. Indeed, a newspaper advertisement for the sale of land across the river from Drayton Hall notes that the parcel affords a view of John Drayton's "palace" (CLS 1758). The inclusion of a two-story Palladian portico and the embodiment of other Georgian–Palladian concepts two decades before its widespread adoption in the colonies makes it a splendid example of surviving early Georgian architecture in the United States (Nichols 1976:101, 107–108).

In addition to the main house, two two-story brick dependencies (flankers) were constructed to either side of the west facade of the house, forming an enclosed forecourt that also contained the land-side driveway. This is in keeping with the plantation layout most typical in the Southeast (Lewis and Haskell 1980:40–42). That there were numerous other out-buildings is made clear in Charles Drayton's diaries where he notes the construction of, or repairs to, at least 20 other buildings on the property. Today only one building from the earliest period of construction remains, a brick privy.

While John was a planter by occupation, he also served as an assistant judge for the Court of General Sessions and a justice for the Court of Common Pleas in 1753, as well as serving as a member of the Royal Council to the Governor from 1754 until the outbreak of the Revolutionary War (CCC 1751–1754:833).

Like many wealthy planters of the time, John sent his sons to England to be educated. Charles, who acquired Drayton Hall from his stepmother in 1783, graduated from the University of Edinburgh as a medical doctor in 1770 (WHL 1770:n.p.), although architecture, horticulture, and agriculture were of particular interest to him, as illustrated in the meticulous diaries he kept between 1789 and his death in 1820.

Charles Drayton, Jr. inherited Drayton Hall from his father in 1820 and he, also a medical doctor, evidently directed his energies toward the maintenance of the family holdings. His death in 1844 left Drayton Hall to his wife and their four sons, and by 1855 she had sold her interest to two of these sons, Thomas Henry and John (CCC 1855:273, 399). Not much is known about the fortunes of Drayton Hall during this period, but there had been neglect and decline. An article written in 1860 for the *N.Y. Spirit of the Times* stated "until within a few years the property has been neglected. . . . We believe it is the intention of the present owner [John] to restore everything, as nearly as possible, to its original perfection, and workmen are now busy in restoring the building and grounds" (Anonymous 1860:4).

The Civil War and its aftermath put an end to these plans. In 1865 John Drayton, by then sole owner of Drayton Hall, wrote to Williams Middleton describing the situation. John considered that it might be wise to "quit the country if we can the better for us, if I can possibly raise the money to get me out of it I will, but unfortunately there is none here, and you can't get any in no manner or shape" (MPF 1865:n.p.).

After the Civil War, the property was leased to phosphate-mining companies; the main house was used as office space (CCC 1866:23; 1868:473; 1875:64). The revenues generated by this extensive mining were probably responsible for preventing Drayton Hall's sale or destruction and enabled Charles Drayton (the fourth one) to plan the restoration of the property. "The restoration of Drayton Hall is already mapped out and before many years have lapsed the old mansion will shine forth resplendent with original beauty and completeness" (Bowen 1885:n.p.). Many of these restorations, including the present terne roof, are still in place today.

Miss Charlotta Drayton, coowner and finally full owner between 1915 and 1969 (CCC 1915:150), respected the significance of Drayton Hall and even refused to modernize it, thus bearing the inconvenience of no plumbing, electricity or modern heating during her stays. It is in this condition that the property was acquired from the Drayton family by the National Trust for Historic Preservation in 1974.

It is believed that for a large part of its history, Drayton Hall was used as a business and entertainment center for the family. It is not until the period of Charles Drayton's ownership (1783–1820) that the first evidence appears that would indicate the use of the property as a working plantation. Several mentions in C. Drayton's diaries (HCF 1789–1820) indicate that at this time he was growing cotton as a cash crop. The entertainment aspects still continued and to a great extent influenced the nature of the lifestyle and, correspondingly, the material possessions that would have been found in the house.

Unfortunately, little is known about this aspect of Drayton Hall. The record of furnishings is sparse, and neither the will nor the inventory survive for John, the builder of Drayton Hall. It is known, however, that he bought several pieces of furniture from Thomas Elfe, a well-known Charleston cabinet maker. The Elfe account books from 1769 to 1775 list purchases such as "a Breakfast Table, a Tea Table" (CLS 1772:47), "a Filed Mahy [Mahogany] Bedstead, a Close Stoole Chair + pan, 6 Mahogany Chairs hair bottoms" (CLS 1772:53), although it is not known if any of these pieces were used at Drayton Hall. A list of furnishings left to Charles Sr. by his father, and which he in turn sold to his stepmother Rebecca, included such items as "nine mahogany Tables, one library Table, two marble slabs and stands, [and] one large gilt framed looking glass" along with numerous pieces of silver (SCSA 1783:477–479).

In Charles Drayton's diaries he notes purchases of furniture for Drayton Hall from his London factors, "Messr. Bourdieu & Chollett" (HCF 1801). Specific items from London that are mentioned include "books, saddles, a 'grand Forte piano,' a Barbarini Vase, a mahogany 'Duchesse' consisting of two bamboo caned chairs and two caned stools covered with fine canvas, a sopha bed and Chinese screen leaves" (HCF 1803). It is known, however, that not all furnishings were imported from London. In 1809 Charles Drayton notes that "Quash and his gang came to make large Tables for kitchen and serv. hall" (HCF 1809). These were slave laborers and it can be assumed that they made other everyday furnishings.

Other than the Barbarini vase, ceramics are mentioned only in two other places. One reference to "crockery ware" appears in the lot of furnishings sold to Rebecca by Charles and the other to the "delft" tiles in the fireplaces, noted in the 1875 *Harper's New Monthly Magazine* (Woolson 1875). A study of these tiles (many still in existence) indicates that they are eighteenth-century tiles and may be contemporary with the construction of the main house.

Altogether it can be established that, at least through the first 120 years, Drayton Hall housed a wealthy, socially prominent family of the planter class. With this background serving to establish the wealth and social standing of the Drayton family, the archaeological record is examined in an attempt to discern how it reflects the wealth of the family, if indeed it does.

ARCHAEOLOGY AT DRAYTON HALL

During the period between 1975 and 1982, several seasons of archaeological investigation took place at Drayton Hall.[2] This work concentrated in the area of the main house, at the two no-longer extant flanker buildings, and at the brick privy. Additional areas throughout the lawn were tested, including a complete survey of the north lawn in 1980 by a New York University field school under the direction of Bert Salwen. These excavations resulted in the recovery of almost 240,000 artifacts, along with 833 pounds of construction material (brick, mortar, and so on) and over 300 pounds of unidentifiable bone fragments and oyster shell (Table 6.1).

---

[2]The archaeological research at Drayton Hall was funded in part by the National Park Service's Historic Preservation Grants-in-Aid Program.

Table 6.1
DRAYTON HALL ARTIFACT TOTALS

	Fragment count	Minimum number of individuals
Household Items		
Maintenance and repair		
Sewing equipment	550	420
Flat irons	2	2
Preparation and consumption of food		
Ceramics	43,575[a]	2,529
Cooking utensils	145	28
Eating utensils and handles	127	95
Table glass	5,987	202
Furnishings		
Furniture hardware	426	419
Mirror and furniture glass	658	20
Lighting equipment	74	15
Ceramic tile	267	24
Other	27	24[b]
Storage		
Barrel bands	77	6
Tin cans	302	24
Wine bottle	23,179	237
Other bottle	8,682	140
Other	68	73[c]
Hygiene		
Pharmaceutical bottle	3,014	115
Ceramic hygiene items	—	86
Total household items	87,160	4,459
Personal Items		
Clothing		
Buttons	1,022	1,011
Buckles	53	50
Other clothing fasteners	87	82
Shoe	5	3
Other	12	12
Adornment		
Beads	252	252
Jewelry	51	43
Other	5	4
Grooming		
Brush/comb	35	21
Perfume bottle	22	4
Other	3	3
Tobacco		
Pipe	4,463	211
Snuff bottle	65	5
Other	11	11

(*continued*)

Table 6.1 (*Continued*)

	Fragment count	Minimum number of individuals
Recreation and activities		
Toys	85	54[d]
Pen/pencil	32	15
Clasp knife	18	13
Other	25	18[e]
Total personal items	6,246	1,812
Architectural Items		
Hardware		
Nails	50,020	20,574
Spikes	417	285
Screws	172	172
Window glass	55,366	—
Door and window hardware	159	82
Construction hardware	304	150
Supplies		
Brick	1,184 and 469 lb 12 oz	
Plaster	89 and 7 lb 7.5 oz	
Mortar	491 and 99 lb 3.5 oz	
Plaster/mortar	6 and 6 lb 1 oz	
Slate	459 and 69 lb 10 oz	
Paving stone	134 and 125 lb 14.5 oz	
Cement	28 and 9 lb 3 oz	
Architectural stone	39 and 41 lb 11.5 oz	
Oyster shell	14 and 2 lb 2.5 oz	
Other	563 and 1 lb 12 oz	
Total architectural items	109,445	21,263 and 833 lb 13.5 oz
Craft/Activity Items		
Arms		
Gun flints and chips	329	79
Munitions (lead)	785	785
Munitions (other metal)	240	240
Gun parts and other	31	17
Acquisition of subsistence resources		
Fishing gear	20	20
Agriculture tools	65	29
Whetstones	8	8
Horticulture	—	24
Commercial		
Bale seals	18	18
Fleams	2	2
Coins	25	25
Scale weights	7	7

(*continued*)

Table 6.1 (*Continued*)

	Fragment count	Minimum number of individuals
Skill or craft		
Lead casting residue	271	—
Construction tools	39	39
Other tools	29	29
Miscellaneous hardware	1,301	453
Coal	168	—
Transportation		
Stable and barn hardware	35	31
Harness buckles	30	19
Total craft/activity items	3,403	1,825
Subsistence Items		
Faunal remains	21,084 and 301 lb 6 oz	
Floral remains	434	
Total subsistence items	21,518 and 301 lb 6 oz	
Miscellaneous Items		
Miscellaneous (unidentifiable and other)	10,353 and 11 lb	
Native American (ceramics)	1,703	
Native American (lithics)	85	
Total miscellaneous items	12,141 and 11 lb	
Total all artifacts	239,913	29,361

[a]Includes all ceramics fragments except tile and toys.
[b]Includes vases, fine flower pots, and a figurine.
[c]Includes ceramic bottles.
[d]Includes ceramic toys.
[e]Includes ceramic inkwells.

The artifact collection derives basically from the first 120 years of occupation of the property. Although there is evidence of twentieth-century activity at the surface level and scattered around the perimeter of the lawn, very little artifactual evidence of occupation after about 1860 is found. This is the product of the changing usage of the property after the Civil War and may also be a reflection of changing trash disposal patterns as the farther one goes from the main house, the more modern the trash deposits become. The mean ceramic date (South 1977:217–221) computed for the fill levels at Drayton Hall is 1802.0. This is compatible with the dates of the most intensive occupation of the property, 1742 to 1860 (the median date for which would be 1801), and serves to confirm the preceding observations.

THE ARTIFACTS

The following discussion compares the results of Drayton Hall excavations with three major plantations in the Southeast that also have been excavated and studied.

Hampton and Middleton Place, located in South Carolina, were rice plantations. Middleton Place, four miles upriver from Drayton Hall, was the home of the socially and politically prominent Middleton family, to whom the Draytons are related by marriage. Hampton, located on the South Santee River about 40 miles northeast of Charleston, was owned by the Horry and Rutledge families (Lewis and Haskell 1980:3, 11, 16). Hampton was constructed circa 1750 and occupied intermittently until 1968 (Lewis and Haskell 1980:13, 22). Middleton Place is traditionally given the date of 1741 for construction. The main house and several other buildings were burned by Federal troops in 1865 (Lewis and Hardesty 1979:13). In 1867 Williams Middleton began reconstruction of the south dependency and this building was used as a residence on an irregular basis into the 1970s (Lewis and Hardesty 1979:18–20).

The third plantation, Cannon's Point, is located on St. Simon's Island, Georgia, and was a major cotton plantation owned by the Couper family from 1794 to 1861 (Otto 1975:1). At this plantation three specific areas—the planter's kitchen and main house, the overseer's house, and a slave cabin area—were all studied and compared.

Among the artifact types suggested as being status indicators are: architectural remains, certain types of buttons, and other personal and recreational items (Lewis and Haskell 1980; Otto 1975); horse equipment (Otto 1975); table glass (Lewis and Haskell 1980; Otto 1975); and most frequently, ceramics (Herman *et al.* 1975; Lewis and Hardesty 1979; Lewis and Haskell 1980; G. Miller 1974, 1980; J. Miller and Stone 1970; Noël Hume 1972; Otto 1975; Stone 1970).

Architectural Remains

In relation to architecture, Kenneth Lewis discusses both Hampton and Middleton Place and notes that their style and ornamentation are indicative of high-status dwellings (Lewis and Hardesty 1979:65; Lewis and Haskell 1980:55). John Otto also notes differences in durability and discusses available living space in terms of status (1975:133–137). In terms of building hardware, Otto notes that because of the nature of the sample taken at Cannon's Point, the evidence is not conclusive, but feels that it could very well be an indicator of status (1975:153). Hence, lower-status sites hypothetically will produce fewer architectural artifacts than higher ones.

In several cases of archaeological investigation this has proven to be the case. Leslie Drucker (1981) investigated a site at Spiers Landing in South Carolina and through various evidences concluded that it was a slave cabin site. She compared the artifacts recovered to the Carolina Artifact Pattern developed by South (1977) and the kitchen and architecture groups of artifacts differed noticeably from those found by South. In the South pattern (as revised by Garrow [1980] to include colonowares with the kitchen group artifacts rather than the activities group), the architecture group ranged from 25.2 to 31.4% (median 27.6%) and the kitchen group ranged from 51.8 to 65.0% (median 59.5%). At the Spiers Landing site the kitchen group constituted 73.7% of the total artifacts and the architecture group 20.2% (Drucker 1981:61). At the slave sites excavated on the Cooper River (Yaughan and Curriboo plantations, Garrow 1980), the kitchen groups were 84.2 and 70.9% for the two Yaughan sites and 80.0% for Curriboo. The architecture group was 11.8 and 24.8% for Yaughan and 13.5% at Curriboo. Garrow (1980) then generated a Carolina Slave Artifact pattern with the kitchen group ranging from 70.9 to 84.2% (median 77.5%) and the architecture group ranging from 11.8 to 24.8% (median 17.7%). Lack of sufficient data does not permit putting Otto's slave site into this form. At Hampton, the refuse attributed to a slave site produced the figures of 69.0% for the kitchen group and 23.4% for the architecture group (Lewis and Haskell 1980:71), the former only slightly below the slave pattern range and the latter within it, all of which points to a greatly reduced percentage of architecturally related items on a low-status site.

In contrast, the figures for the Hampton main house area are 32.6% for the kitchen group and 39.5% for the architecture group (Lewis and Haskell 1980:80–94). This is below the range for South's modified kitchen group and above the range for architecture. Middleton Place, again a site associated with an owner of high socioeconomic status, has 46.0% kitchen group and 28.2% architecture group artifacts (Lewis and Hardesty 1979:71–76), which is intermediate; the architecture group is within South's range and the kitchen group is slightly below. The shift from an emphasis on kitchen group artifacts to architecture group artifacts is also present at Drayton Hall but is even more exaggerated, with the kitchen group comprising only 36.3% and the architecture group 45.6%.

In all three cases the kitchen group falls below the range for the modified pattern, while at both Hampton and Drayton Hall the architecture group is above the modified pattern. (Table 6.2 summarizes this data.)

The presence of 10 purple, hand-painted, tin-glazed earthenware tile fragments is recorded from the main house area of Hampton (Lewis and Haskell 1980:52) and this particular ceramic type is generally associated with homes of the wealthy. At Drayton Hall, of the 266 tin-glazed earthenware tile fragments found, there were undecorated, blue decorated, and blue-and-purple decorated tiles. A total of 23 individual tiles were identified. That more were not found may be due to the fact that they remained in place until the twentieth century when they were removed by the Drayton family to prevent vandalism (many of the tiles have since been donated to Drayton Hall).

Thus it appears that in the coastal Southeast, one of the most reliable indicators of the status of a site's occupants may be the relationship between architectural artifacts and kitchen artifacts, with a high percentage of architectural remains being indicative of high status.

Table Glass

Both Otto and Lewis mention table glass as an indicator of status, particularly lead glass and cut and engraved specimens (Lewis and Haskell 1980:52; Otto 1975:235). Noël Hume mentions that cut glass is usually associated with the wealthy, particularly during the nineteenth century (1972:193).

Table 6.2
KITCHEN AND ARCHITECTURE GROUPS:
SLAVE VERSUS PLANTER SITES

	South modified pattern[a]		Slave artifact pattern[a]	
	Range (%)	Median (%)	Range (%)	Median (%)
Kitchen group	51.8–65.0[b]	59.5	70.9–84.2	77.5
Architecture group	25.2–31.4	27.6	11.8–24.8	17.7

	Kitchen group[h]	Architecture group[h]
Slave sites		
Spiers Landing[c]	73.7	20.2
Yaughan 1[d]	84.2	11.8
Yaughan 2[d]	70.9	24.8
Curriboo[d]	80.0	13.5
Hampton[e]	69.0	23.4
Planter sites		
Hampton[f]	32.6	39.5
Middleton[g]	46.0	28.2
Drayton Hall	36.3	45.6

[a]Garrow 1980:n.p.
[b]All figures rounded to nearest tenth.
[c]Drucker 1981:61.
[d]Garrow 1980:n.p.
[e]Lewis and Haskell 1980:71.
[f]Lewis and Haskell 1980:80–94.
[g]Lewis and Hardesty 1979:71–76.
[h]Percentages.

Although table glass appeared at all the sites being considered here, the percentages vary widely. At Hampton table glass represented 8.2% of all glass containers in the main house area; this was composed of 37 fragments of lead-glass drinking glasses and 3 other wine glass fragments (Lewis and Haskell 1980:52). At the Couper kitchen, Otto reports the presence of 37 cut and pressed glass tumbler fragments, 1 stemmed wine glass fragment, and fragments of 2 glass covers, thus comprising 6.9% of all glass container fragments (1975:226, 235). At the slave site table glass composed 6.6% of the glass containers, only slightly lower than the planter's kitchen, while the overseer's site produced the least table glass, 5.0% (Otto 1975:226, 235).

Drayton Hall, however, had 5987 fragments of table glass, representing 14.6% of all glass containers. Thus it appears that table glass, in amounts of less than 10%, is not a reliable indicator of wealth, but in amounts greater than 10% may be a reflection of high socioeconomic status.

Even more significant seems to be the variety of form within the category of table glass. In the Hampton main house area only tumbler and wine glass fragments were recovered (Lewis and Haskell 1980:52); at Cannon's Point (Couper kitchen) only tumbler, wine glass, and glass cover fragments were found. At the overseer's site only tumbler fragments and a glass handle were recovered while the slave site, oddly, showed the most variety with decanter and cruet-type glass appearing as well as tumbler, wine glass, and fragments of a cut-glass container and cover (Otto 1975:235).

Drayton Hall produced the widest variety of table glass forms. In addition to 42 vessels whose form could not be determined, 160 other vessels were identified, including 50 tumblers. Further, although Otto mentions only 1 stemmed wine glass from the Couper kitchen (1975:235) and Lewis and Haskell report 3 from Hampton (1980:52), 58 stemmed wine glasses were recovered at Drayton Hall, including those with air twist, opaque air twist, and cut faceted stems, as well as 4 engraved bowls. Finally, other table glass vessel forms recovered included 6 decanters (and 10 decanter/cruet stoppers, not counted as vessels), 4 plates, 3 flask/cruets, 3 compote/salvers, 2 bowls, 1 salt cellar, 1 candlestick, and 5 footed vessels. These data lead to the conclusion that table glass—not only in amounts greater than 10%, but also in forms other than tumbler and wine glass—is a sensitive indicator of status.

Buttons

One abalone shell button from the main house area was recovered at Hampton and is suggested as a high-status artifact (Lewis and Haskell 1980:52). Otto, in dividing buttons on the basis of possible function, notes that the four- and five-hole bone and four-hole iron buttons are more common on both the slave and overseer sites (representing 41% and 44% of all buttons, respectively), while at the planter site they comprised only 15% (1975:256). Drayton Hall parallels this with such buttons representing only 20.1% of the total range of clothing fasteners. Shell, porcelain, metal and one-hole bone buttons (most likely associated with shirts, coats, vests, dresses, and so on) comprised 78% of the buttons at the planter site, but only 38% at the slave site and 44% at the overseer site (Otto 1975:256). At Drayton Hall, these types of buttons comprised 70.0% of all buttons recovered.

Personal and Recreational Items

Among items mentioned by Otto as possibly representing recreation and status consumption were ornaments, games and toys, and personal possessions (1975:259).

At both Hampton and the Couper kitchen ornaments consisted entirely of beads (2 and 6 respectively, Lewis and Haskell 1980:93 and Otto 1975:274). At Middleton Place ornaments consisted of 5 beads, 2 "ornaments," and 1 modern earring (Lewis and Hardesty 1979:72–73). At Drayton Hall, in addition to 252 beads, there were 51 items identified as jewelry and 5 other ornaments for a total of 308 ornaments. Taking ornaments as a percentage of total personal possessions (excluding tobacco pipes), there is a remarkable similarity between the three sites. Hampton ornaments represent 20% of all personal possessions, Couper kitchen 18.2%, and Drayton Hall 17.3%. In contrast, the slave site at Cannon's Point is 12.7% and the overseer site 2.6%. In this instance adornment seems to be a definite status indicator, and variety in adornment even more so. Among the jewelry items identified at Drayton Hall were rings, sequins, rhinestones, chains, brooches, pendants, and a possible earring. Most of the items were of brass although many were gold- or silver-plated at one time.

No toys were recorded from Hampton or Middleton Place (Lewis and Hardesty 1979; Lewis and Haskell 1980), and only 2 from Cannon's Point—a partial doll's head and a clay marble, both from the slave cabin area (Otto 1975:276). At Drayton Hall a total of 85 items met this classification and included fragments from 5 porcelain dolls, a lead toy flintlock pistol, and 37 marbles (5 glass, 32 clay). Two Jew's harps and several fragments of toy creamware vessels (3 cups, a saucer, and a teapot) also were found.

Only 1 personal possession is noted from the Couper kitchen (the side plate of a flintlock pistol), 2 from the slave site and 5 from the overseer site (Otto 1975:276). At Hampton no personal possessions were noted from the main house area (Lewis and Haskell 1980) and none were found at Middleton Place (Lewis and Hardesty 1979). At Drayton Hall personal possessions, in addition to the ones mentioned earlier, included writing instruments, clasp knives, brush and comb parts, and perfume bottles. The Couper kitchen personal possessions comprised only 0.03% of all artifacts while at Drayton Hall they comprised 0.07% of all artifacts. At the Couper slave site personal possessions constituted 0.08% of the artifacts, which Otto assumes is due to the slaves claiming the discards from the planter's site (1975:282, 285).

Horse Equipment

The presence or absence of horse equipment on a site has been suggested as an indicator of status, however, analysis of the figures from Drayton Hall, Hampton, Middleton Place, and Cannon's Point do not support this contention. The most horse equipment was found at Hampton, where it represented 0.22% of all artifacts (Lewis and Haskell 1980:93). At Drayton Hall such items represented only 0.03% of all artifacts, while none were found at Middleton Place (Lewis and Hardesty 1979). At Cannon's Point both the planter and slave sites produced horse equipment, representing 0.04% of the artifacts at the slave site and 0.05% at the planter site (Otto 1975:282).

Ceramics

Ceramics as an indicator of socioeconomic status is probably the most thoroughly studied artifact class. Various approaches to the study of ceramics include types of ceramics, decorative techniques, vessel forms, utilization, and price scaling.

The presence of Chinese export porcelain is often mentioned as an indicator of wealth (Herman *et al.* 1975; J. Miller and Stone 1970; Stone 1970). At Drayton Hall the collection of Chinese export porcelain is particularly fine, and is dominated by eighteenth-century forms and styles (e.g., no Nanking and virtually no Canton porcelain was recovered from the site).

Porcelain at Drayton Hall represented 11.0% of the Euro-American ceramics collection. At Hampton, using comparable areas of the site (area 6 and the main house area), porcelain was 14.0% of the Euro-American ceramics (Lewis and Haskell 1980:54) while at Middleton Place it comprises 12.0% (Lewis and Hardesty 1979:32). English or continental porcelain—which is not present at Hampton (Lewis and Haskell 1980) and only one sherd of which was found at Middleton Place (Lewis and Hardesty 1979:76)—may also be a sensitive indicator of status. At Drayton Hall all other porcelain represented 0.7% of the Euro-American ceramics. In examining the presence of reexported ceramics on British colonial sites, K. Lewis found that the presence of Chinese export porcelain in amounts comprising up to 20% of all Euro-American ceramics was typical (1976:79), and that amounts ranging between 10% and 28% might be indicative of higher-status occupation (Lewis and Haskell 1980:75).

The porcelains at Cannon's Point differ substantially from the other plantation sites, most likely due to the fact that they represent exclusively nineteenth-century varieties. Porcelain represented 1.7% of all ceramics at the slave site, 3.2% at the overseer site, and 2.2% at the planter site. European porcelains are more common at Cannon's Point, with 0.7% of all ceramics at the slave site represented by European porcelain, 1.7% at the overseer site, and 0.7% at the planter site (Otto 1975:178).

Within the porcelains themselves, the presence or absence of certain decorative techniques would also be a status indicator. The most costly porcelains were those that were decorated with overglazed enameled painting, a technique that required extra steps and hence raised the price of production (J. Miller and Stone 1970:86). Overglazed porcelain constituted 29.1% of all the porcelains at Drayton Hall, while at both Hampton and Middleton Place it represented 7.2% of the total site porcelain (Lewis and Haskell 1980:90; Lewis and Hardesty 1979:76). When porcelain that was both blue underglazed and overglazed is added to the Drayton Hall total, the figure becomes 39.7% of all Chinese export porcelain; this then would seem to be an even more reliable indicator of wealth than just porcelain itself.

In ceramics other than porcelain, decorative techniques and their dominance as well as their presence or absence also may be a reflection of status (G. Miller 1980; Otto 1975).

In his work at Cannon's Point, Otto noted that among the nineteenth-century ceramics certain decorative techniques seemed to be indicative of status. In particular, the distinction between transfer-printed wares and banded wares was quite noticeable. At the Couper kitchen site 75.0% of all the ceramics recovered were transfer-printed, while only 1.0% were banded wares. Conversely, at the slave cabin site 21.6% were banded and 22.8% were transfer-printed. The overseer's house had 16.8% banded wares and 17.8% transfer-printed, even fewer transfer-printed ceramics than at the slave site (Otto 1975:194–195).

At Hampton plantation (for the total site) 4.2% of the ceramics were banded while only 2.0% were transfer-printed (Lewis and Haskell 1980:89–90), and at Middleton Place there were 2.8% banded and 1.1% transfer-printed (Lewis and Hardesty 1979:75–76). At Drayton Hall 5.8% of all Euro-American ceramics were banded and 7.8% were transfer-printed. Although transfer-printed wares are higher at Drayton Hall than at Hampton or Middleton Place, they made up only a small fraction of the total ceramics, while they were dominant at the Couper kitchen. Hampton and Middleton Place produced even less transfer-printed than banded ware. George Miller noted in his study of nineteenth-century ceramics that transfer-printed wares were the most costly, with banded wares being only slightly more expensive than undecorated wares (1980:3–4). Thus, although large quantities of transfer-printed wares on a site dating from the first half of the nineteenth century may indeed be an indicator of wealth, it does not necessarily follow that its lack demonstrates the reverse.

Distinctions in vessel form have been utilized by several people, particularly the comparison of porcelain table and service wares to teawares (Lewis and Haskell 1980; Stone 1970), as well as the comparison of serving vessels (bowls) to flatware (plates, platters) in the pearlware/whiteware continuum (Otto 1975) in an effort to determine socioeconomic status.

As mentioned earlier, porcelain itself, while to some degree an indicator of status, occurs so commonly on British colonial sites that it in itself does not serve as a reliable indicator of wealth (Lewis and Haskell 1980:53). However, as noted by G. W. Stone in the Massachusetts inventories studied, it appeared that while even the poorer households had some Chinese export porcelain, it usually was in the form of teawares, while the upper-class families had dining and serving pieces of Chinese export porcelain in addition to teawares (1970:83–84). In the main house area at Hampton, 18.0% of the 49 porcelain vessels recovered were teawares and 82.0% were heavy wares (plates and serving vessels, Lewis and Haskell 1980:76). At Cannon's Point there was 75.0% heavy ware and 25.0% teaware at the Couper kitchen, an intermediate figure and apparently confirming this correlation (Otto 1975:217).

When a similar breakdown was made for Drayton Hall, the heavy wares again dominated. Of the 289 Chinese export porcelain vessels designated as serving or consumption related (eliminating toys and decorative objects as well as generalized hollowware/flatware forms), 64.7% were heavy ware and 35.3% were teaware. While not as definite as the distinction at Hampton, almost two-thirds of the porcelain recovered from Drayton Hall was heavy ware. In the more expensive overglazed porcelain, the dominance of heavy ware over teaware is even more pronounced, with 73.1% heavy ware and 26.9% teaware.

In his comparison of the slave, planter, and overseer sites at Cannon's Point, Otto noted that in the pearlware/whiteware spectrum the differences in vessel form reflected status more reliably than decorative technique (1975:219). In particular, he noted that banded serving bowls predominated at the slave and overseer sites, while at the planter site only 8.0% of the tableware was represented by serving bowls (1975:204).

At Drayton Hall the picture is slightly different. Transfer-printed tableware comprised only 8.8% of the total tableware found at the site, while serving bowls (of all patterns) represented 6.7% of the tablewares (the latter figure in keeping with that found at the planter site). Thus it seems that while the low percentage of bowls is distinctly representative of a high-status site, the transfer-printed ware is a less reliable indicator. There was more variety in banded vessel forms at Drayton Hall. At Cannon's Point the banded items consisted of only common bowls (93.3%) and cups (6.7%) (Otto 1975:205, 209, 213). At Drayton Hall 43 bowls (common and regular) represented 70.5% of the identified banded vessel forms recovered. The other forms present at the site included cups, mugs, jugs, and saucers.

At variance with reports from other high-status sites, at Drayton Hall the largest majority of tableware among the pearlware/whiteware group consisted of blue and green edgeware vessels. For example, considering plates only, there were a total of 192 identified, of which 60 (31.2%) were transfer-printed, while 98 (51.0%) were edgewares. Indeed, all edgeware table forms constituted 25.6% of all pearlware/whiteware tableware, just slightly less than the 28.8% that transfer-printed wares represented. The biggest difference was in variety; of all edgeware tablewares, 95.1% were plates (including twifflers and muffin plates) while among the transfer-printed tablewares only 51.7% were plates. At Cannon's Point, edgewares comprised only 8.1% of all tablewares, and edgeware plates only 11.1% of all pearlware/whiteware plates (slightly high because this percentage includes some platters not given separate number from plates) (Otto 1975:213–217).

The significant factor is that a reduced number of serving bowls in the pearlware/whiteware assemblage does indeed appear to reflect high-status occupants. At Hampton figures are given only for a feature believed to represent a slave occupation and bowls constituted only 15% of the nonporcelain European tableware (Lewis and Haskell 1980:77–78). However, colonoware, a ceramic type not found at Cannon's Point, produced a great number of vessels, about 80% of which were bowl forms (Lewis and Haskell 1980:77), again showing that bowls predominate at lower-status sites. At Drayton Hall only 38.5% of the colonoware vessels identified were bowls.

An important factor in ceramics that seems to indicate socioeconomic status is the presence of vessels that serve purposes other than the preparation and consumption of food. Such categories as hygiene (wash basins, chamber pots, ointment pots), horticulture (flower pots and trays), architectural furnishings (tiles), and personal/decorative items (toys, vases, figurines) either will not appear or will appear in greatly reduced quantities among the lower-status groups.

Otto mentions "that lower percentage of tableware and greater diversity of shapes seems to be indicative of higher status" (1975:219). This certainly would seem to be borne out at Drayton Hall. Using figures given by Otto (1975:208, 212, 217), but eliminating the category of unknowns, the figures are as reported in Table 6.3. The "Other" category includes such forms as decorative items (vases, figurines), toys, inkwells, and horticultural and architectural items. The only ceramic of this nature mentioned at Cannon's Point was the doll found at the slave site (Otto 1975:276).

Table 6.3
CERAMIC VESSEL FORMS

	Cannon's Point[a]			
	Slave	Overseer	Planter	Drayton Hall
Tableware	80 (68.4%)	78 (60.9%)	161 (55.3%)	1,080 (55.6%)
Teaware	26 (22.2%)	42 (32.8%)	83 (28.5%)	242 (12.5%)
Dairy/kitchen	0 (—)	1 (0.8%)	4 (1.4%)	404 (20.8%)
Storage (including bottles)	6 (5.1%)	5 (3.9%)	35 (12.0%)	56 (2.9%)
Hygiene	4 (3.4%)	2 (1.6%)	8 (2.8%)	87 (4.5%)
Other	1 (0.9%)	0 (—)	0 (—)	73 (3.8%)

[a]Modified from Otto 1975:208, 212, 217.

The most dramatic difference is that if one combines tablewares and teawares, over 90% of the ceramics at the slave and overseer sites belong to these categories, while at the planter site only 83.8% are teawares and tablewares. At Drayton Hall only 68.1% of the ceramics belong to these categories. Hence, although the slave site has an oddly elevated percentage of hygiene items, less than 10% of all ceramics are not tablewares or teawares, while at Drayton Hall 31.9% of the ceramic collection is available for a wide variety of other usages.

While a reduced percentage of colonoware (less than 40%) seems to indicate high status, an elevated percentage at a site does not necessarily indicate the reverse. This is exemplified at Hampton where the ceramics from the fill identified as related to a slave household were 74.1% colonoware, while the ceramics from the main house area were only 33.0% colonoware (Lewis and Haskell 1980:75). At Drayton Hall colonoware represented 28.9% of all historic ceramics and at Middleton Place it represented 53.9%. At the Spiers Landing site the colonoware represented 56.0% of all ceramics (Drucker 1981:66) (very similar to the figure for Middleton Place), while at Yaughan colonoware was 90.1% and 73.0% of the ceramics at the two sites excavated (Garrow 1980:n.p.).

SUMMARY AND CONCLUSIONS

The archaeological record of socioeconomic status has proved to be surprisingly elusive, even when dealing with a site where the occupants are known to have been wealthy and socially prominent. Indeed, it becomes clear that no one artifact in itself, even the traditional Chinese export porcelain, serves as a definite marker of status.

Although considerations of status may be complicated by the fact that those artifacts normally considered as high status are deposited less frequently and as the result of accidental loss rather than discard, a careful study of the variety and form of those artifacts recovered can be fruitful. Additionally, in regard to artifacts other than those associated with architecture, the picture of socioeconomic status may be complicated by the channeling of wealth into other segments of plantation life. In particular, it is known that the Draytons were constantly buying and selling land and that they owned an extensive plantation system in South Carolina. It is very likely that wealth that could have been channeled into material possessions was being diverted to the land and its production of cash crops.

In analyzing and comparing those artifact classes that have been suggested as status-related, some, such as horse equipment, do not seem to have the hypothesized relationship. Others, such as ceramics, table glass, and buttons, do provide a better picture of status but only when carefully analyzed for the various attributes within that class. For example, Chinese export porcelain itself, even in fairly large quantities, is not a valid indicator of high status. However, a breakdown into decorative techniques and vessel forms does elucidate status. A preponderance of tableware over teaware and a high percentage of overglazed enameled decoration both indicate high status.

In table glass, it is not only the number of vessels represented, but also the variety of forms that indicate high status. Again, in artifact classes such as buttons and personal possessions, the variety of forms rather than the number provides the clues to the site occupant's status.

In contrast to the findings of Bonner for the Deep South in the nineteenth century, the presence of vast quantities of architectural remains such as nails, spikes, construction hardware, and window glass is the most sensitive indicator of status in the sites analyzed. The sites studied had large, substantial, and hence more architecturally productive dwellings, thus producing high concentrations of architectural debris that are likely to be the result of extensive, constant, and planned repair, alteration, and rehabilitation of the dwelling.

REFERENCES

Anonymous

1860 St. Andrew's parish. In *New York Spirit of the Times,* April 7, 1860. Reprinted in *Charleston Mercury,* 10 April 1860. P. 4.

Bonner, James C.

1945 Plantation architecture of the lower south on the eve of the Civil War. *Journal of Southern History* 11:370–388.

Bowen, William Shaw

1885 Drayton Hall and Magnolia Garden: a South Carolina floral paradise. *Providence Journal,* Saturday, April 4, 1885. Providence, Rhode Island.

Charleston County Courthouse (CCC), Charleston, S.C.

1738 Mesne conveyance office, book T.

1751–1754 Probate court, miscellaneous records, Volume 80B.

1855 Deed book T-11, July 2 and 7.

1866 Deed book A-14, No. 6, January 16.

1868 Deed book H-15, August.

1875 Deed book S-16, January 26.

1915 Will book Y, December 27.

Charleston Library Society (CLS), Charleston, S.C.

1758 *South Carolina Gazette,* December 22.

1768–1775 Thomas Elfe account books.

Cornforth, John

1974 The future of Drayton Hall. *Country Life,* August 1. Reprinted by Waterlow (Dunstable) Ltd., England.

Deetz, James J. F.

1973 Ceramics from Plymouth, 1620–1835: the archaeological evidence. In *Ceramics in America.* Ian M. G. Quimby, ed. Charlottesville: The University Press of Virginia. Pp. 15–40.

Drucker, Leslie M.

1981 Socioeconomic patterning at an undocumented late 18th century low-country site: Spiers Landing, South Carolina. *Historical Archaeology 15(2):58–68.*

Garrow, Patrick H.

1980 Investigations of Yaughan and Curriboo plantations. Paper presented at the Southeastern Archaeological Conference, New Orleans, November.

Herman, Lynne L., John Sands, and Daniel Schecter

1975 Ceramics in St. Mary's County, Maryland during the 1840's: A socioeconomic study. *The Conference on Historic Site Archaeology Papers, 1973* 8:52–93.

Historic Charleston Foundation (HCF), Charleston, S.C.

1789–1820 Diaries of Charles Drayton.

Lewis, Kenneth E.

1976 Camden: a frontier town in eighteenth century South Carolina. Occasional Papers of the Institute of Archeology and Anthropology, Anthropological Studies No. 2, University of South Carolina, Columbia.

Lewis, Kenneth E., and Donald L. Hardesty

1979 Middleton Place: initial archeological investigations at an Ashley River rice plantation. Institute of Archeology and Anthropology, Research Manuscript Series No. 148, University of South Carolina, Columbia.

Lewis, Kenneth E., and Helen Haskell

1980 Hampton II: further archeological investigations at a Santee River rice plantation. Institute of Archeology and Anthropology, Research Manuscript Series No. 161, University of South Carolina, Columbia.

Middleton Place Foundation (MPF), Charleston, S.C.

1865 Letter from John Drayton to Williams Middleton, June 2.

Miller, George M.

1974 A tenant farmer's tableware: nineteenth-century ceramics from Tabb's Purchase. *Maryland Historical Magazine* 69:197–210.

1980 Classification and economic scaling of 19th century ceramics. *Historical Archaeology* 14:1–40.

Miller, Henry M.

1979 Pettus and Utopia: a comparison of the faunal remains from two late seventeenth century Virginia households. *The Conference on Historic Site Archaeology Papers, 1978* 13:158–179.

Miller, J. Jefferson, II, and Lyle M. Stone

1970 *Eighteenth-Century Ceramics from Fort Michilimackinac: A study in historical archaeology.* Washington, D.C.: Smithsonian Institution Press.

Nichols, Frederick D.

1976 Palladio in America. In *Palladio in America.* Walter Muir Whitehill, ed. Milan, Italy: Electra Editrice.

Noël Hume, Ivor

1972 *Guide to Artifacts of Colonial America.* New York: Knopf.

Otto, John Solomon
1975 Status differences and the archeological record: a comparison of planter, overseer, and slave sites from Cannon's Point Plantation (1794–1861), St. Simon's Island, Georgia. Ph.D. dissertation, Anthropology Department, University of Florida. Ann Arbor: University Microfilms.

South Carolina Historical Society (SCHS), Charleston, S.C.
1817 History and genealogy of the Drayton family, John Drayton Journal, No. 1. Transcribed by Charlotta Drayton, ca. 1923.

South Carolina State Archives (SCSA), Columbia, S.C.
1783 Miscellaneous records and bills of sale, Volume YY, September 10.

South, Stanley
1977 *Method and Theory in Historical Archeology*. New York: Academic Press.

Stone, Gary Wheeler
1970 Ceramics in Suffolk County, Massachusetts inventories 1680–1775: a preliminary study with divers comments thereon, and sundry suggestions. *The Conference on Historic Site Archaeology Papers, 1968* 3:73–90.

Stone, Gary Wheeler, J. Glenn Little, and Stephen Israel
1973 Ceramics from the John Hicks site, 1723–1743: the material culture. In *Ceramics in America*. Ian M. G. Quimby, ed. Charlottesville: University Press of Virginia. Pp. 103–139.

Waring Historical Library (WHL), Medical University of South Carolina, Charleston, S.C.
1770 Biographical file folders, Charles Drayton folder. Disputatio Medica Inauguralis "De Venenis." Carolus Dreyton, Edinburgh: Apud Balfour, Auld et Smellie, Academiae Typographos. M. DCC, LXX.

Woolson, Constance Fenimore
1875 Up the Ashley and Cooper. *Harper's New Monthly Magazine*, December.

7

Social and Economic Status on the Coastal Plantation: An Archaeological Perspective

Sue Mullins Moore

INTRODUCTION

The study of slavery has, in recent years, gained valuable new data from anthropologically oriented archeological studies of plantation sites (see Drucker and Anthony 1979; McFarlane 1975; Otto 1975; Singleton 1980). Research on the plantation system of the American South has been subject to the biases inherent in primary source material. Contemporary accounts of the plantation system often suffered from falsification and from the fact that they were told from the perspective of the educated white observer. The later slave narratives suffered from the passage of time and the inability of the informants to recall details of their day-to-day lives. By combining the evidence from the historical accounts and contemporary documentation with that from archaeology, it is hoped that perhaps a more accurate and complete picture of the plantation system is possible.

Plantation archaeology has focused primarily on the excavation and discussion of single plantation sites. Other than a one-to-one comparison, usually with John Otto's (1975) work at Cannon's Point, almost no attempts have been made to look for general patterns within the plantation system. Because of the differences that existed in organization and environment on the plantations in different cash-crop regions, the focus of this study was narrowed to only one of these systems, the barrier island cotton plantation. Because a great deal of the plantation archaeology undertaken has been in this region, it was clear that the coastal situation was a fitting start. The purpose of this pattern recognition, in turn, was to discover regularities in the artifact configurations reflective of underlying cultural processes. In this sense, process is being used to understand and explain variation in the material culture as it

ISBN 0-12-646480-4

is influenced by the economic system operative on the antebellum coastal cotton plantation. Primary research was undertaken on St. Simon's Island, Georgia, from 1978 to 1981 with funding from Sea Island Foundation and the National Register of Historic Sites.

PATTERN RECOGNITION IN HISTORICAL ARCHAEOLOGY

The beginnings of the search for patterns in the archaeological record can be seen in the rise of scientific or problem-oriented archaeology. Patterns had long been a focus of study in anthropology (Benedict 1934; Kroeber 1948; Steward 1955), although the concept and use of the word was somewhat different. At this point, patterns were used to *describe* regularities of human behavior, rather than to *explain* similarities and differences. With Julian Steward can be seen the beginnings of the search for laws or generalities that were generated by cultural systems (South 1977). There was a need to see through superficial cultural differences and find more underlying similarities that were reflective of similar cultural processes.

Stanley South has been the foremost proponent of pattern recognition in historical archaeology (South 1975, 1977). South has presented several patterns: the Brunswick refuse disposal pattern, the Carolina artifact pattern, and the frontier pattern (South 1977). Application of South's Carolina pattern has been made at several sites. At the Spiers Landing site in South Carolina, the artifact frequencies of a probable slave site were compared and found to differ significantly in the clothing, activities, and kitchen categories (Drucker and Anthony 1979). From this evidence it was suggested that new patterns might be necessary for nonurban or plantation sites.

The Carolina artifact pattern was tested at another South Carolina slave site and a different Carolina slave artifact pattern was proposed (Garrow 1981). The original Carolina pattern was revised to include colonoware ceramics (of possible slave manufacture) in the kitchen category rather than under "activities" where South categorized them. This made a significant difference in the two patterns.

Theresa Singleton also proposed a slave artifact pattern for four sites in Florida and Georgia (Singleton 1980:216). This pattern appears much more like the frontier pattern than the Carolina or Carolina slave artifact patterns. Singleton offered no real explanation for this except to suggest that there was a scarcity of midden deposits in her sample which probably biased her results.

The quantification of these patterns has been a fundamental part of their utility in testing hypotheses and in comparisons with other patterns, but it has also been used to mask one of the primary problems in pattern recognition—the failure to go beyond the pattern to the processes that are responsible for the pattern (see Honerkamp 1980:29). The pattern in itself is merely another particularistic description. Once the processes that create the pattern are understood, then the differences or similarities between patterns can be explained from a process-oriented viewpoint. So far, this approach has scarcely been applied.

At this point, it is felt that it is not possible to derive a single pattern applicable to all barrier island plantation sites, but the derivation of patterns specific to individual sites or components (planter, overseer, slave) will allow quantitative comparisons to be made. Pattern recognition, then, will be used as a methodological approach (Honerkamp 1980:28–29). The inability to derive one pattern may perhaps be the most significant finding of this study and is implied in the following hypotheses. These hypotheses were designed to explore the processes responsible for the patterns, particularly status, both social and economic. This work examines status both within and between plantations because it is hypothesized that the size of the plantation (based on number of slaves) and, therefore, the economic status of the planter, will affect the material goods available to a plantation's inhabitants.

STATUS ON THE SOUTHERN PLANTATION

Status can be described by a number of qualifiers—age, sex, biological relationship, social class, and economic level (Linton 1973:187–200). Status, without one of these descriptions, generally refers to the sum total of all of the statuses an individual possesses (Linton 1973:187). Each individual, therefore, can have a number of different statuses, none necessarily dependent on any of the others (cf. Nash 1970:3).

Social status in southern plantation society has been discussed extensively by historians and recently by archaeologists (Eaton 1961; Otto 1975; Stampp 1956). Basically, ethnic caste (black and white) divided this society into two social strata. Blacks occupied the lowest stratum and were lumped together, whether free or slave (Genovese 1974:398–413). Whites, regardless of economic position, were considered to be of a higher social status. Slave ownership, in particular, was correlated with social prestige and political power (Wright 1970:68). Three levels of social status can be seen within the white social strata, "poor whites," yeoman farmers and merchants, and large planters (Bonner 1965:58; Stampp 1956:29). Small planters (those with fewer than 20 slaves) were considered part of the yeoman farmer group (Bonner 1965:58). Otto notes that even though the poorer whites were assigned the same broad social status as the yeoman farmers and planters, they often endured material living conditions comparable to slaves (Otto 1975:14). This is one indication of how economic position should affect the archaeological remains of a site.

Historical archaeology is fortunate in that status can many times be determined from the documents (cf. Otto 1975:12–13), rather than having to rely on material remains as the sole indicator. Using the number of slaves owned as the most sensitive indicator of plantation size and thus economic rank (Menn 1964; Stampp 1956:30–31) for each site in this study, an attempt is made to correlate and compare social status with economic status. It has already been pointed out that these are not necessarily the same (Nash 1970:3; Otto 1975:14). It is expected that the archaeological record will demonstrate how these differences are manifested in the material culture of the plantation South.

HYPOTHESES

1. The artifact patterns or configurations on a plantation site, regardless of whether it is within a planter, overseer, or slave context, will vary with the size of the plantation. These pattern variations are believed to be a function of the planter's economic status. Larger plantations should have greater access to preferred goods. These differences should be reflected in the frequencies of the artifact groups. As plantation size increases, there should be larger quantities of kitchen-related artifacts at the expense of architectural artifacts (cf. Otto 1975:13). The other groups usually have comparatively small frequencies, and may therefore be difficult to assess as far as the significance of any differences. It is tentatively proposed that: (1) personal and tobacco group artifacts, which represent luxury items, will increase with plantation size, and (2) activities, arms, and clothing will decrease with increase in plantation size since they are more representative of necessity items.

It should be pointed out that as any system grows larger, it becomes more complex. Applied to this study, this premise would be presented as: the larger the plantation, the more varied the activities carried out there, resulting in more material goods and resources available to the plantation inhabitants. Some plantations, such as the Butler estate (one of the study sites), were almost entirely self-sufficient. This phenomena is not unique to cultural systems and has been extensively treated in the literature on systems theory (Chapman 1979; Von Bertalanfy 1975).

2. When large and small plantation sites are compared, it is hypothesized that the artifact patterns *within* a small plantation (planter and slave components) will be more similar than the intrasite patterns of the large plantation. This hypothesis will be tested by comparing the artifact frequencies within the prescribed categories already discussed. It is hypothesized that differences in frequency and range will be less within the small estate than those on a larger plantation. This again is proposed to be a function of the economic status of the planter. On a small plantation, more of the surplus money would be directed towards the production of a crop and less toward nonessential items for the planter or his dependents (Flanders 1933), which should be reflected in the material culture.

3. The artifact patterns of the domestic and field slave are proposed to differ because of the supposed higher status of the domestic slave (Owens 1976:106–120; Stampp 1956:337–338). It is hypothesized that the domestic slave will have greater access to preferred artifacts. The same artifact categories used for Hypotheses 1 and 2 are used.

In order to define the sizes of the plantations, historical sources were consulted (Eaton 1961; Flanders 1933:128). Initially the division was threefold: large—those over 100 slaves; medium—those with 20–100 slaves; and small—those under 20 slaves. The vast majority of the South's plantations fall into the small category (Eaton 1961; Flanders 1933:129). Problems with gathering the field data necessitated the combination of the medium and small categories for the purposes of this study. The planter component of a small plantation was excavated, but a slave site of similar size could not be located.

PROJECT SITES

Comparative data come from three sites, partially excavated during the project (Hampton, Sinclair, and Pike's Bluff plantations). All three are antebellum plantations located on St. Simon's Island (Figure 7.1). Both the size of the plantations and the size of the components excavated vary.

Hampton Plantation on Butler Point is the largest plantation studied, with, at one point, more than 300 slaves. Its owner was Major Pierce Butler, one of the original delegates to the Constitutional Convention. Hampton was probably the most pros-

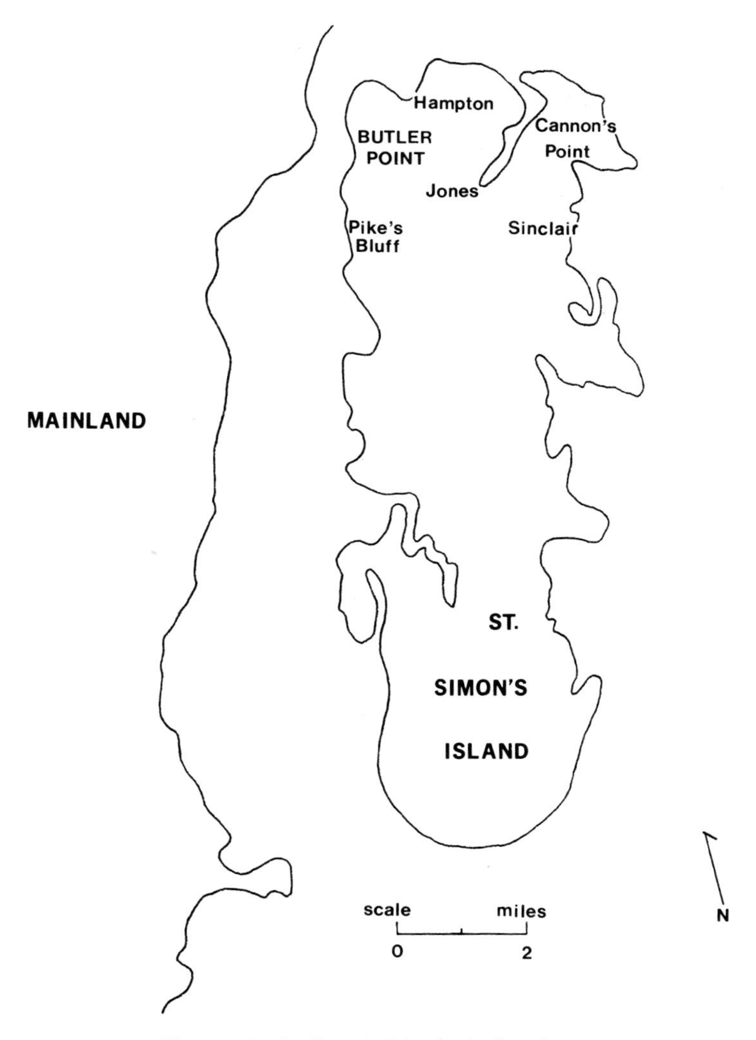

Figure 7.1 St. Simon's Island: site location.

perous of St. Simon's estates producing the staple crop of sea island cotton. There were four slave settlements at Hampton. One was in the immediate vicinity of the planter's house while the other three were scattered, one being over 3 miles from the main complex. The overseer's house was, at various times, located within the main complex and later at one of the outlying settlements. The overseer in the case of Hampton served more as a manager since Pierce Butler hardly ever resided on his Georgia estate (Vanstory 1970:144).

Excavations at Hampton were conducted almost exclusively at Jones, one of the outlying slave settlements. Limited information from a previous survey was available on the big house and the overseer's complexes. The slave settlement excavations included work at one slave cabin; an auxilliary structure, probably a tool shed; a well; and a cotton barn. Several nonstructural areas were also tested. The material from Jones was expected to yield data on the slave pattern. It was thought that Jones would vary from Cannon's Point because of its size and possibly management differences. Cannon's Point Plantation had, at various times, between 100 and 200 slaves and had an owner who resided on the estate. The overseer, then, would not have been as important as at Hampton Plantation.

The second plantation included in the study is Sinclair (or St. Clair). It also grew sea island cotton, though not to the scale of Hampton. Sources indicate that between 10 and 50 slaves resided on this estate (Hawes 1956:U.S. Bureau of the Census 1820). It was owned by General Lachlan McIntosh, of Revolutionary War fame, and began operation under the management of his son William around 1790 (Hawes 1956). The plantation changed hands several times before finally coming under the ownership of Pierce Butler about 1820 (Vanstory 1970:156). When Fanny Kemble visited in 1839, she described the house as being in a ruinous state (Kemble 1961:246). The house burned in 1857 (Vanstory 1970:156).

The excavations at Sinclair consisted of tests in two midden areas,—one believed to be the kitchen trash area for the big house, and a small house that was probably a domestic slave cabin. There were almost no surface indications of the site, therefore the overseer's house (if there was one) or additional structures were not located. The remains from these excavations were expected to yield data on both the domestic slave and the planter. The slave data can be compared to try to detect differences in the artifact patterns of field and house slaves. The planter site is used in conjunction with the others of the study to derive information on the range of planter material culture.

The final plantation being considered is Pike's Bluff, a small estate. There were probably no more than 20 slaves employed and it is believed that there was no overseer. The owner of the plantation was Dr. Thomas F. Hazzard who purchased the land in 1827 (Glynn County Superior Court 1827). His brother, William, owned the adjacent plantation. Documentary evidence on this site is very scanty, but the date of abandonment appears to have been 1857 when Thomas Hazzard died. The site was used as a military outpost during the Civil War (Heard 1938) and was not occupied after that date.

The site today consists of looted ruins of what is presumed to have been the planter's house, a privy, and several middens. No slave cabins could be located.

Excavations were carried out in three of the middens, the privy, and a small test at the house. The privy and middens provided large quantities of material that were expected to illuminate the life of a small planter.

Other comparative data comes from excavations at Kingsley Plantation—a slave importing station (approximately 100 slaves) on the coast of Florida (Fairbanks 1974), Cannon's Point Plantation on St. Simon's Island (Otto 1975), and Butler Island Plantation (up to 500 slaves)—the "sister" plantation of Hampton (Singleton 1980). Butler Island was a mainland river delta rice plantation also belonging to the Butler family (Figure 7.2).

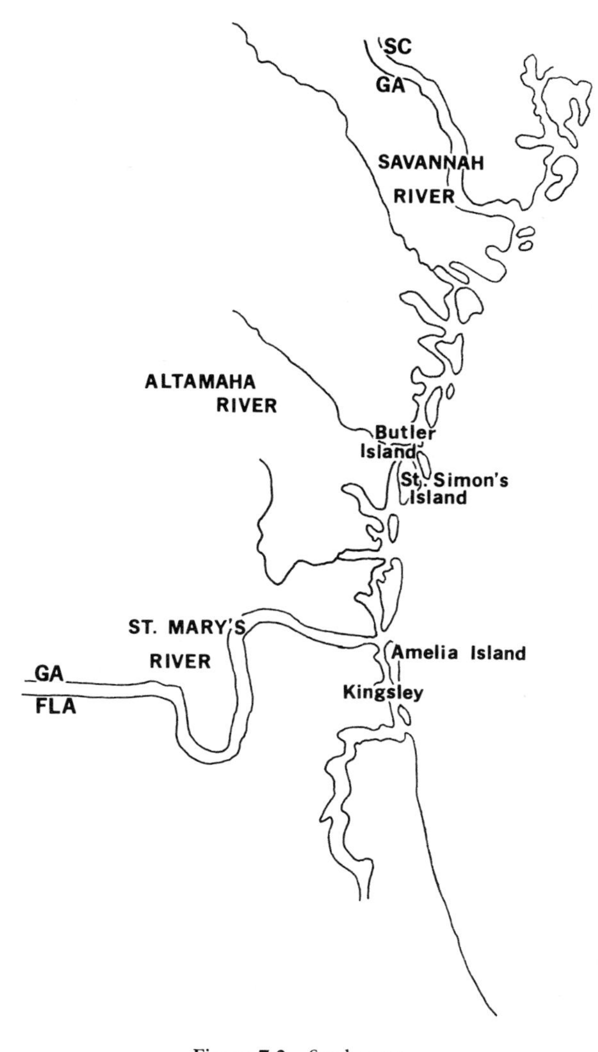

Figure 7.2 Study area.

The sites used for this study, then, can be ranked in descending size as follows:

1. Hampton and Butler Island (same owner)
2. Cannon's Point
3. Kingsley
4. Sinclair
5. Pike's Bluff

This ranking should be reflected in the artifact patterns in the manner specified by the research hypotheses.

ANALYZING THE DATA

In order to test the hypotheses previously stated, artifact patterns for each of the sites were derived (Table 7.1). From these, comparisons were made and statistics computed.

It must be noted that the artifact profiles for Kingsley and the Sinclair slave context were corrected to allow for the fact that these were tabby constructions. The Sinclair correction was done in the same manner as the correction previously made for Kingsley, by adding an amount of nails proportionate to what would have been present if the structure were frame (Singleton 1980:213). There are, admittedly, problems with making such an adjustment, but it seems to give a more comparable artifact profile.

One problem noted in the comparison of the artifact profiles in Table 7.1 is the small sample size in the "rare" artifact groups. It is difficult to assess the significance of any differences in this group because of the scarcity of artifacts. These artifact groups are particularly sensitive to biases of sample size or site function.

Kitchen Artifact Group

The percentage of kitchen group artifacts ranges from 21.01% at Butler Island to 67.24% at the Cannon's Point planter site. Within the slave sites considered, kitchen artifacts account for no more than 30% (using the adjusted profiles for Sinclair and Kingsley). This relatively low amount of kitchen group artifacts is almost certainly indicative of the low social and economic status of the slave. It is significant to note that the highest percentage of kitchen group remains in the slave sites occurs at Jones, the largest plantation site. This would, at this point, support Hypothesis 1, that plantation size, as a reflection of the planter's economic position, would affect the material living conditions of plantation inhabitants. At the same time, the lowest percentage of kitchen artifacts occurs at Butler Island, part of the same plantation. Singleton (1980:217) suggests that one factor accounting for this very low amount of kitchen-related artifacts is the fact that the Butler Island slaves were depositing most of their trash in the river, leading to a disproportionate amount of architectural items. Such would seem to be the case from the artifact profiles. At Sinclair, the

Table 7.1
COMPARISON OF ARTIFACT PROFILES

Location	Kitchen	Arch.	Activ.	Arms	Cloth.	Pers.	Tob.	Total
Cannon's Point								
Planter	2492	1156	1	1	29	1	26	3706
%	67.24	31.19	.03	.03	.78	.03	.70	
Sinclair								
Planter	2329	1083	10	2	14	5	54	3497
%	66.60	30.97	.28	.06	.40	.15	1.54	
Pike's Bluff								
Planter	886	955	12	0	19	3	57	1932
%	45.86	49.43	.62		.98	.15	2.95	
Cannon's Point								
Overseer	687	868	7	5	33	4	47	1651
%	41.61	52.57	.42	.30	2.00	.24	2.85	
Cannon's Point								
Slave	2771	7613	25	8	112	12	178	10754
%	25.84	70.84	.23	.08	1.05	.11	1.67	
Jones								
Slave	1740	3915	31	20	76	11	151	5944
%	29.27	65.86	.52	.34	1.28	.18	2.54	
Sinclair								
Slave	550	1875	8	1	16	2	29	2482
%	22.16	75.54	.32	.04	.64	.08	1.17	
Butler Island								
Slave	1325	4494	26	15	111	5	642	6619
%	20.01	67.90	.39	.23	1.68	.08	9.70	
Kingsley[a]								
Slave	1385	3950	12	10	18	5	15	2198
%	25.66	73.23	.22	.18	.34	.09	.28	

[a]See noted correction for architectural group count in text.

percentage of kitchen artifacts in the slave context is 22.16%. Since this is the smallest slave site represented, the lower proportion of kitchen artifacts was expected according to Hypothesis 1. Kingsley and Cannon's Point have almost the same percentage of kitchen group artifacts in the slave context and because they are almost the same size, this was expected.

The next socioeconomic level, that of the overseer, is represented by only one site, Cannon's Point. Access to the overseer's site at Hampton was limited to architectural data and it is likely that neither Pike's Bluff nor Sinclair had overseers; in the case of Kingsley, this is unknown. As expected, the proportion of kitchen group artifacts at the overseer's site falls between the slave and planter range, at 41.61% of the total assemblage. This indicates that while the overseer had larger quantities of nonessential items than the slave (i.e., ceramics, wine), he still did not have the economic ability of the planter to purchase a larger number of such items.

When considering the planter contexts, it is significant to note that at Pike's Bluff, probably the smallest plantation, kitchen artifacts are less numerous when compared to other planter sites. In fact, at 45.86%, they come closer to the Cannon's Point overseer site than to any other context. This again would tend to support Hypothesis 1 since it was anticipated that the planter at Pike's Bluff would have less to spend on nonnecessity items than the larger planters. Cannon's Point and Sinclair show almost the same amount of kitchen-related artifacts. It was expected that the percentage of kitchen artifacts at Sinclair would fall somewhere between Pike's Bluff and Cannon's Point. No reason for this larger-than-expected frequency was apparent.

Within the kitchen artifact group, ceramics appear to be a sensitive indicator of plantation size and relative socioeconomic status. As Otto had previously noted, both form and type were diagnostic factors. When examining types, it was found that proportions of annular and transfer-printed wares were the most sensitive to the social and economic nature of the site (Otto 1975:220; Singleton 1980:148). Table 7.2 gives the percentages of these ceramics out of the total ceramic assemblage of each site. As can be seen, it seems that, with the exception of Sinclair, the annular wares are much more numerous on slave sites, while tranfer-printed wares are more prevalent in planter contexts. Sinclair is a problem primarily because it was inhabited earlier than the other sites and not occupied as late—transfer-printed ceramics had not yet reached their peak of production. Butler Island shows a particularly large quantity of annular wares, especially when compared to Jones. Because they had the same owner, it would be expected that if the planter were providing their ceramics, the percentages would be comparable. The disproportionate amounts would lead to the suggestion that the slaves were purchasing at least part of their ceramics themselves. The Butler Island slaves, being close to the port of Darien, had a much better opportunity to do so (Singleton 1980:154). Annular wares being relatively inexpensive would have been purchased more often than transfer-printed wares which were more expensive. This is reinforced by the comparable percentage of transfer-printed wares at Jones and Butler Island.

Recently a pricing scale for decorative types (regardless of ware) has been developed for nineteenth-century sites (Miller 1980). The scale is divided into four levels: (1) plain undecorated ceramics; (2) minimal decoration such as edged, banded, sponged, and mocha; (3) hand-painted, both polychrome and blue; and (4) transfer-printed ceramics. This scaling, with "plain" being the cheapest and "transfer-printed" the most expensive, is based on price lists from merchants and potters.

Miller also generated a scaling level for forms available in these decorative types (Miller 1980). It was found that bowls were the least expensive, plates, next, and cups were the most costly. This largely reinforces the pattern that Otto found at Cannon's Point (Otto 1975).

Table 7.3 presents comparative site data on ceramic pricing levels. This seems to reinforce the annular ware–transfer-printed dichotomy. Again, Sinclair is an anomaly for the same reasons. If levels 1 and 2 are combined and levels 3 and 4 are also added together, the difference in ceramic assemblages can best be seen. At Cannon's Point 85% of the ceramics come from levels 3 and 4, while at no other site did these

Table 7.2
COMPARISON OF PERCENTAGE OF ANNULAR AND TRANSFER-PRINTED WARES ON COASTAL SITES

Site	% Annular[a]	% Transfer-Printed[a]
Cannon's Point Planter	1.1	74.9
Sinclair Planter	3.2	7.8
Pike's Bluff Planter	2.8	21.9
Cannon's Point Overseer	16.9	17.8
Cannon's Point North Slave	21.6	22.7
Cannon's Point South Slave	16.3	8.4
Jones Slave	14.6	7.1
Sinclair Slave	1.9	19.6
Butler Island Slave	52.9	6.7

[a]Out of total ceramic assemblage.

two levels account for more than 36%. Even at Pike's Bluff, levels 3 and 4 were only 31% of the total. While it was not expected that this figure would be so low, this does point out that small planters could not afford the more expensive ceramics and that their tableware was much the same type as the overseer and slave.

The Cannon's Point northern slave group had a relatively high percentage of levels 3 and 4 ceramics. One reason for this may be in the probable domestic status of these slaves (Otto 1975). Hypothesis 3 examines this evidence more fully.

Form, as well as type, has been found to be a status indicator on plantation sites. For the purpose of comparison, ceramics forms were grouped into holloware and flatware. This was necessitated largely by the different cataloging of the sites (Otto 1975; Singleton 1980). No data was available on Kingsley. The results of this examination are presented in Table 7.4. As can be seen, ceramic form does seem to be an accurate indicator of site status. The highest percentage of flatware seems to occur on high-status sites with the exception of Pike's Bluff. Again, the small planter appears to have a lower-status material culture resulting from the fact that he had less money to spend on nonessential items. The quantity of flatware at Pike's Bluff is comparable to the northern slave site at Cannon's Point. As previously mentioned, pricing levels for some forms have been developed (Miller 1980:10–11). Flatware forms are more expensive than holloware, with the exception of cups. The archaeological assemblage appears to reflect this difference. At Jones and Butler Island,

Table 7.3
COMPARISON OF SITES BY CERAMIC PRICING LEVELS

Site	Level 1	Level 2	Level 3	Level 4	Total
Cannon's Point					
Planter	221	64	79	1520	1884
%	11.7	3.4	4.2	80.7	
Sinclair					
Planter	719	338	69	110	1236
%	58.2	27.3	5.6	8.9	
Pike's Bluff					
Planter	308	116	29	158	611
%	50.4	19.0	4.7	25.9	
Cannon's Point					
Overseer	232	119	30	94	475
%	48.8	25.1	6.3	19.8	
Cannon's Point					
North Slave	107	232	35	154	528
%	20.3	43.9	6.6	29.2	
Cannon's Point					
South Slave	56	59	25	15	155
%	36.2	38.1	16.0	9.7	
Jones					
Slave	346	197	93	58	694
%	49.9	28.4	13.4	8.3	
Sinclair					
Slave	211	30	34	67	342
%	61.7	8.8	9.9	19.6	
Butler Island					
Slave	217	190	48	17	472
%	46.0	40.2	10.2	3.6	

hollowares are 80% of the identifiable ceramic forms. Both of these are field slave sites. At Cannon's Point (north) and Sinclair, which are both probably domestic slave sites, there are higher percentages of flatware. It is possible that some of these are planter discards (Otto 1975:173), or it is possible that their favored status allowed them greater access to these forms, either by issue or purchase (Owens 1976:106–120). The ceramic forms of the Cannon's Point overseer are much like the forms at the Sinclair and Cannon's Point planter sites. The fact that they indicate a higher-status site than those at Pike's Bluff is puzzling, such was neither expected nor indicated by the other data. It is known that the sons of coastal planters occasionally acted as overseers on these plantations. This happened for a short period of time at Cannon's Point and this may at least partially explain the higher-status ceramics at the site.

The ceramic data from these sites would tend to support hypothesis 1,—that the size of the plantation affects the material culture assemblage of the site's inhabitants. In the status indicators of ceramic type and form, there appears to be a continuum of

Table 7.4
COMPARISON OF SITES BY CERAMIC FORM

Site	Holloware	Flatware	Total
Cannon's Point			
Planter	134	160	294
%	45.6	54.4	
Sinclair			
Planter	93	118	211
%	44.1	55.9	
Pike's Bluff			
Planter	68	37	105
%	64.8	35.2	
Cannon's Point			
Overseer	57	70	127
%	44.9	55.1	
Cannon's Point			
Slave	69	43	112
%	61.6	38.4	
Jones			
Slave	234	55	289
%	81.0	19.0	
Sinclair			
Slave	35	14	49
%	71.4	28.6	
Butler Island			
Slave	44	11	55
%	80.0	20.0	

availability (or presence) from slave to planter with overlap where the economic positions of the site inhabitants overlap. In other words, the planter at Pike's Bluff had much the same material culture as the overseer at Cannon's Point because they had similar economic resources.

Architectural Group

The architectural group, for the most part, responds in an inverse manner to the kitchen group. On sites where there are high percentages of kitchen-related artifacts, there are low percentages of architectural group artifacts. Conversely, a low percentage of kitchen artifacts corresponds to a high percentage of architectural artifacts. It has been shown that at high-status sites, there are high percentages of kitchen artifacts, therefore there would be lower percentages of architectural artifacts. At low-status sites the reverse would be true—a high proportion of architectural artifacts corresponds to a low proportion of kitchen artifacts. What this artifact pattern suggests is that the architectural assemblage at low-status sites is magnified because such individuals had fewer kitchen and nonessential artifacts (i.e., ceramics, glassware, personal use items).

On the slave sites presented in this study, there were high percentages of architectural items (66–76%) while planter sites were concomitantly lower in percentages of these items. Pike's Bluff and the overseer's site at Cannon's Point show similar amounts of architectural items, another indication that while these inhabitants may not have been of the same social status, they occupied the same economic position.

Activities, Arms, Clothing, Personal, and Tobacco Groups

These groups are considered together because they are generally a small proportion of the artifact assemblage, and their significance is difficult to assess (as previously discussed). It is proposed that activities, arms, and clothing might be grouped together under the heading of "subsistence and maintenance artifacts," while personal and tobacco items can be grouped under the heading of "personal use items."

It was expected that when these items were grouped together as suggested, a pattern might indicate more use of personal items at high-status sites. Such did not prove to be the case; in fact, there appeared to be a rather random distribution of these artifacts. Butler Island presented a particular anomaly with 9.78% tobacco pipes, far outside the range of any other site. None of the other groups (activities, arms, clothing, personal, or tobacco) are of significant size to indicate a pattern related to social or economic status. Perhaps larger samples containing more sites may better determine this.

TESTING THE HYPOTHESES

At this point, it is necessary to note two conditions that may bias the interpretation of results derived from this study. The first is that there was slave incentive to improve material conditions through the sale of produce and handicrafts, slave hire (particularly self-hire), and pilferage. These activities were often possible under the task labor system because there was frequently free time after the completion of assigned chores. Second, there was no code by which all planters treated their overseers or slaves. Some planters treated their charges better than others. Unfortunately, there is no way to make adjustments to allow for either problem in this study, but they should be kept in mind when interpreting these findings.

Hypothesis 1

To reiterate Hypothesis 1, it was proposed that artifact patterns on plantations, whether in planter, overseer, or slave context, would vary with size of the plantation. The larger the plantation, the greater the quantity of artifacts, particularly nonessential goods. This was proposed to be a function of the socioeconomic status of the planter. It was hypothesized that these differences would be reflected in the frequencies of the various artifact groups. It was expected that as plantation size increased, there would be larger quantities of kitchen-related artifacts at the expense of architectural items. The affect on the other groups was tentatively proposed that as plantation size increased, there would be an increase in personal and tobacco group artifacts, and a decrease in activity, arms, and clothing group items.

The comparison of artifact profiles in Table 7.1 presents evidence for the support of Hypothesis 1. It can be seen that at Cannon's Point, the largest planter site, the kitchen groups artifacts were much more numerous than at Pike's Bluff, the smallest planter site. To test the significance of this difference, a *Z*-test statistic was computed:

$$H_o: u_1 = u_2$$
$$H_a: u_1 > u_2$$
$$a = .05$$
$$z = \frac{(\bar{Y}_2 - \bar{Y}_1)}{s\bar{Y}_2 - \bar{Y}_1} \bar{Y}_2 - \bar{Y}_1$$
$$z = \frac{(45.86 - 67.24)}{2.04}$$
$$z = -10.48$$

H_0, the null hypothesis, proposed that the mean number of kitchen group artifacts at Pike's Bluff and Cannon's Point would be the same or of insignificant difference. If Hypothesis 1 was correct, H_0 should have been rejected in favor of H_a which proposed that the kitchen group artifacts at Cannon's Point would be more numerous than at Pike's Bluff. A level of significance of $\alpha = .05$ was chosen so that there would be only a 5% chance of obtaining an incorrect conclusion.

At the .05 level of significance, the H_0 was rejected and it was concluded that the difference in frequency of kitchen-related artifacts at Cannon's Point and Pike's Bluff was significant. Therefore, it is felt that plantation size, and the concomitant economic rank of the planter, is reflected in the artifact profile and that kitchen group artifacts are at least one indication of this. When the same process was repeated for architectural group artifacts, the same results were reached,—that there was a significant difference between Pike's Bluff and Cannon's Point. This was expected because of the apparent inverse relation of the two artifact groups.

Because of the small sample size of the other artifact groups, a *Z*-test statistic could not be computed. It has been previously noted that these groups do not appear to act in any patterned manner and, therefore, at this point, they are not believed to be reliable indicators of site status or size.

With only one overseer site studied, there was insufficient data to assess any difference within this socioeconomic level. It is perhaps more significant to note the similar artifact profiles of Pike's Bluff and the Cannon's Point overseer. It appears, then, that despite the fact that these individuals do not occupy the same social status, they do have similar economic positions. It can be suggested, then, that the economic level of a site's inhabitants, as well as social status, is a determinant of the artifact pattern or profile. As previously mentioned, the Cannon's Point overseer site may be somewhat biased because of its use by the owner's son. This question needs to be addressed by additional data.

The Z-test procedure was, again, applied to the slave sites, particularly Jones and Sinclair. Jones represented the upper end of the size scale while Sinclair was the smallest slave site available. Again, it was found that the differences were significant. This would indicate that the economic level of the planter can be seen not only in his artifact profile, but also in the artifacts of the slaves under his control. The larger the plantation, the more varied the material culture (in the sense of the number of nonessential items).

Hypothesis 2

It was proposed that within sites, artifact profiles would be more comparable (similar) on small plantations than on large. In other words, the artifact frequencies of the kitchen and architecture groups would show less difference between planter and slave contexts on a small site than between planter and slave contexts on a large estate.

For this hypothesis the artifact profiles of Cannon's Point (planter and slave) were compared to the artifact profiles of Sinclair (planter and slave). Tests of significance (Z tests) were computed for kitchen artifact frequencies within each site and it was found that, from this data, Hypothesis 2 cannot be supported. The fundamental problem was felt to be that data from a smaller site (i.e., Pike's Bluff) was needed. Sinclair, from the documentary data on Alexander Wylly, could be considered a medium-sized plantation with approximately 40 slaves. A smaller site might yield different results.

Hypothesis 3

Hypothesis 3 proposed that there would be significant differences in the artifact profiles of domestic and field slaves.

For the purpose of testing this hypothesis, the artifact profiles of Jones and Cannon's Point (north slave cabin group only) were compared. It had been previously planned to use the artifact profile from Sinclair for this test, but because of the already demonstrated effect of plantation size on the artifact profile, a slave site from a more comparably sized plantation was needed. The northern group of slave cabins at Cannon's Point was judged to be the best choice.

It was not necessary to compute a test statistic for this hypothesis. Jones had a 3.5% greater frequency of kitchen-related artifacts than the Cannon's Point north group. This figure did not indicate a higher status for domestic slaves. Instead, it indicated that the Jones inhabitants were enjoying better material living conditions. Domestic or field status did not seem to have any effect. Hypothesis 3 is, therefore, not supported by this data. It is felt, however, that when more data become available, this hypothesis should be tested again. The extremely large size of Hampton

Plantation may place Jones at the upper end of the slave economic scale and this may have affected the results.

SUMMARY AND CONCLUSIONS

The barrier island plantation system was among the richest groups of plantations in the antebellum South. This resulted in some extremely wealthy planters and very large plantations. These planters were able to control not only their own material living conditions, but to affect those of their hired help (overseers) and those of their chattel property (slaves). In addition to very large planters, this region had both moderate and small planters. While they occupied a lower economic level, they, too, were able to affect the material living conditions of their charges. The archaeological record has been able to demonstrate ample evidence of the effect economic position had on these plantation sites.

At Jones, one of the slave settlements of a very large plantation, slaves had a rather sparse material culture, but when compared to other slave sites of smaller plantations, these slaves were found to have a higher standard of living indicating greater access to goods and services.

At the Sinclair slave site, data again presented a low-status material culture. It had been predicted that these slaves might enjoy a higher standard of living because of their supposed occupation as domestic servants. Such was not apparent from the artifact assemblage.

The planter occupants of Sinclair appear, from the documents, to have occupied a medium level economically. This is reflected in the archaeological assemblage, as is the lower economic status of the planter at Pike's Bluff. From the available information, it seems that the material culture of the Pike's Bluff planter was dominated more by items of necessity.

These sites were compared to other coastal sites and it could be seen that there was a continuum of economic levels, from the slave on a moderate-sized plantation to a large planter. It is hoped that additional data can be obtained to fill in the missing or underrepresented parts of this scale.

The derivation of one artifact pattern for the barrier island plantation would be a useless gesture. Economic resources were controlled by the planter who distributed them among the people in his charge—the overseer and slave. The data presented in this study have indicated that the material culture assemblage, and therefore the pattern, is partially a function of the wealth of the planter. As the economic resources of the planter increased (number of slaves being used as the economic index), there was a rise not only in the material living conditions of the planter, but in those of his charges as well.

The status indicators of ceramic form and type proposed by Otto (1975:220) have been shown to be reliable indicators of both social and economic position on the sites of this study. They compare with the artifact patterns in their confirmation of Hypothesis 1. Higher status ceramic forms (flatwares) were shown to occur more on higher status sites, but plantation size controlled their relative frequency. Smaller planter sites have smaller quantities of flatware when compared with larger planters. The same results occurred when examining ceramic types. Annular and transfer-printed wares were shown to be indicators of site status. As site status increased, the percentage of transfer-printed wares increased, but again plantation size controlled their relative frequencies.

From the data presented, Hypotheses 2 and 3 cannot be supported. It is highly recommended that as further data becomes available, these hypotheses be reexamined. It is possible from the data presented to derive patterns for the planter, overseer, and slave, but it might be better to label these patterns "upper, middle, and lower economic level artifact patterns." It would be very difficult for someone working with a site of unknown social status to tell whether they had material from a small planter or an overseer, but by examining the profiles presented in this study, they would be able to assess the relative economic position of the site inhabitant.

The purpose of this study was to demonstrate that the fundamental utility of patterns or pattern recognition (profiles) lies in their ability to indicate underlying cultural processes. By examining the artifact profiles of this study, it was shown that the economic system, as well as the social system, affected the material living conditions on plantation sites. Future excavations on other plantations should be able to build upon these data.

ACKNOWLEDGMENTS

I wish to thank Chad Braley, Tim Moore, and Charles H. Fairbanks for their aid in the preparation of this manuscript. The latter is truly the pioneer of plantation archaeology and provided much needed criticism and support during the research.

REFERENCES

Benedict, Ruth
1934 *Patterns of Culture.* New York: Houghton-Mifflin.

Bonner, James C.
1965 Plantation and farm: the agricultural south. In *Writing Southern History—Essays in Honor of Fletcher M. Green.* Arthur S. Link and Rembert W. Patrick, eds. Baton Rouge: Louisiana State University Press.

Chapman, G. P.
1979 *Human and Environmental Systems: A Geographer's Appraisal.* New York: Academic Press.

Drucker, Lesley M., and Ronald W. Anthony
1979 *The Spiers Landing Site: Archeological Investigations in Berkeley County, South Carolina.* Columbia, South Carolina: Carolina Archeological Services.

Eaton, Clement
1961 *The Growth of Southern Civilization, 1790–1860.* New York: Harper & Row.

Fairbanks, Charles H.
1974 The Kingsley slave cabins in Duval County, Florida, 1968. *Conference on Historic Site Archeology Papers.* 7:62–93.

Flanders, Ralph B.
1933 *Plantation Slavery in Georgia*. Chapel Hill: University of North Carolina Press.
Garrow, Patrick
1981 Investigations of Yaughan and Curriboo plantations. Paper presented at the Society for Historical Archeology Meetings, New Orleans, Louisiana.
Genovese, Eugene D.
1974 *Roll, Jordan, Roll*. New York: Pantheon Books.
Glynn County Superior Court
1827 Deed Book H, p. 430.
Hawes, Lila B.
1956 The papers of Lachlan McIntosh. *Georgia Historical Quarterly* 40:170–171.
Heard, George A.
1938 St. Simon's Island during the War Between the States. *Georgia Historical Quarterly* 22:249–272.
Honerkamp, Nicholas
1980 Frontier process in eighteenth-century colonial Georgia: an archeological approach. Ph.D. dissertation, Department of Anthropology, University of Florida, Gainesville, Florida.
Kemble, Francis A.
1961 *Journal of a residence on a Georgian plantation in 1838–39*. John A. Scott, ed. New York: Knopf.
Kroeber, A. L.
1948 *Culture Patterns and Processes*. New York: Harcourt, Brace, Jovanovich.
Linton, Ralph B.
1973 Status and role. In *High Points in Anthropology*. Paul Bohannon and Mark Glazer, eds. New York: Alfred A. Knopf.
McFarlane, Suzanne S.
1975 The ethnoarcheology of a slave community: the Couper Plantation. Master's thesis, Department of Anthropology, University of Florida, Gainesville, Florida.
Menn, John K.
1964 *The Large Slaveholders of Louisiana—1860*. New Orleans: Pelican Publishing Co.
Miller, George L.
1980 Classification and scaling of 19th century ceramics. *Historical Archeology* 14:1–40.
Nash, Gary B.
1970 *Class and Society in Early America*. Englewood Cliffs, N.J.: Prentice-Hall.
Otto, John S.
1975 Status differences and the archeological record: a comparison of planter, overseer, and slave sites from Cannon's Point Plantation (1794–1861), St. Simon's Island, Georgia. Ph.D. dissertation, Department of Anthropology, University of Florida, Gainesville, Florida.
Owens, Leslie H.
1976 *This Species of Property: Slave Life and Culture in the Old South*. New York: Oxford University Press.
Singleton, Theresa A.
1980 The archeology of Afro-American slavery in coastal Georgia: a regional perception of slave household and community patterns. Ph.D. dissertation, Department of Anthropology, University of Florida, Gainesville, Florida.
South, Stanley S.
1975 Pattern recognition in historical archeology. *Conference on Historic Site Archeology Papers* 10:153–155.
1977 *Method and Theory in Historical Archeology*. New York: Academic Press.
Stampp, Kenneth
1956 *The Peculiar Institution: Slavery in the Antebellum South*. New York: Knopf.

Steward, Julian
1955 *Theory of Culture Change.* Urbana, Ill.: University of Illinois Press.
U.S. Bureau of the Census
1820 Report of Population Statistics for Glynn County, microfilm.
Vanstory, Burnette
1970 *Georgia's Land of the Golden Isles.* Athens: University of Georgia Press.
Von Bertalanfy, Ludwig
1975 *Perspectives on General Systems Theory.* New York: George Braziller.
Wright, Gavin
1970 Economic democracy and the concentration of agricultural wealth in the cotton south, 1850–1860. *Agricultural History* 44:63–94.

PART IV

Foodways

8

Archaeological Evidence for Subsistence on Coastal Plantations

Elizabeth J. Reitz

Tyson Gibbs

Ted A. Rathbun

INTRODUCTION

The nutritional status and food procurement activities of slaves are of growing interest to historians and anthropologists. Until recently, most of the information about slave diets came from accounts written by planters and travelers as well as from recollections and testimony of former slaves. While these sources are valuable, recent archaeological research provides data on slave foodways missing from them. Ethnobotanists have provided some data on the plant remains recovered from archaeological sites, zooarchaeologists have provided information on the relative numbers and types of animals used by slaves, and biological anthropologists have begun to examine slave and planter skeletal remains for evidence of diseases that are nutritionally related. Archaeological research has demonstrated the variety of wild foods in the slave and master diets. Resources of the sea, rivers, forest, and marsh were used by both slave and master for food. These resources constituted a major supplement to foods from domesticated sources. While unequivocal evidence of specific nutritional diseases is rare, there are signs of health problems that might have been exacerbated by poor nutrition.

ISBN 0-12-646480-4

This chapter presents the archaeological evidence of subsistence, nutritional status, and food procurement activities of plantation residents using data primarily from the sea island region of Georgia. Data from the tidewater areas of Florida, South Carolina, Virginia, and Louisiana supplement the Georgia data and reference is also made to upland regions. Emphasis is placed upon information provided by vertebrate remains rather than upon plant or human skeletal evidence because more work has been done on this aspect of slave nutrition.

THE SEA ISLANDS ENVIRONMENT

The Atlantic coastal plain lies south and east of the piedmont fall line. The fall line represents the inland limit of ancient marine submergence. The coastal plain terminates at the Atlantic Ocean in a series of barrier or sea islands. These islands extend from Anastasia Island, Florida, to North Island, South Carolina. These two islands roughly coincide with the maritime Carolina province. This is a transitional region between a temperate marine province to the north and a tropical province to the south (Briggs 1974; Ekman 1953). Species composition varies considerably in the waters of these three provinces and the expectation is that subsistence activities reflected these differences although data are not available to document this at this time. In the Carolina province a rich estuarine environment lies between the sea islands and the mainland (A. Johnson *et al.* 1974). The estuaries are composed of a maze of tidal creeks, sounds, and salt marshes inhabited by a wide variety of marine fishes as well as those freshwater taxa that can tolerate the fluctuations in water level, salinity, dissolved oxygen, and water temperatures typical of this area. The seaward side of each sea island is typically marked by beaches and dunes while the landward side is bordered by estuarine salt marshes. The mainland shore is dotted with marsh islands isolated by creeks and rivers which drain the coastal plain into the Atlantic Ocean. Brackish estuarine waters are more diluted at deltas formed where these streams flow into the estuaries, but still are subject to tidal action. The streams that flow into the estuaries are usually subject to tidal fluctuations for several miles inland, although water salinities decrease the farther one goes upstream into the coastal plain. Within the mainland tidewater region, the fish and reptile taxa found in streams and lakes are fewer and substantially different from those taxa of the estuarine/sea island region. Beyond the tidewater area, streams of the coastal plain are not subject to tidal influences and the species inhabiting them are freshwater taxa. Soils of the coastal plain are generally sandy, extensively drained, and moderately-to-severely leached. For purposes of this essay, the upland region includes the freshwater area of the coastal plain beyond the tidal influence as well as those regions above the fall line. It can be expected that when more data are available from these nontidewater locations, this organization will be revised into more environmentally appropriate categories.

Climate on the sea islands is mild. Normal annual rainfall varies from 43 to 52 inches per year, with the greatest rainfall in the summer (Bradley 1978; Carter 1978;

Landers 1978); spring generally is a dry season. Normal annual mean temperatures in coastal Georgia reach or slightly exceed 65°F with highs in the 80s and lows in the 40s. Occasionally summer temperatures reach the 100s. Snow is rare, although frosts occur regularly each winter. The growing season is 228–247 days, from approximately March 13–15 to November 8–15 (U.S.D.A. 1930a, b). The Florida coast is somewhat warmer than the Georgia sea islands, and the South Carolina coast is somewhat cooler. Moderately high mean annual temperatures and abundant rainfall make the coastal setting favorable for long-growing crops and multiple harvests, as well as for a large number of human pathogens.

Resources of the sea islands include a wide variety of wild plants and animals, as well as domestic ones. Abundant estuarine fish species include sea catfishes (Ariidae), sheepshead (*Archosargus probatocephalus*), drums (Sciaenidae), and mullets (*Mugil* spp.) (A. Johnson *et al.* 1974). Some freshwater turtles (Emydidae) are capable of tolerating brackish estuarine conditions, or live in freshwater ponds on the islands (Gibbons and Coker 1978). Diamond-back terrapins (*Malaclemys terrapin*) inhabit estuarine waters regularly, as do alligators (*Alligator mississippiensis*). Sea turtles (Cheloniidae) nest on the island beaches and forage in tidal creeks during the summer. A variety of water fowl, sea birds, and shore birds inhabit the sea islands. Mammals are relatively few, however, but include opossum (*Didelphis virginianus*), rabbit (*Sylvilagus* spp.), raccoon (*Procyon lotor*), deer (*Odocoileus virginiana*), and a number of bats, rats, and mice. Large numbers of edible invertebrates are found in the estuarine setting, including crab (*Callinectes* spp.), oyster (*Crassostrea virginiana*), quahog (*Mercenaria* spp.), conch (*Busycon* spp.), and shrimp (*Peneus* spp.). Edible plants include red maple (*Acer rubrum*), sea oxeye (*Borrichia fretescens*), pignut hickory (*Carya glabra*), persimmon (*Diospyros virginiana*), pickerel weed (*Pontederia cordata*), mulberry (*Morus rubra*), and pennyworth (*Hydrocotyle bonariensis*). Domestic plants include cotton, indigo, rice, corn, olives, citrus, peaches, and a number of vegetables. Pigs (*Sus scrofa*), cows (*Bos taurus*), and chickens (*Gallus gallus*) did well although sheep (*Ovis aries*) and goats (*Capra hircus*) did not thrive in the humid environment (Gray 1933).

PLANTATION LIFE

During plantation days the major cash crops grown in the sea island area of Georgia were cotton and rice. Sea island (or long-staple) cotton was a special variety of cotton that required more care in harvesting and packing than the short-staple cotton grown elsewhere. Rice was also a labor-intensive crop. Both usually commanded good market prices (Eaton 1961; Flanders 1933; Gray 1933). Long-staple cotton was grown on the sea islands and rice along the tidal river deltas as well as on the islands where possible.

As a result of emphasis on crops needing careful attention, most coastal rice and cotton plantations operated mainly on a task system rather than on the gang system, although both may have been used in combination when the need arose (Gray

1933:551; Morgan 1982). Under the *gang system* a team of slaves worked together for a specified period of time, usually from dawn to dusk. Under the *task system*, slaves were assigned a specified task or individual plots of land to tend. When this task was completed to the satisfaction of the supervisor, each slave was finished for the day. Tasks were divided into heavy, moderate, and light categories (Flanders 1933). Slaves were classified as full, three-quarters, half, or quarter hands according to the amount of task units they performed. With sea island cotton each slave might be responsible for 3 to 4 acres and could finish work sometime after noon. Healthier or younger slaves were expected to do more work than children, nursing mothers, the ill, or elderly slaves. As a result of being required to complete a task rather than work for a specified amount of time, slaves might finish their work by mid-day, with time to devote to gardening, stock-raising, fishing, hunting, or other activities (Flanders 1933; Kemble 1961; Morgan 1982). It should be noted, however, that even under the task system the work day might be 15 or 16 hours long during the peak of the harvest season (Gray 1933:557).

There is some documentary information on slave subsistence (Cade 1935; Genovese 1974; Katz 1968; Olmsted 1856; Savitt 1978). Documents indicate that often the rations were issued to a cook who prepared meals for the slaves at a central kitchen (Bonner 1964:198); however, no archaeological evidence for such kitchens has been found (Singleton 1980:142). The foodstuffs given to the slaves were allotted daily or weekly and consisted of some combination of pork, beef, cornmeal, seasonal vegetables, corn bread, sweet potatoes, onions, molasses, rice, salt, and pumpkins. There is no consensus on the amount of food each slave family received. Although documentary evidence is scanty, rations were apparently enough in most cases to maintain the slaves while they worked in the fields and reproduced (Fogel and Engerman 1974; Gibbs *et al.* 1980; Savitt 1978). The amount of food each slave received appears to have depended upon such variables as the size of the plantation; the amount of concern felt by the master or overseer for the welfare of the slaves; the location of the plantation; the size of the slave family; the presence of children; the ability of slaves to produce food themselves; the time available to procure wild foods; and the amount of food slaves could barter, purchase, or steal. It is the combination of these multiple sources of food that makes it difficult to assess the ingredients and adequacy of the slave diet on the coastal plain solely from documentary sources.

Some information is available on rations issued to slaves on sea island plantations. Adult slaves at Cannon's Point, St. Simons Island, Georgia, were issued 9 quarts of maize per week. They received no bacon, but salt fish and beef might be issued (Otto 1975:291). Rice or sweet potatoes could substitute for maize, and both rice flour and molasses were sometimes given to the slaves. Slaves at Cannon's Point and on Cumberland Island could also plant gardens and raise livestock (Ehrenhard and Bullard 1982; Otto 1975:294). Slave livestock included cows, pigs, horses, and poultry (Morgan 1982). On some plantations, such activities were forbidden since slaves were suspected of buying whiskey or their freedom from the profit of these enterprises. On many coastal plantations slaves also fished (G. Johnson 1930:142) and hunted (Morgan 1982). Foods raised or hunted by slaves were not considered substitutes for the master's allocations, but surpluses that belonged to the slaves to do with as they chose (Morgan 1982).

ARCHAEOLOGICAL EVIDENCE FOR SUBSISTENCE

Most information on the diet of slaves is derived primarily from plantation records, eyewitness accounts, slave narratives, and other historical documents. While these sources have proven fruitful for describing many aspects of slavery, they do not adequately document slave subsistence. Not only are they incomplete, but they are probably subject to intentional or unintentional biases. Moreover, much of the previous research into slave foodways assumed that the slave diet was limited, monotonous, and uniform throughout the South.

Archaeological investigations at slave sites have been able to offer a clearer view of local food consumption, food gathering, food preparation, and food storage practices than do the documentary sources (Gibbs *et al.* 1980; Singleton and Gibbs 1983). Slaves had a number of food sources from which they could supplement their core diet of corn, pork, and beef (Gibbs *et al.* 1980). Through their studies of the fauna, flora, and human remains found at plantation sites, archaeologists have demonstrated that a variety of animals and plants were eaten by slaves on coastal plantations (Moore 1981; Otto 1975; Singleton 1980). Many if not all of these may have been obtained through the efforts of the slaves themselves. These efforts resulted in a subsistence pattern that was very similar to that of the plantation elite. Therefore, in researching the activities related to slaves and food consumption patterns, a review of the written documentation and an examination of oral transcripts from slaves and their children, combined with a review of the data from archaeological excavations, provides a more complete picture. In this Chapter, we review the archaeological evidence for subsistence on coastal plantations.

Archaeological evidence for subsistence is found in three forms: in the food remains deposited, in subsistence gear discarded or lost, and in the human skeletal remains. Food remains include bones of animals, shells from invertebrates, and seeds or other inedible parts of plants. Obviously all of these remains are not uniformly preserved in the archaeological record; very little plant material has been identified from coastal plantation deposits. This is partly due to the failure of archaeologists to consult experienced specialists and partly due to poor preservation. Many identifiable plant parts are lost as the plant is consumed or disappear from the archaeological record during decomposition. Preservation of plant parts is enhanced if the material is burned. (Hopefully more attention will be paid to botanical remains in the future.) Invertebrates recovered have also not been extensively studied. Invertebrates found at coastal slave sites could represent construction debris (i.e., tabby floors, walls, and so on) rather than kitchen refuse, or both. Some invertebrate identifications, however, have been made.

Human skeletal remains have been avoided except in a few cases (Corruccini *et al.* 1982; Thomas *et al.* 1977). One reason for the neglect of human skeletal data is that legal, religious, and moral factors frequently discourage scientific examination of recent Christian burials. Due to the limited number of studies of human skeletal remains, much of the data to be presented in this Chapter are drawn from the Caribbean and other locations. More work needs to be done before it is safe to conclude that the nutritional status reflected in these Caribbean data is similar to that experienced by slaves on the sea islands. Vertebrate data have been more extensively studied, although the samples are almost always small and subject to postdepositional disturbances.

Subsistence gear, being classified as part of the material culture, has received more attention from archaeologists. Where such equipment was recovered archaeologically, it has been consistently reported in the literature. Interpretation of archaeological data is also hampered by problems of context. Many of the contexts identified as "slave" for purposes of this study may also have been occupied by tenant farmers or unknown persons after emancipation, even into the twentieth century. It is frequently difficult, if not impossible, to distinguish such deposits from antebellum ones with our present knowledge of these time periods.

BIASES AFFECTING ZOOARCHAEOLOGICAL EVIDENCE

For the above reasons most of this discussion of the archaeological evidence of slave subsistence will focus on zooarchaeological data. Zooarchaeologists employ a variety of techniques when analyzing faunal material from archaeological sites (Wing and Brown 1979). They may count the bone fragments and weigh them. A third method is to determine the minimum number of individuals (MNI) represented in the collection. MNI is based on the principle of paired elements, that is, if the archaeological collection contains two right scapulae of a deer, at least two deer are represented in the collection. There may, of course, actually have been more than two deer consumed at the site. Alternatively, only portions of the deer, rather than two entire animals, may have been used there, but the analyst minimally knows that at least two individuals were involved. One of the hazards of using MNI for comparison is that small species, particularly fish, are usually represented by more individuals than large animals such as cows at estuarine historic sites. MNI also does not reflect the quality or quantity of nutrients contributed by each animal. While there are zooarchaeological techniques for assessing the nutritional contribution of identified species to the human diet, these techniques have not been uniformly applied in the studies being reviewed, so that MNI remains the best method for intersite comparisons.

A serious problem with plantation zooarchaeological data is small sample size. It has been reported that samples with less than 200 individuals will be incomplete and biased (Casteel 1977; Grayson 1979; Wing and Brown 1979). These small samples are the result of limited field time and difficulties inherent in finding samples in closed contexts for the time period under consideration. A quick review of the samples being surveyed in this Chapter shows that many of them are extremely small and that much more work needs to be done before plantation subsistence patterns can be discussed with confidence.

In addition to sample size problems the archaeological deposits also have been biased by a series of cultural and natural processes and methodologies, the effects of which usually cannot be accurately assessed. These biases hamper interpretation. Prior to deposition, capture and processing techniques cause many bones to be lost from the archaeological record. After deposition taphonomic factors such as bioturbation, soil acidity, fluctuations in soil temperature and moisture, and trampling further destroy the archaeological evidence.

Decisions made by the archaeologist on where to excavate and methods used during excavation further influence the faunal sample, as do the analytical methods employed by the zooarchaeologist. Recovery methods have rarely been duplicated by archaeologists excavating at plantation sites. For these reasons the interpretations made of human subsistence activities from archaeological evidence must be approached with caution. We can never know with certainty that the interpretations made from the faunal record are accurate reflections of previous foodways, therefore, it is important to duplicate each archaeological excavation at several similar sites in order to test the accuracy of various interpretations. If archaeological excavations are replicated at a number of sites and result in similar faunal assemblages and subsistence interpretations, we can speak with more confidence about the validity of our knowledge about plantation subsistence. At this stage in plantation archaeology, enough work has been done that it is possible to synthesize the data and develop tentative conclusions. In spite of the problems found in these generally small samples subject to unknown taphonomic biases and recovered with uncomparable methods, they show surprising uniformity and consistency in diets on sea island plantations. Much more work needs to be done to test these opinions, however, before it can be said that our interpretations of subsistence on plantations are complete.

A final bias in the archaeological record is posed by preserved meats. Bones of hogs and cattle have been found routinely in slave contexts. Although the historical record indicates that slaves were given larger allotments of salt pork than beef, at most historic coastal sites cattle bones and individuals are at least as common as pig remains. Cattle are often more abundant in these collections based upon bone weight and meat weight or biomass, but this does not necessarily mean that beef was consumed at a much higher rate than pork. While smoked pork may contain bone, brine-cured meats not subsequently smoked are prone to spoilage if the pieces are too big. Hence most salt pork should be either deboned or smoked. However, prior to canning, spoiled meat was apparently a common occurrence as were complaints of bone in the meat (Wilson and Southwood 1976). Recent excavations in Europe and Australia have shown that bone might remain when left in barrels of salt meat (Henderson 1980; Poplin 1982; Schmid 1982; Wijngaarden-Bakker 1982). Generally speaking the bacon or side meat documented as rations for slaves probably left few identifiable bones or other remains (Singleton 1980), but other fresh or preserved meat rations might have contained bone. While the brining process might have discouraged survival of bone from the preserved meat rations, there remains the probability that some pork rations issued to slaves did contain bone and that such bone might survive to become part of the archaeological assemblage. If part or all of the slave pork and beef rations contained bone, then the archaeological prominence of beef at coastal sites may indicate that more beef than pork was consumed at slave sites or that combinations of fresh bone-containing beef and preserved boneless pork was consumed. Neither of these possibilities is supported by documentary evidence to the extent that it appears in the archaeological record. This problem cannot be resolved at this juncture, although the prominence of cattle remains does indicate the need for further research into the contribution of beef in the slave diet, as well as serious reevaluation of documentary evidence on the role of pork in coastal diets.

ESTUARINE PLANTATION SITES

Archaeological evidence for subsistence on plantations is available from sites on the sea islands and lower estuarine mainlands of Georgia and Florida (Table 8.1 and Figure 8.1). Some data are also available from plantations in tidewater regions of Virginia, South Carolina, and Louisiana and from sites above the fall line in Tennessee and Georgia. While sites located above the lower reaches of the sea island estuaries are not the focus of this essay, they are included in order to demonstrate the validity of defining an estuarine subsistence pattern. The data to be reviewed indicate a regional similarity among the sea island assemblages in contrast to collections from other environmental zones. While these sites do not encompass the entire South, there is enough regional diversity among them to support some general statements about slave food habits. Interpretation of the archaeological record suggests that slaves living on most plantations consumed wild foods to some extent and that some of these foods may have been obtained through their own efforts. Furthermore, the slave diet may not have been dissimilar to the planter's diet. Slaves living on the estuarine plantations used far more fish than did slaves living outside that area, even those living on mainland tidewater plantations. These phenomena are largely invisible in the written record.

Kingsley Plantation (Ft. George Island, Florida)

Kingsley Plantation was owned by Zephaniah Kingsley, a slave importer. It was occupied from approximately 1813 to 1850. Archaeological tests were conducted at Kingsley Plantation in 1968 by C.H. Fairbanks (1974). Faunal materials were not quantified, but they included raccoon, pig, cow, turtle, fish, and shellfish remains. The only floral remains identified were three corn cob fragments. Several lead balls and a musket flint were recovered as were perforated lead weights and a number of ceramic containers and cooking equipment fragments.

Rayfield Plantation (Cumberland Island, Georgia)

Rayfield Plantation was owned by Robert Stafford, who grew sea island cotton in the early 1800s. Testing at one slave cabin by A. Ascher and C. H. Fairbanks (1971)

Table 8.1
SUMMARY OF SITES

Plantation site	Location	Occupation[a]	Context	MNI
Belleview	Charleston Co., SC	1738–1756	slave, planter	17
Bray	Kingsmill, VA	1770–1790	planter	135
Butler Island	Darien, GA	1804–1861	slave	NA[b]
Campfield	Georgetown Co., SC	1865–1900	slave, freedman	11
Cannon's Point	St. Simon's Is., GA	1794–1866	slave (south)	55
Cannon's Point	St. Simon's Is., GA	1794–1866	slave (north)	69
Cannon's Point	St. Simon's Is., GA	1794–1866	overseer	42
Cannon's Point	St. Simon's Is., GA	1794–1866	planter	181
Clifts	Westmoreland Co., VA	1670–1730	slave, planter, servant	16
Elmwood	Jefferson Parish, LA	1790–1840	unknown	44
First Hermitage	Davidson Co., TN	1804–1850s	mixed	121
Hermitage	Davidson Co., TN	1821–1888	A. Jackson and family	104
Jones Creek (Hampton)	St. Simon's Is., GA	1801–1870s	slave	145
Kings Bay out-building	Camden Co., GA	1790–1840	slave	110
Kings Bay	Camden Co., GA	1790–1840	slave	26
Kings Bay	Camden Co., GA	1790–1840	planter	60
Kingsley	Ft. George Is., FL	1813–1850	slave	NA
Millwood	Abbeville Co., SC and Elbert Co., GA	1860–1925	tenant	109
Parland	Colonel's Island, GA	1830–1880	planter	70
Parland	Colonel's Island, GA	1860–?	freedman	46
Pettus	Kingsmill, VA	1600s	planter	50
Pike's Bluff	St. Simon's Is., GA	1827–1857	planter	68
Rayfield	Cumberland Is., GA	1834–1865	slave	NA
Sinclair	St. Simon's Is., GA	1790–1820	slave	17
Sinclair	St. Simon's Is., GA	1790–1820	planter	148
Spiers Landing	Berkeley Co., SC	1700–1800	unknown	15
Stafford	Cumberland Is., GA	1800–1865	slave	16
Utopia	Kingsmill, VA	1600s	tenant	71

[a]Dates are approximate.
[b]Minimum Number of Individuals not available.

produced some animal bones. The faunal remains were not quantified; however, the excavators reported that animal bones were evenly distributed among three categories: mammals, birds, and fish. Pigs, chickens, and catfish were identified as were wild birds, small mammals, and shellfish. Ascher and Fairbanks concluded their report by surmising that the slaves added protein to their diet through their own efforts, and prepared it in their cabins. Evidence to support this interpretation was provided by a gunflint, lead bullets, a chunk of lead, and cooking equipment fragments.

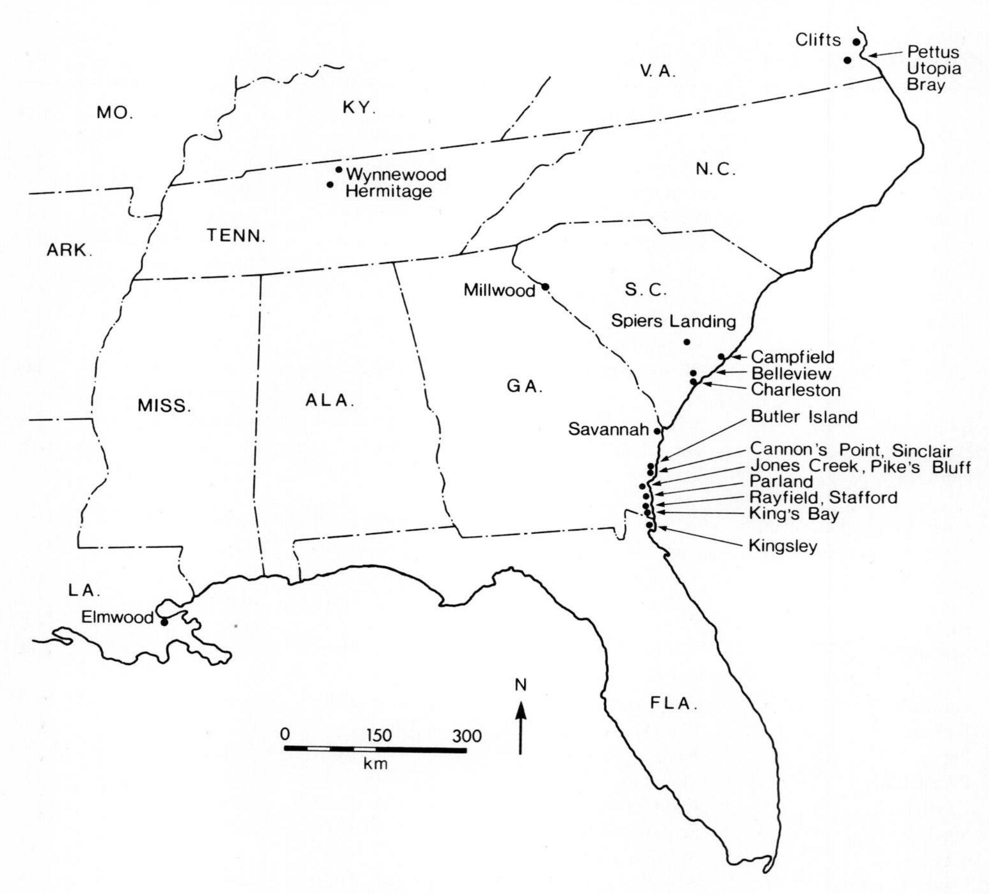

Figure 8.1 Location of sites.

Stafford Plantation (Cumberland Island, Georgia)

Stafford Plantation was also owned by Robert Stafford, the owner of Rayfield. It was the largest plantation on the island, with 348 slaves in 1850 (Ehrenhard and Bullard 1981). The plantation was founded in 1800 and operated into the 1860s. Stafford owned 148 slaves in 1830, 160 slaves in 1840, and 110 slaves in 1860. A slave cabin on the Stafford Plantation was excavated by J. Ehrenhard (Ehrenhard and Bullard 1981) who ascertained that domestic animals contributed 31% of the individuals, and wild fauna comprised 69% of the collection. A rabbit (Leporidae) and a mallard (*Anas platyrhynchos*) may have been domestic rather than wild, but their presence with raccoon, deer, drum, and mullets indicates that a diversity of other species were consumed in addition to one pig, two cows, and a goat. Two gunflints were found associated with the cabin.

Kings Bay Plantation (Camden County, Georgia)

This plantation lies directly behind Cumberland Island (R. Johnson 1978; R. Smith *et al.* 1981). An out-building/slave cabin, a probable slave cabin, and the planter's residence were excavated on the mainland Kings Bay Plantation. Identification of both slave structures is tentative, but the planter's residence was located nearby. At the Kings Bay out-building/slave cabin, 25% of the individuals were domestic animals; the remaining species were primarily estuarine fishes and wild mammals, including deer (Reitz 1978a). Sixteen cows and nine pigs were identified. Two fishnet weights and three gunflints were excavated from the out-building (R. Johnson 1978).

The probable slave cabin was excavated by C. Braley (R. Smith *et al.* 1981) and may predate the out-building occupation. Domestic individuals constituted 23% of the MNI. Most of the wild fauna were estuarine species (53%) and deer (4%). Pigs (12%) outnumbered cattle (8%) at this location. No fishing gear was recovered. Three shot and one gun flint were recovered.

Part of the planter's kitchen was also excavated (R. Smith *et al.* 1981). In this deposit only 13% of the individuals were domestic species. Deer, pig, and cow were each represented by three individuals. Estuarine fishes constituted 40% of the individuals, followed by wild mammals (13%) and aquatic/estuarine turtles (12%). In addition to lead shot and gun flints, cast-net sinkers as well as crimp-on and tie-on line sinkers were recovered.

Parland Plantation (Colonel's Island, Georgia)

Parland Plantation was located on Colonel's Island, a marsh island just south of the Brunswick River (Steinen 1978). Fauna were excavated from two historic contexts: deposits associated with the administrative center directly on the river, and a cabin site about 1 km south. This cabin site was probably a postemancipation residence of black freedmen rather than slaves, based upon the recovery of an 1867 nickel near the base of one of the two excavated chimneys, the unusual construction of the chimneys, and the possibly impoverished nature of the artifacts (Singleton 1978). Domestic species contributed 22% of the individuals recovered from the freedmen site (Reitz 1978b). Pigs were 15% of the individuals and cows only 4%. Wild mammals contributed 43% of the individuals, which is the highest level of use for this category at any of the estuarine plantation sites. Raccoon, opossum, and rabbit were all more abundant in the collection than deer, however. Sea turtles (Cheloniidae) constituted 7% of the individuals and fish 15%. Since Colonel's Island is a marsh island, the amount of sea turtle identified in the collection may seem large; however, they are known to penetrate even further into the upper reaches of the estuaries (Archie Carr, personal communication, 1979).

At the administrative center 37% of the individuals were domestic species (Reitz 1978b). Pigs constituted 19% of the individuals and cows 14%. Deer were consumed (13% of the individuals), as were turtles (13%). Wild terrestrial animals constituted 27% of the individuals and estuarine fishes only 14%. The use of fish at the Parland sites is the lowest of all the estuarine collections.

Cannon's Point Plantation (St. Simon's Island, Georgia)

Cannon's Point Plantation was owned by members of the Couper family, who had an average of over 100 slaves in residence. S. McFarlane (1975) excavated in a southern series of slave cabins while J. Otto (1975) excavated at a northern series of cabins, at the overseer's residence, and at the planter's house. McFarlane's faunal collections included deer, opossum, rabbit, raccoon, sheepshead, sea catfish, drum, gar, mullet, alligator, musk turtle, diamond-back terrapin, sea turtle, and crab. Of the 55 individuals, 20% were domestic species including pig (11% MNI), cow (6%), sheep (2%), and chicken (2%). Wild terrestrial species (deer, opossum, rabbit, and raccoon) constituted 36% of the individuals and estuarine fish 27%. Hickory nuts were also identified. Fish hooks made of nails, net weights, and lead shot indicated to McFarlane that slaves were responsible for obtaining some of these animals themselves. Shell deposits behind the cabin might delineate the location of garden plots (McFarlane 1975:80).

J. Otto's excavations supported this interpretation and found evidence for differential use of domestic resources among planter, overseer, and slave contexts. Faunal remains from the slave cabin included opossum, wild and domestic rabbit, raccoon, mink, pig, cattle, sheep, chicken, diamond-back terrapin, soft-shell turtle, stingray, gar, sea catfish, sheepshead, perch, sea trout, kingfish, croaker, black and red drum, and flounder. The overseer's and planter's debris contained similar species, with the noteworthy difference that only the planter's refuse included deer. In fact, the species identified from the planter's collection contained fewer domesticated animals than found at the slave or overseer cabins. The slave diet included 13% domestic individuals (cow, pig, sheep, and chicken) while the overseer's diet included 9% and the planter's 9%. The slave refuse included equal numbers of pig and cow, but no deer. The overseer deposit likewise did not include deer, and contained more pig individuals than cows. While the planter's refuse did include deer as well as sheep, pigs were slightly more abundant than cows. Food preparation equipment was found in the slave cabins, as were weights, sinkers, lead shot, a percussion cap, and a gunflint. A spring trap element was found at the overseer's house.

Sinclair Plantation (St. Simon's Island, Georgia)

Sinclair was a modest-sized plantation with approximately 10 to 15 slaves and was owned by the Butler family (Moore 1981). The excavations conducted by S. Moore recovered faunal remains from planter and domestic slave contexts. Most of the subsistence artifacts were excavated from the slave cabin. These included lead weights, a hoe, and cooking equipment. According to Moore slave contexts had a higher percentage of domestic animal biomass than did planter contexts. Domestic fauna at the planter's kitchen included 32% of the individuals, with more beef than pork. Venison was almost as heavily used as pork. This collection is unique in containing remains of a domestic duck (*Cairina moschata*).

Jones Creek Settlement (St. Simon's Island, Georgia)

The Jones slave settlement was located on Hampton Plantation. This plantation was owned by the Butler family also. At one point over 300 slaves worked at Hampton (Moore 1981). Moore's excavations at Jones focused on several slave contexts. She found that domestic fauna contributed 32% of the individuals with wild species, primarily estuarine fish, providing the remaining species. Raccoons contributed 15% of the individuals, deer 2%, cows contributed 14% of the individuals, and pigs 13%. Cooking equipment as well as fishing weights and lead shot were recovered. Gunflints, a brass trigger guard, and a copper ramrod holder were also found at Jones.

Pike's Bluff (St. Simon's Island, Georgia)

Pike's Bluff was part of a small estate of no more than 30 slaves (Moore 1981). Moore's excavations here concentrated on the probable main house kitchen and midden area. Although most of the individuals were wild species (63%)—particularly opossum, rabbits, and turtles,—most of the meat came from beef. Pigs and cows were represented by 8 and 11 individuals respectively; 1 deer was identified and 1 caprine. Several lead weights, possibly used for fishing, were discovered.

Butler Island (Darien, Georgia)

Butler Island was also owned by the Butler family. At one point more than 919 slaves worked here and at Hampton Plantation on nearby St. Simons Island (Moore 1981). Butler Island was a rice plantation located on a river delta island just south of the Altamaha River. T. Singleton excavated three slave cabins on the plantation (Singleton 1980). Since the faunal collection was in poor condition MNI could not be determined, but the identifiable species indicate a heavy use of wild resources (9 of the 12 genera). By bone weight, domestic animals contributed 60% of the collection. Most of the weight (20%) was from cow bones, while pigs contributed only 9% of the weight. Buckshot, musket balls, gunflints, and a brass trigger guard were found during excavations as were lead net sinkers. Peach pits were the only floral remains recovered. The species list from Butler Island reflects the reduced salinity of the marsh island/river delta setting by containing species such as gar, bowfin, and freshwater catfish. There were also fewer drum and sheepshead, and no sea catfishes.

TIDEWATER SITES

Campfield Settlement (Georgetown County, South Carolina)

The Campfield settlement was located on Campfield plantation, a rice plantation located on the Black River about 10 miles inland from the Atlantic Ocean. The plantation was a small one that operated as a rice plantation from some time prior to

1791 until recently. The vertebrate component was probably deposited primarily by slaves working on the plantation, although with some freedmen debris probably mixed in with the slave materials (Zierden and Calhoun 1983). Although the collection is very small (11 individuals), it suggests that the subsistence of slaves living even slightly outside of the estuarine environment may have been different from that of slaves living on plantations on sea or marsh islands. No wild terrestrial fauna were identified in the collection and only one aquatic fish, a largemouth bass (*Micropterus salmoides*). Domestic animals (pigs, cattle, a caprine, and chickens) comprises 45% of the individuals. The most prominent single species was the pond slider (*Pseudemys scripta*) which comprised 27% of the individuals. This basking turtle is easily captured in traps and probably was common in the rice drainage canals.

Utopia Cottage (Kingsmill, Virginia)

Utopia Cottage was associated with the Pettus Plantation, and was occupied either by a slave or a tenant (Miller 1979). H. Miller concluded that the collection was probably that of a tenant farmer due to the similarity of the Utopia deposit with that of Pettus. Domestic fauna contributed 66% of the individuals with pigs contributing 31% and cows 23%. The Utopia collection also included a few fish, wild birds, and turtles as well as deer, sheep, goose, and horses. Fish and aquatic turtles constituted 10% of the individuals. These materials were recovered without the aid of a screen, which might have mitigated against the recovery of small animals of nondomestic taxa.

Pettus Plantation (Kingsmill, Virginia)

Materials recovered from the Pettus Plantation were probably deposited between 1640 and 1700 when the Pettus family was quite wealthy (Miller 1979). Domestic fauna contributed over 76% of the individuals: pigs represented 42% of the individuals and cows 26%. Sheep were also identified, as were deer and a horse. Fish and aquatic turtles constituted 6% of the individuals. The materials from Pettus were also recovered without screening.

Bray Plantation (Kingsmill, Virginia)

Faunal materials from a well closely associated with the main house of eighteenth-century Bray Plantation have been identified (Barber 1976). In his analysis, M. Barber determined that 38% of the individuals were domestic: pigs constituted 8% of the individuals, followed by cattle at 5%. In contrast to the other collections from which caprines are generally absent, 11% of the individuals from this well were caprines. Bray's well included over 40 taxa. Although wild birds were used extensively (22%), few fishes and turtles were identified (12%). No deer were identified but a horse was found in the collection. No screen was used in collecting these materials.

Elmwood Plantation (Jefferson Parish, Louisiana)

Elmwood Plantation was originally occupied by French colonists prior to 1790, but has Spanish and American deposits dating through 1840. The site was excavated by R. C. Goodwin (Goodwin *et al.* 1983). Its location places it in the Mississippi delta, but not actually in an estuarine setting. The small faunal collection contained 45% domestic individuals and 55% wild individuals (Reitz 1983). Considering the small sample size, the use of species was fairly diverse. The diversity came from wide use of wild terrestrial animals such as opossum, rabbit, squirrel, and deer rather than a variety in the use of fish or turtles. The striking aspect of this collection is that caprines constituted 11% of the individuals. This is a level of use similar to that found in the Bray well, which was also an early site from the coastal plain. Cattle and hogs both contributed 14% of the individuals in the Elmwood collection.

UPLAND SITES

Spiers Landing (Berkeley County, South Carolina)

Spiers Landing is an undocumented site that was occupied in the late eighteenth/ early nineteenth century. The site was excavated by L. Drucker (1981). It is different from the previous sites in that it is an interior coastal plain site located on the south shore of Lake Marion on the Old Santee River channel. The small faunal assemblage contained 50% wild individuals and 50% domestic individuals. Cows (25%) were equal to pigs (25%) in the species identified. The striking difference between samples from this upland site and those from the coast is the limited range of fauna utilized at Spiers Landing. Only six taxa were identified. These included a bird, bowfin, raccoons, deer, pigs, and cows. This is a sharp contrast to coastal deposits that frequently include 30 or more species. This could also be a reflection of small sample size. Plant remains identified included peaches, corn, beans, acorns, hickory nuts, walnut, and wild grapes.

First Hermitage (Davidson County, Tennessee)

Several excavations have been conducted at the site of the First Hermitage (S. Smith 1976). The cabins excavated were first used by Andrew Jackson as a residence, later as a guesthouse, and finally as slave cabins. Although some of the deposits are probably those of nonslaves, most of the fauna were interpreted as representing slave subsistence. E. Breitburg found no significant differences between food debris associated with Jackson's use of the cabins as a residence and guesthouse and that associated with the slave occupation (S. Smith *et al.* 1977). Domestic mammals contributed 17% of the individuals recovered from the east, west, and south cabins studied by Breitburg (in S. Smith 1976). Domestic birds, primarily chickens, contributed 17% of the individuals also. Aquatic reptiles (2% of the individuals) and freshwater fishes (11% of the individuals) were not major components. Hogs alone contributed 14% of the individuals while chickens were 15%. An interesting aspect of this collection is that the Norway rat, (*Rattus norvegicus*) was represented by 25 individuals (21%). This seems high for a commensal species, but could indicate a rat problem in a slave house or storeroom.

The Hermitage Mansion (Davidson County, Tennessee)

The deposits from Jackson's Hermitage Mansion were more diverse than those of the First Hermitage and slave cabins and there were fewer domestic individuals (Breitburg in S. Smith *et al.* 1977). Domestic mammals constituted 13% of the individuals, domestic birds 18%, wild mammals 19%, and wild birds 33%. The mansion material did seem to differ from the slave deposits by containing a greater variety of avian species, particularly medium-sized passerines. Interestingly, fish contributed 11% of the individuals just as they had at the cabins, although aquatic reptiles were more abundant at the Mansion (4%). Wild mammals included raccoon, skunk, squirrel, rabbit, and opossum, but no deer. Pigs were more abundant than cattle or sheep (10% of the individuals versus 2% each).

Millwood Plantation (Abbeville County, South Carolina, and Elbert County, Georgia)

Millwood Plantation was owned by James Edward Calhoun from 1832 until his death in 1889 (Orser *et al.* 1982). The plantation is located on the Savannah River in the Appalachian piedmont. The two structures excavated on the plantation were tenant/sharecropper houses occupied after 1860. Hogs (17%) outnumbered cattle (6%) and caprines (9%) in the collection. Domestic animals comprised 45% of the individuals. Wild resources were primarily terrestrial species (15%) and fish (16%). The use of fish by tenants at Millwood was very similar to that of freedmen at Parland Plantation. Wild terrestrial species included opossum, rabbit, squirrel, but no deer. A domestic goose (*Anser anser*) was identified in the collection.

HUMAN SKELETAL EVIDENCE

While zooarchaeology, ethnobotany, and artifact inventories provide a great deal of information about plantation subsistence, these studies cover only some of the available data. Human skeletal remains provide evidence of both nutrition and of disease. Evaluations of health and disease for a particular population of the past must be approached with the understanding that the skeleton reflects influences of the environmental, biological, and cultural realms. A number of models have been generated for medical and ecological analyses (Armelagos *et al.* 1980; Armelagos *et al.* 1978; Hunt 1978). These models indicate the need to approach such questions with the biocultural nature of humans in mind. Especially important factors to be considered are environmental constraints, the cultural buffering system, the resistance of the population to infection, the nature of physiological disruptions, and the impact of general biological stress.

The paucity of skeletal material excavated from plantation contexts precludes adequate analysis of physical indicators of subsistence and diet. Just as the reconstruction of past cultural systems with typical archaeological data depends upon patterns seen in adequate samples, so too does the analysis of skeletal remains. Very few archaeological samples have been studied from plantations although such studies are important for a comprehensive examination of slave subsistence. The following review of human skeletal evidence, therefore, draws upon all available data regardless of location and follows a somewhat different format from the preceding review. It is hoped that in the near future enough data will be available to review floral, faunal, and skeletal evidence excavated from the same plantation.

Considerable progress has been made in paleopathological studies. Although not all aspects of subsistence for a group are reflected in the skeletal system, many health and disease factors can be determined from such analysis. Cook (1979) provides a good example of the direct application of skeletal data to questions of subsistence and health. R. Huss-Ashmore and her colleagues (1982) reviewed many of the basic paleopathological indicators of nutritional status. This type of analysis is especially suited for a reconstruction of health and disease states for past groups. Documentation of particular pathological conditions and differential diagnosis from dry bone can be difficult, but even general patterns reflected in the skeleton suggest environmental and cultural influences. J. Buikstra and D. Cook (1980) synthesized and critically reviewed many of the developments within this field and a text by D. Ortner and W. Putschar (1981) illustrates the methodology and types of data needed for productive analysis. Rathbun (1981) documented the range of information that can be provided by viewing human skeletal remains as an archaeological resource. Examples of findings with prehistoric populations in the Southeast and other considerations of interest to archaeologists were illustrated. Many of these aspects are directly applicable to attempts to understand subsistence and diet in plantation systems for both slaves and masters. Coordinated research with historical sources and archaeological information will strengthen both disciplines.

Many of the diseases present in the slave population (respiratory diseases, infectious diseases, and some parasitic diseases) often did not leave detectable evidence on skeletal remains and must be inferred from other data. E. Wing and A. Brown make another point when discussing nutritional diseases. They say:

> Although examination of human skeletal remains can suggest *patterns* of nutritional disease, the limitations on the use of human skeletal material are great. The nature of nutritional diseases within a population cannot be deduced from one or two skeletons. Individuals may manifest nutritional diseases because of uniquely high nutrient requirements, disease states unrelated to dietary intakes, or malabsorption syndromes. (Wing and Brown 1979:73)

Anomalies in the skeletal materials, therefore, could be the result of a number of different or interrelated health problems, and some diseases will leave no evidence in the skeleton (Corruccini *et al.* 1982; Gibbs *et al.* 1980: Wing and Brown 1979).

Skeletal remains are often the only basis for establishing one important indicator of nutritional stress: demographic variables. T. Gibbs and his colleagues (1980) survey historical information on demography from census information. Such data do not necessarily cover all socioeconomic segments of the society. Archaeologically derived materials, however, frequently are limited due to inadequate reporting and recovery of subadult individuals. Often historical records and cemetery materials are not congruent. For example, historical demographic information indicated a lower life expectancy and higher infant mortality than would have been deduced from the archaeological materials recovered from slave burials on Barbados, West Indies (Corruccini *et al.* 1982). It is important to consider systemic relationships among biocultural systems affecting human groups (Hassan 1979).

If sufficiently large samples are obtained, life tables can be generated that indicate age-specific biocultural influences. Using documentary and skeletal evidence, Angel (1976) found that the average age at death of individuals over 15 years during the Colonial-to-Civil War periods was higher for white males than females, but that black females died somewhat later than black males. Although the sample size is very small, Rathbun and Scurry (1983) found that the average age at death of blacks at the Belleview colonial plantation in South Carolina was above that of whites and that white females lived longer than males using archaeological evidence. At Clifts Plantation in Virginia (Aufderheide *et al.* 1981), archaeological evidence indicates that females of both groups lived longer than males. Workers of both sexes on this plantation died slightly earlier than the elite residents. The average age at death for most adults during the plantation system, as indicated by skeletal data, was during the fourth decade of life. When sufficient data are available, age-specific mortality may indicate the effect of nutritional deficiency on the pattern of mortality.

Mortality can often be directly associated with general patterns of pathology in a population. Dietary deficiencies, infection, and parasitism are usually linked in synergistic ways. The availability of iron from the diet is especially important. Iron deficiency is frequently expressed in the skeleton by porotic hyperostosis. The problem of differentiating evidence of nutritional iron deficiency anemia from the genetic anemias (such as sickle-cell and thalessemia) in skeletal remains restricts the type of interpretations that can be made. Historical sources suggest that many of the foods issued to slaves were poor in iron. Due to a heavy reliance on cornmeal, the slave population may have faced nutritional problems similar to those of prehistoric Indian groups who relied heavily on maize as a dietary staple. By supplementing their diet with their own livestock and wild resources, slaves modified the effects of this potential dietary deficiency. Isolation of specific dietary deficiencies such as iron deficiency is difficult to ascertain, however, because malnutrition generally derives from multiple nutrient deficiencies and a high infective load may precipitate nutritional deficiency in a population.

Localized as well as generalized infective patterns are frequently seen in skeletal materials. An epidemiological approach that considers the pathogens in the area, the relative resistance of the human host, and cultural factors for buffering the effects of the infection must be adopted. Historical sources indicate a wide range of infections during the plantation period, but not all of these will be indicated in the skeleton. In fact, skeletal evidence is usually seen only when the host has sufficient immunities to survive long enough for skeletal reactions to occur; epidemic episodes resulting in immediate death will probably not be reflected in skeletal tissue. Although the specific infective organism may not be diagnosed from the skeleton, skeletal responses are detectable. For these, the pattern and degree of the infective load can be estimated. Preliminary analysis of skeletal indicators of infection of colonial groups revealed that black and white males had a higher frequency of infections than the females, but that differences between slaves and planters were minimal (Rathbun and Scurry 1983).

Parasitism was a ubiquitous problem in the Southeast. The historical documentation of these parasites include hookworm and other intestinal worms. The presence of hookworm in South Carolina has been documented from prehistoric coprolites (Rathbun, Sexton, and Michie 1980). The dietary malabsorption problems and systematic drain from parasite infestation are well known. Bacillary and amoebic infections also probably contributed to the death rate through diarrhea and dysentery for both elite and slave groups.

The value of adult stature as an indicator of nutritional states remains unclear. Angel (1976) illustrated that increases in stature from colonial to modern times should not be assumed to be either a steady or a large increase. Higman (1979) analyzed slave stature and growth in the Caribbean from historic sources and Politzer (1958) studied stature among the descendants of slaves in the Charleston, South Carolina area. Blakely and Beck (1982) also provide data from early nineteenth-century groups in Atlanta. No specific trends in stature change were apparent in comparisons of plantation groups in the colonial period (Rathbun and Scurry 1983).

Interruption of normal growth from either disease or periodic nutritional inadequacies is reflected in the long bones of the skeleton and the teeth. Radiographic examination of the long bones often reveals the existence of transverse lines. These lines are formed during the recovery phase of interrupted metabolic development. In conjunction with other indicators, the frequency and age of occurrence of these growth interruptions may be attributed to periods of inadequate diet or disease episodes. Few skeletons from plantation contexts have been examined radiographically. Rathbun and Scurry (1983) found that white males at Belleview Plantation had an average of 4.5 lines and the females had an average of 2.5 lines. The single black male examined had 7 lines and the black female only 1. (Males are typically more susceptible to metabolic insult.) The multiple occurrence of these "Harris" lines generally coincided with dental defects also associated with developmental interruption. It is probable that these metabolic insults were from disease and periodic parasite infestations rather than from periods of near starvation.

Dental defects of the enamel with linear hypoplasia was extremely common among Barbados slave groups (Corruccini *et al.* 1982) These dental anomalies were interpreted as reflecting a poor nutritional episode, especially associated with weaning at 3 to 4 years of age. In American groups these lines are also frequent but are found in both slave and elite groups. At Clifts Plantation in Virginia, 6 of 15 individuals exhibited at least 1 line and at Belleview teeth from elite skeletons had an average of 2.8 lines. Planter females were less frequently affected than males and the lines were less severe. Line formation peaked at approximately 3 to 4 years of age and may be attributed to the synergistic effects of parasites and fevers rather than to nutritional inadequacy alone.

Tooth loss and especially dental caries can be associated with nutrition and the subsistence base. Tooth loss, which may have resulted from trauma as well as alveolar disease, was very high among the Barbados slave groups (Corruccini *et al.* 1982). Comparisons of dentition from small samples of planters and slaves suggest that the elite had a higher rate of tooth loss than the slaves. The differential frequency in these two groups may reflect differences in subsistence and the amount of carbohydrates and sugars available. Carious lesions of the crown and interproximal areas are relatively common in both groups, but are less frequent than among American descendants of both groups.

Analysis of the amount of lead in human bone has been applied to plantation samples. Aufderheide *et al.* (1981) and Rathbun and Scurry (1985) documented a difference between the status groups at two plantations. At both sites the elite groups had significantly higher levels of lead in the bone. Food and drink preparation is suggested as the source for elevated levels of lead among the elite. An analysis of regional differences in lead burdens (Rathbun and Scurry 1985) revealed that Middle Atlantic white groups had a slightly higher lead burden than those of the Southeast. While no differences of lead levels associated with gender were detected among the white groups, within the black sample females had significantly higher levels than did males.

One key to the determination of slave food procurement behavior is an attempt to understand the adaptive behavior of the slave family to different natural environments and plantation systems. Such analysis involves studies of childhood eating habits. These determine the nutrients the child receives, and thus the bone growth and disease states (Kiple and Kiple 1977). While it is not always possible to determine nutritional status through studies of bone growth or remodeling, general overall nutritional status information can be inferred when data on eating habits are also studied. Many anthropologists believe that the most useful data about nutritional status will not be found in a single study of adult bone remains (Corruccini *et al.* 1982); the most useful information, they believe, will come from studies of the younger population, using many individuals, in combination with data on the availability of food. It is this kind of analysis which demonstrates that while coastal slaves suffered from a number of diseases and illnesses, most were not directly related to the amount or kinds of food they ate (Gibbs *et al.* 1980). It is possible that where slaves lived in areas with few wild resources and small weekly ration allotments, diseases of a nutritional origin were rampant and will be evidenced in their skeletal remains.

There is little archaeological evidence to indicate widespread nutritional deficiency syndromes among slaves who inhabited coastal regions. Many of the health problems that indicate the presence of a nutritional deficiency can also be the end result of a number of nonnutritionally related pathogens. The interaction between poor nutrition, disease, and sometimes death is well documented. K. Kiple and V. Kiple (1977) write that malnutrition was more prevalent in the younger population than among adults. Further, they point to the high infant and child mortality rate and blame it on the problems associated with malnutrition and the synergism between undernutrition and disease. Parasitism also contributed to high mortality rates. Data from Charleston, South Carolina, averaged over the years from 1822 to 1848 show a mean mortality rate of 19.4/100 per year for black infants, compared to 9.2/100 per year for white infants (computed based on Waring 1967). Both E. Wing and A. Brown (1979) and R. Huss-Ashmore *et al.* (1982) have indicated that evidence of nutritional stress can best be seen in children.

Adult slaves seemed to die more often from tuberculosis, respiratory diseases, nervous system disorders, diarrhea, old age, and cholera (Savitt 1978). While it is possible that poor nutrition could complicate any one of the above diseases or disorders, it cannot be stated that undernutrition or malnutrition was the ultimate cause of death. In the adult population, it would be extremely difficult to detect an underlying nutritional problem as a cause of death, but the problems of bone growth and bone disease can be easily detected in juveniles and young adults. The lack of protein, minerals, and vitamins can sometimes be detected in bone through appropriate osteological techniques (Huss-Ashmore *et al.* 1982). The only study available in which slave skeletons were examined for nutritional stress indicates that there were no major differences in skeletons of high-and low-status groups (Rathbun and Scurry 1985).

SLAVE SUBSISTENCE STRATEGIES

Data from the sites surveyed in this Chapter point to the widespread use of wild foods by the slave populations on plantations of various sizes throughout the sea islands, as well as in other environmental zones. These data confirm the belief of some historians, archaeologists, and cultural anthropologists that slaves did not passively accept their allotment of food, but actively sought to ensure that other food items were available. Evidence from coastal/estuarine plantations indicates that planters, slaves, and freedmen all used wild resources extensively. The evidence that wild plants, invertebrates, terrestrial and aquatic mammals, freshwater and marine fishes, terrestrial, aquatic, and marine turtles, and birds were used illustrates the fact that slaves exploited many environmental niches with a variety of technological methods. The task system—used to guide the daily activities of slaves on the plantations along the South Carolina, Georgia, and Florida coastal regions—afforded slaves the opportunity to hunt, trap, and fish (Morgan 1982). While planters may have obtained their wild resources through the efforts of slaves, Otto's interpretation of the Cannon's Point data was that slaves and overseers were probably responsible in large part for supplementing their domestic rations through their own efforts although slaves used fewer wild resources than did planters and overseers. The Parland data suggest that former slaves may have increased their use of wild mammals after emancipation.

In narratives given during the 1920s and 1930s, former slaves indicated that they exploited nondomestic food resources (Blassingame 1977; Yetman 1970). The extent to which this was done, however, is not reflected in these documents. Slaves living on estuarine plantations were able to supplement their food allotments in a year-round basis through gathering, hunting, and fishing in the rich estuarine environment and through raising crops, pigs, cows, and chickens. It is estimated that reptiles, wild birds, wild mammals, shellfish, and fish may have contributed as much as 40% of the meat in the slave diet (Ascher and Fairbanks 1971; Fairbanks 1972; McFarlane 1975; Singleton 1980). Based upon the Minimum Numbers of Individuals (MNI) calculated for collections from estuarine plantations, between 69% and 87% of the individuals used by slaves were wild taxa. For overseers and planters between 63% and 91% of the individuals were wild taxa. The animals that the former slaves said they hunted included wild mammals, wild birds, reptiles, amphibians, and fish. Most noteworthy among these were deer, opossum, rabbit, raccoon, alligator, and turtle. These animals have also been identified in the faunal collections from coastal plantations. However, the range of taxa slaves on the sea islands exploited was much greater than this. The list is too long to innumerate here, but other important taxa such as crabs, clams, oysters, sea catfish, stingrays, sharks, sea turtles, and mullets have also been found archaeologically. Although less adequately documented, a variety of wild plants were also consumed.

The fact that most of the information presented here represents coastal areas does not mean that slaves living in the interior plantations were incapable of pursuing wild game. While it is possible that under the gang system practiced on interior plantations slaves may have had fewer opportunities to personally exploit their surroundings for additional food, the limited data cited here indicate that slaves on interior plantations also had access to wild resources either through their own efforts or as rations. Further studies on these plantations will have to be conducted so that more conclusive evidence can be presented.

Many of the resources of the estuarine setting could easily be captured with minimal expenditure of effort or time. Many of the mammals are garden or barnyard raiders and could have been captured by nets or traps as part of the farming chores. Others are nocturnal scavengers best caught by traps. Most of the fish and turtles could be captured using traps, nets, basketry scoops, or trot lines set in tidal creeks and tended during nonwork hours. It is not possible to tell from the species identified, however, whether each individual slave or family unit was responsible for the subsistence effort or whether the wild foods were captured by slave specialists and issued as rations. Many of these same techniques would be appropriate for capturing species on the coastal plain as well as in the uplands, although the number of fish taxa available for use are substantially reduced once the estuarine environment is left behind.

Data from nonestuarine sites are rare. Information from the early tidewater sites of Pettus and Utopia indicates heavy use of domestic resources by planters and tenants alike. Analyses of faunal samples from Bray's well, the Hermitage, and Millwood, however, indicate that wild resources were heavily used by both slaves and masters even at some interior sites. An interesting aspect of the Bray and Hermitage faunal collections is the absence of deer at all three while wild fauna contributed over 60% of the individuals. The bulk of the wild animals at these sites are small mammals and wild birds. The use of wild birds in particular suggests more active hunting at interior sites than was required to obtain the wild fauna, primarily fish and turtles, found at sites in the lower reaches of the estuaries. Perhaps designated hunters actually provisioned these mainland sites while slaves in estuarine settings took advantage of the time made available by the task system to hunt and fish for themselves.

While archaeological techniques demonstrate that particular plants and animals were eaten, without more research the quantity, quality, and adequacy of food consumed by each biological and cultural group can only be estimated. Additional research should include analyzing human skeletal remains for stable isotopes and trace elements (Chisholm *et al.* 1973; Gilbert 1977). Archaeologists have been able to clearly illustrate that the slave diet of cornmeal, pork, and beef was supplemented by other foods. Many of the nutrients not available in the slave diet as traditionally understood from documentary sources were probably supplied by wild plants and animals and from the slaves' gardens and livestock. Without the chance to supplement their rations with other foods, many slaves would have surely died from diseases that are exaggerated by undernourishment. However, we do not know from the species identified just how satisfactorily slave rations were supplemented by these measures.

The measurement of the nutritional adequacy of the slave diet has been a source of great contention. This is so partly because the adult male has been used as the standard for estimating caloric requirements (Fogel and Engerman 1974; Genovese 1974; Gibbs *et al.* 1980; Sutch 1976). In fact, in many instances the protein and calcium needs of children and pregnant or lactating women exceed those of adult males. Even for an adult male the documented core diet may not have been adequate. It is difficult to estimate the nutritional requirements of slaves given that nutritional requirements are based upon age, sex, health, the amount of work performed, as well as environmental variables such as humidity and temperatures. The quantity of nutrients contained in the core diet is also difficult to determine without knowing exactly what that diet contained. The caloric intake from the core diet of slaves has been estimated at 2348 (Savitt 1978) or 2392 calories (Gibbs *et al.* 1980). This would not have been enough to supply the appropriate nutrients for an adult male if it is correct that such an individual expended over 6000 calories per day while performing moderate work (Gibbs *et al.* 1980).

Another problem with determining nutritional adequacy is that we do not know enough about slave health, particularly about diseases related to nutrition. The presence or absence of nutritionally related diseases is difficult to study because of the problem of access to slave skeletal material on which to perform appropriate tests. While there have been some examinations of slave remains, the number of individuals examined is very small (Corruccini *et al.* 1982). Therefore, much of the data about disease comes from inferences made about slave health based on death records, and from surviving plantation medical records that are generally not sufficiently detailed to provide the types of quantifiable data being sought. Furthermore, the diseases related to nutritional deficiencies are extremely difficult to detect in adults (Wing and Brown 1979). Nutritional studies will be greatly enhanced by studies done on the remains of children (Huss-Ashmore 1982). It appears that slave children suffered from many nutritionally related diseases along with other problems associated with poor nutrition and growth. This indicates that malnourishment was rampant in many places (Kiple and Kiple 1977). The skeletal evidence, however, indicates that these problems were not necessarily universal. In order to learn more about slave life from this source of information, it is necessary to demonstrate to the public at large the importance of such studies for a more accurate understanding of plantation systems and slavery.

Other important factors in slave nutrition were the resources available to them for storing, preparing, and cooking food. The chance for nutrient loss was great given the simple methods used for processing, cooking, and preserving foods during the period of slavery. Archaeological evidence indicates that slaves had few storage facilities or cooking vessels compared to those of the plantation master and the overseer (Beaudry *et al.* 1983). Slaves lacked long-term storage facilities and relied heavily on salted or smoked meats, or freshly killed animals cooked within a short period of time after death. Highly smoked and salted meats added very few essential nutrients to the slave diet while increasing their intake of sodium chloride and nitrates. At best, slaves had the use of only a kettle, frying pan, cast iron pot, pails, and possibly a saucepan. While iron absorbed from the iron pots might have increased this mineral in the slave diet, those foods cooked in the form of stews and soups lost vitamins with repeated warming and reheating.

Archaeologists do know from the evidence that slaves supplemented their diet with home-grown livestock and wild foods and that the practice appears to have been widespread. Further, evidence from estuarine plantations demonstrates a wider variety of wild animals used there than at plantations located outside of the estuarine system. This may be due to the variety found in the environment and to the prevalence of the task system on sea island plantations. Beef was apparently at least as frequently used in the diet as pork. Human skeletal evidence suggests that rampant malnutrition was not necessarily always experienced by slaves and that slaves were not necessarily less well nourished than whites. However, many of the cases reviewed in this Chapter suffered from small sample sizes, inappropriate recovery methods, incomplete or incomparable analysis, uncertain identification of socioeconomic affiliation, or other problems. Further work is needed on all aspects of plantation subsistence in order to better assess the reliability of the data summarized here.

ACKNOWLEDGMENTS

The authors wish to acknowledge the assistance of the following people in the preparation of this manuscript: Sue Mullins Moore, Theresa A. Singleton, Samuel D. Smith, Charles E. Orser, Martha Zierden, Robin L. Smith, Lesley M. Drucker, John E. Ehrenhard, R. Christopher Goodwin, Karl T. Steinen, Henry M. Miller, Chad O. Braley, and Stephen Kowalewski. We also gratefully acknowledge our debt to Dr. Charles H. Fairbanks, who initiated our research into plantation archaeology with his excavations at Kingsley and Rayfield plantations.

REFERENCES

Angel, J. Lawrence
1976 Colonial to modern skeletal change in the U.S.A. *American Journal of Physical Anthropology* 45(3):723–735.

Armelagos, George J., Alan Goodman, and S. Bickerton
1980 Determining nutritional and infectious disease stress in prehistoric populations (abstract). *American Journal of Anthropology* 52:201.

Armelagos, George J., Alan Goodman, and Kenneth Jacobs
1978 The ecological perspective in disease. In *Health and the Human Condition.* M. Logan and E. Hunt, eds. North Scituate, Mass: Duxbury Press. Pp. 71–84.

Ascher, Robert, and Charles H. Fairbanks
1971 Excavations of a slave cabin: Georgia, U.S.A. *Historical Archaeology* 5:3–17.

Aufderheide, Arthur C., F. D. Neiman, L. E. Whittmers, G. Rapp
1981 Lead in bone II: skeletal lead content as an indicator of lifetime lead ingestion and the social correlates in an archaeological population. *American Journal of Physical Anthropology* 55:285–291.

Barber, Michael
1976 The vertebrate fauna from a late eighteenth century well: the Bray Plantation, Kingsmill, Virginia. *Historical Archaeology* 10:68—72.

Beaudry, Mary C., Janet Long, Henry M. Miller, Fraser D. Neiman, and Garry Wheeler Stone
1983 A vessel typology for early Chesapeake ceramics: the Potomac typology system. *Historical Archaeology* 17(1):18–43.

Blakely, Robert L., and Lane A. Beck
1982 Bioarchaeology in the urban context. In *Archaeology of Urban America.* Roy S. Dickens, Jr., ed. New York: Academic Press. Pp. 175–207.

Blassingame, John
1977 *Slave Testimony.* Baton Rouge: Louisiana State University Press.

Bradley, James T.
1978 Climates of the states: Florida. In *Climates of the States.* J. A. Ruffner, ed. Detroit: Gale Research. Pp. 211–242.

Briggs, John C.
1974 *Marine Zoogeography.* New York: McGraw-Hill.

Buikstra, Jane E., and Della C. Cook
1980 Paleopathology: an American account. *Annual Reviews in Anthropology* 9:433–70.

Cade, J. B.
1935 Out of the mouths of ex-slaves. *Journal of Negro History* 20:294–337.

Carter, Horace S.
1978 Climates of the states: Georgia. In *Climates of the States.* J. A. Ruffner, ed. Detroit: Gale Research. Pp. 244–265.

Casteel, Richard W.
1977 Characterization of faunal assemblages and the minimum number of individuals determined

from paired elements: continuing problems in archaeology. *Journal of Archaeological Science* 4(2):125–134.

Chisholm, B. S., E. R. Nelson, and H. P. Schwarca
1973 Marine and terrestrial protein in prehistoric diets on the British Columbia coast. *Current Anthropology* 24(3):396–398.

Cook, Della C.
1979 Subsistence base and health in prehistoric Illinois Valley: evidence from the human skeleton. *Medical Anthropology* 4:109–124.

Corruccini, Robert, Jerome S. Handler, Robert J. Mutaw, and Frederick W. Lange
1982 Osteology of a slave burial population from Barbados, West Indies. *American Journal of Physical Anthropology* 59(4):443–459.

Drucker, Lesley M.
1981 Socioeconomic patterning at an undocumented late 18th century lowcountry site: Spiers Landing, South Carolina. *Historical Archaeology* 15(2):58–68.

Ehrenhard, John E., and Mary R. Bullard
1981 Stafford Plantation, Cumberland Island National Seashore, Georgia: archaeological investigations of a slave cabin. Tallahassee: Southeast Archaeological Center, National Park Service.

Ekman, Sven
1953 *Zoogeography of the Sea.* London: Sidgwick and Jackson.

Fairbanks, Charles H.
1974 The Kingsley slave cabins in Duval County, Florida, 1968. *Conference on Historic Sites Archaeology Papers* 7:62–93.

Flanders, Ralph B.
1933 *Plantation Slavery in Georgia.* Chapel Hill: University of North Carolina Press.

Fogel, Robert W., and Stanley L. Engerman
1974 *Time on the Cross: The Economics of American Negro Slavery.* Vol. 1. Boston: Little, Brown.

Genovese, E. D.
1974 *Roll, Jordon, Roll: The World the Slaves Made.* New York: Random House.

Gibbons, J. Whitfield, and John W. Coker
1978 Herpetofaunal colonization patterns of Atlantic coast barrier islands. *American Midland Naturalist* 99(1):219–233.

Gibbs, Tyson, Kathleen Cargill, Leslie Sue Lieberman, and Elizabeth J. Reitz
1980 Nutrition in a slave population: an anthropological examination. *Medical Anthropology* 4:175–262.

Gilbert, Robert I.
1977 Application of trace element research to problems in archaeology. *Southern Anthropological Society Proceedings* 11:85–100.

Goodwin, R. Christopher, Jill-Karen Yakubik, Cyd H. Goodwin
1983 The historic archaeology of Elmwood Plantation. Submitted to Department of Culture, Recreation, and Tourism of Louisiana, Baton Rouge.

Gray, Lewis C.
1933 *History of Agriculture in the Southern United States to 1960.* Washington, D.C.: Carnegie Institute.

Grayson, Donald K.
1979 On the quantification of vertebrate archaeofaunas. In *Advances in Archaeological Methods and Theory.* Vol. 2. M. B. Schiffer, ed. New York: Academic Press. Pp. 200–238.

Hassan, Fekri A.
1979 Demography and archaeology. *Annual Review of Anthropology* 8:137–160.

Henderson, Graeme
1980 Indiamen traders of the east. *Archaeology* 33(6):18–25.

Higman, B. W.
1979 Growth in Afro-Caribbean slave populations. *American Journal of Physical Anthropology* 50:373–386.

Hunt, Edward E., Jr.
1978 Ecological frameworks and hypothesis testing in medical anthropology. In *Health and the Human Condition.* M. Logan and E. Hunt, eds. North Scituate, Mass.: Duxbury Press. Pp. 84–100.

Huss-Ashmore, Rebecca, Alan H. Goodman, and George J. Armelagos
1982 Nutritional reference from paleopathology. In *Advances in Archaeological Method and Theory.* Vol. 5. M. B. Schiffer, ed. New York: Academic Press. Pp. 395–474.

Johnson, A. S., H. S. Hillestad, S. F. Shanholtzer, and G. G. Shanholtzer
1974 An ecological survey of the coastal region of Georgia. Scientific Monograph Series 3. Washington, D.C.: National Park Service.

Johnson, Guion G.
1930 *A Social History of the Sea Islands.* Chapel Hill: University of North Carolina Press.

Johnson, Robert E.
1978 Archaeological excavations of 9Cam167 and 9Cam173 at Kings Bay, Camden County, Georgia. Report for the Department of the Navy. Department of Anthropology, University of Florida. Unpublished manuscript.

Katz, W. L., ed.
1968 *The American Negro—His History and Literature—Five Slave Narrations.* New York: Arno Press.

Kemble, Fanny A.
1961 *Journal of a Residence on a Georgian Plantation in 1838–1839.* John Schott, ed. New York: Knopf.

Kiple, K. F., and V. H. Kiple
1977 Slave child mortality: some nutritional answers to a perennial puzzle. *Journal of Social History* 10:284–309.

Landers, H.
1978 Climates of the states: South Carolina. In *Climates of the States.* J. A. Ruffner, ed. Detroit: Gale Research. Pp. 873–891.

McFarlane, Suzanne S.
1975 The ethnoarchaeology of a slave community: the Couper Plantation site. Master's thesis, Department of Anthropology, University of Florida, Gainesville.

Miller, Henry M.
1979 Pettus and Utopia: a comparison of the faunal remains from two late seventeenth century Virginia households. *Conference on Historic Sites Archaeology Papers* 13:158–179.

Moore, Sue Mullins
1981 The antebellum barrier island plantation: in search of an archaeological pattern. Ph.D. dissertation, Department of Anthropology, University of Florida, Gainesville.

Morgan, Phillip D.
1982 Work and culture: the task system and the world of low country blacks 1700–1880. *William and Mary Quarterly* 39 (Series 3) 4:563–599.

Olmsted, F. L.
1956 *Journey in the Seaboard Slave States: With Remarks on Their Economy.* New York: Dix and Edwards

Orser, Charles E., Jr., Annette M. Nekola, and James L. Roark
1982 Exploring the rustic life: multidisciplinary research at Millwood Plantation, a large plantation in Abbeville County, Georgia. Submitted to the Archaeological Services Division, National Park Services, Atlanta.

Ortner, Donald J., and Walter G. Putschar
1981 Identification of pathological conditions in human skeletal remains. Contributions to Anthropology, No. 28. Washington, D.C.: Smithsonian.

Otto, John Solomon
1975 Status differences and the archaeological record—A comparison of the planter, overseer, and slave sites from Cannon's Point Plantation, (1794–1861), St. Simon's Island, Georgia. Ph.D. dissertation, Department of Anthropology, University of Florida, Gainesville.

Pollitzer, William S.
1958 The Negros of Charleston (S.C.): a study of hemoglobin types, serology, and morphology. *American Journal of Physical Anthropology* 16:241–263.

Poplin, Francois
1982 Le probleme de la conservation et du transport des viandes dans le passe: la contribution des epaves de navires. Paper presented at the Fourth International Council for Archaeozoology, London.

Rathbun, Ted A.
1981 Human remains as an archaeological resource. *South Carolina Antiquities* 13(1 and 2):17–39.

Rathbun, Ted A., and James D. Scurry
1983 Status and health in colonial South Carolina: Belleview Plantation, 1738–1756. Paper presented at the 52nd Annual Meeting of the American Association of Physical Anthropologists, Indianapolis.
1985 Status and health in colonial South Carolina: Belleview Plantation, 1738–1756. In *Skeletal Analysis and the Effects of Socioeconomic Status on Health*. D. Martin, ed. Research Report No. 25. Amherst: Department of Anthropology, University of Massachusetts, in press.

Rathbun, Ted A., Jim Sexton, and James Michie
1980 Disease patterns in a formative period South Carolina coastal population. *Tennessee Anthropological Association Miscellaneous Paper,* No. 5 Pp. 52–74.

Reitz, Elizabeth J.
1978a Faunal remains from a coastal Georgia plantation (KBS-12), with reference to KBS-8. *In* Archaeological Excavation of 9Cam167 and 9Cam173 at Kings Bay, Camden County, Georgia. R. Johnson, ed. Appendix B. Report for the Department of the Navy. Department of Anthropology, University of Florida. Unpublished manuscript. Pp. 116–151.
1978b Report on the faunal material excavated from Colonel's Island, Georgia. *In* Cultural Evolution and Environment of Colonel's Island, Georgia. K. Steinen, ed. Carrollton, Georgia: Department of Sociology and Anthropology, West Georgia College. Unpublishd manuscript. Pp. 135–162.
1983 Vertebrate fauna from Elmwood Plantation, Jefferson Parish, Louisiana. Zooarchaeology Laboratory, Department of Anthropology, University of Georgia. Unpublished manuscript.

Savitt, T. L.
1978 *Medicine and Slavery: The Disease and Health Care of Blacks in Antebellum Virginia.* Urbana, Ill. University of Illinois Press.

Schmid, Elizabeth
1982 Two Archaeological Miscellanies. Paper presented at the Fourth International Council for Zooarchaeology, London.

Singleton, Theresa Ann
1978 Report on the historic excavations, Colonel's Island, Glynn County, Georgia. *In* The Cultural Evolution and Environment of Colonel's Island, Georgia. K. Steinen, ed. Carrollton, Georgia: Department of Sociology and Anthropology, West Georgia College. Unpublished manuscript. Pp. 70–133.
1980 The archaeology of Afro-American slavery in coastal Georgia: a regional perception of slave household and community patterns. Ph.D. dissertation, Department of Anthropology, University of Florida, Gainesville.

Singleton, Theresa, and Tyson Gibbs
1983 Archaeology of slave sites: nutrition and diet. *Journal of Negro History* (in press).

Smith, Robin L., C. O. Braley, N. T. Borremans, E. J. Reitz
1981 Coastal adaptations in southeast Georgia: ten archaeological sites at King's Bay. Department of Anthropology. University of Florida, Gainesville. Unpublished manuscript.
Smith, Samuel D., ed.
1976 An archaeological and historical assessment of the First Hermitage. Division of Archaeology, Tennessee Department of Conservation Research Series No. 2.
Smith, Samuel D., F. W. Brigance, E. Breitburg, S. D. Cox, and M. Martin
1977 Results of the 1976 season of the Hermitage archaeology project. Nashville: Tennessee Division of Archaeology. Unpublished manuscript.
Steinen, Karl T., ed.
1978 The cultural evolution and environment of Colonel's Island, Georgia. Department of Sociology and Anthropology, West Georgia College, Carrollton, Georgia. Unpublished manuscript.
Sutch, R.
1976 The care and feeding of slaves. In *Reckoning with Slavery*. P. A. David, ed. New York: Oxford Press. Pp. 231–301.
Thomas, David Hurst, S. South, and C. S. Larsen
1977 Rich man, poor men: observation on three antebellum burials from the Georgia coast. *Anthropological Papers of the American Museum of Natural History* 54:395–420.
United States Department of Agriculture, Weather Bureau
1930a Climate summary of the United States: Section 103—central and eastern Georgia.
1930b Climate summary of the United States: section 104—northern Florida.
Waring, J. J.
1967 *History of Medicine in South Carolina, 1825–1900*. Charleston: South Carolina Medical Association.
Wijngaarden-Bakker, Louis H. Van
1982 Faunal analysis and historical record. Paper presented at the Fourth International Council for Archaeozoology, London.
Wilson, John P., and Linda D. Southwood
1976 Fort George on the Niagara: an anthropological perspective. *Parks Canada History and Archaeology* 9.
Wing, Elizabeth S., and Antoinette Brown
1979 *Paleonutrition: Method and Theory in Prehistoric Foodways*. New York: Academic Press.
Yetman, Norman, ed.
1970 *Voices from Slavery*. New York: Holt, Rinehart, and Winston.
Zierden, Martha, and Jeanne Calhoun
1983 *An Archaeological Assessment of the Greenfield Barrow Pit, Georgetown County*. Charleston: The Charleston Museum.

PART V

Afro-American Traditions

9

The African-American Tradition in Vernacular Architecture

Steven L. Jones

INTRODUCTION

Usually when one thinks of "architecture" the first impression that comes to mind is the contained space of some kind of structure. On the vernacular or folk idiom level, this impression would imply defining research concerns in terms of the house unit. Instead, what is needed is a concern for relationships—of the parts of any structure to the whole, of the structure to its corollary structures in a functional complex (such as the farmstead), and the cultural tie-in of all these parts.

In America, vernacular architecture research, the stepchild of geography and folklife studies, has been defined by some scholars solely in terms of monolithic cultural forces. Instead, this architecture should be seen as the product of a kaleidoscopic diffusion of influences that are manifested in various manners. When it comes to the African impact on American culture, this diffusion has been offered at times in terms of plan, spatial definition, materials used, and form.

Some of the African analogies used in this essay are derived from my own fieldwork in Africa in 1969 and 1970. Although there are problems with using contemporary African culture to trace the origins of African-American culture traditions, this approach appears to be warranted in the interpretation of African-American vernacular architectural patterns under discussion here. The persistent presence of traditional Central and West African elements in terms of plan, spatial distribution, materials, and form in New World architectural patterns from the seventeenth to the nineteenth centuries suggests indeed that the origin of these patterns is African.

Afro-American vernacular architecture is defined for present purposes as the instances of building and environmental design in the United States at a particular time when Africans, either directly or indirectly, had an influence on the manipulation of space. Central to any analysis in this area is the recognition of the interactional

ISBN 0-12-646480-4

mechanisms and the cultural and socioeconomic context in which individuals as a culture group were operating.

In America persons of African descent, acting essentially as captives until after the middle of the nineteenth century, were severely limited in the parameters within which self-expression and personal traditions were elaborated (Driskell 1976:30). As such, surviving examples of structures that drew upon the African past should be seen as exemplary symbols that are likely to represent far more extensive attempts at self-expression, which were summarily preempted. The attempt of a black man named Okra to build in such a manner is vividly recalled in the 1930s by residents of St. Simons Island, Georgia: "Ole man Okra he say he wahn a place lak he hab in Africa so he buil im a hut . . . . But Massuh make im pull it down. He say he ain wahn no African hut on he place" (Georgia Writers' Project 1940:179). Numerous blacks remembered the building traditions of Africa through relatives and friends who "use tuh talk . . bout weah he come frum" (Georgia Writers' Project 1940:188).

Historically, blacks were the predominate craftsmen of the American South and represented 80% of the antebellum skilled labor of that region (Peniston 1978:284). They were widely skilled artisans, as Booker T. Washington, the preeminent spokesman for black craftsmen at the turn of the twentieth century, is quoted many times as saying:

> If a southern white man wanted a house or a bridge built, he consulted a negro mechanic about the plan and the actual building of the house or bridge . . . every large plantation in the South was, in a limited way, an industrial school. On these plantations, there were scores of young colored men and women who were constantly being trained, not only as common farmers, but as carpenters, blacksmiths, wheelwrights, plasterers, brickmasons, engineers, bridge-builders, cooks, dressmakers, housekeepers, etc. (Bratton 1922:105).

A primary hindrance to blacks infusing more of their traditions into the built environment seems to have been the lack of opportunity. Ultimately, opportunity of expression becomes a question of the application of power.

To what degree did the Europeans see the physical expression of the African presence in America as a threat to their continued control? Certainly in areas like music and dance, open expressions of African tradition were at times severely circumscribed (Blassingame 1972:29). Initially, the slave owner mentality seems to have been one of wondering how best to control the slaves, and whatever seemed to work was given a try. Thomas Coram's late eighteenth-century miniature portrait of Mulberry Plantation (just outside Charleston, South Carolina) shows an axially situated owner's main house fronting two parallel rows of high-pitched roof slave quarters. J. D. B. DeBow, in his *DeBow's Review*, which was commonly read by plantation masters, admonished owners to build their "big houses and quarters" using this hierarchical arrangement because slaves seemed to be controlled better with this plan (also see Skipper 1958). Memories passed down through the Black community reflected the symbolic power significance of such an arrangement. It was remembered that in Africa "they live in 'boo-boo-no' . . . (and) they buil a big 'boo-boo-no' fuh the chief" (Georgia 1940:188). Thus orally transmitted images like the one of a "Bamileké (Cameroun) chefferie," with its great house at the end of a street flanked by women's houses (Spini 1974:72), would have served to help subjugate an already captive population. In both the Mulberry and Bamileké cases, the location of the large unit is used to reinforce the power position identified with that unit.

Laterally symmetrical layouts were not unfamiliar in Europe; however, what is significant is that this is a commonly shared tradition familiar to West Africans. For the Africans at Mulberry, their tradition is abused and used in a way not unknown to the holder of power because of the European tradition (see Anthony 1976). Thus, the masters used a familiar architectural solution to aid them with a difficult problem—control and dominance of the slaves. It is doubtful that slave owners were familiar with the African prototypes or even considered themselves as reinforcing an African design form. They were simply responding to their own needs within the context of the cultural imperatives in which the African slaves operated. For the owners the source of the control mechanism was irrelevant. So both Europeans and Africans in America are caught up in and affected by the creolization process.

This phenomenon highlights the concept that culture is indeed the context within which architectural/environmental imperatives operate. All parties within a situation of cultural interaction bring a background of cultural "givens" to the situation. No person is cultureless. The relative power of the participants is not the exclusive determinant of which "givens" will predominate. Rather, a complex evolution of combinations of cultural habits—reflecting the relative diversity of the interactants as well as the exigencies of environment—mean that no prediction of historical sequence is automatic. This sharing process is reflected in the thinking of scholars from C. Vann Woodward to Eugene Genovese to George McDaniel (McDaniel 1982:xvi). Therefore the question of source is opened up for the many craft aspects with which Africans, even as slaves, and their descendants were involved. Historically, this includes a range from the decorative ironwork of the coastal ports to the repetitive decorative woodwork of inland buildings. Whether that involvement relates to the direction in which ceiling beams are laid or to the painstakingly wrought delicate details of a huge fireplace, as occurred in 1712 in the Jansen House in the Hudson River Valley, hopefully the discussion began by James Porter with his references to such "clearly African" influences of construction and ornamentation will continue to be expanded and broadened (Porter 1943:19).

In pursuing the emergence and development of an Afro-American vernacular architectural tradition, this essay will examine the following: (1) African influences in land-use development, building materials, and building design, (2) the origins and evolution of the shotgun house in light of new research, and (3) the work of Thomas Day, an architectural interior woodworking designer and cabinetmaker.

LAND-USE DEVELOPMENT

Pursuing the "cultural context" line of thought could provide clarification as to the development of several of the all-Black communities begun in the latter third of the nineteenth century in Kent County on the eastern shore of Maryland (see Sullivan 1978). There, in settlements such as Bigwoods, Melitota, Uptown, and Washington

Park, what started as a number of farm plots nestled together grew, not in boundary expansion, but in housing density. The parameters of the land of these black-owned communities remained stable, but areas were built up more intensively within these plots. The seemingly random character of this development within a fixed space contrasts sharply with the nearby white communities which developed linearly. In the latter communities, houses were added at either end of the existing group along a road with a constantly expanding geographical boundary. In the black settlements, houses generally were not located next to each other originally like those in the white communities, but instead had an area of land surrounding them. And for the most part black people owned their own houses (Sullivan 1978:28). Although an outside observer might reason that this density development on the part of the Black settlements was due to the economics of land costs (McDaniel 1982:190), knowledge of the culture and social interaction of members of the black community is important information. One local black resident named Fred described the present community feeling there like this: "Now colored people, most of them live in bunches. They like to live close together, but not too close. They like to live back in places like this" (Sullivan 1978:16).

A more quickly intensified clustering of units seems to have been the pattern of the residents of the late eighteenth-century Afro-American community of Parting Ways near Plymouth, Massachusetts. For at least four families who lived on a total of 94 acres, the separate rights the government gave each of them to portions of the parcel did not cause them to locate their houses apart with each scattered on its own plot as was the contemporary placement pattern of their Anglo-American neighbors. Instead, these black families grouped their structures together in the center of the entire entire plot, even though the town clerk's map explicitly shows separate portions of the plot cleared by each household head. Archaeologist James Deetz has suggested that beyond mutual reassurance, such a settlement pattern likely reflects a "more corporate spirit" than their Anglo-American contemporaries (Deetz 1977:152); as such the similarity to an African pattern is greatly heightened.

In a broad area of West Africa, one finds communities where the living compound is also defined flexibly with additional structures being added as more people join the unit. The nature of the people of these areas is similarly one of heightened social interaction, with the built environment reflecting that attitude (Jones 1970c). The habitat area "usually expressed physically the social structure of the group of people living in them" (Denyer 1978:19). And the housing pattern reflecting this structure was often a very flexible one, changing year by year with births, deaths, marriages, or whatever condition affected the needs and allocation of space. Clusters of units in a compound would intensify, or sometimes thin out by natural attrition, as the particular demands required. Though the specific character of the West African development might not be exactly the same as that in Maryland or Massachusetts, the general feeling and approach is the same. What is important is that similar attitudes about the relationship with the members of one's community is a significant part of producing a similar land-use development.

BUILDING MATERIALS

As a labor force, African-Americans and their cultural reservoir were used in whatever ways necessary to benefit the slave owner. If the African knowledge pool could be exploited for so significant a development as the introduction of rice cultivation on the southeast coast of the United States (see Wood 1974), so too could it be tapped for the materials to construct the buildings of that area. The Spaniards had used the West African's knowledge of localized building materials in constructing Caribbean fortresses such as El Morro in San Juan, Puerto Rico, as indicated by the records of fortress construction in the Archivo General de Indias in Seville, Spain. The English settlers of the Sea Island coast also used their African-derived labor for a building material called "tabby," a burnt lime-and-seashell aggregate that found diverse application as building material for walls, fences, and roadways. While Lorenzo Turner has traced the morphological origins of the term *tabby* (Turner 1974:202), extant historical sources of tabby usage can be cited from the slave church at St. Helena, South Carolina, to The Slave Hospital at the Retreat Plantation on St. Simons Island, Georgia (see Gritzner 1978). Burnt lime (or sometimes local clay) was used as the mortar while seashells were used as a reinforcing agent for strengthening the hard-dried resulting substance. One large area might be handled as a unit, or tabby might be worked into "bricks" that were then used over a large area. The prototype for this material is found throughout the Guinea Coast region of West Africa, where it also functions for a variety of construction types (Jones 1970a).

Black Americans also occasionally have used local building materials similar to those utilized by their African ancestors. Besides tabby, the prevalent leaves of the palmetto tree were a popular favorite. In the 1930s Rosa Grant of Possum Point (near Darien, Georgia) remembered her grandmother (named Ryna) telling her about domestic architecture in Africa: "She tell me dat in Africa she lib in a palmettuh house" (Georgia 1940:145). During the same period, Shadwick Randolph from near Woodbine, Georgia, remembered that his grandfather (Jim) "come ovuh tuh this country from Africa. He tell me that ovuh theah they have houses made of palmettuh" (Georgia 1940:193). On St. Simons Island, Okra's house, according to Ben Sullivan, had "a flat roof wit he made from bush an palmettuh" (Georgia 1940:179). In Florida in 1830, it is reported that "the dwellings of the slaves were palmetto huts, built by themselves of stakes and poles, thatched with the palmetto leaf" (quoted from Weld's *Slavery As It Is* in DuBois 1908:49).

Descriptions of the clay-plastered wattle-and-daub walls of some of these vernacular structures also reflect African counterparts. Ben Sullivan remembered that Okra built the side walls of his structure "lak basket weave wid clat plastuh on it" (Georgia 1940:145). Henry Williams of St. Marys, Georgia, remembered hearing Daddy Patty, who he thought was an Igbo, talk about the "boo-boo-no" in which he lived in Africa, and how it was "made out uh sticks an straw thas plastuhed with mud" (Georgia 1940:188). This wattle-and-daub wall construction is quite commonly found throughout the Igbo areas of Nigeria (see Aniakor 1978) as well as in houses of African descendants in the Caribbean (see Beckwith 1929:10–13; Peterson 1965:40–41; Vlach 1978:127).

Another example of an African-derived building material is rammed-earth (pisé), which survives in two examples in the James River Valley of Virginia. Both at Bremo and at Four Mile Tree Plantation the slave quarters were constructed using this West African building method (Cohn 1970:270). Although vernacular building materials are directly related to the geography of what is available, important too is the knowledge of the ways to combine and handle those materials for effective usage.

BUILDING DESIGN

The early European landowners in America were particular about the design of their living quarters. They were less particular, though, about overseeing the exact construction details of the out-buildings of their complexes as long as these were harmonious with their overall plan for the main house. In terms of the general form and scale of these dependency structures, most often built by the African slave labor of the plantation, it is no wonder that the results bear striking resemblance to some African forms. Compare the smokehouses of eighteenth-century Williamsburg, Virginia, with the Dogon (Mali) granaries, which are the "out-buildings" of that culture (see Anthony 1976). Many of the dependency structures of the American plantation resemble, in scale size and form, structures that the Africans were familiar with. One such example is the circular Rosewell (Virginia) icehouse, now demolished. In Africa, the round form was found to be best for keeping the inside of the building cool during the hot day. The circular form disperses the sun's rays most evenly over the surface of the building so that the inside remains at the lowest temperature possible. This form has been used as a building type throughout coastal areas of West Africa, and the example from the Guinea Coast rain forest is just one type that shows the antecedents of this particular form (Jones 1970b). In the United States the outbuilding was constructed in wood, brick, or stone by workmen familiar with the ways of manipulating all of these building materials. One can only speculate to what degree this historically fragile building element is an African image on American soil. Robert F. Thompson has shown how such a form could be borrowed from African sources and spread throughout Latin America, especially Mexico (Thompson 1983:197–206).

For the early English landowners the design of their living unit would have been used to reinforce, through close similarity, what they remembered from Europe. It provided them a sense of security in an essentially hostile environment. In the middle of the eighteenth century in Virginia this meant living in a rectilinear structure as opposed to a round one (David G. Orr, personal communication, 1977). But what about the round slave quarters at Keswick Plantation near Midlothian, Virginia (Figure 9.1)? Constructed around 1750, it has been seldom written about within its Afro-American context (an exception is Driskell 1976:28, 32) and is usually misunderstood. The materials used, burnt clay bricks hand-made by the plantation slaves,

Figure 9.1 Keswick Plantation slave quarters, Midlothian, Virginia. (Photograph: by author, 1971.)

are the same as for the Georgian-style owner's house. But in the slave quarters they were ordered in a circular structure with a large, triple-fluted central chimney some 9 feet across at the base. This single living unit—some 25 feet in diameter with a wooden floor laid in a chevron pattern, and having an interior pitch of over 20 feet—was probably the best several families could do for space. Its three fireplaces also aided them in surviving the sometimes cold winters. From marks around the circular wall, there appears to have been an upper gallery with 16 compartments originally, which may have been sleeping areas for children (see Jones 1973b:28–37). The use of this round arrangement is reminiscent of the circular structures of Kasai Province in Zaire, with their central smoke holes for the venting of inside fires (Cohn 1970:270). It is a different place with different building materials, but it utilizes the same form with the same function. In eighteenth-century Virginia only one with an African tradition could have envisioned living in such a space as the Keswick slave quarters.

Another place where African tradition was brought to bear on the physical design of a plantation was in Natchitoches, Louisiana (Jones 1973b:5–21). There, in the late eighteenth century, at what eventually became known as Melrose Plantation, an African-born ex-slave named Marie Therese Coincoin took a virgin tract of land granted to her by the Spanish government and turned it into a thriving enterprise. By

1838, her grandson, Jean Baptiste Louis Metoyer, had built the family fortunes into one of the largest for free blacks in the country, being worth over $100,000 (Dejoie 1975:41). The matriarch of the Metoyer clan originally constructed three principal buildings sometime after 1778, once her expanding operations in timber and indigo had proven fruitful. In a west-to-east line, parallel to but well back from the Cane River, she erected Yucca, the so-called African House (Figure 9.2), and a third building now destroyed. Yucca, her two-story ample residence, was built of heavy hand-hewn cypress beams, uprights, and sleepers. The walls were filled in with moss and mud (from the river bottom) mixed with deer hair. The broad overhanging hipped roof, shadowing each side of the upper floor, was covered with shingles of hand-split cypress. African House is a two-story structure whose first floor is made of bricks baked on the property. The upper story is fashioned of thick hand-hewn cypress slabs. A hand-split cypress shingle-hipped roof also covers the entire upper floor, providing a 39 by 35-foot overhang for the 22½ by 17-foot building beneath it (Figure 9.3). The original purpose of African House remains clouded, and locally it was said to be a slave fort or a provision house. The third structure housed all the plantation gear and a grist mill. It probably compared favorably in size to the first two as it was said to have been the largest barn in the parish. It was constructed exclusively of cypress.

Marie Therese Coincoin, said to have been from "the Congo," possibly fashioned her structures as she or her older relatives remembered their first home. Since she had to direct others in the building process, the use of the materials at hand and

Figure 9.2 African House, Melrose Plantation, Natchitoches, Louisiana. (Photograph: Library of Congress, ca. 1940.)

Figure 9.3 African House, Melrose Plantation, detail of overhang. (Photograph: Library of Congress, ca. 1940.)

Figure 9.4 Traditional Bamileké housing, Cameroun. (Photograph: L'Habitat au Cameroun.)

construction methods familiar to the local builders would have been the most logical approach to this process. But the resulting effect of her efforts recalls a house type represented in several variations throughout Central and West Africa. A photograph from the Fisk University (Tennessee) Department of Art shows eighteenth-century houses in Zaire that correspond accurately to the facade lines of Yucca (Driskell 1975:43). African House is reminiscent of the truncated pyramid roof structures of the Bamileké (Cameroun) in terms of form, scale, and the use of brick construction (Figure 9.4) (Beguin 1952:88). The 1940 view of African House shows what appear to be West African ceramic pots in front of the structure (Robert Thompson, personal communication, 1978). In spite of the number of possible sources for the Natchitoches grouping, they still represent the strong memory of the African panorama. This is the same kind of retention of images that likely inspired the Edgefield, South Carolina, house built by Tahro, a Bakongo enslaved in 1858 (McDaniel 1982:34–37; Montgomery 1908:611–623).

THE SHOTGUN HOUSE

A housing type identified with black Americans, and found in exceptional numbers in the United States, is the "shotgun" house, so named, according to folk sources, because one could stand at the front door and fire a shotgun through the house and have the bullet come out the rear door without having hit anything within (Figure 9.5). It is composed of three or more rooms arranged linearly with no hallway, and having the doorway in the street-oriented gable end. This doorway location—rather than having the door in the side of the house and that end oriented to the street—immediately distinguishes the shotgun from the usual American folk house. The shotgun is found in both rural and urban areas throughout the southern United States, from the Mississippi and Ohio River valleys to the architecturally conservative eastern shore of Virginia. Over 10% of the housing stock in New Orleans, Louisiana, and in Louisville, Kentucky, is composed of shotgun houses. The rural shotguns usually have a front porch and are thus distinguished from their urban counterparts that are often without it (Glassie 1968:218–221). The front porch is a common house feature in many areas of West and Central Africa, and may well be an African contribution to American architecture as a whole (Anthony 1976:12). Space in the shotgun house is defined in terms of degrees of privacy. There is "superpublic" space a distance away from the house, public space right in front of the house, semipublic space on the front porch, semiprivate space in the front room, and increasing privacy as one goes further into the house (Jones 1973a, 1975). In this respect the socialization pattern clearly parallels that of parts of southern Nigeria, especially in the area of Benin (Paula Ben-Amos, personal communication, 1979).

Judging from eighteenth-century prints in Charleston, South Carolina, the shotgun-house type appears to have been in this country since at least that time (Scott M. Wilds, personal communication, 1978). John Vlach has done extensive research on the shotgun house, and he traces its origins in the United States to New Orleans after 1810, when waves of immigrants from Haiti quickly expanded the population of the city (Vlach 1978:122–131, derived from Vlach 1975). Vlach places the origin of the shotgun house in Haiti, where it is supposed to be an amalgamation of Arawak Indian and Yoruba (Nigeria) sources. Although this geographic origin contains some

Figure 9.5 A shotgun house (right), Raleigh, North Carolina. (Photograph by author.)

diachronic impossibilities for its dispersion in the United States (since the presence of the shotgun house form is identified on the eastern coast of the United States before 1810, and the pattern of architectural style movement was generally east to west [Glassie 1968:38]), the Haitian source does point out how an already existing tradition can be significantly reinforced at another time. Vlach's Haitian theory of the shotgun's origins also is apparently nullified by the research of Carl Anthony, who found and photographed a Yoruba religious building in Nigeria that is a multiroomed hallwayless structure with the door in the gable end and with a front porch (Anthony 1979). There even appears to be a Yoruba word very similar to *shotgun*, the term *to-gun* meaning "place of assembly" (Ferris 1982:221).

By far the most important aspect of Vlach's research is the identification of an African architectural volumetric context that continues in America. The 10-feet-on-a-side square room size is an average that typifies much of the West and Central African region, and is carried over in both Caribbean and American derivations (Vlach 1978:124). This spatial figure is significant not only for the shotgun, but also in understanding the numerous references to "small" slave quarters and the apparently smaller scale of black houses in many areas of the South today (Gregory Day, personal communication, 1972). Archaeological evidence indicates that these smaller spaces were preferred by other Afro-Americans, notably the free Black community of Parting Ways (near Plymouth, Massachusetts) established around 1792 (see Deetz 1977:138–154). A group of escaped slaves in Virginia, in 1727, is known to have built one-room houses of a similar size as plantation cabins, and they were, in an architectural sense, completely misunderstood (Vlach 1978:135). The Anglo-American room size was more frequently 16 to 18 feet on a side square, and cultural ethnocentrism usually regarded the black dwelling as humble, too small, and inferior. Even seasoned observers failed to realize the different definition of space operating when confronted with African traditional structures (Griaule 1965:69).

Nearly as interesting as the shotgun house itself are its evolution and variations in New Orleans. Very popular as dwellings for the middle-class by the middle of the nineteenth century, it was modified into the "double shotgun" and the "camelback" house. The double shotgun is two shotguns built side by side under one roof. The camelback is a shotgun with a second-story room added above the rear room. Supposedly, the camelback development was influenced by economic considerations as the real estate tax in New Orleans at the time was determined according to the number of floors, and the camelback counted as a one-story house. After 1870, these type modifications were decorated with elaborate Victorian "gingerbread" jigsaw cutouts. Although advertised as early as 1867, pretentious prefab shotguns under the name "Maison Portative de la Louisiana" were being assembled by 1880. Although existing as early as 1850, the double shotgun became the most popular form of the shotgun by 1880, and numerous examples are still extant in neighborhoods like the Creole Faubourgs. It is possible that by 1900 this style had evolved into an American bungalow.

In the late nineteenth and early twentieth centuries shotguns came to be used as workers' housing in a wide area of the United States due to the expanding needs of a rapidly increasing European immigrant labor pool. This, even though the house type was identified often with poorer people. It is important to consider to what degree this construction by an entirely different power source influenced the use and propagation of the shotgun house. It is estimated that today there are more than a million houses of this type in this country, and for sheer numbers alone this is a form that cannot be ignored (Vlach 1978).

THOMAS DAY

For either production output or design results, one cannot ignore the work of Thomas Day, a cabinetmaker and architectural interior woodwork designer from Milton (Caswell County), North Carolina (all Thomas Day material from Jones 1973b:38–88). Although vernacular studies do not usually focus on specific individuals unless their products are obviously part of a local popular tradition, an exception should be made with Day, whose entire life was ironic and exceptional.

Details of the 1801 birthplace of Thomas Day are unclear, with local tradition emphasizing Caribbean beginnings while federal census schedules indicate a Virginia birthplace. It is clear, though, that he arrived in the piedmont town of Milton in the northern part of the state in the mid-1820s, and today remains an enigma and anachronism. As a free black, his life was severely circumscribed. For example, he had to get a special legislative dispensation in order to bring his free black wife into North Carolina from a few miles away across the state line in Virginia. Yet he is listed as an early stockholder in the local bank and remained prominent in the town.

In his lifetime Day saw as many as 40 or 50 other shops similar to his exist at one time in Milton, but his was the only one to outlast them all. The 1850 industrial census schedule listed the value of the output of Day's shop as over one-third of the total output value for all cabinetmaking shops in the entire state of North Carolina. The 1850 federal census recorded Day as the fifth wealthiest man in the county. Yet a little over a decade later, he was dead after being debt-ridden and living in poverty.

In his time he was a man of considerable professional reputation. When competing for a job, his was not often the lowest bid, but he frequently got the work. He was still, however, a black American and subject to the discrimination and segregation that affected all people of color. For instance, in the Milton Presbyterian Church, blacks were relegated to the "colored section," that is, the balcony. There is a story that the church fathers concocted a "deal" for Day. For doing new solid walnut pews for the church, Day and his family would be allowed to sit up front on the main floor. Day apparently did the pews, but in a cheaper walnut veneer, and got the agreed upon seating, with the deception not being discovered until nearly a century later.

Although tied into the styles of his time—a logical necessity considering his near exclusively white clientele—Thomas Day fashioned his products with a decidedly different vision. No two things were ever carved the same, as was so frequently the case with the "pattern book" salesmen of the day. Even though he had steam-run lathes and presses to do any kind of turned piece or fitting, frequently he preferred to carve individual pieces that fit together to form a total product. On the pilaster design of the pulpit of the Milton Baptist Church, he carved separately and inset an oval disk shape into the capital element, rather than simply carving the design into the capital, as was the usual procedure. His treatment recalls the separate "set-in," rather than carved on, eyes of some African sculpture, notably that of the Bakongo of Zaire. There is also an elusive duality to some of Day's work. He juxtaposed parts in an unexpected yet refreshing manner as in the capital of a mantel in the Bartlett Yancy House (Caswell County). In his capital he combined order details of both doric, with an echinus, and ionic, with a volute. In the woodwork of that same house, Day carved door frames that at once seem both concave and convex in their design. The handrails of Day's stairways flow gracefully through space as if the balusters were there by chance. This rhythmic flow is accentuated by various repetitive wavelike patterns added on to the stairway stringer.

The most unexpected Day designs, however, are his variety of stair newel posts, which range from the light, airy S curves of the Holmes Hunt House (near Milton), to the static, solid, silhouettelike cutouts of the Paschal House (Caswell County). In the Paschal posts the Day design seems to take on the proportions of a stylized West or Central African figure with its $\frac{1}{3}$–$\frac{1}{3}$–$\frac{1}{3}$ scale for head-torso-lower body. There are two stairways in this house. The one whose newel is more rectilinear easily

Figure 9.6 Thomas Day's stairway newel post—"male." (Photograph: Tony Wrenn, North Carolina State Archives.)

Figure 9.7 Thomas Day's stairway newel post—"female." (Photograph: Tony Wrenn, North Carolina State Archives.)

suggests male anatomy, with head, penis, and feet highlighted (Figure 9.6). The other's more curvilinear form conforms to female conventions of traditional African sculpture, with head, breasts, and navel highlighted. There is an uncanny similarity between the Day "female" newel post and a female Dogon (Mali) sculpture profile, in terms of hairdress, breast, and navel emphasis (Figure 9.7). Perhaps it is coincidental that these comparisons seem to exist since they raise more questions about how and why than they answer. But the unprecedented designs of this exceptional craftsman whose work was in such great demand warrants creative speculation.

CONCLUSION

W. E. B. DuBois published the earliest survey of African and Afro-American house types in 1908 (DuBois 1908). James Porter was the first scholar to analyze an American building in terms of its African features, in his 1943 book (Porter 1943). Since these pioneering efforts, others have tried to grapple with the difficulties involved in delineating the African component of the multiethnic American architectural experience, with varying degrees of success. The major problems have stemmed from trying to isolate either the people or the artifacts from the broader context in which they functioned. The material products of a culture—architecture being the most monumental example—are the results of a particular world view. A Dagomba (Ghana) griot, when asked why his people built circular houses, answered: "The sun is round, the moon is round, and a woman's womb is round. Graves are rectangular. We build houses of life and not houses of death" (Jones 1971, based on Jones 1970b). The men of Djenne, Mali, are said to treat the building of their houses with the same affection they give their women in producing the smooth, undulating, plastic facades of the structures of their town (Griaule 1965:94). In African tradition, the life force is reaffirmed, the life sense is brought into the physical manipulation of materials, and mental attitudes have visual manifestations.

The potentialities in the mind are not necessarily eliminated because of lack of expression. The black "whittlers" and wood-carvers of the 1930s who had been carpenters earlier when there was work, did not begin a new wood-carving tradition; they merely expressed it, having had that potential all the time. What is important about the architectural artifact is that potentially it can give insight into the world view of a people, and help to understand forces operating in a culture. Folklorist Henry Glassie has often postulated that ideally the whole of a culture can be "read" through the entirety of its material output (Henry Glassie, personal communication, 1976). But nowhere near an "entire" output is known for much of past Afro-American experience. Those larger, more monumental structures most directly related to the power forces in the society are the ones most likely to survive the years. This means that vernacular and popular buildings can all too easily be downplayed in or erased from the pages of architectural history (for comparative survival rates of "popular" and "polite" architecture, see Brunskill 1971:25–29). Black history can thus be victimized by the fragility of its objects. So attempts are therefore made to fill in the "missing pages" with the hope that enough can be pieced together to provide an accurate, broader context by indicating a pattern. The demography of black building craftsmen in the United States indicates that such a pattern should exist. More in-depth local studies on the city and county level—of the kind being done by Worth Long in Mississippi—should provide the illumination for this. As folklorist/curator for the Mississippi Folklore Project in more than 10 counties in that state over the past decade, Long has accumulated a vast reservoir of information interconnecting the architecture, crafts, and other material culture of black Mississippians with the cultural patterns of their lives (see Long 1975, 1983; Long and Freeman 1976, 1977; and Long *et al.* 1983). The degree to which African-American architecture is successfully understood will be a direct result of the degree to which the broader context of the pattern defined by and correlated with African-American culture is correctly understood.

REFERENCES

Aniakor, Chike C.
1978 Igbo architecture: a study of forms, functions and typology. Ph.D. dissertation, Department of Fine Arts, Indiana University, Bloomington, Indiana.
Anthony, Carl
1976 The Big House and the Slave Quarters: part II. African Contributions to the New World. *Landscape* 21(1): 9–15.
1979 Oral presentation to the Afro-American Architecture seminar (February), Tuskegee Institute, Alabama.
Beckwith, Martha W.
1929 *Black Roadways: A Study of Jamaican Folk Life.* Chapel Hill: University of North Carolina Press.
Beguin, Jean-Pierre, Michel Kalt, Jean-Lucien Leroy, Dominique Louis, Jacques Macary, Pierre Pelloux, Henry-Noël Peronne
1952 *L'Habitat au Cameroun.* Paris: Editions de l'Union Française.
Blassingame, John W.
1972 *The Slave Community.* New York: Oxford University Press.
Bratton, Theodore D.
1922 *Wanted—Leaders!: A Study of Negro Development.* New York: Presiding Bishop and Council Department of Missions and Church Extension.
Brunskill, Ronald W.
1971 *Illustrated Handbook of Vernacular Architecture.* New York: Universe Books.
Cohn, Michael
1970 Collectors' notes. *Antiques* 98(2):270.
Deetz, James
1977 *In Small Things Forgotten: The Archaeology of Early American Life.* Garden City, N.Y.: Anchor Press/Doubleday.
Dejoie, Macletus M.
1975 Metoyer: A Planter Family in Louisiana, 1742–1975. Senior paper. Yale University, New Haven, Connecticut.
Denyer, Susan
1978 *African Traditional Architecture: An Historical and Geographical Perspective.* New York: Africana Publishing Company.
Driskell, David C.
1975 *Amistad II: Afro-American Art.* New York: American Missionary Association.
1976 *Two Centuries of Black American Art.* New York: Los Angeles County Museum of Art/Knopf.
DuBois, William E. B., ed.
1908 *The Negro American Family.* Atlanta University Publications, No. 13. Atlanta: Atlanta University Press.
Ferris, William
1982 *Local Color: A Sense of Place in Folk Art.* New York: McGraw-Hill Book Company.

Georgia Writers' Project
1940 *Drums and Shadows*. Athens: University of Georgia Press.
Glassie, Henry
1968 *Pattern in the Material Folk Culture of the Eastern United States*. Philadelphia: University of Pennsylvania Press.
Griaule, Marcel
1965 *Conversations with Ogotemmêli: an introduction to Dogon religious ideas*. London: Oxford University Press.
Gritzner, Janet B.
1978 Tabby in the coastal Southeast: the culture history of an American building material. Ph.D. dissertation, Department of Geography and Anthropology, Louisiana State University, Baton Rouge, Louisiana.
Jones, Steven L.
1970a Field notes in coastal Ghana (June).
1970b Field notes in Tamale, Ghana (July).
1970c Field notes in Ghana, Nigeria, Upper Volta, and Niger (June–September).
1971 Kumasi Summer Project presentation program (May), Howard University, Washington, D.C.
1973a Field notes in North Carolina.
1973b Afro-American Architecture and the Spirit of Thomas Day. Senior paper, Howard University, Washington, D.C.
1975 Field notes in New Orleans.
Long, Worth W.
1975 Mississippi Black Folklife. *Southern Exposure* 3(1):84–87.
1983 Unpublished documents of the Mississippi Folklife Project (covering approximately ten years).
Long, Worth W., and Roland L. Freeman
1976 Leon Rucker: Woodcarver. In *Black People and their culture: selected writings from the African Diaspora*. Linn Shapiro, ed. Washington, D.C.: Smithsonian Institution African Diaspora Program.
1977 Foreward. In *Folkroots: Images of Mississippi Black Folklife (1974–1976)*. Photographs by Roland Freeman. Jackson: Mississippi Department of Archives and History.
Long, Worth, Alan Lomax, and John Bishop
1983 The land where the blues began. Film in production.
McDaniel, George W.
1982 *Hearth and Home: Preserving a People's Culture*. Philadelphia: Temple University Press.
Montgomery, Charles J.
1908 Survivors from the cargo of the Negro slave yacht "Wanderer." *American Anthropologist* 10:611–623.
Peniston, Gregory S.
1978 The slave builder–artisan. *The Western Journal of Black Studies* 2(4):284–295.
Peterson, Charles E.
1965 The houses of French St. Louis. In *The French in the Mississippi Valley*. John F. McDermott, ed. Urbana: University of Illionis Press.
Porter, James A.
1943 *Modern Negro Art*. New York: Dryden Press. (reprint Arno Press 1969).
Skipper, Otis C.
1958 *J. D. B. DeBow, Magazinist of the Old South*. Athens: University of Georgia Press.
Spini, Tito and Sandro
1974 Bamileké: La buona terra cullata dal vento (The good earth cradled by the wind). *Abitare* 127:68–75.
Sullivan, Brian D.
1978 Coping with poverty and prejudice: How rural blacks adapt environmentally to the constraints of society. M.Arch. thesis, Massachusetts Institute of Technology.

Thompson, Robert Farris.
1983 *Flash of the Spirit: African and Afro-American Art and Philosophy.* New York: Random House.
Turner, Lorenzo D.
1974 *Africanisms in the Gullah Dialect.* Ann Arbor: University of Michigan Press.
Vlach, John M.
1975 Sources of the shotgun house: African and Caribbean antecedents for Afro-American architecture. Ph.D. dissertation, Department of Folklore, Indiana University, Bloomington, Indiana.
1978 *The Afro-American Tradition in Decorative Arts.* Cleveland: Cleveland Museum of Art.
Wood, Peter H.
1974 *Black Majority: Negroes in Colonial South Carolina from 1670 through the Stono Rebellion.* New York: Norton.

10

Establishing Historical Probabilities for Archaeological Interpretations: Slave Demography of Two Plantations in the South Carolina Lowcountry, 1740–1820

Amy Friedlander

INTRODUCTION

Since the publication in 1974 of Peter Wood's *Black Majority,* historians of slavery in colonial South Carolina have been sensitive to the significance of blacks in the emergence of the colonial plantation system. Wood emphasized the contributions of slaves to provincial culture, most notably their expertise in rice cultivation, and the presence of African survivals such as Gullah, a dialect that black inhabitants of the sea islands still speak. In *Roll, Jordan, Roll* Eugene D. Genovese, moreover, found that a distinctive, African interpretation of Christianity formed the core of Afro-American slave culture. His study has limited relevance for the eighteenth century, however, since it is admittedly an exercise in antebellum history. Similarly, Herbert Gutman's *The Black Family in Slavery and Freedom, 1750–1925,* although it begins with reference to the mid-eighteenth century and extends to the early twentieth century, applies largely to the mid-nineteenth century. Like the other two studies, however, this also examined the African roots of Afro-American culture and contemporary survivals.

Several recent studies have refined our understanding of the Carolina lowcountry and its distinctive ethnic configuration. Ira Berlin described a phased evolution of Afro-American society in this region. "During the first generation of settlement," he writes, "Afro-American and Anglo-American culture and society developed along parallel lines with a large degree of overlap" (Berlin 1980:57). The advent of inten-

ISBN 0-12-646480-4

sive staple-crop agriculture interrupted progress toward a unified Afro-American culture, polarized Afro-American and Anglo-American cultures, and sharply divided blacks as well. Urban-based blacks, who were frequently more literate and highly skilled than plantation-based blacks, moved intimately in the circuits of white, Charleston-centered life. Plantation slaves, however, became increasingly isolated not only from whites but also from this segment of the Afro-American population. Distributed throughout the large plantations of the lowcountry, these slaves obtained social as well as geographical isolation from their white masters, which helped to insulate them from the harsh conditions of primitive rice cultivation and to perpetuate a large measure of cultural autonomy (Berlin 1980:65–67).

Detailed research by George Terry and Philip Morgan will be discussed in greater detail below. Two more recent studies, however, require mention here, since they address issues raised by the preceding generation of scholars. Working within confines sketched by Philip Curtin (1969) and Wood (1974), Daniel C. Littlefield, in *Rice and Slaves: Ethnicity and the Slave Trade in Colonial South Carolina,* demonstrated that white masters appreciated cultural differences among Africans to a greater extent than has hitherto been realized (Littlefield 1982). As a result, slavers consciously modified their cargos to meet colonial demand, and white masters actively sought specialized expertise in their human purchases. Cheryll Ann Cody elaborated upon the naming patterns of slaves and patterns of slave dispersal in a manner reminiscent of Gutman for the period 1786 to 1833. Working with the papers of Peter Gaillard, a South Carolina cotton planter, she found that he tended to respect the two-parent nuclear family with children under the age of 15 and to treat this as a unit in the subdivision of his large slave holdings among his children. Gaillard's vision of the black family was not, however, congruent with that of the slaves themselves, who tended to construe their families in a broad sense, including extended kin in their definition (Cody 1982).

The historical research discussed in the following text was conducted as a component of a cultural resource investigation undertaken by Soil Systems, Inc., in connection with the Cooper River Rediversion Canal Project in Berkeley County, South Carolina, which was performed under contract with Interagency Archaeological Services—Atlanta (Contract Number C-5950 [79]).[1] Because the work took place within the parameters of a cultural resource management contract, it differed substantially from traditional historical study, both in conception and in execution. Its partner archaeological study set the theme and posited the research question; this concerned the presence of African survivals in a community of slaves on two plantations (Yaughan and Curriboo) in St. Stephen's Parish, Berkeley County (see Wheaton and Garrow, Chapter 11, this volume). The archaeological investigation sought to establish evidence of the process of acculturation in changes perceived in colonoware, a ceramic type associated with slaves. In order to do so, the archaeological

[1]Archaeological and historical investigations of Yaughan and Curriboo Plantations were conducted by Soil Systems, Inc., a wholly owned subsidiary of Professional Services Industries, Inc., under contract to Interagency Archaeological Services—Atlanta (Contract Number C-5950[79]).

researchers posited as an *assumption* that the community of slaves that produced the artifacts was, in fact, culturally stable; changes in the artifact over time, therefore, could be understood to reflect cultural change rather than the infusion of new people into this population. This assumption, however, proved capable of historical investigation. As the work reached conclusion, we were able (through historical, empirical means) to *demonstrate* the continuity of the population on the two plantations rather than to assume that this state existed. Both components consequently obtained greater scientific validity.

In order to address the question of cultural continuity on these two plantations, the historical work reversed its typical stance. Since the creation of the *Annales* school of historians in the early 1930s, social and cultural historians have focused their attention on doing history as understanding past processes. The specific event, person, or phenomenon becomes interesting to the extent that it assists in understanding the larger process. In this study, however, we were interested in bringing the larger historical corpus to bear upon an individual site in order to make statements about that site, that is, whether or not the slave community was stable. We sought, in short, to understand the individual in terms of the current generalizations rather than to abstract the total picture from the accumulation of many separate instances. In addition, we extrapolated upon the basis of a series of site-specific data integrated with relevant generalizations drawn from the literature. Our ultimate statements about the behavior of slaves on Curriboo and Yaughan plantations truly represent probabilities drawn from the preponderance of evidence, buttressed by comparison with the scholarly corpus. These conclusions obtained greater credibility when they were consistent with conclusions drawn from the companion archaeological analysis.

The final, joint product reflects the strengths obtained from genuinely interdisciplinary work. The archaeological investigation stood upon a firmer basis because its primary assumption about the nature of the underlying population had been validated historically. The historical investigations found another set of data from which to evaluate conclusions drawn from traditional sources. From the wider perspective of cultural resource management studies, this collective effort illustrates the strengths of using historical research and analysis of a sophisticated nature in order to develop an interpretation of cultural materials, rather than merely to identify archaeological artifacts and compile descriptive information.

Before the tantalizing question of continuity could be broached, however, certain basic information was collected. Two members of the Cordes family, brothers Isaac and Thomas, set up the two plantations, Yaughan and Curriboo, between 1742 and 1745. Their descendants continued to work the plantations until the early nineteenth century. An overseer was clearly in residence at Yaughan in the 1760s, although the members of the Cordes family that owned the plantations possessed multiple holdings throughout the parishes surrounding Charleston. At some point in the 1760s, Thomas's son Samuel, who inherited Curriboo, moved his principal residence from St. John's Parish, Berkeley, to Curriboo Plantation in St. Stephen's. Thomas Cordes, grandson of Isaac Cordes, probably began to live at Yaughan in the mid-to-late

1770s, although he may not have been in permanent residence until he married after the end of the Revolutionary War.

The progenitor of this family, Anthony Cordes, had been born in France. He and his wife had left the country after the revocation of the Edict of Nantes in 1685 and arrived in the Carolina colony by the 1690s. In general, the Huguenots who migrated to South Carolina immediately after the revocation of the Edict of Nantes did not coalesce into a distinct cultural group that perpetuated itself into future generations in the Carolina lowcountry (Friedlander 1979). Isaac Cordes, the first owner of Yaughan Plantation and initially part-owner with his brother of Curriboo Plantation, married a woman from Barbados. Subsequent generations of this family, like other Huguenot descendants, tended to take spouses from their social and economic class rather than on the basis of their French Protestant background.

After we collected baseline data on the family and the parcels of land and identified the period of occupation (from approximately 1760 through 1810), we began to explore the issue of continuity. The concept resolved itself into a series of considerations: the ethnic background of the community, the interaction between the slave and white communities, and the extent to which we could describe the structure of the black population on Yaughan and Curriboo plantations. The interaction between slave and white communities, further, could be understood by looking at the overall structure of the parish, the impact of inheritance and sale on the slave population, and the extent to which the working of plantation elicited black participation. All of these questions tie directly into the directions of historical research previously described, and we, therefore, found ourselves working in the mainstream of contemporary scholarship.

ETHNICITY

In a now classic definition of the southern plantation system, Lewis Cecil Gray linked the evolution of the plantation to staple-crop agriculture and forced labor (Gray 1933). In South Carolina, "forced labor" meant first Indian but predominantly black labor. Although initial settlement in the 1670s saw rapid enslavements of the aboriginal population, the proportion of Indians in the slave population consistently decreased after 1708, when it peaked at one-fourth of the total slave population (Table 10.1) (Friedlander 1975).

The average number of slaves imported from the West Indies and from Africa grew quickly after 1700, reaching a peak during the period 1735–1749. After a slump in the 1740s, importation of Africans again accelerated in the 1750s, spurred by the prosperity associated with the cultivation of indigo. Between 1752 and 1756, slave imports to Charleston grew by 566%, and between 1757 and 1762, slave imports to the colony grew by another 20% (Bentley 1977:69, 74). Early in the eighteenth century, South Carolinians had begun to bring slaves directly from Africa and not from one of the other colonies on the mainland or the West Indies (Curtin 1969:145).

Table 10.1
POPULATION OF SOUTH CAROLINA, 1703–1724

Year	White	Percentage of total	Black	Percentage of total	Resident Indian slave	Percentage of total	Total
1703	3800	53.1	3000	42.0	350	4.9	7650
1708	4080	42.6	4100	42.8	1400	14.6	9580
1710	4500	39.0	5500	45.6	(1550)	(13.4)	(11550)
1715	6250	33.6	10500	56.5	1850	9.9	18600
1720	5220	27.3	11828	61.9	2060	10.8	19108
1724	(7830)	(30.4)	(15800)	(61.4)	2100	8.2	(25730)

Note: Parentheses indicate estimates based on interpolation; constructed by author.
Source: Friedlander 1975:81.

The settlement of Yaughan and Curriboo plantations in St. Stephen's Parish by Isaac and Thomas Cordes took place between 1742 and 1745 and followed more than 20 years of enormous growth in the black slave population of the colony. The years in which the plantations' slave communities took shape, moreover, accompanied another expansion in the size of the African population in the colony. Although an occasional slave in the inventories of estates entered in probate court included the description "Indian" or more frequently "Mustee" (i.e., half Indian), we have not obtained any information indicating that the constituency of these plantations differed radically from the mainstream, which was overwhelmingly African.

STRUCTURE OF THE POPULATION OF ST. STEPHEN'S PARISH

St. Stephen's Parish was formally created in 1754, but settlement occurred earlier when the area was known as upper St. James, Santee, or English Santee. By 1710, slaves outnumbered free people in South Carolina, and Wood has argued that this imbalance engendered a white mind-set that was anxious about incipient rebellion and defensive in matters relating to the questions of loyalty of slaves to their masters (Wood 1974:274). Research by George Terry (1981) and Philip Morgan (1977) detailed the extent of the black majority and the significance that this demographic structure had upon the provincial society.

Morgan found that in the 1730s slaves tended to become concentrated on larger plantations; half of the colony's slaves lived on plantations with 20 to 50 slaves (Morgan 1977:1). Although a small increase in the size of the slave population apparently occurred from natural causes in the early eighteenth century, the enormous growth due to importation between 1715 and 1739 and again in the 1760s more than accounted for the increase in the slave population (Morgan 1977:288).

By the 1790s, in the Santee region (which included St. Stephen's Parish), three-fourths of the slave population resided on large plantations, that is, plantations of 20 slaves or more (Morgan 1977:1). Terry found a relative scarcity of white population in neighboring St. John's Parish, Berkeley, and considers it among the most distinctive features of the parish in the colonial period (Terry 1981:I:1). He estimates the average ratio of blacks to whites to have been 15:1 during the eighteenth century, and at the close of the century, Morgan found that on large plantations, the ratio of slaves to whites went as high as 27:1 (Morgan 1977:7; Terry 1981:IV:15).[2]

The numbers themselves are less important than their significance relative to black culture. The exaggerated imbalance meant that slaves were in less frequent contact with whites and hence were less likely to be in a position to graft white, colonial customs onto their own practices. Although Terry estimates that the white population in St. John's, Berkeley, never exceeded 600 during the eighteenth century, the black population, by contrast, grew to approximately 4000 in nearly the same period (Terry 1981:IV:2). Blacks, particularly on plantations in outlying parishes such as St. Stephen's (at that time known as upper St. James, Santee) in the 1740s and early 1750s, were also more likely to have been left on their own. Although plantations wholly composed of slaves were the exception rather than the rule, Terry uncovered sufficient evidence to demonstate limited black autonomy within the plantations of St. John's, Berkeley, and a surprising amount of movement within the contiguous parishes along the Cooper River (Terry 1981:IV:15–18).

In 1720, 82% of South Carolina's slaves lived in parishes that were over 60% black (which included St. John's, Berkeley) and 43% lived in parishes that were over 70% black (Morgan 1977:4). By 1790 all but two of the lowland parishes were over 70% black, and these parishes comprised 85% of all the state's slaves (Morgan 1977:7). Black population by density was highest in the Santee region, which included the parish of St. Stephen (Morgan 1977:4, 7). Clearly, the slaves owned by the Cordes family on Curriboo and Yaughan resided in a demographic setting similar to that of the majority of black South Carolinians, although their white masters represented an elite segment of the white population.

Table 10.2 summarizes census data for South Carolina and St. Stephen's Parish from 1790 to 1850 with emphasis on the relationship between the black and white populations. Because St. Stephen's had been an eighteenth-century plantation parish, the ratio of blacks to whites was higher in 1790 than for the state as a whole. Over the course of the first five decades of the nineteenth century, this parish ratio tended to approach the state statistic, although it continued to exceed it as a result of the persistent investment in plantation agriculture with its concomitant adherence to slavery. The ratio of whites to blacks fluctuated, but the most dramatic changes in this ratio occurred between 1790 and 1800. Although legitimate questions concerning the precision of this census can be raised, it is nonetheless quite obvious that contacts between whites and blacks increased substantially at the end of the eigh-

[2]Dr. Terry graciously made relevant chapters of his study available to us in draft in August 1980; citations refer to chapter and page as numbered in this document.

Table 10.2

POPULATION OF SOUTH CAROLINA AND ST. STEPHEN'S PARISH, 1790–1850

	South Carolina							St. Stephen's Parish						
Year	Total	Percentage	White	Percentage	Black	Percentage	Ratio[a]	Total	Percentage	White	Percentage	Black	Percentage	Ratio[a]
1790	249,073	100	141,979	57.0	107,094	43.0	1.3:1	2733	100	227	8.3	2506	91.7	1:11.0
1800	345,591	100	196,255	56.8	149,336	43.2	1.3:1	2512	100	330	13.1	2182	86.9	1:6.6
1810	415,115	100	218,750	52.7	196,365	47.3	1.1:1	(2553)[b]	100	(372)	14.6	(2174)	85.2	1:5.8
1820	502,741	100	244,266	48.6	258,475	51.4	1:1.1	(2503)	100	(427)	17.1	(2063)	82.4	1:4.8
1830	581,185	100	265,784	45.7	315,401	54.3	1:1.2	2416	100	602	25.0	1814	75.0	1:3.0
1840	594,398	100	267,360	45.0	327,038	55.0	1:1.2	2453	100	481	19.6	1972	80.4	1:4.1
1850	668,507	100	274,563	41.0	393,944	59.0	1:1.4	2854	100	689	24.1	2165	75.9	1:3.1

[a]Ratio, whites to blacks.

[b]Brackets indicate estimates based on trend-line analysis.

Sources: U.S. Bureau of Census, 1963/I:22–42.
U.S. Bureau of Census, 1840a,b, Charleston District, St. Stephen's Parish.
U.S. Bureau of Census, 1850, Charleston District, St. Stephen's Parish.
U.S. Bureau of Census 1790:South Carolina:8.
U.S. Bureau of Census, 1820, South Carolina.
U.S. Bureau of Census, 1800:2–3.
U.S. Bureau of Census, 1830:94–95.
U.S. Bureau of Census, 1840a:47, 367.

teenth century, and the demographic conditions conducive to black autonomy during the colonial period began to dissipate as the eighteenth century blended into the nineteenth century.

PARISH AND PLANTATION

Morgan argues that the decade of the 1740s constituted a watershed in the development of the plantation in the lowcountry. After the hard times of these years, he argues, planters consciously tried to promote self-sufficiency within their plantations (Morgan 1977:27–31). He has, however, minimized the extent to which planters supplied each other in a parishwide network of self-sufficiency. A network of local exchanges emerged within which the planters supplied each other with essential goods, ranging from items for the household to extra bushels of corn for the stock. Clearly Thomas Cordes, master of Yaughan Plantation from 1768 to 1809, participated in such a circuit since he obtained rice and indigo seed from his neighbors who also traded with his uncle Samuel Cordes, master of the adjacent Curriboo Plantation; his brother John Cordes of nearby Peru Plantation; and his cousin Francis Cordes, who owned lands in St. Stephen's and neighboring St. John's, Berkeley (Maham 1765–1790:44; Palmer 1777–1811: 6, 7, 50, 74). The geographically restricted scope of the exchanges meant that these transactions also took place within the familiar matrix of neighbors and kindred, which characterized eighteenth-century parish life (Friedlander 1979, Chapter 5).

Systematic analysis of Henry Ravenel's ledger between 1760 and 1771 details this local commerce (H. Ravenel 1760–1774). In the years preceding the Revolutionary War, Ravenel traded consistently with six neighbors: William Moultrie, Daniel Ravenel, James Ravenel, Samuel Richebourg, Samuel Williams, and Stephen Mazyck. Two, Daniel and James Ravenel, were kindred, and two, William Moultrie and Stephen Mazyck, were in-laws. Ravenel dealt in tar, pitch, hides and beef, small quantities of indigo, tallow, bark, and the labor of slaves. None of these items or services were a part of the rice–indigo basis of the colonial economy, but all related to the daily functioning of the plantations. Kinship clearly informed these exchanges, and the picture that emerges reinforces the insular quality of life in the rural parishes.

The account book of the estate of John Cordes presents an even better picture of the subsistence economies of the plantation, its relationship with other plantations, and its interaction with the larger colonial economy. John Cordes inherited Yaughan together with other properties in St. John's, Berkeley, from his father Isaac Cordes in 1745. When he died in 1756, his sons were children so the estate fell to the custody of his brother-in-law and first cousin Samuel Cordes, then master of adjacent Curriboo Plantation (in addition to properties in St. John's, Berkeley). The account book describes Samuel Cordes's administration of John Cordes's estate, with special attention to Yaughan, since this was the last tract conveyed to an heir.

The account lists 112 transactions between 1756 and 1774. Of these, 68 give the name of the firm or the individual involved; 39 of these transactions took place

Table 10.3
JOHN CORDES ESTATE, ACCOUNT BOOK, FREQUENCY OF TRANSACTIONS WITH INDIVIDUALS, 1756–1774

Number of exchanges per individual	Frequency	Percentage	Cumulative percentage
1	17	68	68
2	3	12	80
3	3	12	92
4	2	8	100
	25	100.0	100.0

Source: John Cordes Estate, Account Book, 1757–1798.

between the estate and the individuals; and the remainder were between the estate and a firm in Charleston. In these exchanges with Charleston firms, six of the seven known firms were also involved in the overseas slave trade (Higgins 1964:205–17). Exchanges with these firms concerned almost rice, indigo, and corn in large quantities. Rarely did they involve small consumables (e.g., several bushels of corn or bottles of wine or rum) for the plantation. These firms also acted as bankers for the family. In 1767, Samuel Cordes notes the proceeds of £350 paid to the estate's account with Livingston & Champney for the sale of one crop of indigo. Over £1200 had been carried over to the estate's credit with the firm from the preceding year (John Cordes Estate 1757–1798:26).

These commercial transactions involving the plantation's viability over the long run were conducted in a separate circuit from those involving daily provisioning. As the analysis of Ravenel's ledger implied, these took place almost exclusively among neighbors and kindred. The Cordes's account book listed 39 transactions with 25 individuals. They ranged from one-time exchanges to multiple, the most frequent of which was four (Table 10.3). These relationships were fluid and no permanent relationship or dependency appears to have existed between one or two individuals in the parish. Nine of these 25 men resided in St. Stephen's Parish; one was a kinsman and two were in-laws (Table 10.4). Nearly half (12/25) were exchanges between men who already knew each other and already shared common bonds. In a world in which kinship, marriage, and proximity defined one's scope of contacts, these economic exchanges reinforced this web and heightened the insularity of the parish.

In 29 transactions, both the supplier and item exchanged are known. In this analysis, the two circuits become extremely clear (Table 10.5). Items concerning consumption and provisioning the plantation, including supplying the slaves with goods, are almost entirely local. Eight of the nine exchanges of "Negro" goods involved neighbors (i.e., residents of St. Stephen's Parish), kindred, or in-laws. The two exchanges involving poultry were between neighbors, and six of the nine transactions that involved primarily small quantities of beef or an odd steer took place

Table 10.4
INCIDENCE OF BONDS AMONG PARTICIPANTS IN THE EXCHANGES, JOHN CORDES ESTATE, ACCOUNT BOOK, 1756–1774

	Frequency	Percentage	Cumulative percentage
Neighbor	9	36	36
Kindred	1	4	40
In-law	2	8	48
Unknown	13	52	100
	25	100	100

Source: John Cordes Estate, Account Book, 1757–1798.

between the estate and neighbors. By contrast, the commercial exchanges, which dealt with the colonial export staples, did not involve neighbors.

Slaves occupied an ambiguous position in these circuits. On the one hand, six of the seven firms with which the estate dealt also had interests in the overseas slave trade, implying clearly that the Cordes families were in a position to acquire imported slaves through the Charleston markets, who were most likely to have been brought directly from Africa. Since the acquisition of slave labor was critical to the survival of the plantation, obtaining slaves in this sense resembled marketing indigo, rice, and corn. On the other hand, provisioning slaves with shoes took place within the local trading circuit. This implies that slaves, once acquired, were treated as inhabitants of the plantation. This plantation, in many ways, functioned like a small village, and items such as shoes were matters to be resolved locally. By implication, then, once on a plantation, a slave became nested in an insular setting, and his/her contacts were restricted to a relatively small, predominantly black area.

Henry Ravenel's Day Book, in contrast to his Ledger, was a private record that he kept on a daily basis, detailing primarily small transactions principally within Hanover plantation, his principal residence. The exchanges largely concern trading with his slaves. These transactions, exclusively in cash, were very small—the mean value was £1, 6Sh—and seem to have involved slaves on neighboring plantations as well as from Hanover. The slaves purchased relative luxuries, including flannel and rice, and appear to have supplied the products of their own industry, skill or ability to forge (Table 10.6). Sixty-three percent of the slaves' sales to Ravenel involved fowl, hogs, and corn: 18.5% involved supplying skills (i.e., mending a chair or table) or a product of skill (making a basket or a tub). Finally, 18.5% reflected the slaves' ability to exploit the environment for fish, honey, or wood.

Other records of plantations in St. Stephen's and St. John's, Berkeley, echo this pattern. The whites supplied certain basic items, such as blankets, shoes, and corn, but this was not exclusively a provisioning, and the slaves elaborated upon these staples. In April 1830, for example, another member of the Ravenel family recorded

Table 10.5
CROSS-TABULATION, SELECTED ITEMS[a] BY INDIVIDUAL/FIRM, JOHN CORDES ESTATE, ACCOUNT BOOK, 1756–1774

Item	Total	Neighbor/ kin/in-law	Percentage	Other	Percentage
Negro goods	9	8	88.9	1	11.1
Beef and steers	9	6	66.7	3	33.3
Poultry	2	2	100.0	0	0.0
Rice	1	0	0.0	1	100.0
Indigo	4	0	0.0	4	100.0
Corn	2	0	0.0	2	100.0

[a]2 items, 1 pair of shoes for a member of the family and 1 payment of commission, were deleted.
Source: John Cordes Estate, Account Book, 1757–1798.

giving out "550 yards of colored homespun to the negros for summer clothes" (T. P. Ravenel, 1830–1832). Slaves presumably assisted in weaving the homespun and evidently made their own clothes from the dry goods supplied them. Additionally, they augmented their diet. In 1833 Ravenel listed both debts he owed them for fowl he had purchased and debts they owed him for meat they had "purchased." In still another fragmentary list, he recorded "Money due me from Negroes for items

Table 10.6
GOODS AND SERVICES SUPPLIED HENRY RAVENEL OF HANOVER BY SLAVES, 1763–1766

Item	Frequency	Cumulative frequency	Percentage	Cumulative percentage
Fowl	10	10	37.0	37.0
Hogs	4	14	14.8	51.8
Corn	3	17	11.1	62.9
Mending chair	1	18	3.7	66.6
Mending table	1	19	3.7	70.3
Bricklayer	1	20	3.7	74.0
Tub	1	21	3.7	77.7
Basket	1	22	3.7	81.4
Catfish	1	23	3.7	85.1
Honey	1	24	3.7	88.8
Trees	1	25	3.7	92.5
Rails	2	27	3.7	99.9[a]
Total	27	27	100.0	100.0

[a]Error due to rounding.
Source: Henry Ravenel, Day Book, 1763–1766.

purchased," which included cards, a waistcoat, kerchiefs, calico, and the entry, "Lucy at Ophir [a plantation in St. Stephen's Parish] for a lock" (T. P. Ravenel 1829–1830).

The Cordes and Ravenel papers show that part of the plantation's economic self-sufficiency rested on the *slaves'* input, apart from their forced labor in the fields. Not only, then, did slaves become an element in the insular life of the rural parishes, but the demands of the plantation and the system's quest for self-sufficiency exercised the slaves' abilities, elicited responses that might have perpetuated African customs (e.g., basket-making), and fostered the slaves' sense of community within and an identification with the plantation.

THE IMPACT OF INHERITANCE AND SALE

Demographic structure, occupancy, and provisioning were not the only conditions and behaviors that defined the black experience. Inheritance strategies and sale also affected the formation of a slave community, and with the community the conditions contributing to maintaining an African tradition. Wills and inventories have survived for four male members of the Cordes family: Isaac Cordes (d. 1745), his son John Cordes (d. 1756), Isaac's brother Colonel Thomas Cordes (d. 1748), and his son Thomas Cordes (d. 1763). Additionally, Henrietta Catharine Cordes's (d. 1765) will and inventory are available. The documents constitute a 20-year unit of related individuals, which is augmented by information in the account book of the estate of John Cordes pertaining to inheritance practices and their impact on slaves as well as data on sales. Bills of sale together with Samuel Cordes's will (d. 1796) and inventory, Thomas Cordes's will (d. 1799), and Thomas Cordes's (d. 1806) inventory have survived and represent another block of documents for the turn of the century.

The enormous advantage of having both wills and inventories for the same people is that the *terms* of the division of property are known as well as a precise list of the testator's personal property. This made it possible to determine the "population at risk" and to provide a check on the record linkage of slaves from inventory to inventory. All of this information has been tabulated in Table 10.7. Since the same procedure was followed on each pair of documents (will and inventory), only the sequence analyzing Isaac's relationship with his son John will be detailed.

Isaac Cordes left a slave to each of his three biological daughters, the remainder of his personal property divided equally among his son and three daughters. The appraisers listed 114 names and prices in the inventory of his estate and an additional 11 slaves held with the Curriboo property. Isaac Cordes owned 117 slaves outright and perhaps as many as 128. Eight of the 11 slaves held as Curriboo slaves owned jointly with Colonel Thomas Cordes reappear in Colonel Cordes's inventory, suggesting that he obtained all of the property he had owned with Isaac Cordes. These slaves were, therefore, excluded from the calculation of the population at risk. Since the slaves named and individually left in the will did not reappear in the inventory, the population at risk to be bequeathed among the four heirs was 114.

Table 10.7

TRANSMISSION OF SLAVE PROPERTY BY INHERITANCE, 1745–1765

Name	Date	Total slaves	Slaves at risk to be willed	Slaves at risk per heir	Number found		Number inherited		
					Number of slaves found	Number at risk to be found	Number inherited	Number at risk to be inherited	Total
Isaac Cordes	1745	128	114	28–29	33	$\frac{33}{40} = 82.5\%$			
Colonel Thomas Cordes	1748	127	119	20	39	$\frac{39}{42} = 92.8\%$			
John Cordes	1757[a]	51					25 31[b]	$\frac{25}{29} = 86.2\%$	52.1%
								$\frac{6}{20} = 30.0\%$	64.4%
								$\frac{31}{49} = 95.5\%$	
Thomas Cordes	1763	69					21	$\frac{21}{22^c} = 95.5\%$	30.1%
Henrietta Catharine Cordes	1765	30					18	$\frac{18}{20} = 90.0\%$	60.0%

[a]Although John Cordes died in 1756, the inventory was taken in 1757.
[b]Includes slaves from his father-in-law.
[c]Assumed ±10% in slaves at risk to be inherited from his father.

Sources: Charleston Probate records 1671–1868/5:406–409, 6:141–145, 7:582–584, 10B:450–452, 442–444.
Charleston Probate Records 1736–1776/67A:316–332, B:124–129, S:22–28, V:492–494, W:221–222.

The population at risk to be inherited by any single heir was 114 divided by 4, or 28–29 slaves.

John Cordes died 12 years after his father in 1756. His estate, which was appraised in 1757, included at least 51 slaves, although some ambiguities suggest that the number may have been slightly higher. There appear to have been children (Little Janny, Little Grace, and Little George). Linking names from Isaac's inventory to John's—and checking price as an indicator—matched 25 names. This empirical exercise came extremely close to the predicted estimate of 28–29 names, which did not consider mortality, sale, or relative values; appraisers divided slaves so that *values* were equal, not the numerical size of the lots of slaves. John Cordes also inherited slaves from his father-in-law Colonel Thomas Cordes by right of his wife (who was also his first cousin). Six slaves are a possible match. Since three slaves were apparently children, 38 slaves were at risk to have been inherited from the total population (51) of slaves in John Cordes's estate in 1757. Thirty-one slaves are possible links with other records, and therefore, 30 out of 48 slaves at risk were inherited slaves, or 64.6%.

This procedure was replicated for each documented relationship: from Colonel Thomas Cordes to his son Thomas, from Colonel Thomas Cordes to his wife Henrietta Catharine, and from Isaac Cordes to his brother Colonel Thomas Cordes. Seven of the eight slaves in Colonel Cordes's will appear in the inventory of 126 slaves. The total number of the estate's slaves was 127, but the population at risk to be bequeathed according to the terms of the will was only 119 because 8 were individually earmarked for certain heirs. Cordes left one-sixth of his personal property to his wife, and the remainder in fifths to his five children. Between 19 and 20 slaves were at risk to appear in his wife's inventory, and 20 were at risk to show up in his son Thomas's inventory.

In 1763 Colonel Thomas Cordes's son Thomas died, leaving 76 slaves. Of these, 7 were children, and therefore, the population at risk to have been inherited from his father 15 years earlier was 69. Twenty-one slaves in the inventory of Thomas Cordes are a possible match with slaves listed in Colonel Thomas Cordes's inventory. There are several possible explantations. Thomas may have inherited a larger number of children from his father, and although the value of his portion would have equaled the values of his siblings' lots, there would have been a larger population at risk in his share. Slaves tended to name their children for their kin, frequently for the father (Gutman 1976:190–201). Therefore, the linkage from one inventory to the next may have matched too many names, assuming, then, that the linked name was that of a child and the name to which it was linked in the 1745 inventory belonged to a slave who went to another lot. At any rate, clearly the empirical linkage of names from list to list and the predictions of the size of the lots on the basis of the wills are sufficiently close to validate the method as a means of assessing relationships between lists of slaves, although the statistics must not be construed as a precise measurement. Subject to these restrictions, slightly more than 30% (30.4%) of Thomas Cordes's (d. 1763) slaves were inherited.

Henrietta Catharine Cordes's estate was less complicated. She owned 30 slaves when she died in 1766 and was in a position to have inherited property from her father as well as from her husband, Colonel Thomas Cordes.[3] Considering only the slaves she may have inherited from her husband, she stood to inherit a possible 19–20 slaves. Eighteen names from her inventory match names in her husband's inventory so that 60% of her slaves were inherited.

These relationships can be viewed in two directions. On the one hand, the continuity from testator to heir can be measured. Out of all of Isaac Cordes's slaves, for example, how many were tracked to later owners within the family, and by implication, how many disappear, presumed sold or died? On the other hand, the numbers can be construed from the perspective of the heir. Of his/her total estate, how many did he/she acquire from potentially distant sources?

The concept of population at risk again is critical. Since not all heirs were considered, the population at risk to be discovered is not equal to the population at risk to have been bequeathed by the testator. Thus, a total of 33 slaves belonging to Isaac Cordes, including those in which he had an interest in Curriboo, were discovered either in Colonel Thomas Cordes's inventory (8) or in his son John's inventory (25). Using the assumptions previously outlined, that 114 ÷ 4 was the population at risk per heir enumerated in Isaac Cordes's will, and that the slaves at Curriboo were handled separately, the population at risk to reappear in the documents in hand (Colonel Thomas Cordes's inventory and John Cordes's inventory) is 29 + 11 = 40. Of these, 32, or 82.5%, resurface in a later document. This is an extremely high degree of continuity since a null hypothesis—that a slave had equal probability of being kept or sold—would yield 50% of the slaves as having been inherited. A similar procedure involving Colonel Thomas Cordes's estate shows 92.8% of the 42 slaves at risk to appear in Henrietta Catharine's and Thomas's inventories do, in fact, match.

Conservation of slaves as well as real property within the family meant that slaves were protected, since ownership of slaves appears to have been strongly influenced by systems of inheritance. Thus, an amazingly high percentage of a testator's slave property reappears in the estates of his heirs. As the heirs prospered, though, the impact that the father's slaves had on his son's total slave property diminished. Patrimony in slaves, so to speak, became the basis of a slave quarter but not necessarily the totality of it, since the larger the slave population, the more likely it was that there were "foreign" slaves in it. Foreign slaves might be slaves acquired from sources within the colony as well as from abroad since the expansion of slave holdings among members of the family took place during the years of enormous importations of Africans and since the family traded with Charleston-based firms known to have been involved in this commerce.

Heirs appear not to have sold the slaves that they inherited. Careful consideration of the account book that Samuel Cordes kept for John Cordes's estate provided

---

[3]Henrietta Catharine Cordes was the daughter of Philippe Gendron, a prominent planter in St. James, Santee Parish, located immediately down the Santee River from St. Stephen's Parish. His surviving will does not list slaves individually.

additional information on the impact of inheritance and sale of slaves directly associated with Yaughan Plantation. According to the terms of John Cordes's will, the estate was to be kept intact until the occasion of his daughters' marriages or until his sons reached their majority. When Ellinor Cordes married Theodore Gaillard in 1764, a total of 14 slaves were drawn off and turned over to her husband. Three years later, Catharine Cordes married Samuel Prioleau, a Charleston merchant who dealt with the family; he sold the 13 slaves belonging to his wife back to Samuel Cordes, who acted on behalf of the estate. Samuel then divided the Prioleau lot between the two remaining heirs, John and Thomas Cordes, who later inherited Yaughan Plantation.

In order to explore the question of how conscious whites were of the bonds among blacks and how interested they were in maintaining and protecting those bonds, relationships among the slaves in John Cordes's estate whose names are known were investigated. Herbert Gutman demonstrated that patterns in slaves' names are a key to understanding familiar success inusing naming patterns as a proxy for understanding dispersal (Cody 1982:194; Gutman 1976:189–90). Considering only namesakes in the five lots of slaves selected from John Cordes's estate, names from one list that matched with names on the same or another list were considered to mark a kinship relation. No effort was made to guess the nature of the relationship beyond inferring that the prefix *Little* meant a child, *Young* meant a young or middle-aged adult, and *Old* meant a grandfather or grandmother.

These assumptions obtained the following results. No namesakes were divided in the widow's share, withdrawn in 1764. In the Gaillard share, also withdrawn in 1764, three slaves, who were evidently prime or elderly, were separated from namesakes and two women were kept together. In the Prioleau share, separated out in 1767, three slaves were separated from namesakes. When this share was divided between John and Thomas Cordes, two—a woman and a child—were not reunited with their namesakes, and one, Old Harry, was put back in the lot that contained Little Harry. Both Old Harry and Little Harry were separated from Big Harry, who was probably the adult, father to Little Harry and son to Old Harry. Since John's and Thomas's lots came last, several separations had already been made. Five slaves in John's lot had already been parted from namesakes, and one new separation was made when drawing off his share in 1768. In John Cordes's share, thee were at least two sets of namesakes, although one of these sets was presumably a grandfather/grandson relationship. Four slaves, Old Culley and Little Culley, possibly grandparent and grandchild, remained together.

Although whites recognized black family organization, particularly in their attention to mothers and their young children, they did not respect it entirely when confronting the needs of the plantation. The practices governing the decisions of a given individual (localism, kinship) worked to restrict the damage to black familial bonds that further divisions might have made. White inheritance practices, in this way, tended to stabilize slave ownership within the extended white family, although they possibly affected the immediate slave population from plantation to plantation. Since the extended white family tended to group their plantations within a restricted

Table 10.8
BILLS OF SALE AND MORTGAGE, 1790–1836

Year	From	To	Identification	Number of slaves
1790	Thomas Cordes, of St. Stephen's	Timothy Ford William Henry DeSaussure	Merchants of Charleston	2
1798	Thomas Cordes, of St. Stephen's	Catharine Cordes	Mother, St. John's, Berkeley, Parish	22
1800	Thomas Cordes, of St. Stephen's	Margaret Cantey	Sister-in-law, St. Stephen's	15
1814	Charlotte Cordes for estate of Thomas Cordes	Philip Porcher	Planter, St. Stephen's	28
1834[a]	Dr. Samuel Cordes, of St. James, Santee	Gibby & Waring	Bank of South Carolina	63 (13)
(1836)	M. Catharine Cordes, of St. Stephen's	Solomon Clarke	Planter, St. Stephen's	18

[a]Mortgage of 63 slaves; 13 match with slaves known left him in Charlotte Cordes's will. (Charleston Probate Records, 1671–1868: Will of Charlotte Cordes, 12 June 1826, recorded 26 May 1827, Vol. 37, 1826–34, pp. 238–41).

Sources: South Carolina Secretary of State 1671–1973/OOO:270–272, 50:239, LLL:40, ZZ:137, 5R:147, 3W:255.

geographic area in the late eighteenth century, dislocation among blacks was not as drastic as it might have been. Finally, the pattern of divisions evident in separating lots in John Cordes's estate indicates that although the black nuclear family's bond between parent and child was strained, the bond between grandparent and grandchild could be preserved when the former was broken. The pattern of division, therefore, was conducive to the preservation of an extended black family within a restricted area, although the nuclear family was attenuated.

The preceding discussion related to the impact primarily of inheritance strategies on the slave populations. In the early nineteenth century, Thomas Cordes (d. 1806), master of Yaughan, and his heirs began to sell slaves. Some bills of sale have survived, listing different types of information about the slaves. These are summarized in Table 10.8. Four of these six exchanges took place either within the parish or involved kin in the parish or the two adjoining parishes. The 17 slaves sold to Solomon Clarke probably resided on Yaughan since he purchased Yaughan in January 1836. Only two slaves were sold away from the area and away from the circle of kindred/neighbors. Sixty-one (excluding the 13 slaves known to have gone from Charlotte Cordes, Thomas's widow, to her son Dr. Samuel Cordes) stayed within the familiar circle of kindred and neighbors. This early nineteenth-century pattern of sale echoes the restricted network of exchanges of the mid- and late eighteenth century. In this instance, as had been the case with inheritance strategies, it was conducive to stabilizing the pool of slaves who resided in a limited area, although the community of slaves on a single plantation might suffer periodic, short-distance dislocation.

THE BLACK COMMUNITY

The preceding sections outlined the structure of the population in the parish and detailed practices among whites that defined the boundaries of the slaves' world: occupancy, provisioning, and ownership. Conventions bounding white behavior, namely localism and kinship, were found to have a profound impact on the slave experience. Both heightened the insularity of the parish, which was reinforced by the economic autonomy of the plantations. The black rural majority was relatively insulated from the white world, and the degree of independence and travel that blacks did enjoy facilitated communication within the slaves' world of plantations. This softened the impact of the sale of slaves within the parish or between adjoining parishes and is consistent with a pattern that strengthened, according to Gutman, an African identification with the wider kinship network (Gutman 1976:211–12). The needs of the plantations, moreover, elicited responses from slaves that exercised their traditional skills, and the organization of labor by tasks on many plantations may also have continued to insulate blacks from their white masters even after the ratio of blacks to whites decreased dramatically in the early nineteenth century (for a discussion of the cultural implications of the task labor system, see Berlin 1980:66).

The continuity in ownership demonstrated earlier indicated that the slave communities on these plantations were not entirely determined by the slaves a slaveholder inherited from the parent generation. Rather, growth was probably brought about in the 1750s by acquiring slaves who were very probably recently imported from Africa, as well as through natural increase. This conclusion has two significant features. First, the chance for social discontinuity as a result of *sale* was small, and second, importation provided recontact with Africans for slaves born in South Carolina.

Except for Curriboo in 1796, the ratio of men to women tended to become more equal on the plantations over the course of the eighteenth century. The ratio of men to women among Isaac Cordes's 114 slaves in 1745 was 1.6:1. In 1756 the ratio of men to women among John Cordes's 65 slaves was 1.3:1, but in 1796 among Samuel Cordes's 408 slaves distributed among several plantations, the ratio of men to women was 1:1, although the ratio at Curriboo itself (then owned by Samuel Cordes) was 1:1.4. On Yaughan in 1807, the ratio of men to women was 1:1.

This is consistent with Morgan's findings. In the 1730s, the imbalance between men and women was greatest, reflected the preference for African males in the importation of slaves. This preference, he argues, was also responsible for the relatively low rate of natural increase in the black population in the mid-eighteenth century. Later decades, however, were not as seriously affected, despite the massive influx of Africans in the 1750s, because a core group of females existed. The 1760s and 1770s, therefore, saw a higher fertility rate, which partially offset the effect of increased importation in the 1750s (Morgan 1977:187–291). Relying on data derived primarily from the mid- to late eighteenth century, Littlefield suggests that the conventional wisdom stressing South Carolinians preference for male Africans over females may overstate the case and that South Carolinians may have imported a more equitable ratio of men to women than has been realized (Littlefield 1982:60). In either scenario—that posited by Morgan, in which higher fertility offset preferential importation of males over females, or that posited by Littlefield, in which more equal numbers of men and women were imported into the colony—the result is a more equal ratio of men to women on plantations in the later eighteenth century.

The Cordes family documents do not lend themselves to reconstructing either the age or the family structure of the plantations' slave populations. The records of the neighboring Palmer family for the late eighteenth century, however, do include lists for the distribution of blankets that suggest the parameters of slave family life. Admittedly, this involves certain assumptions (outlined below) that may not be valid. Nonetheless, since we have not found a better proxy for gauging the groupings that slaves formed in St. Stephen's, the exercise proved useful.

In a plantation ledger spanning the years from 1777 to 1811, an anonymous member of the Palmer family noted six distributions of blankets. In three of these distributions, 42–43 people accepted blankets, suggesting that the same people took the item. These three distributions occurred in the 6-year period from 1796 to 1802. The principal change in number of people occurred in the 11-year span from 1785 to 1796 (35 to 43). There was thus a longer period of time during which changes might have occurred, resulting in an increase in the number of slaves on the plantation.

Table 10.9 summarizes data on size of family for four of the six distributions for which information is complete. The tablulations make the following assumptions:

1. The head of the household took out as many blankets as he or she could.
2. The master allowed only one blanket per person.
3. The master gave out blankets to the heads of slave families, recognizing in this way both the household structure among the slaves and the person held responsible for the unit.

For purposes of this analysis, we recognized that a "family" was not necessarily a two-parent, two-generational nuclear family. We do believe, however, that the groupings reflect ways in which the *slaves grouped themselves*.

Family size for the period as a whole ranged from one to six. In only one instance, December 1796, did more than half of the families consist of one person. In all cases, close to three-quarters of the population lived in families of two or less. The mean size of a family hovered around two. This implies that this population was dominated by young adults in the process of forming families. The tendency for household size to increase during this period is consistent with this observation as is the statewide trend toward a more equal ratio of slave men to slave women. Family life produced within the confines of slavery was still truncated. A significant part of the

Table 10.9
MEAN SLAVE FAMILY SIZE AND DISTRIBUTION OF SLAVE FAMILIES BY SIZE, PALMER FAMILY RECORDS, 1785–1802

	Size	Number	Percentage	Cumulative percentage
February 1785	1	11	31.4	31.4
	2	14	40.0	71.4
	3	6	17.2	88.6
	4	4	11.4	100.0
	5	0	0.0	100.0
	6	0	0.0	100.0
Total		35	100.0	100.0
Mean	2.1			
December 1796	1	22	51.1	51.1
	2	10	23.3	74.4
	3	10	23.3	97.7
	4	1	2.3	100.0
	5	0	0.0	100.0
	6	0	0.0	100.0
Total		43	100.0	100.0
Mean	1.8			
February 1799	1	17	40.5	40.5
	2	14	33.3	73.8
	3	5	11.9	85.7
	4	5	11.9	97.6
	5	1	2.4	100.0
	6	0	0.0	100.0
Total		42	100.0	100.0
Mean	2.0			
November 1802	1	17	39.5	39.5
	2	16	37.5	76.7
	3	4	9.3	86.0
	4	2	4.7	90.7
	5	3	7.0	97.7
	6	1	2.3	100.0
Total		43	100.0	100.0
Mean	2.1			

Source: Palmer Family, Ledger, 1777–1811:1, 2, 3, 167.

slave population lived in families greater than one, but it was largely homogeneous with respect to age. Children were present, however, and evidently brought up in households with parents and/or grandparents.

Since the generation of the mid- and late eighteenth century was the last to experience contact with Africans freshly imported to South Carolina, these children were in a setting conducive to transmitting traditions within households still close to its African sources. Earlier, changes in the ratio of whites to blacks in St. Stephen's in the early nineteenth century was discussed, concluding that after 1800, blacks came into contact with whites far more frequently than they had in the mid-eighteenth century. Taking the longer view of the relationsip of the black family to the black community and to the wider parish population, both white and black, it is clear that more stable black families came to dominate the social organization of South Carolina's black population in the decades during which migration from Africa lessened and ended, and contact with whites increased. Although a social mechanism existed that might have transmitted African practices—and in the case of Gullah successfully *did* convey a modified linguistic tradition from one generation to the next—it was set in a context that rendered tradition more vulnerable to adaptation. Thus, at the turn of the century, after which the artifacts exhibit substantive evidence of acculturation, the evolution of the demographic structure of the black population, and profound changes in the structure of the parish's population as a whole, appear to have created an environment susceptible to modification yet sufficiently stable to perpetuate altered African traditions.

CONCLUSION

The evidence we sought to understand in this project was primarily material. Historians typically draw conclusions on the basis of the preponderance of evidence and regularly speculate as to the implications of carefully reconstructed, frequently statistical descriptions. This information and type of argument, however, only describes the structure of the black population on Yaughan and Curriboo plantations, relying heavily on parishwide patterns and patterns discerned on adjacent plantations and in adjacent parishes. It is, for example, more probable that slaves were African rather than Indian and that the typical slave in a rural parish saw his/her cultural isolation decrease after 1800. The slaves themselves, on the other hand, produced the colonoware, which represents direct expression in contrast to the inferences extrapolated from historical evidence. The material evidence of the acculturation of slaves, independently analyzed, also indicated that the watershed in this process occurred around 1800. In addition to confirming the dating of this change, the material evidence confers an immediacy and a visual impact lacking in a recital of numbers and careful extrapolation from written sources.

The historical argument is compatible with the archaeological analysis and provides an explanation that makes sense not only of the archaeological data but also sets them and the historical information in their appropriate historical perspective. The demographic information presented shows a high degree of continuity in the slave population on these plantations, accompanied by the opportunity for demographic recontact with Africa until the turn of the century. The slave population became more stable over the course of the eighteenth century in both ratio of men to women and in its social organization. The underlying population was not static, but moving toward greater stability from relative instability implied by a single sex and age bracket, which is implicit in the relative absence of children characteristic of the early eighteenth century. Finally, blacks dominated the countryside, at least in numbers, and the plantations in the eighteenth century were relatively isolated from frequent contact with Charleston in their daily routines. This relative economic isolation on a daily basis was supported by a social localism—expressed in the nexus of neighbors and kindred—that characterized parish life. Inheritance strategies and the ways in which slaves were sold minimized dislocation in the population, and geography restricted the effect of these behaviors. The self-sufficiency of the plantation, moreover, elicited black participation and fostered a sense of identity. In the absence of frequent contact with whites, the needs of the plantation itself created a setting conducive to perpetuating African practices.

These demographic parameters changed in the nineteenth century as the ratio of blacks to whites decreased. Family life became more stable and some work practices, such as the task system, became a buffer, protecting some degree of cultural autonomy. Although the setting still permitted the transmission of traditions over generations, the extraordinary demographic, social, and geographic isolation that had characterized the eighteenth century dissipated, rendering the slave community more vulnerable to outside influence.

REFERENCES

Published Sources

Bentley, William George
1977 *Wealth distribution in colonial South Carolina.* Ph.d. dissertation, College of Business Administration, Georgia State University, Atlanta.

Berlin, Ira
1980 Time, space, and the evolution of Afro-American society on British mainland North America. *American Historical Review* 86:44–78.

Cody, Cheryll Ann
1982 Naming, kinship and estate dispersal: notes on slave family life on a South Carolina plantation, 1786 to 1833. *William and Mary Quarterly* 82:192–211.

Curtin, Philip D.
1969 *The Atlantic Slave Trade: A Census.* Madison/London: University of Wisconsin Press.

Friedlander, Amy
1975 Indian slavery in proprietary South Carolina. Master's thesis, Department of History, Emory University, Atlanta.
1979 Carolina Huguenots: a study in cultural pluralism in the low country, 1679–1768. Ph.D. dissertation, Department of History, Emory University, Atlanta.

Genovese, Eugene D.
1976 *Roll, Jordan, Roll: The World the Slaves Made.* New York: Vintage Books.

Gray, Lewis Cecil
1933 *History of Agriculture in the Southern United States to 1860.* Washington, D.C.: Carnegie Institution of Washington.

Gutman, Herbert G.
1976 *The Black Family in Slavery and Freedom, 1750–1925.* New York: Pantheon Books.

Higgins, W. Robert
1964 Charles Town merchants and factors dealing in the external Negro trade, 1735–1775. *South Carolina Historical Magazine* 65:205–17.

Littlefield, Daniel C.
1982 *Rice and Slaves: Ethnicity and the Slave Trade in Colonial South Carolina.* Baton Rouge: Louisiana State University Press.
Morgan, Philip D.
1977 The development of slave culture in eighteenth century plantation America. Ph.D. dissertation, University College, London.
Terry, George D.
1981 "The champagne country lies chiefly on the river"; a social history of an eighteenth century lowcountry parish in South Carolina. Ph.D. dissertation, Department of History, University of South Carolina, Columbia.
Wood, Peter H.
1974 *Black Majority: Negroes in Colonial South Carolina from 1670 Through the Stono Rebellion.* New York: Norton.

Manuscript Sources

Charleston Probate Records
1671–1868 Record of Wills. South Carolina Department of Archives and History, Columbia; Charleston County Public Library, Charleston; Charleston Probate Office, Charleston.
1736–1776 Inventories. South Carolina Department of Archives and History, Columbia; Charleston County Public Library, Charleston; Charleston Probate Office, Charleston.
Cordes, John, Estate of
1757–1798 Account Book. W.P.A. transcript of original in possession of Philip G. Porcher, 1932–1937. Library of the College of Charleston, Charleston.
Maham, H.
1765–1790 Plantation ledger. Manuscript on file in Manuscripts Division, South Caroliniana Collection, University of South Carolina, Columbia.
Palmer Family
1777–1811 Ledger. W.P.A. transcript of original. South Carolinana Library, Manuscript Room, University of South Carolina, Columbia.
Ravenel, Henry
1760–1774 Ledger. South Carolina Historical Society, Charleston.
1763–1766 Day Book. South Carolina Historical Society, Charleston.
Ravenel, Thomas Porcher
1731–1906 Family Papers. South Carolina Historical Society, Charleston.
1829–1830 Fragment, "Records due . . . from Negroes for Articles Purchased." Manuscript in Family Papers, South Carolina Historical Society, Charleston.
1830–1832 Crop Book for Planting. Manuscript in Family Papers, South Carolina Historical Society, Charleston.
South Carolina Secretary of State
1671–1973 Miscellaneous Records, Main Series. South Carolina Department of Archives and History, Columbia.
United States, Bureau of Census
1790 Heads of families at the first census of the United States taken in the year 1790. Microfilm on file at the National Archives, Washington, D.C.
1800 Return of the whole number of persons in the second census of the United States. On file at the Robert W. Woodruff Library for Advanced Studies, Emory University, Atlanta.
1820 Compendium of the fourth census of the United States. On file at the Robert W. Woodruff Library for Advanced Studies, Emory University, Atlanta.
1830 Compendium of the fifth census of the United States. On file at the Robert W. Woodruff Library for Advanced Studies, Emory University, Atlanta.

1840a Compendium of the sixth census of the United States (1840). On file at the Robert W. Woodruff Library for Advanced Studies, Emory University, Atlanta.

1840b Sixth census of the United States, 1840. Microfilm on file at the on file at the National Archives, Washington, D.C.

1850 Seventh census of the United States, 1850. Microfilm on file at the National Archives, Washington, D.C.

1963 *U.S. Census of Population: 1960. Vol. 1. Characteristics of the population* (part 42), *South Carolina.* Washington, D.C.: Government Printing Office, Published compendium available at Documents Center, Robert W. Woodruff Library for Advanced Studies, Emory University, Atlanta.

11

Acculturation and the Archaeological Record in the Carolina Lowcountry*

Thomas R. Wheaton

Patrick H. Garrow

INTRODUCTION

Acculturation studies have received much more attention from cultural anthropologists than archaeologists. Redfield *et al.* (1936:149) defined acculturation as "those phenomena which result when groups of individuals having different cultures come into first-hand contact, with subsequent changes in the original cultural patterns of either or both groups." Those authors not only defined acculturation, but also summarized those aspects of the process that deserved attention by anthropologists. Subsequent anthropological literature has therefore been devoted to the acculturation of nonmaterial/ideational systems versus material/behavioral systems; to the relative speed of acculturation of different aspects of culture; and to how varying degrees of social integration of both societies determine which society changes most and how rapidly. Articles on acculturation have included discussions of the types of acculturation (Freed 1957), of specific cases (Bruner 1956), and of ethnic groups in the United States (Spiro 1955). Aspects of acculturation have been examined archaeologically on several occasions as part of larger discussions, but

*The research and analyses reflected in this essay were conducted by Soil Systems, Inc. through funds provided by the Charleston District of the U.S. Army Engineers. Contract administration was provided by the National Park Service, Southeast Regional Office, Archaeological Services Branch, under contract number C-5950(79). The artifacts and other materials generated by this project are curated by the Institute of Archeology and Anthropology of the University of South Carolina, Columbia, South Carolina.

ISBN 0-12-646480-4

rarely has acculturation been addressed exclusively or in detail (Henry 1980; White 1975).

The literature on Afro-American archaeology probably can be best characterized by repeated attempts to archaeologically define aspects of acculturation, although no single work in the existing literature can be accurately characterized as an acculturation study. The earliest substantive effort in the area of Afro-American archaeology was the Black Lucy's Garden site reported by Bullen and Bullen (1945). That project did not represent an attempt to study acculturation, but the search for artifacts that were distinct from those found on Euro-American sites appears to have been inherent in that project. The pioneering work conducted by the University of Florida had the stated goal of identifying African "survivals" (Ascher and Fairbanks 1971; Fairbanks 1974).The Parting Ways excavations conducted by Deetz (1977) studied differences between Afro-American architecture and the architecture of Euro-American sites, while research by Handler and Lange (1978) on Barbados and by Combes (1974) in coastal South Carolina dealt with changing burial practices among persons of African descent. A number of investigators have studied colonoware ceramics as distinct expressions of Afro-American potters (Anthony 1979; Ferguson 1978, 1980; Henry 1980; Lees 1978; Lees and Kimery-Lees 1979). Distinct differences among Afro-Americans as expressed by the material culture surrounding food preparation and service have been studied by Otto (1975). Perhaps the most comprehensive study of a site presumed to be occupied by Afro-Americans published to date has been the Spiers Landing report authored by Drucker and Anthony (1979). Many other studies (cf. Geismar 1982; Mullins-Moore 1979; Schuyler 1974; and Singleton 1979) in Afro-American archaeology have become available in recent years, and differences between Afro-American and Euro-American occupied sites have been dealt with at some level within each of those studies.

HISTORICAL AND ARCHAEOLOGICAL EVIDENCE

The archaeological investigations of Yaughan and Curriboo, conducted in Berkeley County, South Carolina (Figure 11.1), were carried out under a research design (Wheaton *et al.* 1983:5–7) that did not explicitly state that acculturation of Afro-Americans would be an integrative feature of the research. Instead, as in the case of virtually all other Afro-American studies, the study of acculturation and its effects were inherent in the research hypotheses stated for the project. The research hypotheses employed for this investigation dealt with site architecture, colonoware ceramics, and artifact patterning within and among the sites. Two possible lines of inquiry were posited for the site architecture. Under one hypothesis, the observed changes in architectural modes on the plantations were explained as reflections of the gradual acculturation of the Afro-American slave residents. Under the second hypothesis, which was not supported by analysis and research, the unusual architectural modes found within the plantations were attributed to differences in frontier and nonfrontier settings. Two research hypotheses were also devoted to the study of

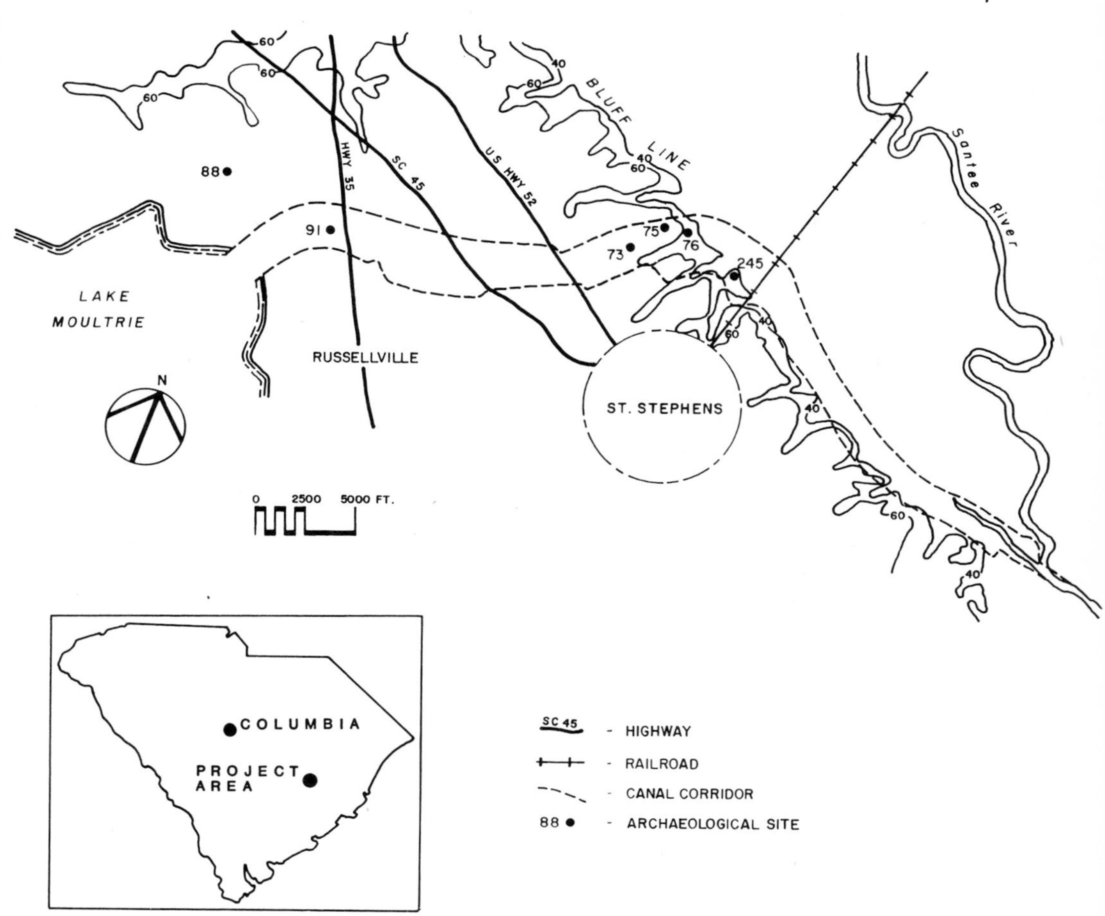

Figure 11.1 Location Map of Yaughan (75 and 76) and Curriboo (245) in Berkeley County, South Carolina.

the colonoware ceramics recovered from the sites. The first colonoware hypothesis stated that those ceramics were made by the residents of Yaughan and Curriboo plantations for their own use, and that the colonoware ceramics recovered from those plantations would be typical of colonoware ceramics produced elsewhere in the South Carolina lowcountry. The second colonoware hypothesis stated that those ceramics declined in importance from the eighteenth to the nineteenth centuries, and were gradually replaced by nonlocally produced ceramics. The single hypothesis devoted to artifact patterning stated that sites occupied by Afro-Americans should produce different artifact patterns than sites occupied by Euro-American.

The research design did not contain a formal hypothesis concerning the subsistence base of the inhabitants of Yaughan and Curriboo plantations. Faunal and floral studies were conducted on recovered bone and seed samples, and upon completion of those studies it became evident that the subsistence base on the plantations varied from that described for Euro-American sites. The subsistence evidence was then combined with data gained from the archaeological and historical research on the project to conclude that the variance in the archaeological record at Yaughan and Curriboo plantations, and the manner in which the record changed through time, could best be explained through the process of acculturation.

Yaughan and Curriboo plantations were established in the 1740s by descendents of French Huguenots who came to the colonies to escape religious persecution. Curriboo Plantation operated until around 1800, while occupation of Yaughan by Afro-American slaves continued until the 1820s. The historical research established a number of factors that were key to the interpretation that acculturation was indeed reflected by the archaeological record. First, the slave populations of both plantations were remarkably stable during the study period. Slaves were passed on within an extended family system, and there was a strong tendency for inherited slaves to be kept within the area where they had always lived. Second, there was no evidence for mass infusions of slaves through time and, except at Yaughan, for the period immediately after the Revolutionary War, the numbers of slaves on the plantations appeared to remain at the same level throughout the study period. Third, the historical record indicates that the slave populations on the plantations were overwhelmingly, if not totally, Afro-American slaves. Fourth, the historical evidence indicates that prior to the Revolutionary War the slaves at Yaughan had very little contact with whites, and that that same situation existed at Curriboo to a lesser extent. Significantly, the research indicated that prior to the Revolutionary War there was little interference from whites, and slaves were allowed to develop and maintain their own family structures.

The historical record did, in summary, confirm that conditions existed on both plantations for the establishment and maintenance of a society based on African or Caribbean models. It is not possible to determine with great accuracy if the artifact and architectural forms originated in Africa or were based on a creolized culture that developed when individuals of different tribal backgrounds were thrown together in the Caribbean. Sidney Mintz and Richard Price (1976) have presented an impressive case to support the development of creolized slave culture in the Caribbean during early settlement, but their argument has been countered to a degree by Ira Berlin (1980), who has built an equally impressive case for preservation of strong African traits in the Carolina lowcounty. The disagreement between those researchers is germane to the study of Yaughan and Curriboo plantations since most of the slaves in that area of South Carolina appear to have been imported into the state by way of the Caribbean. That disagreement does not change the fact, however, that the slaves who inhabited Yaughan and Curriboo maintained a material culture that was distinct from that extracted from Euro-American sites. The historical record does indicate that there was an infusion of whites as well as changes in the economy of Berkeley County following the Revolutionary War, and that this time period also exhibited accelerated acculturation of the slaves who inhabited Yaughan and Curriboo plantations.

ARCHITECTURAL REFLECTIONS OF AN AFRO-CARIBBEAN ORIGIN

Archaeological criteria for studying acculturation necessarily relate to material culture. Keesing and Keesing (1971:353–354) have noted that some segments of material culture are more easily changed than others, and that some artifact changes may indeed be superficial indicators of acculturation. It is possible to establish a relative scale based on that concept, under which one end of the scale is replacement of an artifact with a new type that fills the same functional niche, while the opposite end of the scale represents the acceptance of a wholly new world view with rejection of the original world view and all or most of its material and nonmaterial associations. This means that any attempt to study acculturation archaeologically must go beyond individual artifacts (what Ascher and Fairbanks [1971] and Fairbanks [1974] termed *survivals*), and build a case for acculturation based on the total material culture expression recovered from a site.

The acculturation of the Afro-American slaves from an Afro-Caribbean (or West African, or Afro-Caribbean-American Colonial) cultural model within Yaughan and Curriboo plantations to a more Euro-American cultural model can be demonstrated through a study of architectural evidence, recovered artifacts, and subsistence data. Further, change in the artifact assemblages within the study units can be viewed in totality through use of the South (1977) artifact pattern model concept.

The archaeological investigations of Yaughan and Curriboo centered on three distinct slave quarters. Unfortunately, the plantation main houses were not available for excavation because the main house at Curriboo had been destroyed before the fieldwork, and the Yaughan main house fell outside the Army Corps of Engineers' boundary. The earliest slave quarter at Yaughan Plantation (38Bk76) spanned the period from the 1740s to the 1790s. The younger Yaughan slave quarter (38Bk75) was established immediately after the Revolutionary War, and was occupied until the 1820s.The single slave quarter at Curriboo was occupied from the 1740s to shortly after 1800.

The earliest slave quarter at Yaughan was occupied at a time when Euro-American influence within the plantation was minimal. The plantation was run by a series of white overseers from the 1740s to around 1775, when Thomas Cordes took possession of the plantation from his father's estate. Thomas Cordes married Charlotte Evance in 1784, and had apparently constructed the main house by that time. His influence within the plantation was probably minimal until the close of the Revolutionary War since he was actively engaged in that struggle. The earliest Yaughan slave quarter was occupied until the 1790s; Thomas Cordes doubled the number of slaves on the plantation in the 1780s, but after financial reverses, cut the number in half in the 1790s. The second Yaughan slave quarter was constructed during the time the number of slaves was increased, and the earliest slave quarter was abandoned in favor of the second when the slave force was reduced.

The earliest Yaughan slave quarter was completely excavated through a combination of hand-excavated blocks and machine stripping. Nine structural areas were found at the early Yaughan slave quarter (Figure 11.2), while 13 structures, including structural replacements and apparent nondomestic structures were identified. One structure (76D–M) was interpreted as an overseer's house, on the basis of the size of the structure, the recovered artifacts, and the strategic position of the structure within the slave quarter. This left 8 structural areas for occupation by slaves. Assuming 3–4 slaves per structure or 50 square feet per slave (Morgan 1977:47, 49), approximately 30 slaves could have been housed in this slave quarter. This agrees with the historical record, which indicates that 20–30 slaves were present by the 1750s.

The later slave quarter at Yaughan Plantation was constructed in the 1780s, when the slave population was increased to approximately 80. That slave quarter was partially excavated (Figure 11.3), using a combination of hand-excavated blocks and machine stripping. The later slave quarter was apparently abandoned in the 1820s.

The excavations at Curriboo Plantation revealed a portion of a much larger slave quarter (Figure 11.4), remnants of a brick kiln (not illustrated), and a brick pier structure interpreted as a plantation office overlying an earlier naval store warehouse (not illustrated). Curriboo Plantation was occupied from the 1740s to shortly after 1800, and represented the holdings of a much more affluent planter than did Yaughan Plantation.

The architectural sequence noted at Yaughan and Curriboo indicates that the earliest structures were of wall trench construction, while the later buildings were of post construction. The wall trenches were relatively long and narrow features that were excavated into subsoil. The trenches varied from 0.8 feet to 1.5 feet wide, and were vertically sided and flat-bottomed in profile. The trenches varied from 1.5 feet to 2.5 feet below ground surface in undisturbed areas, and the trenches normally extended at least 1 foot into subsoil. The trench fill appears to have been carefully selected, and consisted of fine red clay subsoil at the early Yaughan slave quarter, with an unusual fine gray clay used at Curriboo. In many cases the trench fill appears to have been puddled, that is, placed in while wet with some mixing while in the ground. Posts were present in the trenches, and averaged 2.2 feet apart where measurements could be taken. The trench structures appear to have mud-walled huts, and evidence of interior fireplaces was absent in all cases.

Post structures predominated at the latest slave quarter at Yaughan, and a post replacement structure was found superimposed over a trench structure at the earlier Yaughan slave quarter. Further, small post-constructed sheds—probably for storage or some other nondomestic function—were also found in the early Yaughan slave quarter. The post molds in all cases were filled with topsoil, and graded clays were absent. The post structures were apparently frame buildings—the postholes averaged approximately 3.75 feet apart and represent a familiar building style on sites of the period occupied by Euro-Americans.

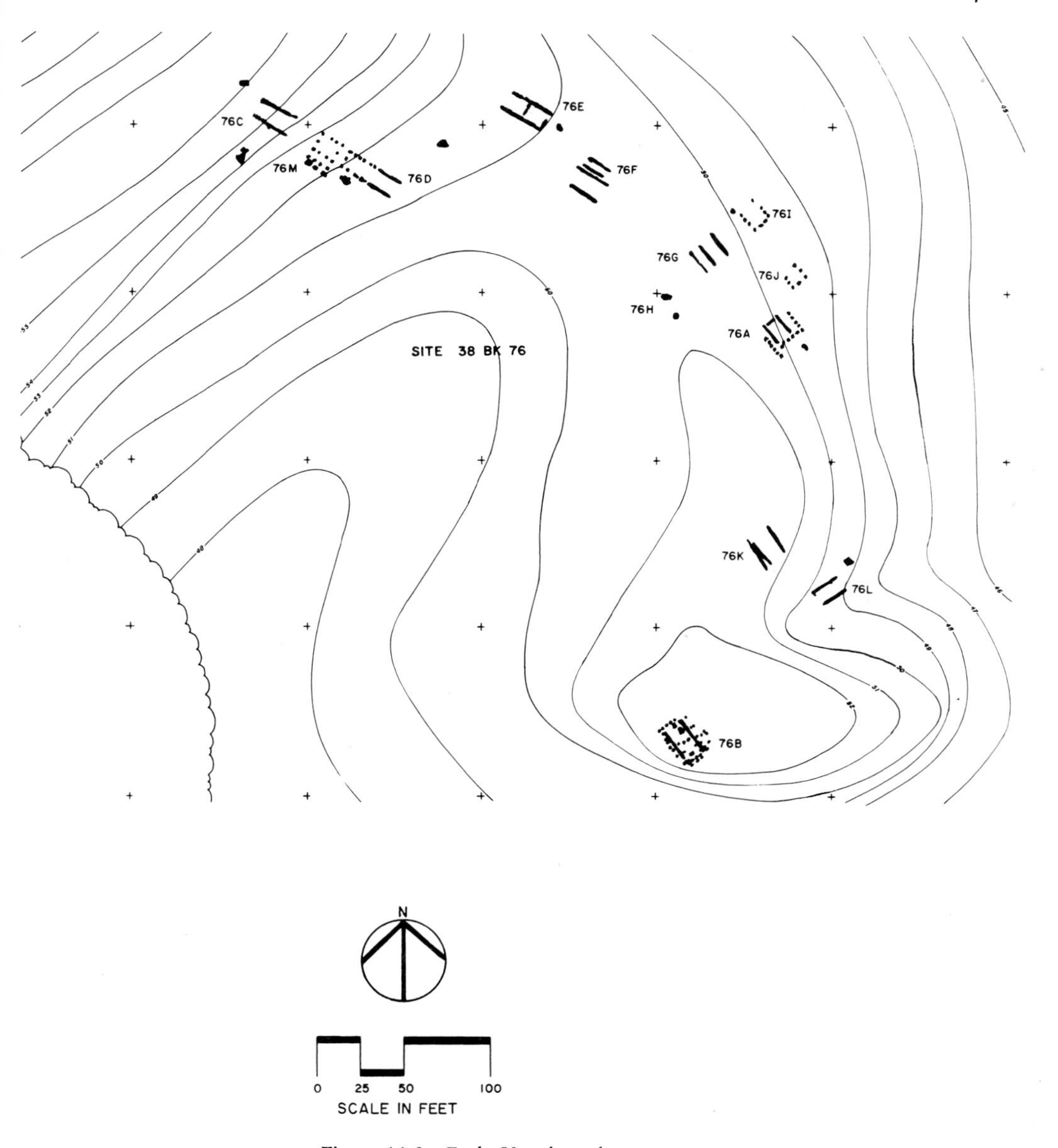

Figure 11.2 Early Yaughan slave quarter.

The only brick pier construction encountered on the sites occurred at Curriboo Plantation. The dearth of artifacts around this structure, and the presence of brick pier construction with an attached fireplace, led to the interpretation of that ruin as a plantation office building. The brick pier building was outside of the slave quarter and it contained the only fireplace found on either plantation.

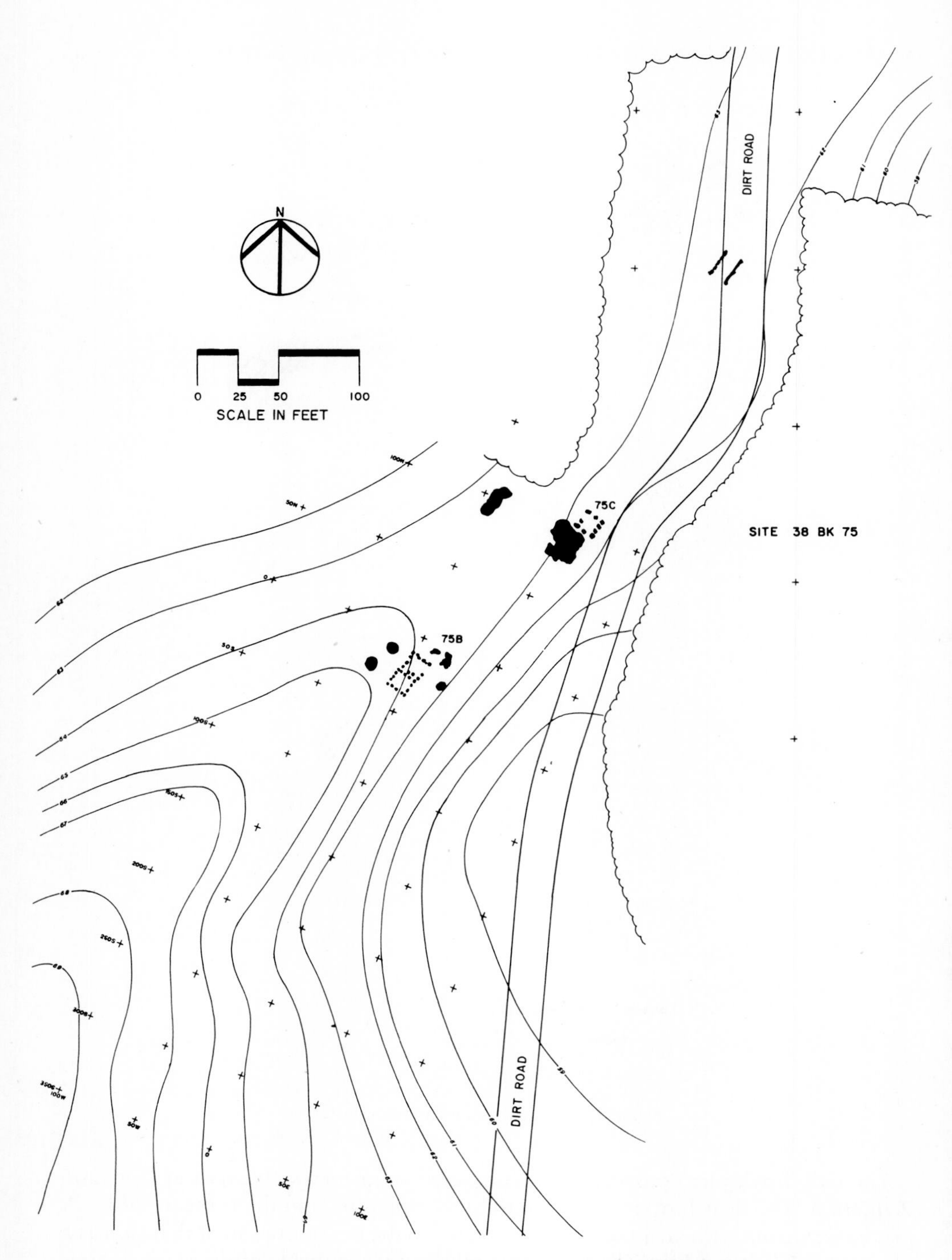

Figure 11.3 Excavated portion of late Yaughan slave quarter.

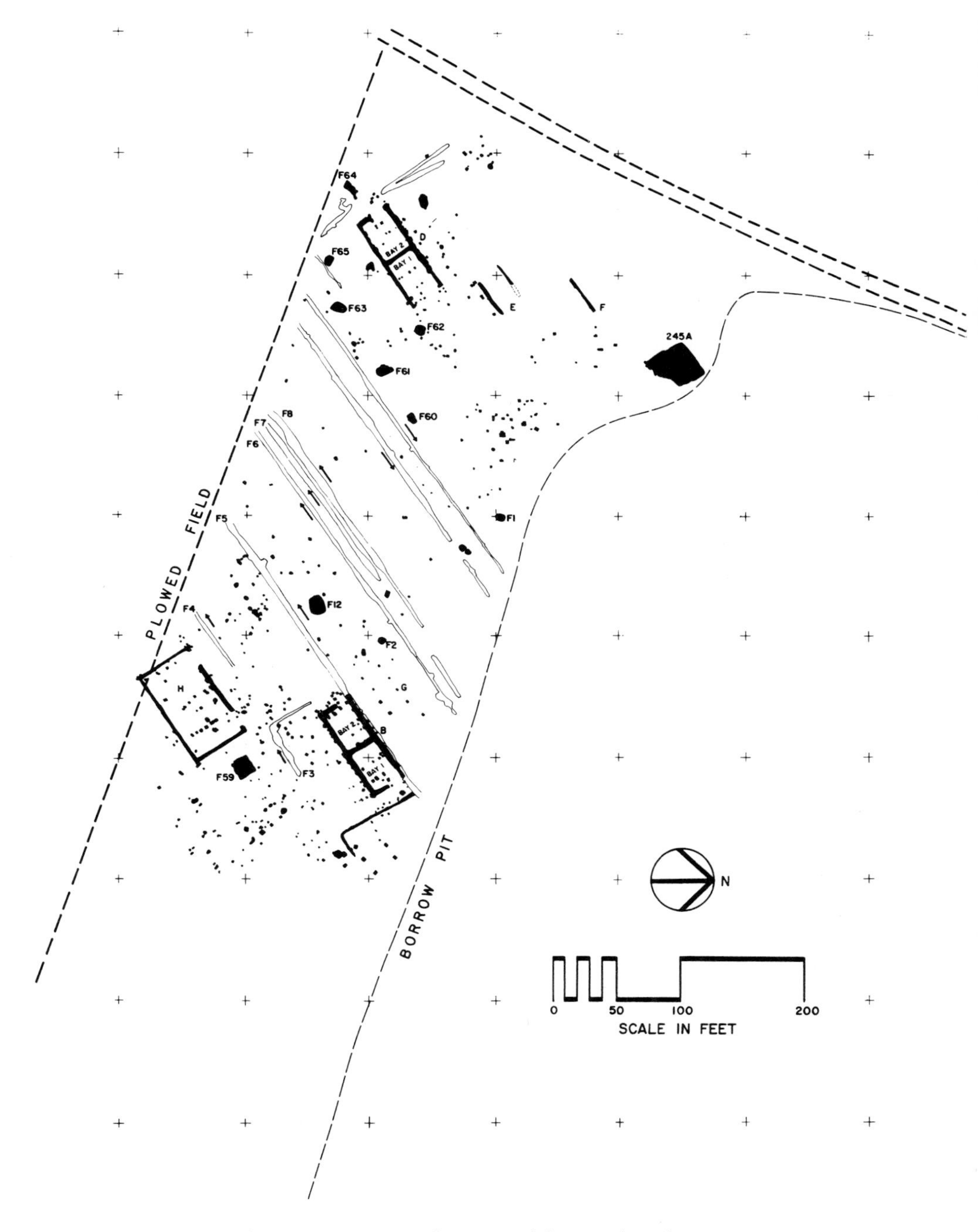

Figure 11.4 Excavated portion of the Curriboo slave quarter.

The type of construction reflected by the Yaughan and Curriboo plantations (Figure 11.5) is a familiar architectural mode in West Africa, where it is referred to as "cob-wall construction" (Williams-Ellis and Eastwick-Field 1919, cited in Greene 1983). It is interesting to note that the hypothesized overseer's house within the early Yaughan slave quarter (Fig. 11.2, 76D–M) included a wall trench section, but was primarily constructed of posts. The significance of that factor is not known at this time, but it does reflect that the major portion of the building thought to have been occupied by white overseers was indeed constructed in a style familiar on Euro-American sites, and had doubtless been a frame dwelling. In short, the archaeological evidence within the plantations supports the idea that an architectural shift took place through time in which West African styled mud-walled huts were replaced by more familiar Euro-American style frame buildings.

THE ARTIFACT EVIDENCE

Colonoware ceramics (Ferguson 1980) were the most common artifacts recovered from the Yaughan and Curriboo slave quarters. One of the stated research goals of this project was to determine if indeed colonowares were being made at the plantation by slaves for their own use. Proof that the ceramics were made on the plantations was found during the analysis. Two unfired sherds were recovered from the Curriboo slave quarter, while a fired lump of clay with finger marks was recovered from the early slave quarter at Yaughan. Further, three lumps of fired clay with colonoware paste were also recovered from the early Yaughan slave quarter. Perhaps the best argument, however, for local manufacture was the sheer bulk of colonoware sherds recovered from the slave quarters. Colonoware sherds accounted for more than 50% of all artifacts at the early slave quarter at Yaughan and at Curriboo, and made up 40.6% of all artifacts at the late slave quarter at Yaughan.

A persistent problem that has plagued colonoware studies has been differentiating between those wares made by Afro-Americans and Indians (Ferguson 1980). Analysis of the artifacts from Yaughan and Curriboo indicated that it is indeed possible to

Figure 11.5 Conjectural view of a structure from Curriboo Plantation with associated shed.

Table 11.1
DIFFERENTIATION OF AFRO-AMERICAN (COLONOWARE) AND INDIAN (CATAWBA) WARES AT YAUGHAN AND CURRIBOO

	Colonoware	Colono-Indian (Catawba)
Thickness	Average 0.725 cm thick up to very uneven on individual vessels and even single sherds.	Average ±0.5 cm thick; 1.1 cm, regular and even.
Form	Generally open, incurving bowls and small flared-mouth jars; lips were crudely rounded, or flattened with a finger or stick.	Generally straight-sided, open, outflaring bowls, and small well-made jars; lips were tapered and well finished.
Body	Wide variation in size, amount, and type of nonplastics; generally various water-washed sands, oxidation was usually not complete leaving a dark core.	Limited variety of nonplastics; generally fine particle size and completely oxidized or completely reduced.
Surface	Ranged from crudely smoothed to polished with obvious evidence of the polishing tool; generally interiors of bowls and exteriors of jars were polished; color ranged from black to dark brown to reddish-orange; great variation on individual vessels and sherds.	Usually highly polished on interior and exterior of bowls and wide-mouthed jars, polish marks were often evident; color ranged from black to gray to buff; little variation on individual sherds, some vessels were intentionally reduced.
Decoration	0.3% had decoration on interior of bowls including prefiring notched rims, reed punctate, thimble-impressed, incised lines; postfiring incision in the form of a cross in a square and a circle occurred on the interior bottoms of a few bowls.	3.5% of Catawba had undulating "day-glo"-red painted lines on the exterior of jars and the interior of bowls applied after preliminary or final firing of the vessel; occasionally red dots were placed around the undulating line, or around small regular facets taken out of the interior lip, or both.
Method of manufacture	Bases occasionally coil-made and body was hand-modeled; poor control over firing temperature and firing time; handles appeared to be attached to the surface of the vessel.	Evidence supports hand-modeling but sample is too small for definite conclusions; firing temperature and time were well controlled; reduction when it occurs was intentional; handles had plugs on the end that were inserted in the wall and smoothed from the inside.

differentiate those types based on sherd thickness, vessel forms, temper, surface finish, and decoration. Table 11.1 summarizes the traits that were employed to separate the two types of wares at Yaughan and Curriboo, while Figure 11.6 illustrates rim and vessel profiles from the two types. Further, study of the collections from the three slave quarters indicated that the smallest percentages of colono-Indian sherds (in this case Catawba-made) occurred at the early slave quarter at

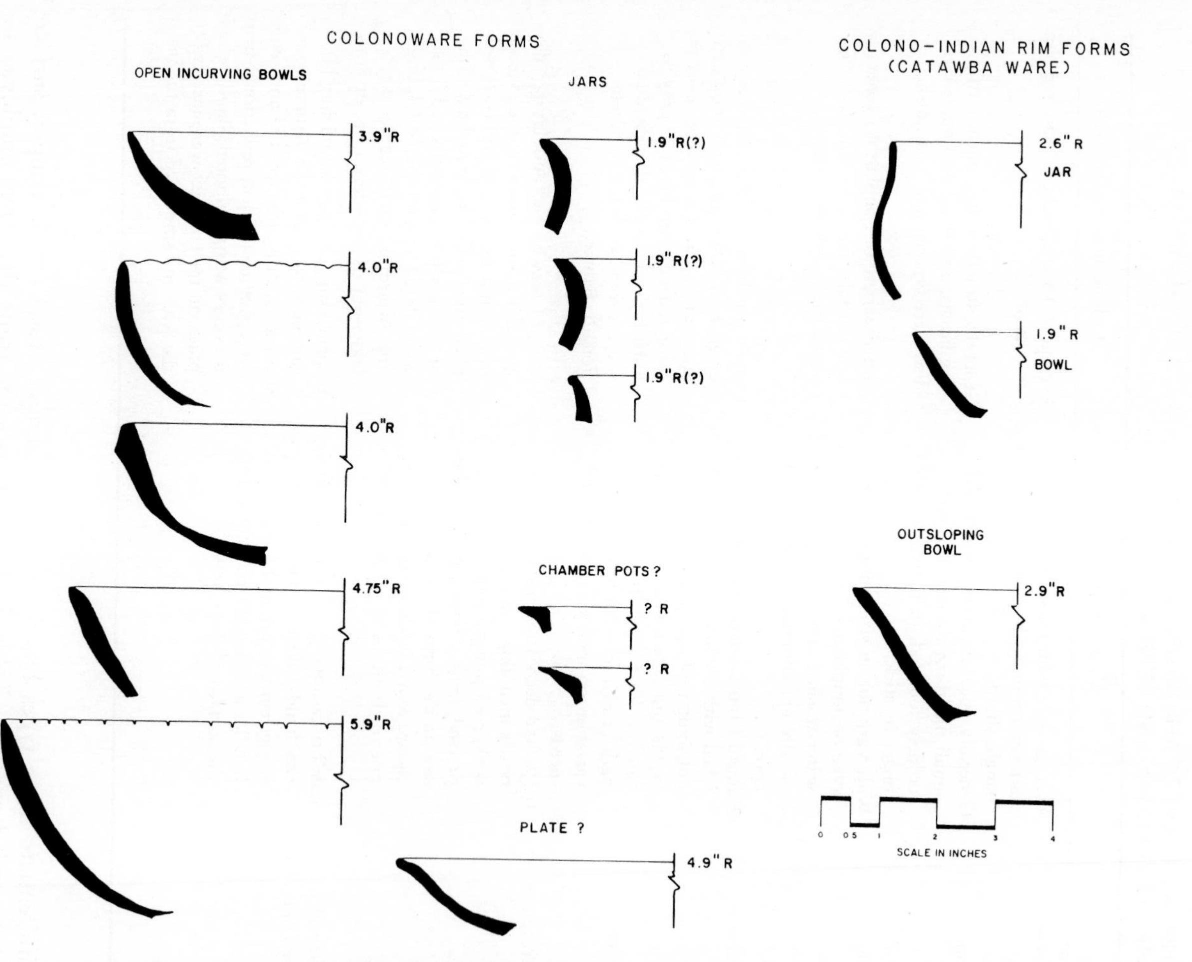

Figure 11.6 Colonoware and Catawba rim forms.

Yaughan, while the greatest percentage occurred at the latest slave quarter at Yaughan.

The non-Indian colonoware recovered from Yaughan and Curriboo plantations bears a striking resemblance to Afro-Cruzan wares as defined in the Virgin Islands by Richard Gartley (1979:47–61). Gartley links those wares to similar ceramics recovered from Barbados, Jamaica, St. Kitts, St. Vincent, and St. Martin. In all cases, those ceramics are attributed to African or African-descent potters. It is doubtful that colonoware (or Afro-Cruzan, Afro-Jamaican, or its other Caribbean types) developed in place in that area. Instead, it appears that the many forms of colonoware (not including that directly attributable to American Indian groups) may have derived from West Africa or from an amalgam of West African cultures.

It is evident that the importance of colonoware in the overall artifact assemblages of the slave quarters declined through time. The earliest slave quarter at Yaughan yielded an artifact assemblage that included 67.4% colonoware ceramics. Curriboo Plantation—which began at the same time as the early Yaughan slave quarter, but lasted longer—yielded 56.9% colonoware sherds. The later slave quarter at Yaughan, and the youngest site in the sample, contained 40.6% colonoware sherds. Significantly, while nonlocal (mainly British) ceramics increased in percentage of occurrence at the later slave quarters, so did almost all other items of material culture. That increase was at the expense of colonoware. The decrease in colonoware and the increase in virtually all other categories of nonlocal artifacts again points to increased acculturation of the Afro-American slaves through time.

ANALYZING THE DATA

The artifact patterns (Table 11.2) from the three slave quarters add further substantiation to the idea that the slaves' culture changed to something closer to a Euro-American model through time. The earliest slave quarter returned the highest kitchen group percentage, and conversely the lowest architecture figure. All nonlocally produced items and bottle glass increased in percentage of occurrence within the kitchen group from the earliest to latest slave quarter. Further, the lowest percentage of occurrence of all architecture group classes was found at the earliest slave quarter. The furniture group percentages showed a small increase from the earliest to latest slave quarter, but in that instance the numbers of artifacts involved were too small to support a conclusive statement. The arms group artifact classes remained fairly constant from the earliest to latest slave quarter, but again the numbers of artifacts were exceedingly small. The total percentage of clothing group artifacts nearly doubled from the earliest to latest slave quarter, and nearly one-third of the clothing group artifacts from the earliest slave quarter were glass beads. Strangely, one of the most unusual artifacts found in the entire project—a solid gold button—came from the earliest occupation. Very few personal group artifacts were found during the project, but it may be significant that the only coin came from the late Yaughan occupation. The tobacco pipe group percentages did not follow the general trend

Table 11.2
THE YAUGHAN AND CURRIBOO SLAVE ARTIFACT PATTERNS

	Early Yaughan (1740s to 1790s)		Curriboo (1740s to ca. 1800)		Late Yaughan (1780s to 1820s)	
	Number	Percentage	Number	Percentage	Number	Percentage
Kitchen group						
Nonlocal ceramics	1,627	7.29	445	7.64	1,022	16.28
Colonoware ceramics	15,043	67.38	3316	56.92	2,545	40.55
Catawba ceramics	141	0.63	17	0.29	295	4.70
Bottle glass	1,946	8.72	685	11.76	544	8.67
Tumbler	3	0.01	0	0.00	3	0.05
Glassware	13	0.06	4	0.07	10	0.16
Tableware	7	0.03	7	0.12	7	0.11
Kitchenware	20	0.09	6	0.10	13	0.21
Total	18,800	84.2%	4480	76.90%	4,439	70.73%
Architecture group						
Window glass	101	0.45	114	1.96	72	1.15
Nails and spikes	2,529	11.33	844	14.49	1,489	23.73
Construction hardware	10	0.04	4	0.07	5	0.08
Door-lock parts	0	0.00	3	0.05	3	0.05
Total	2,640	11.82%	965	16.65%	1,569	25.00%
Furniture group	12	0.05%	4	0.07%	5	0.08%
Arms group						
Balls, shot, and sprue	2	0.01	8	0.14	10	0.16
Gunflints, spalls	2	0.01	8	0.14	1	0.02
Gun parts	1	0.01	1	0.02	0	0.00
Total	5	0.02%	17	0.29%	11	0.18%
Clothing group						
Buckles	6	0.03	2	0.03	2	0.03
Thimbles and pins	2	0.01	1	0.02	0	0.00
Buttons	38	0.17	13	0.22	29	0.46
Bale seals	0	0.00	2	0.03	0	0.00
Glass beads	20	0.09	3	0.05	1	0.02
Total	66	0.30%	21	0.36%	32	0.51%
Personal group						
Coins	0	0.00	0	0.00	1	0.02
Keys	3	0.01	2	0.03	0	0.00
Personal	2	0.01	0	0.00	3	0.05
Total	5	0.02%	2	0.03%	4	0.06%
Tobacco pipe group						
Pipe parts	774	3.33	306	5.25	182	2.90
Colonopipes	8	0.03	4	0.07	0	0.00
Total	752	3.37%	310	5.32%	182	2.90%
Activities group						
Construction tools	15	0.07	14	0.24	11	0.18
Farm tools	3	0.01	4	0.07	7	0.11
Toys (colonoware)	4	0.02	0	0.00	1	0.02
Fishing gear	5	0.02	0	0.00	0	0.00
Horse tack	3	0.01	4	0.07	2	0.03
Miscellaneous hardware	10	0.04	1	0.02	9	0.14
Other	6	0.02	4	0.07	4	0.06
Total	46	0.21%	27	0.46%	34	0.54%
Grand totals	22,327	99.99%	5826	99.99%	6276	100.00%

established for the other artifact groups, but this is hardly surprising in view of the eccentric nature of that group. The percentage of activities group artifacts more than doubled from the earliest to latest component, although once again the numbers and percentages of artifacts present were small.

The trend exhibited by the comparison of the artifact patterns from early Yaughan, Curriboo, and late Yaughan seems to indicate that the slaves consumed and discarded proportionately larger percentages of Euro-American produced goods as time passed. That trend, coupled with a direct increase in consumption and discard of African-related goods, appears to further reinforce the interpretation that the slave inhabitants of Yaughan and Curriboo were undergoing accelerated acculturation to a Euro-American cultural model as time passed. The triggering mechanism for this trend may have been increased Euro-American presence in Berkeley County following the Revolutionary War, which decreased the isolation of the slaves and placed pressure on them to conform to Euro-American cultural models.

The differences between the slave material culture and Euro-American 'material culture of the same period can be delineated through application of a revised version of the Carolina Artifact Pattern Model proposed by Stanley South (1977:83–139). The Revised Carolina Artifact Pattern Model, as proposed by Garrow (1982:57–58) incorporates three of the sites used by South, and shifts certain artifact classes from group to group to produce a more functionally aligned model. Garrow's shift of colonoware ceramics from South's activities group to the kitchen group has particular meaning for the Yaughan and Curriboo artifact patterns. The Revised Carolina Artifact Pattern Model, summarized at the group level, is presented in Table 11.3. The Revised Carolina Artifact Pattern Model exhibits a lower set of kitchen group percentages than the Yaughan and Curriboo sites, with higher representations of the architecture group artifacts. Perhaps most significant, however, is that the average combined representation of kitchen, architecture, and tobacco pipe groups among the three sites of the Revised Carolina Artifact Pattern Model is 94.94%, which leaves 5.06% of the recovered artifacts distributed among the remaining groups. The combined average representation of kitchen, architecture, and tobacco pipe groups among the Yaughan and Curriboo contexts is 98.93%, which leaves a mere 1.07% to be distributed among the remaining groups. Further, the percentages of artifacts not incorporated within the three major artifact groups totaled 0.61% at the early Yaughan slave quarter, 1.22% at Curriboo, and 1.37% at the late Yaughan slave quarter. Those gradual shifts in the artifact percentages are consistent with the other available archaeological and historical data that indicate that acculturation was indeed perceptively increasing during the study period. That trend appears to have continued into the nineteenth century, and Afro-American and Euro-American domestic artifact patterns probably became indistinguishable during that century.

The artifact pattern data extracted from Yaughan and Curriboo plantations appear to be strong enough to suggest that a distinct slave artifact pattern existed in the South Carolina lowcountry during the eighteenth and into the nineteenth centuries. That pattern was characterized by a very high kitchen-to-architecture percentage, with a fraction of the artifact assemblage represented in groups outside of the kitchen, architecture, and tobacco pipe groups.

Table 11.3
THE REVISED CAROLINA ARTIFACT PATTERN[a]

Artifact group	Brunswick S25 (1732 to 1776)		Brunswick S10 (1728 to 1830)		Cambridge 96 (1783 to 1820)	
	Number	Percentage	Number	Percentage	Number	Percentage
Kitchen[b]	22,710	61.77	6,795	51.80	12,916	64.97
Architecture	9,620	26.17	4,116	31.38	5,006	25.18
Furniture	83	0.23	82	0.63	35	0.18
Arms	34	0.09	45	0.34	27	0.14
Clothing	1,070	2.91	72	0.55	1,069	5.38
Personal	71	0.19	20	0.15	108	0.54
Pipes	2,830	7.70	1,829	13.94	349	1.76
Activities[c]	347	0.94	159	1.21	370	1.86
Total	36,765	100.00	13,118	100.00	19,880	100.01

[a]Modified from South (1977:83–139).
[b]Includes colonoceramics.
[c]Colonoceramics deleted.

Fortunately, at least some comparative data do exist within the literature that can be used to cross-check the Yaughan and Curriboo artifact pattern data. Those data come from the Spiers Landing site which was excavated and reported by Drucker and Anthony (1979). Spiers Landing was apparently a single slave cabin that was also located in Berkeley County, South Carolina. The dating evidence for that site was not clear-cut, but it is probable that the site was occupied between 1790 and 1830. The site excavation included a post-constructed dwelling (which may have been superimposed over a wall trench structure) and associated features. The excavation methods employed on that site were comparable to those used within Yaughan and Curriboo, and the resultant artifact pattern derived from the site does appear to have comparative value.

The Spiers Landing artifact pattern, summarized at the group level, is presented in comparison with the Yaughan and Curriboo artifact patterns in Table 11.4. The kitchen and architecture groups from Spiers Landing were intermediate to those from Curriboo and the late Yaughan slave quarters, and the combined kitchen, architecture, and tobacco pipe groups accounted for 98.03% of all artifacts. That left 1.97% to be distributed among the other artifact groups, which is slightly higher than the Curriboo or Yaughan examples. That figure is still significantly lower than the 5.06% among the Euro-American occupied sites of the Revised Carolina Artifact Pattern Model.

The artifactual evidence from Yaughan and Curriboo plantations provide consistent results at the level of both individual artifacts and combined assemblages. Again, ample evidence of cultural change is present from the artifact studies, and it

Table 11.4

THE CAROLINA SLAVE ARTIFACT PATTERN[a]

Artifact group	Yaughan 38Bk76 (1740s to 1790s)		Curriboo 38Bk245[b] (1740s to ca. 1800)		Yaughan 38Bk75 (1780s to 1820s)		Spiers Landing[c] (1790s to 1830s)	
	Number	Percentage	Number	Percentage	Number	Percentage	Number	Percentage
Kitchen	18,800	84.20	4,420	79.77	4,439	70.73	2,275	74.84
Architecture	2,640	11.82	757	13.66	1,569	25.00	631	20.76
Furniture	12	0.05	4	0.07	5	0.08	2	0.07
Arms	5	0.02	15	0.27	11	0.18	6	0.20
Clothing	66	0.30	20	0.36	32	0.51	24	0.79
Personal	6	0.03	2	0.04	4	0.06	2	0.07
Pipes[d]	752	3.37	300	5.41	182	2.90	74	2.43
Activities[e]	46	0.21	23	0.42	34	0.54	26	0.86
Total	22,327	100.0	5,541	100.0	6,276	100.0	3,040	100.0

[a]Colono included in kitchen group.
[b]Does not include structure 245C.
[c]Modified from Drucker and Anthony (1979).
[d]Includes colonopipes.
[e]Unidentified metal deleted.

further supports the idea that acculturation was taking place within the plantations under study.

A study of the subsistence base of the slave inhabitants of Yaughan and Curriboo plantations was conducted through an analysis of recovered faunal and ethnobotanical remains. The soils within both plantations were quite acidic, with an average pH of 6.17 at the early Yaughan slave quarter, 3.78 at Curriboo, and 5.78 at the late Yaughan slave quarter. This factor probably biased the faunal and ethnobotanical samples, but it was possible to draw at least some conclusions about the subsistence base of the occupants.

The excavations returned a very small amount of bone from all three slave quarters. Surprisingly, however, the largest amount of bone was returned from Curriboo, which had the most acidic soils. Curriboo also had the widest range of species represented of any of the slave quarters, with cow, pig, dog, snake/lizard, opossum, quahog clam, and the common oyster present in varying amounts. The early Yaughan slave quarter yielded cow, pig, snake/lizard, and the common oyster. The late Yaughan slave quarter contained cow, pig, freshwater catfish, goose, and white-tailed deer. The oyster and clam shells were in all cases found in association with architectural debris, and apparently had been used as constituents in a mortar mix, consequently those species should be regarded as nonfood items. Dog and snake/lizard may have been used as food sources, but it is more likely that they were nonfood species.

Cows and pigs outweighed all other edible animal species in terms of both bone weight and the minimum number of individuals present. Those animals were the major sources of meat within the plantations, but considering the small numbers of bones present, meat must have been a rare constituent of the diet.

Extensive flotation samples were taken and processed from each slave quarter. The ethnobotanical analysis produced relatively small numbers of identifiable seeds. Seeds from plant species that could have been used in the diet included rice, maize, peach, walnut, and hickory from the early Yaughan slave quarter. The Curriboo site yielded rice, maize, peach, hawthorn, bramble, walnut, and hickory. Rice, maize, peach, hawthorn, sumac, walnut, and hickory were all identified from the late Yaughan slave quarter. The small amount of edible plant seeds in the collections from the three slave quarters led to the conclusion that seeds such as rice and maize were thoroughly milled before cooking, and that that factor reduced the likelihood that they would be represented in the archaeological record.

The diet of the slaves within the three slave quarters appears to have been primarily vegetal, and there appears to have been a heavy dependence on rice and maize. Wild species were present but rare in the collections, and the hunting and gathering of wild animals and plants appears to have made relatively minor contributions to the subsistence base.

The subsistence base conclusions drawn for the Yaughan and Curriboo slave quarters contrasts with the high bone-to-artifact counts found on Euro-American sites (South 1977:126–128). Animal protein was apparently much less important in the Yaughan and Curriboo diets than among Euro-Americans of that period. The contrast noted between the subsistence base at the study plantations may well be further proof of cultural level differences between Afro-American slaves and Euro-Americans of that period. If that is indeed the case, those differences were apparently not maintained far into the nineteenth century, as later Afro-American-occupied sites appear to reflect subsistence patterns that are more similar to Euro-Americans (Fairbanks 1974).

CONCLUSIONS

The archaeological and historical data derived from the Yaughan and Curriboo slave quarters clearly indicate that the inhabitants of those sites were going through culture change from the eighteenth to nineteenth centuries. Further, the material culture evidence recovered from those sites stands in sharp contrast to the material culture of Euro-American sites of that period.

The architecture of the early Yaughan, Curriboo, and late Yaughan slave quarters presents a clear picture of the processes that took place within those plantations from the 1740s to the 1820s. Mud-walled huts, evidenced by wall trenches with cob-wall construction, were the earliest slave/domestic structures on the plantations. This architectural form does have antecedents in West Africa, and probably represents a West African architectural form. The presence of iron nails and small amounts of window glass and construction hardware recovered within the area of those structures bears testimony to the fact that some alteration of that architectural form had taken place in response to contact with Euro-Americans. This architectural form appears to have begun to change around the Revolutionary War, and by the late eighteenth to the early nineteenth century, post-constructed frame houses were in use as dwellings. This change appears to have taken place in response to greater contact with Euro-Americans after the Revolutionary War, and because more influence on architectural mode was exerted by the plantation owners or managers.

The changes that took place within the slave quarters were not restricted to architectural expressions. Colonoware ceramics, which appear to have been as distinctly West African as the architecture, declined in importance after the Revolutionary War, and the material culture inventory was broadened by more and more nonlocal artifact types. The artifact patterns extracted from the slave quarters appeared to reflect a change from what can be recognized as a purely slave artifact pattern model to models more similar to those gained from Euro-American sites.

The subsistence data from the three slave quarters appear to add support to the idea that acculturation was ongoing during the time the slave quarters were occupied. The subsistence base of the slaves at Yaughan and Curriboo reflected a heavy dependence on vegetal food sources, with little utilization of animal species. This stands in sharp contrast with subsistence data available from Euro-American sites. Perhaps it is significant that no great degree of change was noted in the subsistence base from the earliest to latest slave quarter since the subsistence base should be one of the most conservative expressions of a culture, and thus highly resistent to change.

This chapter represents an attempt to chronicle evidences of acculturation within three slave quarters in coastal South Carolina. Ample evidence of change was found within the archaeological record of the three slave quarters that were studied, but it is not known at this time if those slave quarters were typical for the eighteenth and early nineteenth centuries. The results of this study are probably applicable for the South Carolina lowcountry of that period, but validation of that assumption must await future research.

REFERENCES

Anthony, Ronald W.
1979 Descriptive analysis and replication of historic earthenware: colono wares: from the Spiers Landing site, Berkeley County, South Carolina. *The Conference on Historic Site Papers 1978* 13:253–268.

Ascher, Robert, and Charles H. Fairbanks
1971 Excavation of a slave cabin: Georgia, U.S.A. *Historical Archaeology* 5:3–17.

Berlin, Ira
1980 Time, space, and the evolution of Afro-American society in British mainland North America. *The American Historical Review,* 85(1):44–78.

Bruner, Edward M.
1956 Primary group experience and the process of acculturation. *American Anthropologist* 58:605–623.

Bullen, Adelaide, K., and Ripley P. Bullen
1945 Black Lucy's garden. *Bulletin of Massachusetts Archaeological Society* 6:17–28.

Combes, John D.
1974 Ethnography, archaeology, and burial practices among coastal South Carolina blacks. *Conference on Historic Site Archaeology Papers 1972* 7:52–61.

Deetz, James
1977 *In Small Things Forgotten*. Garden City, N.Y.: Anchor Press.

Drucker, Lesley M., and Ronald W. Anthony
1979 *The Spiers Landing Site: archaeological investigation in Berkeley County, South Carolina.* Carolina Archaeological Services, Columbia, South Carolina.

Fairbanks, Charles
1974 The Kingsley slave cabins in Duvall County, Florida, 1968. *The Conference on Historic Site Archaeology Papers 1972* 7:62–93.

Ferguson, Leland
1978 Looking for the "Afro" in Colono-Indian pottery. *Conference on Historic Site Archaeology Papers 1977* 12:68–83.
1980 The "Afro-" in Colono-Indian pottery. In *Archaeological perspectives on ethnicity in America.* R. Schuyler, ed. Farmingdale, N.Y.: Baywood Pp. 14–28.

Freed, Stanley A.
1957 Suggested type societies in acculturation studies. *American Anthropologist* 59:55–68.

Garrow, Patrick H.
1982 Archaeological investigations on the Washington, D.C. Civic Center site. Ms. on file, Soil Systems, Inc., Marietta, Georgia.

Gartley, Richard T.
1979 Afro-Cruzan pottery—a new style of colonial earthenware from St. Croix. *Journal of the Virgin Islands Archaeological Society* 8:47–61.

Geismar, Joan H.
1982 *The Archaeology of Social Disintegration in Skunk Hollow, A Nineteenth Century Rural Black Community*. New York: Academic Press.

Greene, Lane
1983 Architectural historian's report. Yaughan and Curriboo plantations: studies in Afro-American archeology, by Thomas R. Wheaton, Amy Friedlander and Patrick H. Garrow. Ms. on file, Soil Systems, Inc., Marietta, Georgia. Pp. 597–606.
Handler, Jerome, and Frederick W. Lange
1978 *Plantation slavery in Barbados: an archaeological and historical investigation.* Cambridge: Harvard University Press.
Henry, Susan
1980 Physical, spatial, and temporal dimensions of colono ware in the Chesapeake 1600–1800. Master's thesis, Catholic University of America, Washington, D.C.
Keesing, Roger M., and Felix M. Keesing
1971 *New Perspectives in Cultural Anthropology.* New York: Holt, Rinehart and Winston.
Lees, William
1978 Pattern and meaning of Colono-Indian ceramics at Limerick plantation, South Carolina. *Pattern and Meaning* 1(4).
Lees, William, and Kathryn M. Kimery-Lees
1979 The function of Colono-Indian ceramics: insights from Limerick plantation. *Historical Archaeology* 13:1–13.
Mintz, Sidney W., and Richard Price
1976 *An Anthropological Approach to the Afro-American Past.* Philadelphia: Institute for the Study of Human Issues.
Mullins-Moore, Sue
1979 The southern coastal plantation: view from St. Simon's Island, Georgia. Paper presented at the 12th Annual Meeting, Society for Historical Archaeology, Nashville.
Otto, John Solomon
1975 Status differences and the archaeological record—a comparison of planter, overseer, and slave sites from Cannon's Point Plantation (1794–1861), St. Simon's Island, Georgia. Ph.D. dissertation, University of Florida. Ann Arbor: University Microfilms.
Redfield, Robert, Ralph Linton, and Melville J. Herskovits
1936 Memorandum for the study of acculturation. *American Anthropologist* 38:149–152.
Schuyler, Robert L.
1974 Sandy ground: archaeological sampling in a black community. *The Conference on Historic Sites Archaeology Papers 7, 1972*: part 2:13–51.
Singleton, Theresa
1979 Slaves and ex-slave sites in coastal Georgia. Paper presented at the 12th annual meeting, Society for Historical Archaeology, Nashville.
South, Stanley
1977 *Method and theory in historical archaeology.* New York: Academic Press.
Spiro, Melford E.
1955 The acculturation of American ethnic groups. *American Anthropologist* 57:1240–1252.
Wheaton, Thomas R., Amy Friedlander, and Patrick H. Garrow
1983 Yaughan and Curriboo plantations. Studies in Afro-American Archaeology. Ms. on file, Soil Systems, Inc., Marietta, Georgia.
White, John R.
1975 Historic contact sites as laboratories for the study of culture change. *Conference on Historic Sites Archaeology Papers, 1974* 9:153–163.
Williams-Ellis, Clough, and Elizabeth Eastwick-Field
1919 *Building in Cob, Pise, and Stabilized Earth.* England: Country Life Limited.

12

An Afro-Jamaican Slave Settlement: Archaeological Investigations at Drax Hall

Douglas V. Armstrong

INTRODUCTION

The proper starting point . . . for any examination of the cultural environment—as indeed, for any study dealing with links between Africa and the Caribbean—must be with the societies constructed as a result of the transatlantic slave trade. And in this it is imperative to deal not just with slavery as an abstract inhumane institution, but the people and the entire social complex of which slavery was a part (Knight and Crahan 1979:4).

An historical archaeology project was conducted at the "Old Village" at Drax Hall Plantation, St. Ann's Bay, Jamaica, during 1980–1982 (Figures 12.1–12.3). In carrying out the project both archaeological and historical investigation techniques were used in a case study examination of the development of Afro-Jamaican cultural systems during the period of slavery through the postemancipation era. Though the majority of the artifacts recovered from the site were imported European materials, artifact pattern analysis (South 1977) and ceramic shape/function analysis (Deetz 1973; Otto 1975) are shown to provide a mechanism by which the Afro-Jamaican cultural context of the site can be demonstrated and a series of research questions regarding the development of an Afro-Jamaican community can be addressed. Results of excavation and artifact data analysis, using these techniques, provide empirical support for the hypothesized development of a distinct Afro-Jamaican cultural system marked by elements of continuity and systems of change.

ISBN 0-12-646480-4

Figure 12.1 A plan and view of Drax Hall Estate (Wilson and Robins 1765), showing acreage of "Negro Houses and Grounds."

The major stimulus for initiating this project came from a growing awareness that transplanted Africans in the New World are underrepresented in traditional histories. Though there are numerous accounts of the institution of slavery, there is comparatively little information on the slaves themselves (Handler and Lange 1978:1). They were for the most part "inarticulate," leaving little documentation on their lives (Ascher 1975). Furthermore, little was written about them except in economic records kept by the plantation owners or managers (inventories, deeds, wills, etc.), along with occasional mention in the planters' journals or brief descriptions by travelers.

While the slaves did not write about their own lives, a record has been preserved and can be reconstructed through the study of the materials they left behind, or what James Deetz has called the "many small things forgotten" (Deetz 1977). Archaeological methods and techniques, combined with a thorough examination of the documents that are available for the period, can be used to get a clearer perspective of the community, their living conditions, and the processes by which their social context changed through time to become "Afro-Jamaican."

This essay was prepared not only as a means of reporting specific findings concerning the development of Afro-Jamaican cultural systems, but also to demonstrate

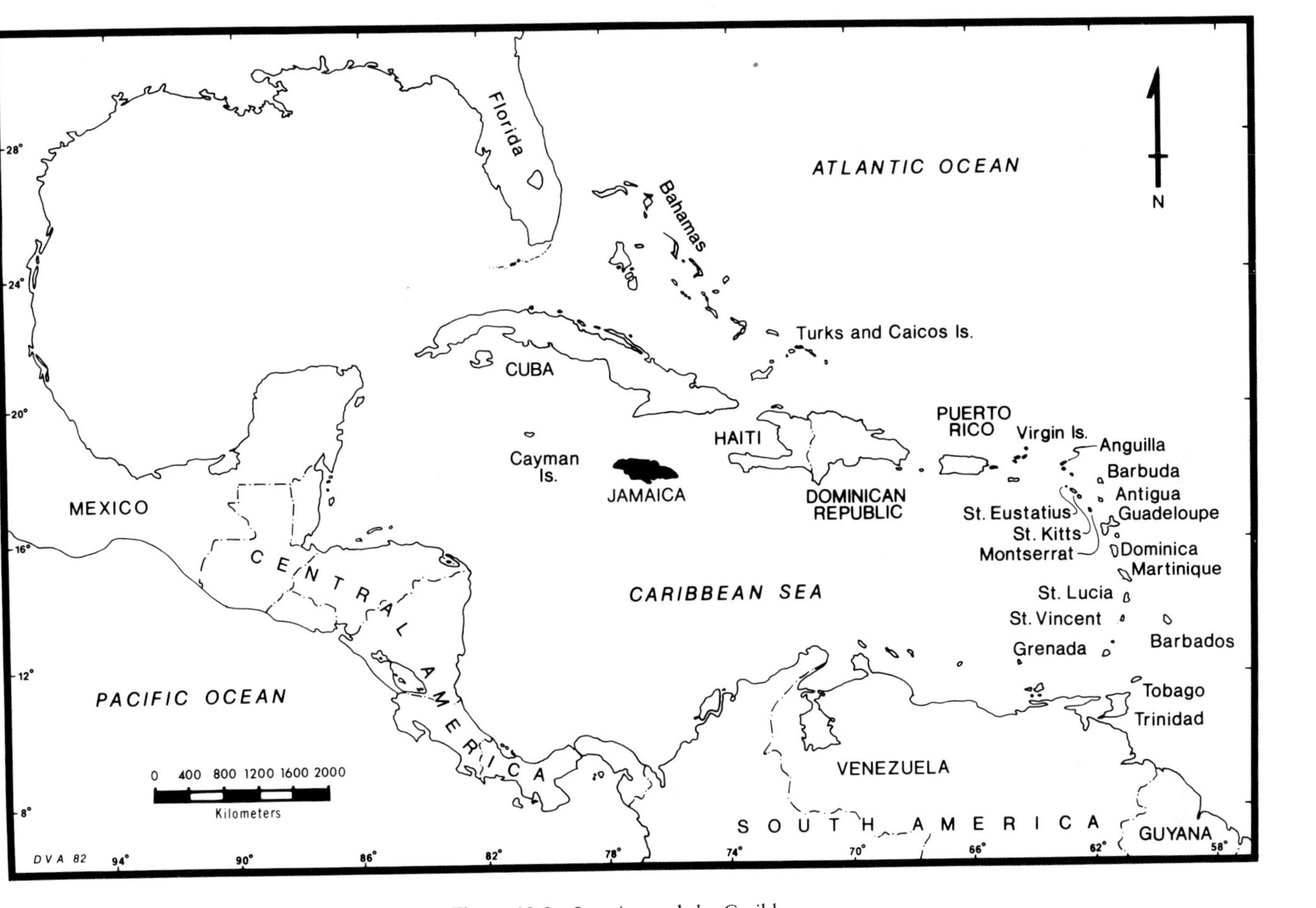

Figure 12.2 Jamaica and the Caribbean.

the utility of historical archaeology to expand on some poorly understood aspects of Caribbean history. In addition, it is hoped that this case study from the Caribbean will provide comparative insights for researchers studying transplanted Africans throughout the New World.

PREVIOUS AFRO-CARIBBEAN ARCHAEOLOGY

Recent studies in Jamaica and the Caribbean have shown the utility of archaeological investigations in examining questions relating to historical archaeology. Mathewson (1972, 1973, citing work by Handler), analyzed the material remains from the Old King's House and Port Royal, Jamaica, and postulated the presence of a distinct and apparently well-developed Afro-Jamaican ceramic and craft tradition.

Based on this preliminary work with the local Afro-Jamaican ceramics, Mathewson (1973) hypothesized that socioeconomic differentiation between slave quarters and manor houses could be demonstrated archaeologically. While this question had not been addressed directly for Jamaica, it had been studied in detail and substantiated for plantations in the southeastern United States (Fairbanks 1974; Ferguson 1978; Moore 1981; Otto 1975, 1977).

In Barbados, Handler (1972) and Handler and Lange (1978, 1979) combined archaeological and historical interpretations of excavations at the slave cemetery at Newton plantation. These studies demonstrate the importance of using documentary and published sources in order to understand the development of Afro-Jamaican living systems. Some of the problems that they encountered in carrying out their archaeological project helped to refine the research strategy employed at Drax Hall.

The first Jamaican archaeological project concerned strictly with a slave settlement on plantations was Barry Higman's study of early nineteenth-century occupations at New Montpelier (Higman 1974; Higman and Aarons 1978; Riordan 1973). While analyses of these findings are not complete, the endeavor showed the utility of the extensive use of documents as a means of locating potential sites for empirical testing using archaeological methods and techniques.

Both Higman (personal communication, 1980) and Handler and Lange (1978) were surprised at the small proportion of locally made artifacts surviving in slave settlement sites that could be attributed to African influences. These observations were taken into consideration when preparing for this project. Still, this author too was surprised by the dearth of "African" remains, or perhaps more correctly, the preponderance of imported European materials found at Drax Hall. Fortunately, shape/function and artifact pattern analyses provide mechansims with which to define and explore distinct Afro-Jamaican cultural patterns within the slave and free laborer community (Armstrong 1980, 1982a, b, 1983).

The research questions addressed in this chapter are defined so as to clarify and explicate some basic assumptions on the development of an Afro-Jamaican community. These are seen as a starting point to Afro-Jamaican studies utilizing archaeological reconnaissance techniques. They focus on areas where it was expected that archaeology could provide an empirical base for understanding what is not readily available in the historical record.

RESEARCH QUESTIONS: ELEMENTS OF CONTINUITY, SYSTEMS OF CHANGE

In preparation for this project the literature on slavery and slave society in Jamaica and the Caribbean was reviewed in order to formulate a "generalized" working hypothesis regarding the development of Afro-Jamaican society (see Braithwaite 1971; Craton 1978; Curtin 1969; Dunn 1973; Higman 1979; Mintz 1974; Mintz and Hall 1960; Patterson 1973; Sheridan 1974). These background readings suggest that the transplanted Africans in Jamaica developed a new and distinct internal social organization within the externally imposed confines of slavery. The living conditions into which the slaves were thrust and the historically "assumed" results of these conditions include:

1. Isolation and disruption from specific, African, ethnic backgrounds, and adaptation of many African elements (individual cultural traits) in modified form and context. These elements have been carried on, and/or rejuvenated, and can be seen in modern folk song, linguistics, and material culture (see Mintz 1974:11–12).
2. Subjugation to a system of divide and rule. Family patterns and lineage systems were broken up (Knight and Crahan 1979; Posnansky, personal communication, 1980; 1982). In the absence of the old systems, modified systems developed within slave settlements in plantation settings.
3. Segregation from the essentials of European cultural heritage (Dunn 1973:250; Goveia 1965). Social and legal sanctions restricted slaves from interacting freely with Euro-Jamaicans. However, while conscious efforts were made to disassociate slaves from their pasts, it was deemed necessary for the perpetuation of the system that their "Africaness" be distinguishable. Hence, they were free, if not encouraged, to retain some elements of their African cultural heritage.
4. Isolation from other island systems and slave systems. While similar island systems developed throughout the Caribbean, each island, and perhaps regions within an island, was influenced by its own physiographic parameters (size, topography, rainfall, soils, and location), as well as by colonial ties (Dunn 1973:25). Furthermore, slaves had restricted mobility with limited interactions from region to region within the island. One would expect at least minor variations from site to site depending on the region inhabited, the type and size of the estate, or degree of isolation (for example, rural versus urban).

Based on these historical and ethnohistorical observations and assumptions, it is hypothesized that transplanted Africans in Jamaica developed a new and distinct cultural context that drew upon a variety of African as well as European and possibly Amer-Indian patterns, and which evolved through time to become strikingly Jamaican or Afro-Jamaican—retaining elements of continuity within a system

Figure 12.3 Jamaica, showing location of Drax Hall Plantation.

of change. This cultural system is marked by elements of *continuity* and systems of *change*. Furthermore, this dual pattern of retention and evolution continued into the transitional apprenticeship period and "free laborer" period in Jamaica.

In order to address the question of continuity and change in an initial study such as this, particular aspects of the problem were selected for a case study examination at the Old Village at Drax Hall (Figures 12.3 and 12.4). The objectives were (1) to test for the presence and continuity of African elements in the material remains recovered from the Old Village; (2) to determine if, and how, the internal structure of the community was influenced by interactions with the Euro-Jamaican and European communities; and (3) to explore the dual relationship of continuity of Afro-Jamaican elements and systems of change (an amalgamation of Afro-Jamaican and Euro-Jamaican systems).

ARCHAEOLOGICAL RECONNAISSANCE

After an intensive survey of the slave settlement at Drax Hall Plantation, 60 probable house area features were identified (Figure 12.4). On the basis of survey data 6 of these house area features were excavated to obtain information on the development of the community. In addition, a trench was dug across another possible house area, identified by a magnetometer survey, in an attempt to identify its location and context. These features are placed in chronological context based on the "working mean dates" obtained for each:

Slave period (1760–1810)	Features 1, 52
Transitional period (1810–1840)	Feature 23
Free laborer period (1840–1925)	Features 15, 26
Mixed context (1690–1925)	Features 64, 48

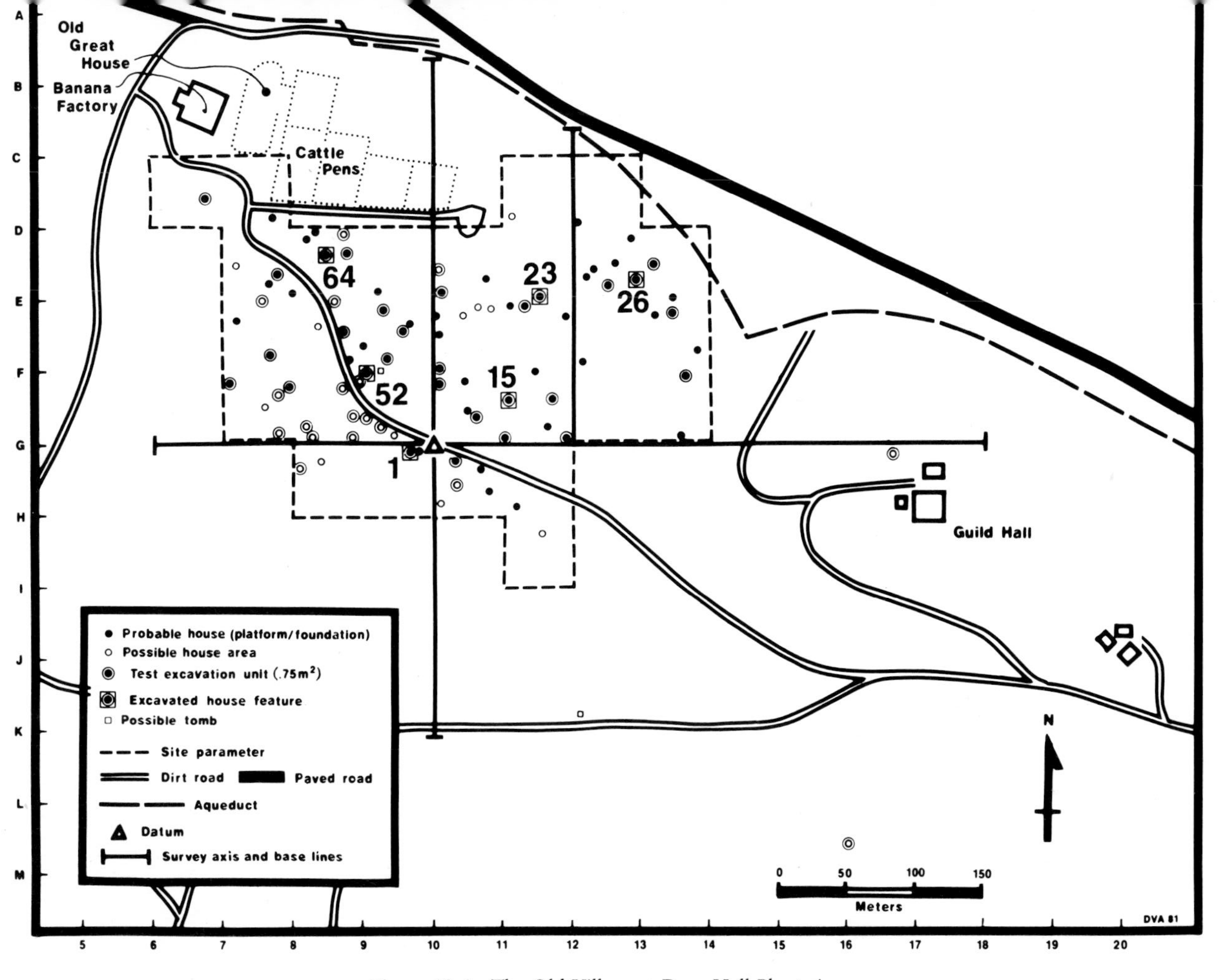

Figure 12.4 The Old Village at Drax Hall Plantation.

ANALYTICAL TECHNIQUES

Dating House Area Features

The dates of occupation for each house area feature were obtained using a combination of historical material dating techniques including South's Mean Ceramic Date (MCD) formula (1977; modified to account for the 1925 terminus date of the site).

The MCD formula was specifically designed for eighteenth-century sites where a rather fine-grained chronological context was desired. The usage of the method at Drax Hall for house areas dating to the late nineteenth century was designed to gain only a relative ballpark estimate. The dates obtained from coins and clay pipes (bowl shapes and marker's marks) refine the average date of occupation for each of these house areas (Figure 12.5).

Shape/Function Analysis

In addressing the research question it is assumed that ceramics constitute a portion of the material remains associated with food preparation and consumption; or what Deetz refers to as the "foodways subsystem" (1973:16, after Anderson 1971:2). This subsystem is only part of a complex cultural system, however; such component subsystems are interrelated and changes in one system usually bring about changes in another (Deetz 1973:16). Hence an examination of ceramic materials can help explain the cultural system of the material users. With respect to the research questions it is the objective of this study to use ceramic analysis to illuminate the existence and persistence of Afro-Jamaican continuities and to help explain cultural processes within the Old Village. In this endeavor the analysis of vessel shape (or attributes of form) is seen as a sensitive indicator of the function of the artifact within the cultural-behavioral system of the user. The examination of frequency and proportions of these forms, through time, is seen as an indicator of cultural processes.

Artifact Pattern Analysis

As Stanley South stated, "A key to understanding cultural processes lies in pattern recognition" (South 1977:3). If we are to derive meaningful comparative data from artifact assemblages, a testable, quantitative method must be employed. In pursuit of pattern recognition, South developed a standardized model of artifact pattern analysis (South 1977).

South (1977:86) assumed that the British (Euro-Americans) brought a basic set of behavioral modes, attitudes, and associated artifacts to the colonies. He attempted to demonstrate this postulate of "regularities in patterning in the archaeological record from colonial sites" through the examination of the material remains from several colonial sites. Based on these analyses South postulated a "Carolina Artifact Pattern." Furthermore, he postulated that specialized behavioral activities

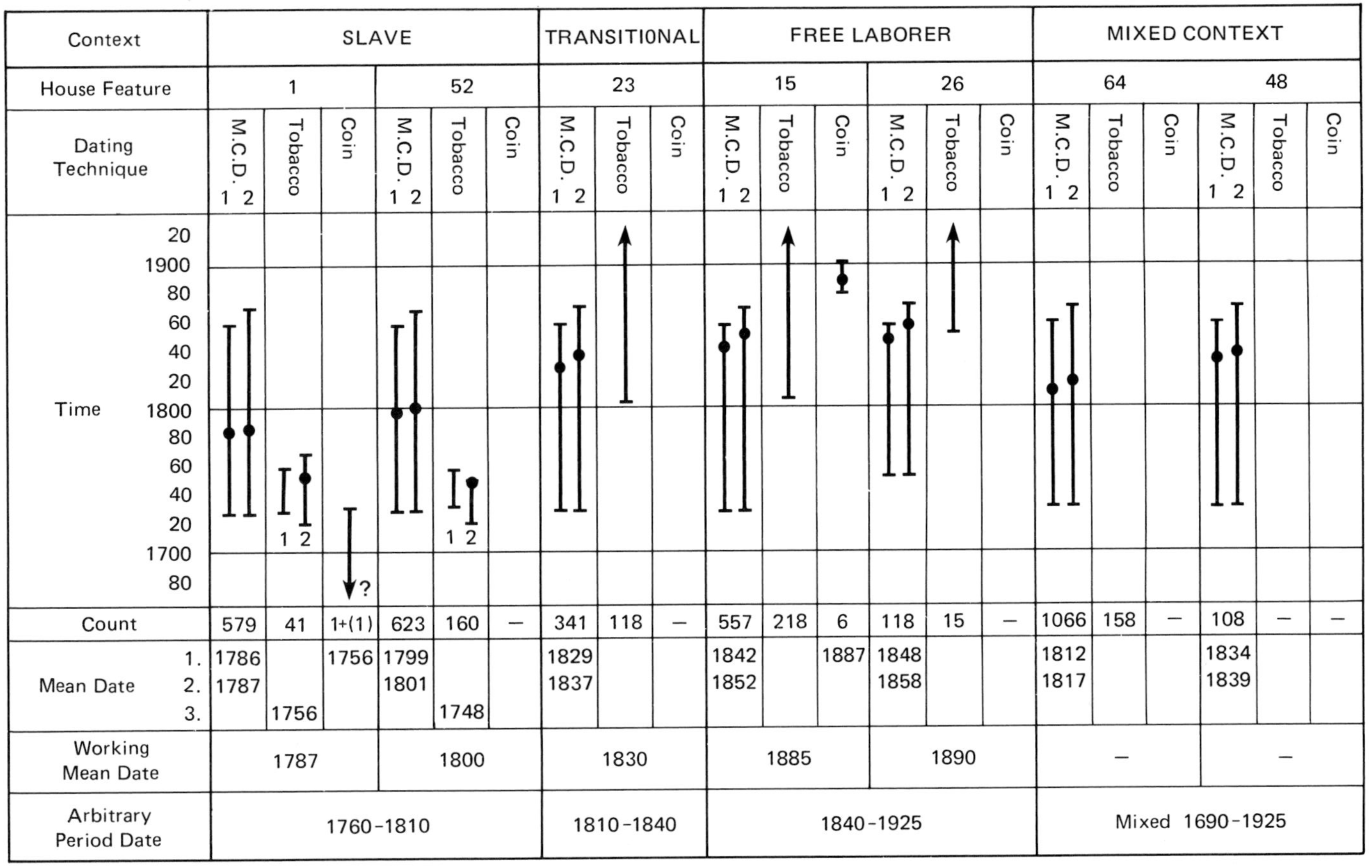

Context	SLAVE						TRANSITIONAL			FREE LABORER						MIXED CONTEXT					
House Feature	1			52			23			15			26			64			48		
Dating Technique	M.C.D. 1 2	Tobacco	Coin	M.C.D. 1 2	Tobacco	Coin	M.C.D. 1 2	Tobacco	Coin	M.C.D. 1 2	Tobacco	Coin	M.C.D. 1 2	Tobacco	Coin	M.C.D. 1 2	Tobacco	Coin	M.C.D. 1 2	Tobacco	Coin
Time (20, 1900, 80, 60, 40, 20, 1800, 80, 60, 40, 20, 1700, 80)		1 2	?		1 2																
Count	579	41	1+(1)	623	160	—	341	118	—	557	218	6	118	15	—	1066	158	—	108	—	—
Mean Date 1. 2. 3.	1786 1787	1756 (3.)	1756	1799 1801	1748 (3.)		1829 1837			1842 1852		1887	1848 1858			1812 1817			1834 1839		
Working Mean Date	1787			1800			1830			1885			1890			—			—		
Arbitrary Period Date	1760–1810						1810–1840			1840–1925						Mixed 1690–1925					

Figure 12.5 Working mean dates for house-area features at Drax Hall. M.C.D. (mean ceramic date): 1, South (1977:210–212); 2, modified in consideration of 1925 terminus date for the Drax Hall site. Tobacco-pipe dating techniques: 1, Oswald (1975); 2, Harrington (1954); 3, Binford (1962).

should reveal contrasting patterns. This latter postulate is supported by significantly different artifact pattern data from frontier sites in the United States—the "frontier pattern" (South 1977:146)—and data from both specialized military outposts and slave settlements for the same period in the southeastern United States (Garrow 1981).

For purposes of comparison some refinements in South's original English colonial Carolina Artifact Pattern were made (following Garrow 1981). These included the elimination of nondomestic occupation sites. Some additional refinements were made in the artifact groupings for Drax Hall in order to more efficiently categorize the data. The most significant alteration was the inclusion of "redware" earthenwares in the kitchen group. In the southeastern United States locally produced earthenwares have been regarded as "Colono-Indian," a term not applicable for the Caribbean (for a discussion of this terminology, see Ferguson 1978; cf. Noel-Hume 1962), and were placed in a generalized activities group by South. More recently these materials have been considered to be kitchen group artifacts based on the assumption that they played a significant role in food preparation and eating practices (Garrow 1981). A further, minor, alteration was the inclusion of "stub-stemmed pipes" in the tobacco group.

An underlying assumption in South's study is that the artifact frequency pattern is a reflection of human behavioral patterns and that these patterns are affected by ethnicity. This ethnic identity in South's model may be examined and defined by studying the frequency patterns of artifacts classified into functional groups. Thus the Carolina Artifact Pattern is a British colonial ethnic pattern. It follows that if we are studying a group with a different ethnic origin—African or Afro-Jamaican—we would expect a "specialized" artifact pattern reflecting elements of an African or Afro-Jamaican identity. The role of pattern analysis is particularly important for our study of Drax Hall and for other slave settlement sites where a surprising paucity of locally made materials have been recovered (see Handler and Lange 1978; Higman and Aarons 1978). The overwhelming majority of artifacts are imported and derive from English sources, yet, as we attempt to show, the overall use pattern within the Drax Hall settlement during the period of slavery varies from the suggested British colonial pattern of the same period.

ADDRESSING THE RESEARCH QUESTIONS AT DRAX HALL

The first step toward addressing the research questions is to demonstrate the presence of African elements (either elements of artifacts, artifacts, or the pattern of artifact frequencies) in the material remains recovered from the village. Once this is established, it is then possible to discuss the problem of continuity and change.

Elements of Continuity

One of the research problems was to demonstrate the presence of African elements in the material remains. Once established, another aspect of this problem was to examine the continuity and significance of these elements to the occupants of the site through time.

The broad category of redware includes all red earthenware ceramics found at the site, both imported and locally produced. To distinguish locally produced pottery and Afro-Jamaican elements, a typological system was devised in consultation with Roderich Ebanks (personal communication, 1982) who has examined collections of local redwares from both modern folk potters and from archaeological contexts. This system includes a variety of elements that establish discrete interval criteria for thickness, sherd size, temper size, along with an expanding numerical key to measurable elements such as shape, type of sherd (rim, body, or base), surface treatment, and surface preparation.

The examination of redware–earthenware elements indicated a distinct dichotomy in redwares. One group consists of thick, fine-grained, and often massive sherds that are fully fired (no core) and show evidence that they were turned on a wheel. This group is made up of what are probably imported redwares used as storage vessels for water or other commodities (27.1% of redwares). In the absence of trace element characterization, it cannot be established that these vessels were actually imported; however, they represent a technological mode of production sharing common elements with "Spanish jars" and other European forms.

The second group of redwares is identified as exhibiting an Afro-Jamaican mode of production. This group includes bowl-shaped (11.5% of redwares) and cooking pot-shaped vessels (31.4% of redwares). Both forms are commonly referred to by Jamaicans as "yabbas." This term has been traced linguistically to the Akan (Twi language) word *ayawa,* which means "earthenware vessel or dish" (Mathewson 1972:55). By analogy to contemporary sites in West Africa, the Caribbean, and the southeastern United States, it is argued that these forms correspond to generalized African "foodways" functions in both technology and social context.

The bowl forms found at Drax Hall are shallow, open vessels, with thick walls (average 10 mm), course-grained temper, and coil construction (Figure 12.6). The internal and external surfaces are smoothened and show some signs of burnishing. The internal surface is covered by an olive or reddish green glaze, an innovation presumably in response to European glazed ceramics. However, they appear to have been fired at fairly low temperatures. Firing probably took place in open hearths since it is an incomplete firing and yields a banded appearance in cross-section. The pot forms are of similar manufacture but the internal surface below the rim/lip is simply smoothened with no glaze. The rim and the lip of some fragments are covered with a thin red slip. All but one of the sherds of both bowl and pot forms are undecorated. The only possible decoration found is a stamped T impressed on a rim sherd. The sample size is small (count 328), however these distinctive redwares are found at all house features.

The Old King's House in Spanish Town, Jamaica, yielded a variety of course earthenwares similar to those found at Drax Hall which Mathewson (1973:28) attributes to the Afro-Jamaican community. A broad range of forms and fabrics were found among the 2000 sherds examined by Mathewson. Where decoration occurs, it is often a simple, incised pattern.

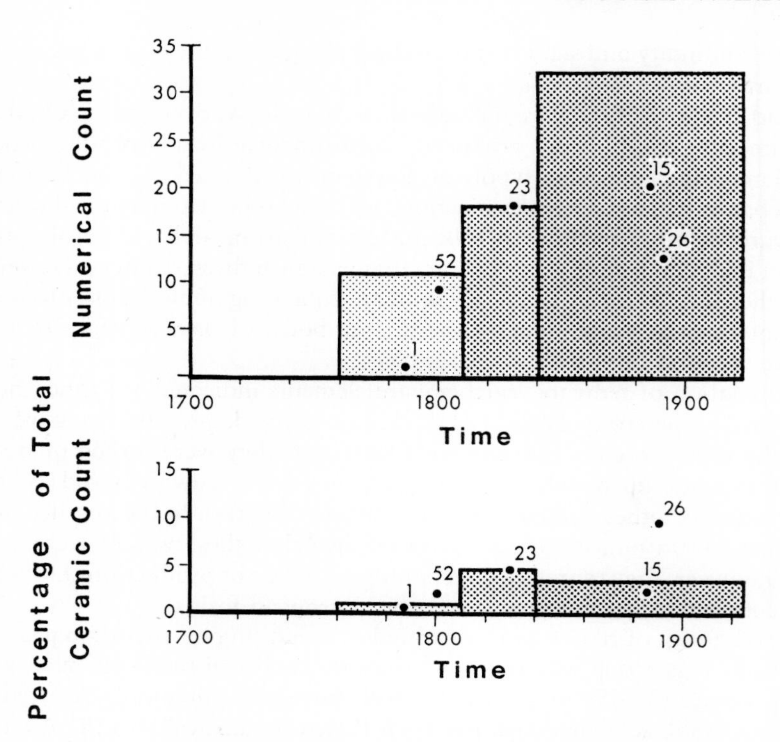

Context	SLAVE		TRANSITION	FREE LABORER		MIXED CONTEXT	
House Feature	1	52	23	15	26	64	48
Count by Feature	2	9	18	20	12	25	2
Percent by Feature	0.4	2.0	6.5	2.8	9.7	2.8	1.8
Count by Period	11		18	32		27	
Percent by Period	0.8		4.3	3.3		–	

Figure 12.6 Retention of redware bowl form.

African techniques and shapes also have been reported at Afro-American sites in the Southeast. Ferguson (1978) suggests that the colonoware found at Afro-American slave sites was probably produced by the slaves. He argues that the flat-bottomed bowl shape, low-firing, coil-and-molded construction, and methods of surface finishing are all found in prehistoric Africa (1978:79). These findings have been supported by recent studies by Garrow (1981) and Drucker and Anthony (1979).

It appears that the Drax Hall bowl and pot forms stem from generalized African forms and manufacturing techniques. These forms are similar to those found in many sites in West Africa. However, this is only a vague comparison since there is much variation, from region to region, in the specific forms and design elements used in West Africa. For example, Crossland (1973) describes the common vessel forms from the site of Begho, Ghana, West Africa, as spherical-bodied pots and hemispherical bowls. At Begho, as at several sites in Ghana, ceramics have a broad variety of surface decorations and a high percentage of them are decorated. However, many sites in Ghana, such as Techiman, Bono Manso, Mompongtin, have ceramics with similar vessel forms but which lack surface decorations (Crossland 1973:217).

Perhaps more significant than the mere presence of a bowl form and a technology that can be tied to African traditions is the sociocultural function of the "yabba" vessels. The bowl and pot represent part of a shared (or communal) food preparation and eating practice (see Deetz 1973). Materials that were probably used along with these ceramic forms include the calabash gourd, wooden vessels, and woven baskets. All are perishable, nonsurvivors in the archaeological record and probably played an important role in the "foodways" subsystem.

Mintz and Hall (1960) refer to an active internal marketing system in Jamaica. The earthenwares found at Drax Hall and other sites, such as the Old King's House, were probably obtained through this internal system along with perishable items and produce from provision grounds and gardens. Although the proportion of red earthenware bowl and pot fragments is relatively small for the periods we were able to study, it is quite possible that in the late seventeenth and early eighteenth centuries, prior to the proliferation of inexpensive imported ceramics, these forms constituted a larger proportion of the kitchen group, or foodways, remains (Armstrong 1983).

The presence of these vessel fragments confirms the continuity of African elements and helps to demonstrate that the site under examination is, as the historical documents suggest, an Afro-Jamaican village. By analogy to contemporary sites in West Africa, the Caribbean, and the southeastern United States, it is argued that these forms correspond to generalized African foodways functions in both technological and social contexts.

Shape/Function Analysis. In regards to retention through time, if the Afro-Jamaican elements persist, there should be a maintenance of the relative frequency of these elements through time. In fact, the yabba bowl form was found at all house features and actually increased in frequency through time (0.8% in house areas dating to the period of slavery; 3.3% from the free laborer period).

A second (independent or complementary) set of information on vessel shape is presented for general comparative purposes. At Cannon's Point Plantation in Georgia, Otto (1975) found the proportion of bowls and tableware ceramics combined (plates and bowls) at the slave settlement to make up a significantly greater portion of the total of ceramics than found in remains from the planter house/living area context. Furthermore, Miller (1980) has shown that the nineteenth-century imported ceramics bowl forms are the least expensive forms with others such as plates and cups relatively more expensive. While we do not have a comparable sample from planter contexts, we can compare the data from the slave settlements at Drax Hall and Cannon's Point. It should be noted that the ceramic samples from these two sites are quite different. The sample from Drax Hall is 4221 sherds, most of which are highly fragmented, compared to 126 from Cannon's Point where only whole or distinguishable vessels were included. Still, a relatively high proportion of tableware was found in both the slave quarters at Cannon's Point (64%) and at the Old Village at Drax Hall (63%).

The proportion of ceramics used to serve tea and coffee is lower in slave (21%) than in planter (27%) or overseer (31%) contexts at Cannon's Point. By comparison, at Drax Hall the proportion (1%) is significantly lower than any of the Cannon's Point sites. Storage vessels at Drax Hall make up a higher proportion than at the slave quarters at Cannon's Point. The significance of this particular statistic is unclear since there is considerable variation in and through time in the proportion of storage vessels at Drax Hall (0.8%–14.9%), while at Cannon's Point the slaves had 4% storage vessels, the planters 11%, but the overseers had only 2% (Otto 1975).

The results of shape/function studies at Drax Hall reinforce the pattern reported by Otto (1975) of a relatively high proportion of tableware and low proportion of tea/coffee ceramic forms in slave/lower-economic contexts. However, significant differences are seen in both the composition of the sample being compared and the overall vessel shape composition (Table 12.1).

Returning to the primary test of the presence of elements of continuity, the data from Drax Hall demonstrate the continued presence of local yabba bowl forms. These forms were produced using technology which was, at least in part, derived from West African potting practices. These data reflect a maintenance of a communal foodways subsystem and a continuity or retention of African elements.

Artifact Pattern Analysis. If an Afro-Jamaican context exists, it should be exhibited not just in a specific class of artifacts, but in the overall pattern of materials used and discarded. The artifacts deposited at Drax Hall should reflect this pattern. The study of artifact patterns (South 1977:83–139, as modified by Garrow 1981) provides a mechanism to demonstrate the Afro-Jamaican presence in the overall material record. After the examination of data collected from three late eighteenth-century slave sites in Georgia (Yaughan and Curriboo plantations) and data reported from presumed slave contexts at Spiers Landing (Drucker and Anthony 1979), Garrow (1981) found a marked contrast between the proportions of artifacts present in eighteenth-century British colonial sites (Carolina Artifact Pattern) versus slave context sites. On the basis of these differences he suggested the existence of a slave artifact pattern (Carolina Slave Artifact Pattern) with the following characteristics:

	A	B
(1) An elevated percentage of kitchen group artifacts	77.49 (70.94–84.18)	59.51 (51.80–64.9)
(2) A lowered percentage of architecture group artifacts	17.74 (11.82–24.83)	27.58 (25.18–31.38)
(3) A higher combination of kitchen/architecture group artifacts	95.23	87.09

A, Carolina Slave Artifact Pattern (Garrow, 1981).
B, Carolina Artifact Pattern (South, 1977; modified by Garrow, 1981).

Table 12.1
SHAPE OF CERAMIC ITEMS

	Drax Hall—Old Village (St. Ann's, Jamaica)[a]								Cannon's Point Plantation (Georgia)[b]		
	Slave		Transition	Free laborer		Mixed					
	1	52	23	15	26	64	48	$\bar{X}$	Slave	Overseer	Planter
Tableware	43.5	63.2	57.2	42.3	88.9	54.6	77.2	54.3 (42.3–88.9)	64	58	52
Tea/coffee	1.1	0.6	3.0	1.3	0	0.6	0.8	1.0 (0–3.0)	21	31	27
Storage	23.0	3.3	3.0	12.6	0.7	13.1	0.9	11.7 (0.7–23.0)	4	2	11
Cooking pot	0.3	0.3	0	27.3	0	0.5	0.8	0.6 (0–27.3)	—	—	—
Other (unidentified)	29.5	32.4	34.6	15.3	10.3	31.1	13.4	27.0 (10.3–34.6)	11	9	10
Sample size (total items)	740	660	422	839	136	1297	127	4221	126	135	309

[a]Fragments, including redwares.
[b]Whole and identifiable forms.

It was expected that the proportions of artifacts from the slave village at Drax Hall would be similar to the Carolina Slave Artifact Pattern.

In fact, a higher proportion of kitchen group artifacts (71.43% versus 59.5%) and a lower proportion of architecture group artifacts (19.56% versus 27.58%) were found in the houses dating to the period of slavery in Jamaica than reported for the Revised Carolina Artifact Pattern (Table 12.2). These data fit well with the Carolina Slave Artifact Pattern. Garrow found this variation from the Carolina Artifact Pattern to be accentuated when the proportions of kitchen and architecture groups were combined. The combined kitchen/architecture groups made up 95.23% of the materials from the four slave sites from the Southeast, but only 87.09% of the material from the sites making up the Carolina Artifact Pattern. Materials from these combined groups accounted for 90.99% of materials from the slave period.

The Drax Hall combined total of kitchen/architecture group artifacts was greater (+3.90%) than that of the revised Carolina Artifact Pattern and fell midway between the Carolina Slave Artifact Pattern and the Revised Carolina Artifact Pattern (Table 12.2). The Drax Hall data, therefore, seem to support a hypothesis of a distinguishable artifact pattern corresponding to a "specialized" slave or Afro-Jamaican (or Afro-American) context. While the data from southeastern slave sites described by Garrow and the data from Drax Hall focus on a common Afro-American and Afro-Jamaican slave pattern, it is possible that this pattern of material use is as much a response to the commonly deprived economic status of the occupants of these sites, as artifact pattern proportions for kitchen and architecture groups. This later proposition could be tested with data obtained from historically known lower-economic British colonial settlements.

Systems of Change

It was expected that the internal structure of the community would be influenced by interactions with the Euro-Jamaican community. The period in question is one of a proliferation of many inexpensive European materials that were transported to the colonies and rapidly distributed, used, and broken (South 1977:206). African elements would constitute only a portion of the artifactual assemblage, and were used along with a variety of European materials.

Shape/Function Analysis. If the occupants adopted and incorporated European or Euro-Jamaican use patterns, then it was expected that ceramic usage would reflect the general Euro-Jamaican pattern. Specifically, in imported ceramics the expected pattern is a decrease in the bowl form and an increase in the plate form corresponding to similar shifts in European form use. Given the absence of comparative data from Euro-Jamaican sites, analogies were restricted to similar evidence from North American colonial sites presented by Deetz (1973) and Brown (1973) which illustrated a shift through time in the form and function of ceramics from seventeenth- and eighteenth-century sites at Plymouth, Massachusetts. The bowl form predominated in the seventeenth century but decreased in popularity through time. By 1800

Table 12.2

COMPARISON OF THE REVISED CAROLINA ARTIFACT PATTERN AND ARTIFACT PATTERNS FROM SLAVE SITE CONTEXTS

Artifact group	A Revised Carolina Artifact Pattern[a]		B Carolina Slave Artifact Pattern[b]		C Artifact pattern at Drax Hall (features 1 and 52)	
	$\bar{X}$	Range	$\bar{X}$	Range	$\bar{X}$	Range
Kitchen	59.51%	(51.80%–64.97%)	77.49%	(70.94%–84.18%)	71.43%	(63.06%–79.10%)
Architecture	27.58%	(25.18%–31.38%)	17.74%	(11.82%–24.83%)	19.56%	(14.54%–25.05%)
Furniture	0.35%	(0.18%–0.63%)	0.07%	(0.05%–0.08%)	0.00%	(0.00%)
Arms	0.19%	(0.09%–0.34%)	0.17%	(0.02%–0.27%)	0.02%	(0.00%–0.05%)
Clothing	2.95%	(0.55%–5.38%)	0.49%	(0.30%–0.79%)	0.46%	(0.18%–0.77%)
Personal	0.29%	(0.15%–0.54%)	0.05%	(0.02%–0.08%)	0.27%	(0.24%–0.31%)
Pipes	7.80%	(1.76%–13.94%)	3.52%	(2.43%–5.42%)	4.64%	(1.82%–7.74%)
Activities	1.34%	(0.94%–1.86%)	0.48%	(0.23%–0.86%)	3.60%	(3.09%–4.07%)
Sample size totals	100.01%	—	100.01%	37,232	100.00%	4,326
A COMPARISON OF COMBINED KITCHEN GROUP AND ARCHITECTURE GROUP MATERIALS						
Kitchen	59.51%	(51.80%–64.97%)	77.49%	(70.94%–84.18%)	71.43%	(63.06%–79.10%)
Architecture	27.58%	(25.18%–31.38%)	17.74%	(11.82%–24.83%)	19.56%	(14.54%–25.05%)
Combined total	87.09%		95.23%		90.99%	(88.11%–93.64%)

[a]South (1977) modified by Garrow (1981).
[b]Garrow (1981).

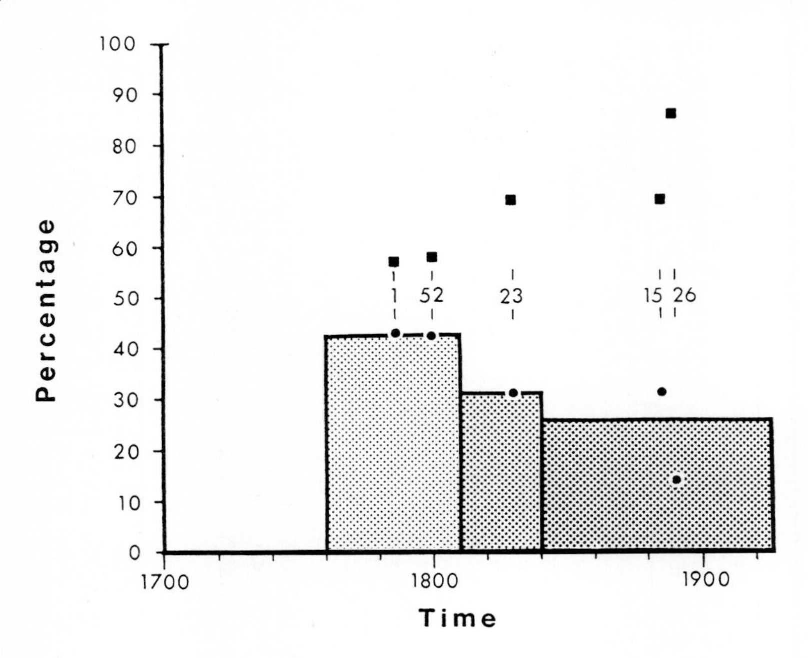

Context	SLAVE		TRANSITION	FREE LABORER		MIXED CONTEXT	
House Feature	1	52	23	15	26	64	48
■ % Plate	57.3	58.0	69.0	69.0	86.7	80.6	82.5
● % Bowl	42.7	42.0	31.0	31.0	13.3	19.4	17.5
Sherd Count	342	417	250	355	121	708	97
% BOWL	42.3		31.0	25.8		-	

Figure 12.7 Overall bowl/plate ratios through time.

the plate form actually outnumbered the bowl form. These archaeological data are interpreted to correspond to changes in the behavior patterns, with the hollow form (including bowls) representing "folk culture" and communal eating practices, and the plate representing the formation of a rather ubiquitous "popular culture" and individual eating practices (Deetz 1973).

Archaeological data from Drax Hall suggest a continuation of the nineteenth-century shift towards plate (flatware) forms. During the period of slavery, 42.3% of all tableware ceramics (both imported and locally made) were in the form of bowls. The overall proportion of bowls decreased through time to 31% in the transition period and to 25.8% in the free laborer period (Figure 12.7). This could be a response to trends in the Euro-Jamaican (and Euro-American) spheres, however such patterns have not yet been defined. The continued trend may also have been the result of a decreased availability of bowl forms as manufactures decreased their production of these forms in response to the use patterns of the dominant Euro-American populations. The increased frequency of yabba bowl forms at a time when the proportion of imported bowl forms was decreasing may reflect an Afro-Jamaican compensation for this decreased availability.

Artifact Pattern Analysis. It was expected that patterns of artifact use would vary through time in response to changes in the external Euro-Jamaican system. Unfortunately this is at present untested due to lack of comparative data from a suitable series of middle-to-late nineteenth-century sites (either Euro-Jamaican or Euro-American). South's model for artifact pattern analysis was defined for eighteenth-century sites and sites analyzed using this procedure have been primarily of eighteenth-century contexts. Still, the examination of Drax Hall artifact patterns reveal trends in material use through time that can be tested and refined in future studies in the Caribbean and elsewhere.

The Drax Hall data suggest a trend toward a decrease in the high proportion of kitchen group artifacts—from 71.43% in slave context to 43.8% in free laborer (Figure 12.8)—and an increase in the proportion of architecture group materials.

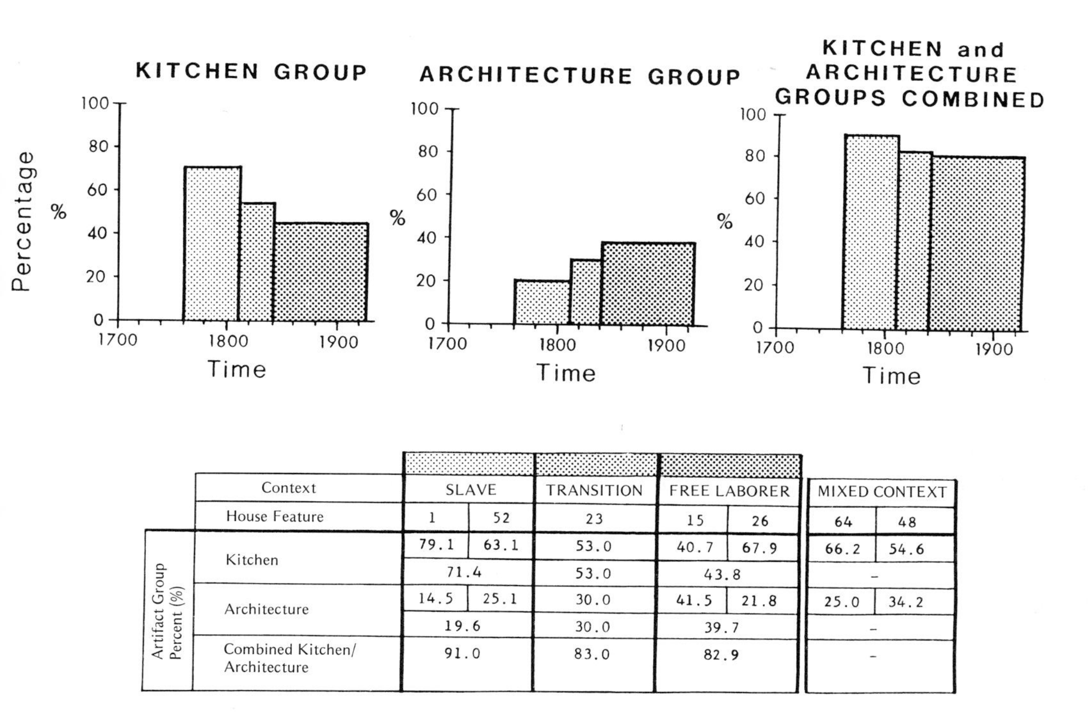

Artifact Group Percent (%)	Context	SLAVE		TRANSITION	FREE LABORER		MIXED CONTEXT	
	House Feature	1	52	23	15	26	64	48
	Kitchen	79.1	63.1	53.0	40.7	67.9	66.2	54.6
		71.4		53.0	43.8		–	
	Architecture	14.5	25.1	30.0	41.5	21.8	25.0	34.2
		19.6		30.0	39.7		–	
	Combined Kitchen/ Architecture	91.0		83.0	82.9		–	

Figure 12.8 Artifact pattern analysis: change through time.

However, the combined kitchen and architecture group retains its relative high proportion. This shift in kitchen and architectural groups could be the result of one or more untested causes. It could result from: (1) a shift towards the "British-Colonial" model; (2) a shift corresponding to a general pattern of nineteenth-century material use associated with worldwide patterns of availability; or (3) a shift corresponding to the documented change from slave to free laborer reflecting a change in status.

The Dual Relationship: Continuity and Change

If both continuity of Afro-Jamaican elements and systems of change occur through time, then these should be exhibited in a dual relationship through time. The preceding examples of vessel shapes, artifact patterns, and changes in their frequency through time are used as a test.

Shape/Function Analysis. Elements of continuity, such as the local redware bowl form, are retained (0.8% of ceramics during the period of slavery increasing to 3.3% in the free labor period) while the overall frequency of imported ceramic bowl forms decreases (42.3%–25.8% over the same period) and the proportion of imported plate form increases (Figure 12.9).

While the overall increase in plate forms found through time at Drax Hall may be in response to European patterns and could be associated with an increase in prosperity (these flatware forms cost more than bowls), the shift may also be a response to what forms were available for sale in the markets. Similarly, the increase in redware bowl forms could be regarded as either a maintenance of traditional Afro-Jamaican ways in response to freedom of choice or increased self-reliance after emancipation. It may also be a reflection of limited purchasing power and the necessity to produce, for use, low-cost items from local resources when, after emancipation, such goods were no longer provided by the plantation. The cost of imported ceramics decreased through the nineteenth century thus making all such wares relatively less expensive (Miller 1980). It is probable, therefore, that the increase in locally produced bowl forms was a reflection of either a retention of communal foodways by choice, and/or that this pattern suggests a continued impoverished condition with restricted access to goods that had to be purchased with cash at the marketplace. While support for the latter possibility is suggested by corresponding faunal data which indicate the increased use of marginal shellfish species, no doubt both choice and economic condition played a part in this pattern.

Artifact Pattern Analysis. Once again the comparative base for European-American and Jamaican settlements is nonexistent. Regardless, a dynamic quality is apparent in the patterns of artifacts from Drax Hall which conform to a similar pattern of change in the slave settlements examined by Garrow (1981). This change is marked by a decrease in kitchen artifacts and an increase in architectural group items, with an overall decrease in kitchen/architecture group combined.

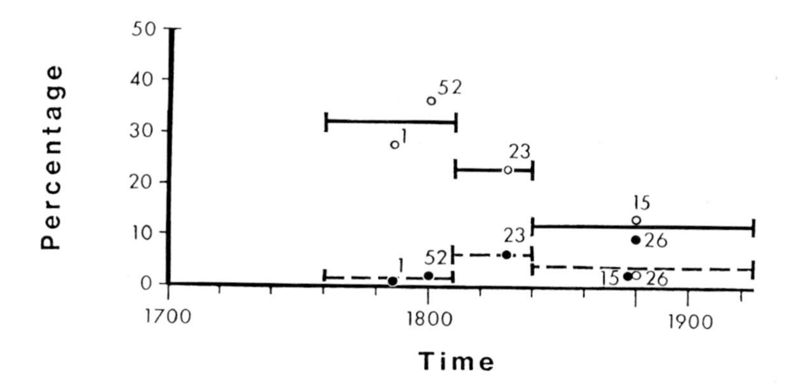

	Context	SLAVE		TRANSITION	FREE LABORER		MIXED CONTEXT	
	House Feature	1	52	23	15	26	64	48
Imported Ceramics	Count	144	164	64	98	4	112	15
	%	27.6	36.8	23.8	13.8	3.2	12.5	13.6
	Combined %	31.8		23.8	12.4		–	
Local Redwares	Count	2	9	18	20	12	25	2
	%	0.4	2.0	6.5	2.8	9.7	2.8	1.8
	Combined %	1.2		6.5	3.9		–	

Figure 12.9 Bowl form: proportions of imported ceramics versus local redwares.

It is suggested that these trends in the patterns of material use through time are in response to both a continuance of Afro-Jamaican elements and assimilative responses to changes in the Euro-Jamaican system. The European industrial production and distribution of goods made products available to the people at Drax Hall at increasingly lower costs through the nineteenth century. However, similar trends in availability and cost of materials should be expected in Euro-American material contexts. It would not be surprising if future studies of Euro-American and Afro-American sites reveal continued "parallel" differences in artifact patterns through the nineteenth century. As previously stated, this expected variance may be as much a function of economic differentiation as ethnic distinction.

The data presented here form a foundation for further examination of questions regarding the behavioral systems of slaves and, later, free laborers in Jamaica. These questions could include comparative studies on the conditions of slaves from one estate to another, on large estates versus small estates, or an examination of slave, maroon, and free black (as well as planter, overseer, poor white, Asian, and East Indian) living conditions as they changed through time in these various settings.

What effect did emancipation have on plantation slaves, and was "freedom" accompanied by increased social status and access to goods? This study provides a baseline of data supporting the assumption that an Afro-Jamaican population can be defined archaeologically.

Summary of Additional Findings

In addition to addressing specific research questions, the dissertation from which this essay is abstracted includes considerable information on slave and free laborer living systems, village and house-yard living areas, and dietary patterns (see Armstrong 1983).

The artifacts that survived in the ruins of the house areas at the Old Village permitted the definition of a tentative plantation slave and/or lower-economic pattern of material use. The basic artifacts also provide some nonquantifiable aspects and insights into the idiosyncracies and complexities of the slave's living systems. A cursory look at the artifacts yields little information on ethnicity or economic condition; however, upon closer examination the persistence of the yabba forms derived from African potting practices can be noted. In the foundations of the houses a variety of borrowed or reused bricks are found, suggesting limited access to supplies. An incised knife handle and inscribed belt buckle provide small clues to individual personalities and perhaps the importance of scarce goods. The presence of glass beads tell of body adornment, and thimbles and spool ends bring to mind the picture of a woman sewing. Rough flint nodules with multiple use-worn surfaces were picked up and used along with bits of scrap iron to light clay pipes and kitchen fires. The inexpensive yet brittle pipes in turn were used until only a stub remained and stem fragments were sometimes reworked to extend the life of the bowl. Immediately behind the thatched wattle-and-daub (or post-fill) house, a fire warmed an evening meal, and through the evening, family and friends filled their calabash from the communal pot. In the yard, well-worn and broken agricultural tools and files were found. These were probably used in both the cane fields and the provision grounds. Finally, a heavy iron object, probably a burden weight, provides a grim reminder of the institution of slavery in which the people were bound. These impressions are in themselves quite limited in scope and no one item provides positive identification of the cultural identity of the village occupants, but the artifact pattern and shape/function studies provide this information.

The fauna, flora, and documentary examination of diet suggest a subsistence system which made use of a combination of domestic and wild foods in a dual relationship of reliance on provisions such as codfish, corn, and flour obtained from the plantation management, and the independent production and procurement of wild and domesticated foods.

A study of remnant vegetation at the site demonstrated the presence of a high proportion of useful wild and domesticated plants among the remnant vegetation at the Old Village. These data, when supplemented with ethnobotanical accounts, give indirect evidence for the continuation of African dietary practices including the continued use of plants such as akee, and the importance of house-yard garden areas described in the historical accounts. These gardens contained a variety of plants for dietary, medicinal, ritual/belief, and asthetic purposes.

Faunal remains were highly fragmented throughout the period under investigation. The condition of these remains suggest a continuation of soup bone/cooking pot foodways and reinforce the artifact shape/function data from the site (Reitz 1982). A change noted in the faunal assemblage is of an increase in the latter periods in the frequency of, and perhaps reliance on, shellfish (protein) from the rocky intertidal area in house areas. This may be due to the probable loss of traditional protein sources in the postemancipation, free laborer era. The "marginal" shellfish resources provided a high nutritional yield, could be quickly gathered, and had no monetary cost (Armstrong 1983).

While the increase in shellfish species in the faunal remains suggests marginality in the community, we do not know if shellfish actually played an important part in the diet. Rodent gnawing on surviving bone and the presence of dogs in the house areas forces only tentative conclusions from the archaeological remains (Reitz 1982). Furthermore, while documents indicate at least some effort was made to procure fish during both the period of slavery and the period of transition, few fish remains were recovered. This leads to questions concerning the survival of food refuse in the archaeological record, and to those considering what part the provisions reported in the historical record actually played in the diet, and thus to our present understanding of slave and free laborer diets.

The question of diet—and what proportion of the diet is contributed by marine resources, domestic fauna, wild and domestic provisions grown by the slaves in the plantations provisioning grounds, and provisions purchased by the estate and supplied to the slaves—remains a problem. Further analysis of historical documents and more intensive examination of the archaeological record, including fine-grained flotation and pollen sampling in house areas, may help to further define the slave and free laborer diets and changing patterns in diet over time. A study using these techniques was carried out in the winter of 1983 and the findings are being analyzed.

DISCUSSION

This project undertook the primary task of using archaeological methods and techniques to help answer some basic questions regarding the development of an Afro-Jamaican community. The results of the analyses of materials recovered from excavations at the Old Village at Drax Hall suggest that the Afro-Jamaican context of the site can be demonstrated and identified archaeologically by the presence of a distinct pattern in material use. This pattern is marked by the retention of elements of African continuity within a system of change. The changes identified at the site were responses to trends in, and an assimilation of, European behavioral patterns and local environmental conditions.

It has been shown that an Afro-Jamaican redware-earthenware bowl form—with its functional implications of African technology and a collective "foodways" system—was retained and increased in frequency, although the overall pattern of ceramic use reflected a European colonial trend of decrease in the bowl form and an increased use of imported plates (imported presumably by individuals).

A problem encountered in slave site studies has been the small proportion of surviving artifacts that can be directly attributed to a specific, or even an generalized, African ethnic identity. These data suggest extensive change from traditional African patterns and extensive assimilation of European behavioral practices within the new cultural contexts of the Afro-Jamaican community. Even the definable Afro-Jamaican redware-earthenware fragments from the Old Village constitute only a small proportion of all artifacts recovered from this site—the majority being imported European materials. However, artifact pattern analysis provides a mechanism for distinguishing and understanding Afro-Jamaican cultural processes. The artifact patterns at Drax Hall suggest a "specialized" variation from the British colonial Carolina Artifact Pattern model (South 1977, as revised by Garrow 1981). Materials from Drax Hall show a relatively high proportion of kitchen group materials, a lower proportion of architecture group materials, and a higher combined proportion of kitchen architecture group materials. These data conform to a pattern found at slave sites in the southeastern United States, and mark a step toward the definition of a distinctive "slave" pattern and/or a pattern of low economic status. The latter (poor economic condition and low status) is apparent in both the material and dietary record, however the dividing lines between ethnic/cultural choices and economic conditions are not clear.

While historical and archaeological techniques are additive partners in the study of the human past, the history of Afro-Jamaicans, and history in general, is often limited by the subjectivity of its recorders. Archaeology, on the other hand, deals with the everyday refuse of those who lived in the past and provides an objective view that allows us to add to our knowledge of a people caught up and lost within the institution of slavery. Artifact pattern analyses (after South 1977) combined with shape/function analysis techniques (after Deetz 1973) are shown to provide a mechanism by which the Afro-Jamaican slave cultural contexts can be objectively defined and explained.

It is hoped that this initial case study will serve as both a model and a port of embarkation for further studies aimed at the investigation of the development of Afro-Jamaica and Afro-Caribbean cultural systems.

ACKNOWLEDGMENTS

The contents of this essay are derived from my dissertation in anthropology completed in 1983 at the University of California, Los Angeles (see also Armstrong 1982b). The Drax Hall Archeological Project was carried out by the author under the supervision and guidance of Professor Merrick Posnansky, and under the joint sponsorship of the University of California, Los Angeles and the Institute of Jamaica. Financial assistance was provided through a Fulbright-Hays Doctoral Research Fellowship (1981–1982) along with funds from UCLA's Chancellor's Council on International and Comparative Studies, and grants from the UCLA Friends of Archeology (1980–1981) and the Regents of the University of California (1980–1981). The Institute of Jamaica provided material support and field personnel.

REFERENCES

Anderson, Jay
1971 A solid sufficiency: an ethnography of yeoman foodways in Stuart England. Ph.D. dissertation, Department of Anthropology, University of Pennsylvania, Philadelphia. (Ann Arbor; University Microfilms.)

Armstrong, Douglas V.
1980 The Drax Hall slave village: an archaeological investigation of slavery on a Jamaican plantation. Preliminary Report: Part 1—Documents Search and Site Selection. Submitted to the Chairman of the Board, Institute of Jamaica. Manuscript on file at the National Library, Institute of Jamaica and at the U.C.L.A. Archeological Survey.
1982a The Old Village at Drax Hall. In *Proceedings of the Ninth International Congress for the Study of Pre-Columbian Cultures of the Lesser Antilles.* Santo Domingo, Dominican Republic, August 1981 (in press, University of Montreal).
1982b The Old Village at Drax Hall: an archeological progress report. *Journal of New World Archaeology* 5(2):87–103. (Institute of Archaeology, University of California, Los Angeles.)
1983 The Old Village at Drax Hall plantation: an archeological examination of an Afro-Jamaican settlement. Ph.D. dissertation in Anthropology, University of California, Los Angeles. Ann Arbor: University Microfilms.

Ascher, Robert
1975 Tin can archaeology. *Historical Archaeology* 8:7–16.

Binford, Lewis R.
1962 A new method of calculating dates from kaolin pipe stem samples. *Southeastern Archaeological Conference Newsletter* 9(1):19–21.

Brathwaite, Edward
1971 *The Development of Creole Society in Jamaica 1770–1820.* Oxford: Clarendon Press.

Brown, Marley
1973 Ceramics from Plymouth, 1621–1800: the documentary record. In *Ceramics in America.* Ian Quimby, ed. Charlottesville: The University of Virginia Press. Pp. 41–74.

Craton, Michael
1978 *Searching for the Invisible Man: Slaves and Plantation Life in Jamaica.* Cambridge: Harvard University Press.

Crossland, Leonard Brighton
1973 A study of Begho pottery in light of excavation conducted at the Begho B-2 site. Master's thesis, Department of Archaeology, University of Ghana, Legon.

Curtin, Philip D.
1969 *The Atlantic Slave Trade—a census.* Madison: University of Wisconsin Press.

Deetz, James
1973 Ceramics from Plymouth, 1620–1835: the archaeological evidence. In *Ceramics in America.* Ian Quimby, ed. Charlottesville: University of Virginia Press. Pp. 15–40.
1977 *In Small Things Forgotten: The Archaeology of Early American Life.* Garden City, N.Y.: Anchor Press/Doubleday.

Drucker, Lesley M., and Ronald W. Anthony
1979 *The Spiers Landing Site: Archaeological Investigations in Berkeley County, South Carolina.* Columbia, S.C.: Carolina Archaeological Services.

Dunn, Richard S.
1973 *Sugar and Slaves—The Rise of the Planter Class in the English West Indies, 1624–1713.* New York: Norton.

Fairbanks, Charles H.
1974 The Kingsley slave cabins in Duval County, Florida 1968. *The Conference on Historic Sites Archaeology Papers, 1972* 7:62–93.

Ferguson, Leland G.
1978 Looking for the "Afro" in Colono-Indian pottery. *The Conference on Historic Site Archaeology Papers* 12:68–86.

Garrow, Patrick H.
1981 Investigations of Yaughan and Curriboo plantations. Paper presented at the 14th Annual Meetings of the Society of Historical Archaeology Conference, New Orleans, January 1981.
Goveia, Elsa
1965 *Slave Society in the British Leeward Islands at the End of the Eighteenth Century.* New Haven, Conn.: Yale University Press.
Handler, Jerome S.
1972 An archaeological investigation of the domestic life of plantation slaves in Barbados. *Journal of the Barbados Museum and Historical Museum and Historical Society* (Barbados, West Indies) 34(2):64–72.
Handler, Jerome S., and Frederick W. Lange
1978 *Plantation Slavery in Barbados; An Archaeological and Historical Investigation.* Cambridge: Harvard University Press.
1979 Plantation slavery on Barbados, West Indies. *Archaeology* July/August 1979:45–52.
Harrington, Jean C.
1954 Dating stem fragments of seventeenth century clay tobacco pipes. *Archaeological Society of Virginia Quarterly Bulletin* 9(1):10–14.
Higman, Barry W.
1974 A Report on excavations at Montpelier and Roehampton. *Jamaica Journal* 8:40–45.
1979 *Slave Population and Economy in Jamaica, 1807–1834.* London: Cambridge University Press.
Higman, Barry W., and G. A. Aarons
1978 A report to the University of the West Indies, Mona, and the Jamaican National Trust Commission, on archaeological work carried out at the slave village site, New Montpelier, St. James. Manuscript dated January 12, 1978. Unpublished manuscript.
Knight, Franklin W., and Margaret E. Crahan
1979 The African migration and the origins of an Afro-American society and culture. In *Africa and the Caribbean: the legacies of a link.* Margaret E. Crahan and Franklin Knight, eds. Baltimore: The Johns Hopkins University Press.
Mathewson, Duncan R.
1972 Jamaican ceramics: an introduction to 18th century folk pottery in West African tradition. *Jamaica Journal* 7(1–2):25–29 (Kingston).
1973 Archaeological analysis of material culture was a reflection of sub-cultural differentiation in 18th century Jamaica. *Jamaica Journal* 7(1–2):25–29 (Kingston).
Miller, George L.
1980 Classification and scaling in 19th century ceramics. *Historical Archaeology* 14:1–40.
Mintz, Sidney
1974 *Caribbean Transformations.* Chicago: Aldine.
Mintz, Sidney W., and Douglas Hall
1960 *The Origins of the Jamaican Internal Marketing System.* Yale University Publications in Anthropology No. 57, Yale University, New Haven, Conn.
Moore, Sue Mullins
1981 The antebellum barrier island plantation: in search of an archeological pattern. Ph.D. dissertation in Anthropology, University of Florida. Ann Arbor: University Microfilms.
Noel-Hume, Ivor
1962 An Indianware of the colonial period. *Quarterly Bulletin of the Archaeological Society of Virginia* 17(1) (Richmond).
Oswald, Adrian
1975 Clay pipes for the archaeologist. *British Archaeological Reports,* No. 14. Oxford, England: British Archaeological Reports.
Otto, John S.
1975 Status differences and the archaeological record: a comparison of planter, overseer, and slave

sites from Cannon's Point Plantation, 1794–1861, St. Simon's, Georgia. Ph.D. dissertation, Department of Anthropology, University of Florida, Gainesville.

1977 Artifacts and status differences: a comparison of ceramics from planter, overseer, and slave sites on an antebellum plantation. In *Research Strategies in Historical Archaeology*. Stanley South, ed. San Francisco: Academic Press. Pp. 91–118.

Patterson, Orlando

1973 *The Sociology of Slavery: An Analysis of the Origins, Development and Structure of Negro Slave Society in Jamaica*. Kingston, Jamaica: Sangster's Book Stores.

Posnansky, Merrick

1982 Towards the archaeology of the black diaspora. In *Proceedings of the Ninth International Congress for the Study of Pre-Columbian Cultures of the Lesser Antilles*. Santo Domingo, Dominican Republic, August 1981; and at the American African Studies Association Meetings at Bloomington in October 1981.

Reitz, Elizabeth J.

1982 Vertebrate fauna from "Old Village," Drax Hall Plantation, Jamaica. Manuscript on file, University of Georgia Zooarcheology Lab and the University of California, Los Angeles.

Riordan, Robert V.

1973 Report on excavations at New Montpelier estate, St. James, 8–12 January 1973. Manuscript on file, Port Royal Project, Institute of Jamaica, Kingston.

Sheridan, Richard B.

1974 *Sugar and Slavery—An Economic History of the British West Indies, 1623–1775*. Aylesbury, Great Britain: Ginn and Co., Ltd., Caribbean Universities Press.

South, Stanley

1977 *Method and Theory in Historical Archaeology*. New York: Academic Press.

Wilson, George, and L. Robins

1765 A Plan and View of Drax Hall Estate and Sugar Plantation in the Parish of St. Ann's the Property of William Beckford Esq. (Survey 1752 view drawn in 1765). National Library, Institute of Jamaica, Kingston.

PART VI

Transformation

13

Archaeological Implications for Changing Labor Conditions

Theresa A. Singleton

INTRODUCTION

Perhaps the most perplexing problem confronting investigators of plantation archaeology, particularly of slave sites, is the difficulty in the identification of an antebellum versus a postbellum deposition. This problem has been mentioned in several studies within this volume, and it is also an important research consideration in the study of other aspects of Afro-American material culture (McDaniel 1982:135–137; Vlach 1978:4–5). Yet the fact that slaves and freedmen contexts are almost indistinguishable has been a significant finding of plantation archaeology as it points to a continuity of Afro-American material life, a consequence conditioned by poverty.

It is, however, important to be able to make distinctions between slave and freemen contexts whenever possible. Archaeological interpretations of either condition cannot be satisfactorily offered if the temporal placement of a site is seriously in question. While the resolution to this problem must await refinements in dating nineteenth century sites, it may be possible as Drucker has suggested to recognize a site as "'slave' or 'free worker' based upon testable field models derived from careful research and compared against historical records" (1981:67). Such an approach forms the conceptual basis for the reexamination of the archaeological data of a black freedmen site discussed in this essay.

In the American South, numerous slave assemblages dating from the eighteenth to the mid-nineteenth centuries have been documented through archaeological resources. The same is true for a growing number of tenant farmer sites of the late nineteenth and early twentieth centuries (Adams 1980; Orser 1983; Trinkley 1983). The gray area in the identification of slave and free contexts appears to date roughly between 1850 and 1880—a 30-year period that includes the last 13 years of slavery

ISBN 0-12-646480-4

and the first 17 years of freedom; a time when plantations survived but plantation life and labor were transformed (Roark 1977:209).

This chapter examines archaeological data that date from the early years of freedom in coastal Georgia (approximately 1865–1880). The discussion centers upon one site located at Colonel's Island in Glynn County, Georgia, where a former slave settlement of a sea island cotton plantation was later reoccupied presumably by black freedmen. Interpretation of the Colonel's Island data as an ex-slave site rests primarily upon excavated architectural features for which a postbellum date was established. In addition, comparative data from both archaeological and historical sources indicate that similar structures were characteristic of the Civil War period. Historical references to ex-slaves at Colonel's Island are sketchy, therefore conclusive documentation is lacking. However, the ex-slave interpretation gains added support from the abundant archaeological data that identify slavery in coastal Georgia (Ascher and Fairbanks 1971; Ehrenhard and Bullard 1981; Goin 1983; MacFarlane 1975; Moore 1981; Otto 1975; Singleton 1980; Smith *et al.* 1981). Comparison of the slavery assemblages with the presumed ex-slave assemblage reveals distinctive differences. Thus, the significance of the Colonel's Island ex-slave site is seen in discernible archaeological resources associated with the transformation from slave to free labor. It also provides tentative suggestions for the immediate material effects of emancipation.

HISTORICAL BACKGROUND

The plantation system that developed along the Georgia coast was based upon the cultivation of two labor intensive crops—rice and long-staple cotton, also known as a sea island cotton (a special variety of cotton cultivated in coastal areas). Georgian plantation society was in many respects an extension of the South Carolina lowcountry. South Carolina planters often through family ties expanded their operations in Georgia in search of new lands (Clifton 1978a:xvii–xviii). By the early 1800s the region had become dominated by a small group of wealthy slaveholders who owned numerous slaves and several plantations engaged in the production of both staples.

Because large slaveholding was essential to both cultures, black slaves soon outnumbered whites creating one of the highest concentrations of blacks in the Old South. This high concentration of blacks, as well as the infusion of African-born slaves long after the ban on the slave trade (for example, see Wells 1967), may account for the retention of African-derived elements evident in present-day Afro-American arts, cuisine, and language. Another unique feature of plantation slavery in the coastal area was the employment of the task labor system.[1] Within this system, slaves were able to hunt, fish, cultivate gardens, raise poultry, and sell

[1]The task system and its impact upon coastal slavery is discussed in several chapters within this volume; see Chapters 7, 8, and 10.

handicrafts. Through these activities, slaves had opportunities to acquire goods such as livestock, produce, and wagons (Morgan 1982, 1983). Moreover, task labor may have permitted a limited degree of autonomy within a slavery system.

After the Civil War, attempts to restore rice and sea island cotton to their former prosperity were disastrous. Rice fared poorly for several reasons: few had the capital to rebuild old irrigation systems; competition grew from rice-producing areas of the Southwest (Clifton 1978b); flooding caused by accelerated erosion in the interior increased (Trimble 1969); and, hurricanes devastated crops several years in the 1880s (Singleton 1980:39). Sea island cotton, on the other hand, had begun to experience a downward shift on the eve of the Civil War (Otto 1979) and its importance continued to decline thereafter (*DeBows Review* 1867:88). In spite of these factors, however, the primary cause for the failure to restore these antebellum cultures appears to have been the reluctance of ex-slaves to work for former masters. Many former slaves had enjoyed their freedom on lands alloted to them by the Union Army. In 1865, a 40-mile-wide belt extending from Charleston, South Carolina, to Jacksonville, Florida, declared "Sherman's reservation" was established exclusively for black settlement. Consequently, both former slaves of the region and those escaping from the interior attempted to settle the area. The reservation, however, ended by 1867, but because of it, many freedmen associated emancipation with the ownership of land (Cimbala 1983:197). When these lands were restored to the planters, some freedmen refused to work, preferring to forage or to cultivate small plots. It has been suggested that work habits of the task labor system established during slavery may have presented obstacles to the development of a plantation-based, free labor system (Armstrong 1980). Additionally, many black men had been attracted to the good wages seasonal employment offered in the lumber and turpentine industries (Bullard 1982:83) which gradually supplanted the agrarian economy of coastal Georgia at the close of the nineteenth century.

ARCHAEOLOGICAL BACKGROUND

Slavery sites from 10 plantations have been investigated thus far in coastal Georgia (Figure 13.1 and Table 13.1). This research has resulted in illuminating data on slave lifeways discernible in quantitative and qualitative patterns. These archaeological data have permitted both the identification of activities and objects associated with life in slave quarters and the comparison of slave activities and objects with those of planter and overseer sites. Comparison of the slave archaeological resources with those of the ex-slave site could aid in understanding the material differences between slavery and freedom, whenever differences exist.

A quantitative slave artifact pattern for coastal Georgia based upon artifact pattern analysis (South 1977) is discussed elsewhere (Moore 1981; Singleton 1980: 211–219)[2] For purposes of comparison with the ex-slave artifact profile, this pat-

---

[2]A slave artifact pattern for coastal Georgia is discussed at length in Chapter 7, this volume.

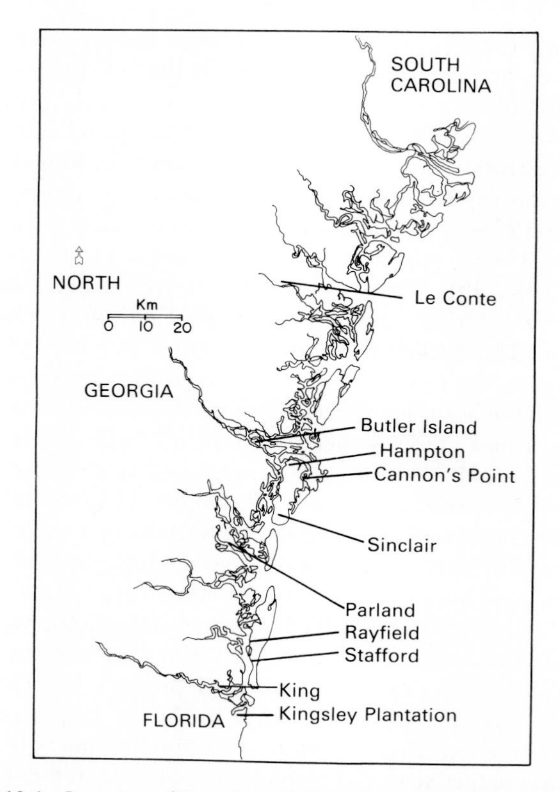

Figure 13.1 Location of investigated plantation sites in Coastal Georgia.

Table 13.1
ARCHAEOLOGICAL INVESTIGATIONS OF PLANTATIONS IN COASTAL GEORGIA

Plantation	County	Report
LeConte-Woodmanston	Liberty	Hamilton 1980
Butler Island	McIntosh	Singleton 1980
Cannon's Point	Glynn	MacFarlane 1975; Otto 1975
Hampton	Glynn	Moore 1981
Sinclair	Glynn	Moore 1981
Parland	Glynn	Steinen 1978
Rayfield	Camden	Ascher and Fairbanks 1971
Stafford	Camden	Ehrenhard and Bullard 1981
King	Camden	Smith *et al.* 1981; Goin 1983
Kingsley	Duval, Florida	Fairbanks 1974

Table 13.2
COMPARISON OF SLAVE ARTIFACT PATTERN WITH EX-SLAVE ARTIFACT PROFILE

Artifact group	Slave pattern[a]	Ex-slave profile[b]	
		%	N
Architecture	70.70	82.45	3351
Kitchen	24.60	14.93	607
Arms	.18	.14	6
Clothing	1.00	1.43	58
Personal	.12	.55	22
Tobacco	3.00	.40	16
Activities	.35	.10	4
Total	99.95[c]	100.00	4064

[a]Mean percent derived from Cannon's Point, Hampton, Sinclair, Kingsley, and Butler Island plantations.
[b]Artifact frequencies from Colonel's Island ex-slave site.
[c]Error due to rounding.

tern is presented in Table 13.2. Comparison of the architecture and kitchen groups (the artifacts most suggestive of socioeconomic status) reveals that the ex-slave pattern is characterized by a higher proportion of architectural artifacts to kitchen artifacts (5:1) than the slave pattern (3:1). This difference may be an indication that the material life of freedmen was below that of slaves based upon interpretations offered for similar proportional differences found between slave and overseer and slave and planter assemblages.[3]

Differences between slave and ex-slave data are most evident in qualitative trends, namely housing and foodways. (These archaeological data are compared later in this chapter.) Coastal slave housing and foodways were characterized by the following attributes.

Slave housing on the eve of the Civil War was characterized by substantial structures that met the standards recommended by antebellum reformers (Genovese 1974:524). Dwellings based upon European models (Otto 1975:103) were either single-family units or duplexes. They were most frequently framed but occasionally were made from poured tabby (a cementlike substance made from burnt lime, oyster shell, and sand) with clay or tabby brick chimneys. Floors were often raised upon building piers, but low-lying supports or even the possibility of earthen or brick-lined floors are also known. The average size of a single-family unit was 16 by 20 feet and 22 by 42 feet for duplexes.

Animal food remains suggest slave diet consisted primarily of domestic foods. Beef and pork have been found to supply 60% or more to slave diet using zooarchaeolog-

[3]See Chapter 7, this volume.

ical techniques which can approximate the relative percentage each animal species recovered from the site contributed to the diet. These domestic foods, however, were abundantly supplemented by a variety of nondomestic foods.

Archaeological evidence of postbellum occupation is also suggested at two other slave sites, LeConte-Woodmanston Plantation (Hamilton 1980:91) and Cannon's Point (Otto 1975:99). At LeConte, postbellum occupation is suggested by varieties of ceramics which may date after the Civil War and at Cannon's Point by an 1877 coin. At both sites, the postbellum occupation was limited and difficult to distinguish from antebellum contexts, suggesting a continuity in the material life from slavery to freedom. Colonel's Island, on the other hand, presents a strong case for change—evident in archaeological resources of the post-Civil War period—which are strikingly different from those of the preceding antebellum period.

COLONEL'S ISLAND EX-SLAVE SITE

Colonel's Island is a 2100-acre expanse of land located approximately 10 miles south of Brunswick, Georgia. It is referred to as a "marsh island" because it is entirely surrounded by and separated from the mainland by a 500-m-wide strip of marsh and estuary (Sheldon 1976:1) (Figure 13.2). Archaeological research was undertaken to test both prehistoric and historic sites potentially endangered by plans to develop the island. The project was funded by the Georgia Ports Authority and reported by Steinen (1978).

Historic Occupation and Land Use

The first recorded owner of Colonel's Island was Joseph Forrestor, who acquired 1450 acres of the island through Royal Grants in 1767 (Chandler 1907:83). After Forrestor, ownership of the island passed through several hands, and by 1810 Colonel's Island had apparently reached its present-day limits (*Georgia Genealogical Magazine* [GGM] 1963:608). The island was functioning as a plantation by 1823, which is indicated by a newspaper advertisement for an overseer placed by William Page (Page 1823), the owner of the island at that time. John Parland presumably acquired the island through purchase after it had been placed on public auction in 1834 (Palmer 1834). The records documenting this transaction could not be found. Parland and his heirs retained ownership for most of Colonel's Island until the 1880s.

Parland, a native Scotsman, served as justice of the inferior court and as a member of the grand jury in Glynn County. In addition to Colonel's Island, he owned at least three other plantations: Longwood, the Dyke, and Gowrie. Parland married Mary Ann Scarlett in 1833, and they had two daughters, Jean Adams and Francis Ann. Parland was killed in a fall from a horse in 1836 and the site of his grave is still located on the island. He died intestate, and his estate was equally divided between his daughters. From 1837 to 1857, Francis M. Scarlett, Mary Ann's father, served as guardian for the management of the estate (GGM 1962:269, 276). Annual reports

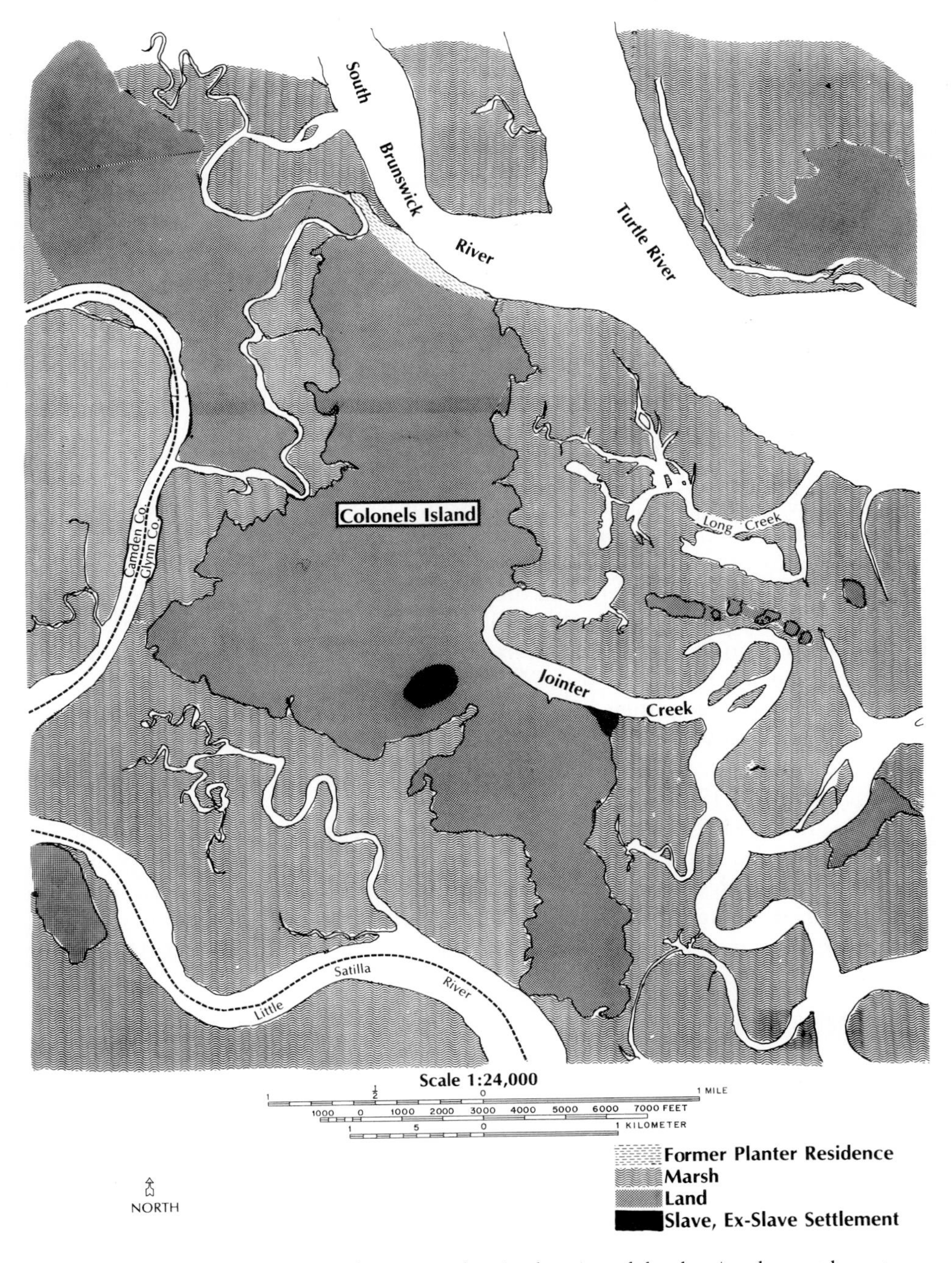

Figure 13.2 Colonel's Island and environs, showing location of the slave/ex-slave settlements.

submitted to Glynn County Court House provide details for the operation of the estate under Scarlett's trusteeship.

Parland's plantations were typical of those found on the Georgia coast. The number of slaves for the entire estate averaged at 160 with 82 present at Colonel's Island (Glynn County Records [GCR], 1810–1842). He had accumulated 159 slaves prior to his marriage. Fifteen of these had been purchased in 1832 from Joseph Demere, Parland's predecessor at Colonel's Island (GGM 1963:615). He acquired the the other slaves prior to 1830 (U.S. Census 1830:537). At the time of his death, he owned 163 slaves (GCR 1810–1842:320–321); after that time, few slaves were brought or sold. The staple at Colonel's Island was sea island cotton, but considerable quantities of poultry, corn, and potatoes were also raised to sell to other plantations (GCR 1843–1851). Additional sources of income included rice and sugar cultivation at the other plantations, the sale of lumber, and the leasing of slaves to other plantations (GCR 1852–1859).

After 1857 the documentary record for Colonel's Island is fragmentary. This is an unfortunate circumstance since the vast majority of archaeological resources date from this time. During the Civil War, in 1862, the island was briefly visited by Union troops who encountered contrabands (refugee slaves who had gone to Union lines), many of whom belonged to the Parland estate. The army took with them food supplies and farming equipment and fired shots at Confederate troops located on a nearby island (Official Records 1901:633–634). When the island was returned to the Parland heirs in 1867, 76 acres were sold to Carl Epping and Henry A. Wayne for "their respective business interest" (GCR 1859–1869:516–518), under the condition that they establish their business at Colonel's Island within a 3-year period. Henry Wayne, a native of New York, was a lumber dealer (U.S. Census 1870a:212). Perhaps, the purchased property was used in the lumber or naval store industries. Between 1874 and 1885 additional portions of the land were leased (GCR 1875–1889:173, 192, 234, 261), but it is not clear how these lands were developed. Finally in 1885 the entire island was sold to a number of entrepreneurs who planned a massive industrial development of the island (GCR 1885–1886:180). In 1888 the Brunswick Harbor and Land Company was formed and established at Colonel's Island. The venture was short-lived and abandoned in 1900 (McVeigh 1969).

Archaeological Investigations

Archaeological research at the historic sites at Colonel's Island was designed to investigate the antebellum occupation of the Parland Plantation. Using John Otto's (1975) research at Cannon's Point Plantation as a model, the archaeological resources at the former planter site were to be compared with those at the slave sites. Excavations at the planter site at the northern end of the island revealed few antebellum contexts. The 1888 development centered on the former planter site disturbed the earlier occupation. The only antebellum feature was a brick-lined well that had been cleaned and filled with late nineteenth-century and modern debris.

Two presumed slave settlements were identified (see Figure 13.2), but time and resources permitted the excavation of only one (WGC903) located near the center of the island. The other settlement (WGC905), located on the river, was surveyed and the structural features cleared and recorded. At the excavated site, the spatial arrangement of the archaeological features, the artifact types, and artifact patterns were suggestive of a slave occupation, yet the nature of the structures, particularly the chimney construction, was unlike slave dwellings excavated at the other Georgian sites. These appeared to have been built as temporary habitations rather than permanent slave quarters. This temporary or perhaps seasonal occupation was further implied from the faunal analysis (Reitz 1978). Recovery of an 1867 nickel near the base of one of the two excavated chimneys established that at least one structure was of postbellum date. Therefore, it was reported that the site represented ex-slave rather than slave remains (Singleton 1978, 1979).

Since the initial report of the Colonel's Island data, an exhaustive effort has been conducted to determine if, in fact, the archaeological resources were representative of a postbellum occupation. This subsequent research has been along three lines: first, the reexamination of documentary sources to establish that ex-slaves occupied the island after the Civil War; second, the careful study of postbellum land use and labor transformations in the area; third, a search for descriptions of similar structures resembling those at Colonel's Island. The first met with few results and those have been incorporated in previous sections of this essay. The second provides the historical framework for the interpretation offered here, while the third uncovered comparative data from archaeological and historical sources of similar construction practices. Although occupation by ex-slaves has not been confirmed, the argument is now strengthened by additional data and insights.

Archaeological Resources

As previously mentioned, the most striking suggestion of postbellum remains were present in the architectural features. These consisted primarily of chimney falls with no associated posts, fittings, or wall trenches, therefore, the approximate size, shape, and construction materials for the remainder of the structure could not be determined. At the excavated slave/ex-slave settlement, three tabby brick chimney falls were uncovered, one completely excavated and another partially tested (see Figure 13.3). Two chimneys were cleared at the unexcavated site which revealed an identical chimney construction to those of the excavated site (Singleton 1978:78).

Construction of these chimneys was inferior to that of slave dwellings excavated at other sites on the Georgia coast. All bricks were laid in place with marsh mud instead of mortar (Figure 13.4). In fact, mortar was completely absent from the horizontal surfaces of the brick. Some bricks did have dried mortar on them from former use or new mortar had been applied to fill in or square off chips, spoils, and missing corners. The use of mortar in this fashion, however, strongly suggests that the bricks were reused, presumably salvaged from structures that were once located on the island.

A similar chimney construction in which clay was used as mortar for salvaged

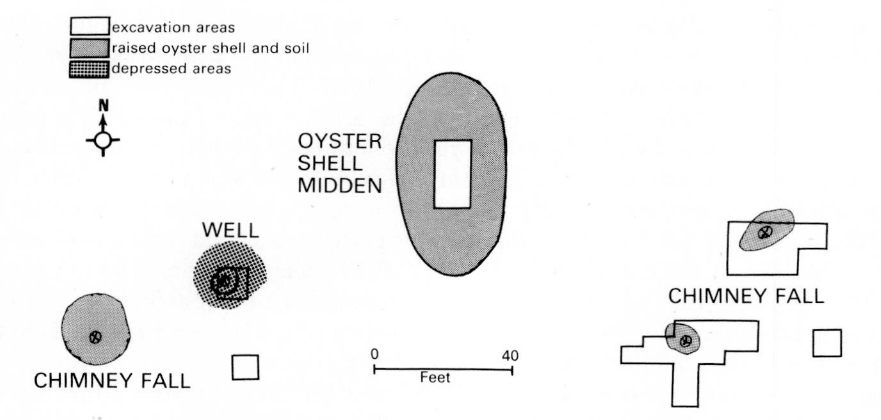

Figure 13.3 Layout of slave/ex-slave site (WGC903).

Figure 13.4 Fireplace construction (note the use of mud for mortar).

bricks and stones has been observed at the Confederate Fort Anderson in Brunswick Town, North Carolina (South 1959). The use of mud or clay sometimes mixed with Spanish moss is a well-established building practice frequently employed by southern blacks in building log cabins (Genovese 1974:524–525) and in mud-and-stick chimney construction (Gonzales 1924:221). Blacks were very likely responsible for the construction of dwellings at both Colonel's Island and Fort Anderson. More important, however, the occurrence of similar construction at a Civil War barracks not only offers an approximate temporal placement for the Colonel's Island structures but also points to their impermanent function.

Hearth construction was similarly substandard. A carefully flattened deposit of whole oyster shell served as a footing for the hearth bricks (Figure 13.5). Below the whole oyster shell in one of the chimneys was a layer of burnt shell and charcoal. This layer may have been the result of an unsuccessful attempt at making tabby by persons apparently unfamiliar with its manufacture. Although oyster shell footings have been found in slave cabins, there they are usually supported by brick. The significance of the oyster shell is that it may have been the only available building material. Makeshift fireplaces and chimneys made from salvaged, flimsy, or other unconventional materials also characterized camp architecture of the Civil War. In such structures, the use of brick, stone, or logs thickly coated with mud was limited

Figure 13.5 Oyster-shell fitting underlying hearth.

to the construction of the fireplace. Split wood adhered with mud, or, more frequently, pork barrels, served to to complete the chimney above the fireplace (Nelson 1982:87). The small quantity of brick debris recovered from the completely excavated structure at Colonel's Island suggests that a similar construction technique was employed in building the remainder of the chimneys. The cabin walls must have been frame or log, with earthen floors.

In addition to the structures, a barrel well and an oyster shell midden were identified and partially excavated. The relationship of these nonstructural features to the structures could not be ascertained. Although few artifacts were recovered from the well shaft and fill, they suggest that both construction and abandonment occurred during the antebellum period. Excavation revealed that at one time an attempt was made to remove the square casing surrounding the barrel but for unknown reasons this action was abruptly stopped (Singleton 1978:104–106). This attempted removal of well wood may be another example of the need to salvage abandoned materials for construction or possibly, in this case, for firewood.

The shell midden appears to have been a deposit initiated during the antebellum occupation but was perhaps continually added to throughout the nineteenth century. Such middens are frequently found at coastal slave sites where the shell was often collected for making tabby (Kemble 1961:257). This feature may have been the source for the oyster shell used in the fireplace construction.

Food remains found in and around structures point to an occupation that is not at all characteristic of slave sites where the mainstay for diet is provided by domestic foods. Although the faunal sample was only 46 individuals, a diet derived from foraging is indicated. Nondomestic foods contributed 98% of the meat to the diet at the ex-slave site compared to 40% or less at slave sites. These nondomestic foods included deer, raccoon, oppossum, fish, and sea turtle. Faunal analysis also suggested that the site may have been occupied briefly or possibly on a seasonal basis from June to October (Reitz 1978:142).

The artifacts consisted of items typically found at sites occupied by slaves or other low-status inhabitants (the artifact profile is given in Table 13.2). Only 267 ceramic fragments were recovered consisting primarily of undecorated whitewares (including ironstones), utilitarian stonewares, and earthenwares. Most of these wares were manufactured and used throughout the nineteenth century and are therefore useless in making distinctions between antebellum and postbellum contexts. Only one ceramic variety was not widely available until after the Civil War; it resembles the yellow earthenwares but is somewhat lighter and has a coat of clear alkaline glaze. Experimentation with its manufacture was extremely limited prior to 1850 and it did not come into wide usage until after that date (Ketchum 1971:120–122). Forty-two sherds (16.5% of the total ceramics) were recovered.

Discussion

To summarize, the archaeological resources at Colonel's Island appear to represent a former slave settlement that was later reoccupied by freedmen. Makeshift structural features constructed from salvaged materials are presumably associated with the postbellum occupation while the well and oyster midden date from the antebellum occupation. Evidence for a postbellum date is suggested by a *terminus post quem* of 1867 for one of the structures, by comparable building practices of the Civil War period, and, to a lesser extent, by ceramics manufactured during the second half of the nineteenth century. A more important basis for this interpretation lies in the dissimilarity between Colonel's Island and other slave sites seen in architectural features and faunal resources. Further, the impermanent or seasonal occupation is more reflective of a contraband, squatter, or seasonal worker camp (all forms of settlement associated with emancipation) than it is of a permanent slave village.

The postbellum date and temporary occupation of the site, however, do not indicate that the site was occupied by ex-slaves. This interpretation must rely upon historic sources. Contrabands residing at Colonel's Island in 1862 may have stayed on the island after it became part of Sherman's reservation in 1865. If this was the case, it may have been a squatter settlement rather than one officially authorized by the Freedmen's Bureau (the agency established to oversee the restoration of land and labor in the South during the War and in the immediate postbellum years), because no ex-slaves were reported on Colonel's Island in Freedmen's Bureau records (Bullard 1982:76). Freedmen frequently squatted on lands and continued to do so even after the demise of "Sherman's reservation" (Cimbala 1983:293).

The Colonel's Island data may represent another form of labor transformation—a seasonal work camp. Immediately after the war, black men were attracted to seasonal employment in turpentine and lumber industries. While few references to these industries are indicated for Glynn County before 1880, small embryonic operations were not always reported (U.S. Census 1870a, b, 1880a, b). The sale of land for the Epping and Wayne business venture and the lands leased between 1874 and 1885 were possibly utilized for these industries. General descriptions of cabins associated with wilderness activities such as lumbering, trapping, and turpentine extraction seem to fit the ephemeral quality of the Colonel's Island data (Olmsted 1962:147; Randolph 1978:6–8).

Assuming that the occupants were ex-slaves, the Colonel's Island data provides insights into the immediate effects of emancipation upon former bondsmen. These data indicate that conditions were worse in freedom than in slavery. Because "ex-slaves chose to manifest their freedom in many different ways" (Litwack 1979:226), material correlates for their new life vary and are elusive. For many freedmen, independence under the most marginal circumstances was preferable to their former existence in slavery or for working for old masters under new, unsettled conditions (Armstrong 1980:44; Bullard 1982:82; Litwack 1979:229; Webster 1916:148–160). The transitory quality of the archaeological resources at Colonel's Island is suggestive of this marginal, unsettled status of recently emancipated slaves.

In conclusion, the archaeological data at Colonel's Island offer a possibility of post-Civil War labor transformation. It is impossible to say what kind of occupation is represented, but the site provides an example of archaeological resources associated with labor changes resulting from emancipation.

CONCLUSION

An attempt has been made in this essay to offer an interpretation of archaeological resources that appear to be associated with ex-slaves during the early years of freedom (1865–1880). Although definitive evidence for this conclusion is lacking, inferences derived from archaeological and historic sources support it. Hopefully, data from future freedmen sites will elucidate the interpretations offered here.

An alternative explanation can be considered. It is possible, for example, that the site was primarily a slave settlement occupied throughout the Civil War and afterward. When compared with other slavery sites, however, this explanation seems doubtful. The full range of slave sites will always remain an unknown, but those recovered thus far have indicated permanent, year-round residences. The structural and faunal resources at Colonel's Island do not provide any suggestion of permanency.

In order to identify archaeological resources associated with emancipation, the archaeologist must first understand what are the material attributes that are likely to characterize this form of occupation. Historical descriptions indicate that ex-slave settlements were occupied briefly, often less than year or two, and the quality of these settlements varied considerably. Ex-slaves that were of the opinion that the land was theirs forever built new, substantial cabins. On the other hand, those squatting may have merely reoccupied abandoned structures or built temporary dwellings. This means that the archaeological resources could potentially range from a trash pit to substantial architectural remains that can be only discerned as emancipation contexts through careful excavation.

The coastal areas of South Carolina, Georgia, and northern Florida offer a unique opportunity to examine the early years of emancipation because of the occupation by Union troops and the establishment of Sherman's reservation. Contraband and squatter villages were established throughout this region frequently at abandoned slave settlements (Bullard 1982). Archaeologists need to be aware of this potential resource and develop ways to identify it. It is incorrect to assume that a postbellum occupation is absent or unimportant at a slave or other plantation site. In recent years, historians have directed a great deal of attention to the early years of freedom in order to better understand slavery and the tenant farmer systems of the late nineteenth and twentieth centuries. The archaeological study of the "transition" could be equally significant to slave and tenant farmer archaeology.

REFERENCES

Adams, William H., ed.
1980 *Waverly Plantation: Ethnoarchaeology of a Tenant Farming Community*. Washington, D.C.: National Technical Information Service.

Armstrong, Thomas
1980 From task labor to free labor: the transition along the Georgia rice coast, 1820–1880. *Georgia Historical Quarterly* 63:432–447.

Ascher, Robert, and Charles H. Fairbanks
1971 Excavation of a slave cabin: Georgia, U.S.A. *Historical Archaeology* 5:3–17.
Bullard, Mary R.
1982 *An Abandoned Black Settlement on Cumberland Island, Georgia.* DeLeon Springs, Fla.: E. O. Painter Printing Company.
Chandler, Allen D.
1907 *The Colonial Records of the State of Georgia.* Vol 9. Atlanta: Franklin-Turner Company.
Cimbala, Paul A.
1983 The terms of freedom: The Freedmen's Bureau and Reconstruction in Georgia, 1865–1870. Ph.D. dissertation, Department of History, Emory University, Atlanta.
Clifton, James M.
1978a *Life and Labor on Argyle Island.* Savannah, Ga.: The Beehive Press.
1978b Twilight comes to the rice kingdom: postbellum rice culture in the south Atlantic coast. *Georgia Historical Quarterly* 62:146–154.
DeBows Review
1867 The sea-island cotton of the South: its history, characteristics, cultivation. (After the War Series.) *DeBows Review* 3:84–88.
Drucker, Lesley M.
1981 Socioeconomic patterning at an undocumented late 18th century low country site: Spiers Landing, South Carolina. *Historical Archaeology* 15(2):58–68.
Ehrenhard, John, and Mary R. Bullard
1981 *Stafford Plantation, Cumberland Island, National Seashore, Georgia: Archaeological Investigations of a Slave Cabin.* Tallahassee, Fla.: Southeast Archaeological Center National Park Service, U.S. Department of Interior.
Fairbanks, Charles H.
1974 The Kingsley slave cabins in Duval County, Florida, 1968. *Conference on Historic Sites Archaeology Papers* 7:62–93.
Genovese, Eugene
1974 *Roll Jordan Roll: The World the Slaves Made.* New York: Pantheon Books.
Georgia Genealogical Magazine (GGM)
1962 Georgia Court House Records, Minutes, Glynn County Inferior Court. Vol. 1(5).
1963 Deeds, Glynn County. Vol. 1(10).
Glynn County Records (GCR), Georgia Archives, Atlanta
1810–1842 Wills and Appraisement, Book D.
1843–1851 Wills and Appraisement, Book E.
1852–1859 Wills and Appraisement, Book F.
1859–1869 Deeds and Bonds, Book C.
1875–1889 Record Accounts, Current Book B.
1885–1886 Deed Book Z.
Goin, Coleman J., Jr.
1983 Historical archaeology at the Thomas King Plantation site. Paper presented at the 40th Annual Meeting of the Southeastern Archaeological Conference, Columbia, S.C., November 3, 1983.
Gonzales, Ambrose
1924 *The Captain Stories of the Black Border.* Columbia, S.C.: The State Publishing Company.
Hamilton, Jennifer M.
1980 Early history and excavation of LeConte-Woodmanston Plantation. Master's thesis, Department of Anthropology, University of Florida, Gainesville.
Kemble, Frances A.
1961 *A Journal of Residence on a Georgia Plantation in 1838–1839.* Edited by John A. Scott. New York: Knopf.

Ketchum, William C.
1971 *The Pottery and Porcelain Collector's Handbook: A Guide to Early American Ceramics from Maine to California.* New York: Funk and Wagnall's.
Leigh, Frances B.
1883 *Ten Years on a Georgia Plantation Since the War.* London: R. Bentley and Sons.
Litwack, Leon F.
1979 *Been in the Storm So Long: The Aftermath of Slavery.* New York: Knopf.
McDaniel, George W.
1982 *Hearth and Home Preserving a People's Culture.* Philadelphia: University of Temple Press.
MacFarlane, Suzanne
1975 The ethnoarchaeology of a slave cabin community: the Couper Plantation site. Master's thesis, Department of Anthropology, University of Florida, Gainesville.
McVeigh, Shaw
1969 The development of Colonel's Island. Paper submitted to State Science Fair, Atlanta, Ga. Manuscript on file, Brunswick Public Library, Brunswick, Ga.
Moore, Sue M.
1981 The antebellum barrier island plantation: in search of an archaeological pattern. Ph.D. dissertation, Department of Anthropology, University of Florida, Gainesville.
Morgan, Philip D.
1982 *Work and culture: the task system and the world of low country blacks, 1700 to 1880. William and Mary* 39(Series 3):563–597.
1983 The ownership of property by slaves in the mid-19th century low country. *Journal of Southern History* 49(3):399–434.
Nelson, Dean E.
1982 "Right nice little house(s):" impermanent camp architecture of the American Civil War. In *Perspectives in Vernacular Architecture.* Camille Wells, ed. Annapolis, Md.: Vernacular Architecture Forum. Pp. 79–93.
Official Records
1901 *Union and Confederate Navies in the War of the Rebellion.* Vol. 12 (Series I). Washington, D.C.: Government Printing Office.
Olmsted, Frederick L.
1962 *The Cotton Kingdom: A Traveller's Observation in Cotton and Slavery in the American Slave States.* Edited by Arthur M. Schlesinger. New York: Knopf.
Orser, Charles E., Jr., Annette M. Nekola, and James L. Roark
1983 Exploring the rustic life. Multidisciplinary research at Millwood Plantation, a large plantation in Abbeville, Georgia. Report on file at Archaeological Services Division, National Park Service, Southeast Regional Office, Atlanta.
Otto, John S.
1975 Status differences and the archaeological record—a comparison of planter, overseer, and slave sites from Cannon's Point Plantation, 1794–1861, St. Simon's Island, Georgia. Ph.D. dissertation, Department of Anthropology, University of Florida, Gainesville.
1979 Slavery in a coastal slave community Glynn County, 1790–1860. *Georgia Historical Quarterly* 64(4):461–468.
Page, William
1823 An overseer wanted. *Darien Gazette,* 6 November.
Palmer, Samuel
1834 Trustee's Sale. *Georgian,* 21 January.
Randolph, Wayne
1978 Wilderness architecture: a trapper's cabin survey. In *14th Annual Traditional Craft Days.* Oneida, N.Y.: Madison County Historical Society. Pp. 6–8.
Reitz, Elizabeth
1978 Report on the faunal material excavated by West Georgia College from Colonel's Island,

Georgia. *In* The Cultural Evolution and Environment of Colonel's Island. Karl T. Steinen, ed. Report on file, Department of Sociology and Anthropology, West Georgia College, Carrollton, Ga. Pp. 135–163.

Roark, James
1977 *Masters Without Slaves: Southern Planters on the Civil War and Reconstruction.* New York: Norton.

Sheldon, Craig T.
1976 An archaeological survey of Colonel's Island, Georgia. Report on file, Georgia Ports Authority, Savannah, Ga.

Singleton, Theresa A.
1978 Report on historic excavations, Colonel's Island, Glynn County, Georgia. *In* The Cultural Evolution and Environment of Colonel's Island. Karl T. Steinen, ed. Report on file, Department of Sociology and Anthropology, West Georgia College, Carrollton, Ga. Pp. 70–135.
1979 Slave and ex-slave sites in coastal Georgia. Paper presented at the 12th Annual Meeting of the Society for Historical Archaeology, Nashville, Tenn.
1980 The archaeology of Afro-American Slavery in coastal Georgia: A regional perception of slave household and community patterns. Ph.D. Dissertation, Department of Anthropology, University of Florida, Gainesville.

Smith, Robin L., C. O. Bradley, N. T. Borremans, and E. J. Reitz
1981 Coastal adaptations in southeast Georgia: ten archaeological sites at King's Bay. Report on file, Department of Anthropology, University of Florida, Gainesville.

South, Stanley
1959 Excavation report—Fort Anderson Barracks Excavation Unit N18. Brunswick Town, N.C. Report on file, State Department of Archives and History, Raleigh, N.C.
1977 *Method and Theory in Historical Archaeology.* New York: Academic Press.

Steinen, Karl T., ed.
1978 The cultural evolution and environment of Colonel's Island. Report on file, Department of Sociology and Anthropology, West Georgia College, Carrollton, Ga.

Trimble, S. W.
1969 Culturally accelerated sedimentation in the middle Georgia piedmont. Master's thesis, University of Georgia, Athens.

Trinkley, Michael
1983 "Let us now praise famous men"—if only we can find them. *Southeastern Archaeology:* 2:30–36.

United States Census
1830 Population Schedule for Glynn County, Georgia. Georgia Archives, Atlanta.
1870a Agricultural Schedule for Glynn County, Georgia. Georgia Archives, Atlanta.
1870b Population Schedule for Glynn County, Georgia. Georgia Archives, Atlanta.
1880a Agricultural Schedule for Glynn County, Georgia. Georgia Archives, Atlanta.
1880b Population Schedule for Glynn County, Georgia. Georgia Archives, Atlanta.

Vlach, John M.
1978 *The Afro-American Tradition in the Decorative Arts.* Cleveland: Cleveland Museum of Art.

Webster, Laura
1916 The operation of the Freedmen's Bureau in South Carolina. *Smith College Studies* 1(#2–3):67–181.

Wells, Tom H.
1967 *The Slave Ship "Wanderer."* Athens, Ga.: University of Georgia Press.

14

Historical Perspectives on Black Tenant Farmer Material Culture: The Henry C. Long General Store Ledger at Waverly Plantation, Mississippi

William Hampton Adams

Steven D. Smith

INTRODUCTION

Black history under slavery has been the subject of considerable literature, most recently centered upon revising misconceptions of slavery (e.g., Blassingame 1972; Fogel and Engerman 1974; Genovese 1974; Gutman 1976; Ransom and Sutch 1977). Historical archaeologists have largely focused their research along similar lines, investigating slave sites (Ascher and Fairbanks 1971; Fairbanks 1974; Handler and Lange 1978; Moore 1981; Otto 1977; Singleton 1980). While attention in American historiography has begun to focus on the South after Reconstruction, only sparse literature exists about the late nineteenth century, especially concerning the invisible poor. We know more about blacks during slavery than we do about their early years of freedom as sharecroppers and tenant farmers. Recent historical studies are beginning to reveal black history during this period, especially surrounding family organization, but most have not yet been published (McDaniel 1979; Nathans 1979). The archaeological study of blacks is of growing interest, but like their

ISBN 0-12-646480-4

historian colleagues, historical archaeologists have only recently turned to the study of late nineteenth-century blacks (Adams 1980; Bridges and Salwen 1980; Geismar 1980; Kern 1980; McDaniel 1979; Riordan 1978; Schuyler 1974, 1980). The information presented here results from a major study of a plantation in Mississippi. This essay compares archaeological and historical data for tenant farmer material culture at Waverly Plantation so that we may better understand poverty and its affects on tenant farmer research.

This study results from research conducted on Waverly Plantation, a National Historic Landmark located on the Tombigbee River, 8 miles upstream from Columbus, Mississippi. Construction of a federal recreation area for the Tennessee–Tombigbee Waterway was to destroy part of the plantation, so the U.S. Army Corps of Engineers and the Heritage Conservation and Recreation Service contracted with a private consulting firm to mitigate the construction impact. This entailed an interdisciplinary study whereby five tenant farmer houses and other sites, were excavated in conjunction with archival research and interviews with over 80 tenants and other former residents. The majority of the archival data pertained to the period prior to 1910, while oral data generally pertained to the period after 1910, with considerable overlap between 1890 and 1910. The result was a comprehensive portrayal of tenant life on the plantation during the 1880-to-1930 period particularly, but also for the historical antecedents and the more recent period (Adams 1980).

WAVERLY HISTORY: A SYNOPSIS

In 1830 Col. George Hampton Young bought the Waverly Plantation from the half-breed Chicasaw Indian, Alexander Pitchlyn. By 1841 he had built a steam-powered cotton gin and gristmill, and a brick warehouse. By 1845 he had added a sawmill and tannery. He lived in a log dogtrot house until finishing a fine mansion in 1857, complete with gas plant and swimming pool. The Civil War action passed very near Waverly but it was largely spared damages. After the war a sharecropping system was attempted, but by the mid-1870s this had shifted to tenant farming. (Apparently most of these people were former slaves from Young's plantation, given the available ledger data. Letters from the 1840s [Young 1848], slave narratives [Works Progress Administration 1941:173–174], and oral data collected from slaves' grandchildren indicate the Young family were good masters to the slaves and later good landowners for the tenants. That they sold land to blacks in the 1880s is a good indication of this.) The plantation owners lived at Waverly until 1913; thereafter, the family lived in Columbus and hired an overseer. Following World War I, black tenant farmers began leaving Waverly and they were replaced by whites with an accompanying shift toward sharecropping. By the end of World War II, the land at Waverly was farmed by whites as sharecroppers.

The Tenant System at Waverly

The term *tenant farmer* has several meanings. Some authors use it to include sharecropping arrangements. At Waverly, a tenant farmer rented the land for cash (or cash equivalent in produce) while sharecroppers provided a percentage of their crop in payment, thus the term *cash renter* could be applied to the Waverly tenant farmers. Several studies of tenant farmers and sharecroppers have been made in Mississippi and elsewhere. In the Bay Springs Mill community white sharecroppers were interviewed by David Barton and Stephen Poyser to provide data on farming practices, farmstead layout, material culture, community, and other aspects of life from the early twentieth century (Adams *et al.* 1981; Smith *et al.* 1982). A few miles upriver from Waverly, near Aberdeen, a similar study was undertaken of Sharpley's Bottom tenants (Kern 1980; Kern *et al.* 1982a, b). Because of a legal dispute over land ownership in the late nineteenth century, a wealth of documents describe that tenant community from 1870–1918. Three books in particular provide poignant portrayals of tenant life (Agee and Evans 1960; Maguire 1975; Rosengarten 1974), while other studies provide contemporary accounts from historical, geographical, and social vantage points (Branson 1923a, b, c; Cates 1917; Johnson *et al.* 1935; Prunty 1955; Thomas 1934; Woofter 1936).

After the Civil War the plantation system in the area took advantage of the new crop lien laws to develop a sharecropper—and later a tenant farmer—system of labor. In the sharecropper system the landowner furnishes all the equipment and supplies and the worker furnishes the labor only; the landowner receives a certain agreed-upon portion of the crop. In the plantations around Waverly, this system was soon replaced by a renting system, whereby the tenant furnishes his own equipment, mule, and labor, and paid the landowner rent in cash or in cotton. This placed more of the risk on the tenant because if a bad year occurred or if a mule died the tenant still owed the rent. "Some years they'd make somethin' and some years they didn't, but then some years when they did make great, they mopped up," said one informant at Waverly. Most likely, however, the net profit and loss balanced out for those tenants remaining several years. The landlord could not afford to lose too many tenants by charging too high a rent, and would have to carry the tenants over in bad years to ensure an available labor force. This system worked at Waverly since considerable evidence exists that a stable black community had developed by the 1870s. While tenants did move in and out of the community, it appears most movement was lateral, whereby a tenant might move to a nearby plantation if it was still in the community. Names of the same tenants from different plantations appear in probate lists from the 1870s and 1880s, the store ledgers of 1878–1879 and 1887–1888, and again on the 1913 probate list of tenants on Waverly. These same individuals were frequently mentioned in the oral history. We suspect those who stayed were the average tenants, those whose judgment, skills, and luck made them neither successful enough to buy land nor failures needing to "skip out."

The tenant was rented a plot of land (usually 15 ha) on which to make his cash crop. The tenants' fields were located in the old plantation fields near the river, but their homes were built on higher ground where possible. This settlement pattern differs slightly from the usual one of having the house and fields on the same plot of land (Prunty 1955). In addition to the 15 ha, the tenant had access to the community pasture and was permitted garden space as well. The tenants also exploited a much larger area for acquiring wild foods, although how this was arranged with the landowner is unknown. Although wild foods played an important role in subsistence at the Waverly sites excavated, the ledger data suggests that much of the diet consisted of purchased items. With 38% of the tenants' expenditures being for food, their needs for food were certainly much greater than they were able to acquire from their own sources, either wild or cultivated. We suspect that the requirements of cotton production prevented full exploitation of wild plants and animals during much of the year.

For comparison, on the Armstead Plantation, a mile west of Waverly, the average tenant (N = 12) in 1880 tilled 14.6 ha in cotton and 1.9 ha in corn, producing 4.8 cotton bales and 59.6 bu of corn. He possessed $9 worth of equipment, 1.9 draft animals, 2.5 cattle, 6.4 swine, and 14.5 poultry. While two-thirds or more of the cropland was devoted to cotton, other crops were of substantial importance. Corn was raised for animal and human consumption. The corn was carted to the nearest miller who charged one peck per bushel for grinding it. (Because of restrictions on liquor sales to blacks, some corn no doubt ended up in moonshine.) Other crops of sufficient importance to warrant their own "patch" included field peas, sweet potatoes, peanuts, sorghum, and watermelon. At the house garden, surrounded by a paling fence, the tenant would grow cabbage, lettuce, beets, turnips, mustard, collard, okra, English peas, and string beans. In a bad year, the house garden meant survival to the tenants. The produce was used fresh or dried. Field peas, beans, peanuts, and corn were dried, while greens could be harvested nearly the entire year. Sweet potatoes were kept in "kilns" in the garden. Hogs were butchered in the fall, salted, and smoked. Fruits were dried and canned. Archaeological sites produced few canning jars or crocks, suggesting little use of such vessels for preservation. Informants stated that the blacks had not yet learned safe canning procedures for meats or vegetables, and hence were limited to canning fruits, presumably in sugar. Whites, however, did can meats and vegetables at Waverly.

The General Store

The Long General Store operated at Waverly from ca. 1877 to 1897 and two ledger books survive from it. One shows the store's purchases of stock and a list (under the planter's name) of purchases by tenants in 1877 and 1878 (Long 1885). The list shows the planter's name at the page's top and below that the monthly accounts of each tenant by dollar amounts rather than product. The 1887–1889 ledger pages were organized differently (Long 1889). An individual name was at the page top and each daily purchase listed below by date, item, quantity, and price. From these we can see Christmas Eve purchases of candy and nuts by a planter and new clothes bought by tenants just before the annual Emancipation Day celebrations. Items listed by date include not only purchases but also entries for renting mules, cotton ginning, ferriage, and legal fees. As typical for most rural American general stores, the storekeeper played an very important role as culture broker (Adams 1977; Carson 1965; Clark 1944).

The storekeeper served many functions other than selling merchandise. Henry C.

Long served the community in a pivotal role as banker, buyer, middleman, and postman. "As a salesman, middleman, issuer of credit, banker, supplier of necessities and some luxuries, as shipper of farm crops and local manufactures, the country trader had contacts with all his neighbors and with the larger commercial world" (Carson 1965:117). "There was, perhaps, no other rural citizen, living within a ten to twenty mile radius of the store, who touched life at as many different places as the retailer" (Carson 1965:118). Tenants' entries occasionally listed "Cash $1.00" or some other amount, but usually in even dollars, indicating Long gave them cash to spend elsewhere. Just as frequently were entries showing that Long served as a middleman in transactions: "Hire mules 13 days $7.80," "fixing wagon $6.25," "By amt due him G.P.R.R. $10.40," "Making coffin Wm Miller $2.50." Long paid their doctor bills, their taxes, and their fees for marriage, divorce, deeds, and lawsuits. He also bought their produce; for example, in October and November of 1888, J. Arnold settled up at the store as follows: fish $2.20, 40 bu seed $3.20, 22 bu corn $16.20, 40 bu corn $18.40, 68 days work $61.20. "The country dealer's principal asset was the produce he collected through the barter trade" (Carson 1965:67) for he was able to profit on its purchase and resale. Through Long, Georgia P. Young, a planter, paid to have tenant (probably) Jasper's chimney built for $4.00 and a well cleaned for $1.50. In 1880 Long paid $1200 for 10 mules which he resold to tenants and collected 15% interest. Thus, Long served an important role in a relatively cashless economy, providing tenants with supplies, buying their cotton and produce, redistributing produce within Waverly, and selling the surplus to outside markets.

The store ledger listed scores of individuals from the surrounding area, resident as well as visitor. Even the construction of the nearby railroad was documented by purchases from various companies and individuals noted with "G.P.R.R." Because of the time available to us for the research and no access to a computer then, we were not able to take advantage of the full wealth of data in these ledgers. For now we have to be satisfied with a sample of 12 tenant years (five tenants for 2 years, plus two tenants for 1 year). Subjectively, we are fairly comfortable with the sample representing the tenant community, for after studying the sample, we scanned the rest of the ledger for differences and similarities. The people selected were ones mentioned in our oral history and for whom in several cases we had census data available. While our first priority was to use those individuals living in the sites excavated, only Henry Goodall occurs in both the ledger and at the specific site. These people are profiled below.

TENANT PROFILES

The following black tenants were chosen for study from the Long ledger. While only the man's name was listed, we must remember the record was for an entire household. One black landowner, Hiram Finney, was identified from land rolls and found listed in the ledger, so he was selected for comparison with the landless tenant, the storekeeper (Henry Long), and the two planters (Capt. Billy Young and his brother, Major Val Young). The objective was to determine the differences and similarities between the landed and the landless, rich and poor, black and white. Were some items exclusive indicators of certain classes of people? Would such items appear in an archaeological context where status might not be known?

Henry Goodall was born in Mississippi in 1861 and married Lou (b. 1862) in 1883. They had four children, Ella (b. 1883), Sarah (b. 1884), Sidney (b. 1885), and Nona (b. 1898) (U.S. Census of Population 1900). We suspect they moved to site 22CL571B at the time of their marriage and stayed until about 1910. He was also the only tenant for which detailed purchase records existed at Long's store for the 1870s. In 1878 Goodall worked for Alexander Hamilton, a son-in-law of Col. Young. Hamilton died that same year and in his probated estate records was a ledger page from the Long store (ledger no longer extant). Each of Hamilton's tenants were listed by their own name and individual purchases, thus we can compare Goodall's purchases for 1878, 1887, and 1888 (Table 14.1). Prices did not change much at those points in time. His 1878 purchases appear similar, but several items stand out: he purchased $6.30 in eggs (probably 63 dozen), as well as, chickens, fish, potash, and fodder. This appears to indicate his status as a young, 17-year-old bachelor, not yet established in his own house. The similarities between his amounts for purchases as a bachelor and those of his married household a decade later were considerable. Married life brought an increase in costs for clothing and medicine, and a decrease in consumption of alcohol, tobacco, and laundry products. Clothing, shoes, and cloth were 22.4% of his purchases in 1878, but 34% the decade later. Thus, between 85% and 94% of his purchases at Long's were for food and clothing, leaving little money to purchase anything else. In 1887 Goodall ginned 5 bales of cotton, selling one bale to Long for $44.70. His rent for the year consisted of one-third of the cotton crop—1.67 bales, worth $74.50—leaving him with 2.33 bales which he apparently sold elsewhere. It is unlikely that he received cash because Long would have known this and asked Goodall to settle his store debt of $149.26. Since those 2.33 bales were worth $148.85, it is possible that Long had set a credit limit of five bales worth of merchandise, knowing Goodall's production capability from previous years, and that those bales settled Goodall's account from the previous year. In any case, Goodall began the year with the $44.70 credit and the $149.26 debt. He added to that debt in 1888, and by the fall sold Long "1/2 of 3 B/C" for $64.15, giving him $108.85 in accumulated credit and $289.38 in debts, a net deficit of $180.53 starting out in 1889.

Clem Mathews lived in a log house a few hundred feet southwest of the store. His son ran the steam-powered gin near the bath house during the early twentieth century. In 1887 his only credit was the $6.75 for corn, while by year's end he had accumulated $132.66 in store debts. In 1888 he earned $12.80 working on the railroad construction, sold $2.50 worth of beef and three bales of cotton for $141.05, for a total credit of $163.10 and an indebtedness of $369.39. This meant he started 1889 owing Long $206.29.

Marshall Sissney was remembered by informants as the ferryman during the early

Table 14.1
COMPARISON OF HENRY GOODALL'S PURCHASES

	1878		1887		1888	
	Dollars	Percentage	Dollars	Percentage	Dollars	Percentage
Clothing	$6.80	5.31%	$16.95	14.09%	$12.05	9.44%
Shoes	7.75	6.06	11.00	9.14	11.25	8.82
Adornment	—	—	—	—	—	—
Grooming	—	—	—	—	.25	.20
Medicine	1.53	1.20	2.15	1.79	3.10	2.43
Tobacco	6.73	5.26	1.95	1.62	—	—
Alcohol	.75	.59	—	—	—	—
Personal	—	—	—	—	.40	.31
Infant care	—	—	—	—	—	—
Furnishings	—	—	—	—	—	—
Food	69.56	54.36	71.05	59.06	64.70	50.72
Culinary	—	—	—	—	.85	.67
Gustatory	.20	.16	—	—	—	—
Cleaning	—	—	.50	.42	.30	.23
Laundry	2.15	1.68	.25	.21	—	—
Illumination	2.25	1.76	.60	.50	.55	.43
Entertainment and Business	.10	.08	—	—	—	—
Construction	.20	.16	—	—	.25	.20
Hardware	1.43	1.12	.80	.66	—	—
Tools	1.00	.78	—	—	1.50	1.18
Agricultural equipment	—	—	.50	.42	.90	.71
Feed/seeds	1.35	1.05	—	—	11.18	8.76
Fishing	—	—	—	—	—	—
Hunting	2.35	1.84	.30	.25	—	—
Transportation	—	—	.20	.17	—	—
Other	9.70	7.58	.15	.12	—	—
Total	$127.97	100.02%	$120.31	100.01%	$127.56	100.00%

twentieth century. In 1887, he made few purchases ($59.78) and sold only one bale of cotton ($44.70) for a carryover of $15.08 into the next year. In 1888 he owed Long $70.62 more, sold a bale of cotton for $39.52, which left him $46.18 in debt carried into 1889.

Walter Ivy lived in the quarters at the Upper Place. He owed Long $31.06 for 1886, plus $3.11 in interest (10%). By the end of 1887 he had increased his debt to $114.17, less $14.00 for 29 days work in February and March. In November of that year he paid (via Long) for cotton picking help, but sold no cotton to Long. Presumably the entire crop went toward rent. The next year was little better, for he began 1889 owing Long $129.55.

George Washington had no cotton picking or ginning charged to him in 1887. Apparently all the crop went toward rent, leaving him owing Long $129.21, less

Table 14.2
HIRAM FINNEY, CREDITS AND ANNUAL DEBTS

	1887	1888
Meat	$22.50	$17.08
Meal	9.75	7.80
Wages	150.00	150.00
Wages	37.50	—
Cash	74.92	52.25
Rebates	6.82	—
Cotton	6.15	—
Error	—	16.85
Error on wagon	—	34.50
Total indebtedness	−307.64	−451.98
Balance forward	−9.90	+41.82

$.85 in credit. In 1888 he received $6.00 for working on the railroad and also paid Long $10.30 in cash. Thus, he began 1889 owing Long $249.76.

William Taylor produced four bales of cotton in 1887, selling half to Long for $83.40, the other half probably going for rent. He also paid $10.00 in cash, leaving him owing only $7.35 to Long. In 1888 no mention was made of his paying Long for ginning or picking, but he did acquire $60.00 in cash somewhere, since he paid cash for part of his settlement. He may have worked on the railroad or have ginned his cotton elsewhere. In any case, he began 1889 owing Long $26.69.

Mort Dudley appeared only in one year, either 1887 or 1888, but he had been trading with Long for three years previously since he owed three years of interest ($1.50) on the house he rented for $5.00 annually. In addition he rented 5 acres of land for $15.00, on which he produced two bales of cotton. One bale he sold to Long for $45.65, the other (less 169 pounds given to Elijah Collins to settle some debt) sold for $29.35. He settled his account at the store at the end of the year for cash, even.

Hiram Finney was the ferryman in 1887 and 1888. He was paid $150.00 each year in wages for "labor at ferry" and was given a ration ("meat allowed at ferry $17.08, meal allowed $7.80"). In addition to this he worked for the railroad in 1888, rented a sweet potato patch from Long, sold sweet potatoes and peas, and raised cotton. The ledgers do not mention how much cotton was raised or sold—perhaps it went to pay for the small farm he had recently bought. He settled his store debt in a variety of ways (Table 14.2).

ANALYZING THE DATA

In this study, we have sampled data on material culture from the 1887–1888 ledger of the Henry C. Long General Store at Waverly (Long 1885, 1889). These data have been subjected to the following kinds of analyses:

1. reconstruction of the store inventory;
2. comparison of pricing structure;
3. comparison of seasonality of purchase by compiling monthly purchases for certain individuals;
4. comparison of tenant farmers' purchases with those of a black landowner, the storekeeper, and two planters;
5. contrasting the store inventory and their purchases with the items' archaeological visibility.

Store Inventory

We reconstructed the store's 1887–1888 inventory by comparing the purchase lists for the tenants surveyed and then adding categories derived from scanning the other pages (Table 14.3). While this inventory may seem like a considerable variety of merchandise relatively few items within any group of items would be purchased by a tenant in any given year and the stock on hand would not have been great. The inventory provided the range of goods available to tenants, travelers, and planters. The terms used in the original ledger are presented in Table 14.3 and their function determined by context within the entry; hence, items like sheeting and bull tongue are in their correct typological locations. This inventory was arranged within the functional typology used for the archaeological materials (Smith *et al.* 1980:263–284). This typology was derived from one developed in the early 1970s by Roderick Sprague (1981) and used for the Silcott studies (Adams 1977:32–69; Riordan 1976). Items were placed into functional categories according to our historical and oral historical knowledge of the most probable *primary* function of the items. Some multifunctional items presented problems solved by consulting historical catalogs or farm almanacs and comparing their prices with those in the ledgers. Illegible items and other transactions, like ferriage, were subtracted from the totals. For the artifacts, we used estimated vessel counts for glass and ceramics, assigning a function on the basis of form, decoration, embossing, and labeling. Unidentifiable items and small unassignable fragments of glass or ceramics were subtracted from totals. Our methods are similar to those of Stanley South for his various artifact patterns, although we did not use his functional typology (South 1977), preferring the Sprague functional typology because its components were far better defined.

Pricing Structure

One way for the storekeeper to earn a higher profit was through a system of differential pricing. This system varied from store to store. Often only a code rather than the prices were marked on items. This allowed storekeepers to charge some people more than others without their knowledge (Carson 1965:93–94). This does not appear to be the case for the Long store. Price differences did occur, but these appear to be related to three variables: seasonal availability, different quality of merchandise, and the credit system.

Table 14.3
THE RECONSTRUCTED INVENTORY OF GOODS SOLD AT HENRY C. LONG'S GENERAL STORE IN 1887 AND 1888

Clothing				
hose	socks	stockings	corset	drawers
undershirt	cravat	balmoral	pants	leggins
coat	overcoat	vest	gloves	cotton veil
hat	shirt	collar	collar button	jersey jacket
overalls	handkerchief	suspenders	suit of clothes	
Footwear				
boots	men's	women's	child's	shoes, general
button shoe				
Adornment				
initial pin	beads	cuff button	breast pin	
Grooming and hygiene				
hair pins	chill tonic	vermifuge	fever specific	paregoric
cologne	quinine	liniment	soothing drops	bitters
beads	pills	syrup	cough medicine	lung balm
castor oil	ague	tonic	liver medicine	eye water
cardui	sweet oil	sulphur	laudanum	turpentine
Indulgences				
tobacco	snuff	drink	McCleans Cordial	
cheroots	cigarettes	flask		
cigars	pipe	paper	1/2 gallon whiskey	
Personal accoutrements				
knife	pocket book	unbrella	parasol	fan
pocket knife	cane			
Infant care				
baby powder				
Furnishings				
furniture				
Food				
molasses	sugar	flour	rice	meal
meat	beef	lamb	chicken	sardines
salmon	fish	oysters	saltpeter	chewing gum
salt	catsup	cider	mustard	baking powder
vinegar	lard	coffee	vanilla extract	butter
mush	grits	peas	crackers	lemon extract
nuts	candy	ginger	cream of tartar	pepper
cheese	apples	eggs		
Culinary				
strainer	sifter	dipper	coffee pot	coffee mill
tin pan	skillet	pan	pie plates	boiler
well bucket	milk bucket			
Gustatory				
plates	dishes	bowls	pitchers	saucer & cup
cup	saucer	goblet	talecloth	bowl & pitcher
knife	fork	spoon	tin cup	set knives/forks
Cleaning				
towel	broom	soap bars	dish pan	blacking
bucket	blacking brush			

Table 14.3 Continued

Laundry				
soap	starch	bluing	bleach soda	iron
Sewing				
calico	osnaburg	jeans	domestic	checks
linsey	black	shirting	black domestic	ribbon
drilling	quilt lining	ticks	stripes	dress patterns
lace	cottonade	lawn	hickory stripes	cotton flannel
cloth	gingham	bed linen	thread	silk thread
scissors	needles	pins	buttons	thimble
Portable illumination				
lantern	lamp wick	lamp	oil can	lamp oil
matches	lamp chimney			
Household entertainment and business				
3rd reader	5th reader	books	passbook	slate pencil
pencil	pen	pen holder	ink	*Chicago Times*
paper	writing paper	envelopes	pack of cards	stamps
harp	harmonica			
Architecture				
plank	sheeting	wood	nails	screws
tacks	hinges	lock	padlock	hammer
axe	steel axe	hatchet	axe handle	file
chisel	linseed oil	mill saw file		
Agriculture				
hoe	shovel	spade	sugar	plow shoes
rope	singletree	buckles	heel bolt	back band
sweep	bull tongue	plowpoint	plow lines	curry comb
plow stock	turning plow	hame	hame strap	beans
corn	seed corn	seeds	onion sets	oats
corn sack	cotton seed	potatoes	turnip seeds	
Fishing				
line	hooks			
Hunting				
powder	shells	shot	caps	ammunition
wads	cardboard	gun cleaner		
Transportation				
saddle	bridle	mule	buggy whip	rod on hack
wagon	axle grease	traces	spring seat	stirrips, girdle, leathers

In order to examine these variables, we compared the unit prices paid by tenants, a black farmer, the storekeeper himself, and two planters (Table 14.4). Three commodities were chosen—meat, meal, and molasses—under the assumption these would not include quality differences; therefore the prices charged different kinds of customers indicate a differential pricing structure. The white storekeeper and planters were paying less than the black farmer and tenants, but this likely reflects credit versus cash prices and ability to pay, not racial prejudices as such. The storekeeper in America usually charged cash prices and credit prices, the latter dependent upon the trustworthiness of the individual (Carson 1965:93). If you paid cash then you paid

Table 14.4
COMPARISON OF PER-UNIT COST FOR MEAT, MEAL, AND MOLASSES

	Meat (lb)	Meal (bu)	Molasses (gal)
Tenant	$.125	$.778	$.603
Farmer	.112	.603	.560
Storekeeper	.106	—	.550
Planter	.105	.545	.533

less than if you charged items. In addition, a 10% interest was charged on any balance remaining after settling the debt at harvest. Even in the hands of a benign and well-meaning merchant such a system creates feedback, and eventually would force most tenants into debt. There are indications of a cash price system in Long's 1887–1888 ledger. One entry mentions an item sold on credit "coat and vest, cash price $1.60." Other entries have two figures marked down, the one owed being 10% higher than the cash price. With such a system the poor in essence lost 10% of their expendable income on every purchase, for few ever paid in cash.

Seasonal differences also were observed in prices, peaking in the summer and lowering as the new corn and sorghum crops became available (Figure 14.1). What

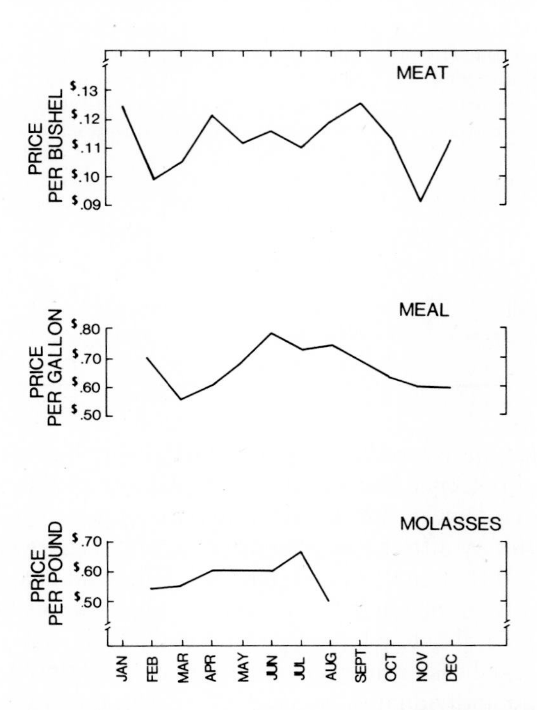

Figure 14.1 Monthly price averages for meat, meal, and molasses.

cannot be determined is whether this resulted from increased demand, fewer supplies, or both. Ledger entries of "meat" are assumed to mean pork since beef and chicken are distinguished by name. Meat prices fluctuated the most.

Seasonality of Purchase

In order to study seasonality, the purchases were compiled on a monthly basis and this then compared to the agricultural calendar. Purchases of certain items were well correlated with seasons; for example, small amounts of nails were purchased in the late winter and early spring, a slack period in the agricultural cycle often used for making general repairs, according to informants. Hoes were bought in the spring for chopping cotton.

Based upon the sample of 12 tenants listed in the 1887–1888 ledger (Table 14.5; Figure 14.2) and the oral history, we may construct the following calendar: *December to January*—worked at sawmills, brickyards, made charcoal, general fix-up of homestead and equipment; *February to late March*—fix-up continues (86.5% of annual nail purchases then), set out onions, buy seeds, early plowing (44.4% of plow points bought in March), planting, weeding begins in garden (12.5% of hoe purchases); *late March to late April*—plant cotton, weed garden (25% of hoe purchases); *May and June*—chop cotton (62.5% of hoes purchased), plow (22.2% of points), shear sheep in May; *July and August*—construction, plant winter vegetables, harvest vegetables; *September to December*—pick cotton, butcher pigs. Similar seasonality was observed for the tenant farmers at Sharpley's Bottom upriver from Waverly (Kern *et al.* 1982b:85–91).

The summer and winter months free from cotton chores were spent gardening and obtaining any extra cash by working at the sawmills, brickyards, or by making charcoal to peddle in town. Those months were spent working on the homestead, fixing leaky roofs, building sheds, making furniture, repairing harnesses, and sewing clothing. Based upon the average thread consumption for 1887–1888, many clothes were made or mended in March (21%) and June (18.2%), with lesser numbers produced in July (12.7%), August (12.7%), and May (10.9%). The least amount of thread was used in April and from September to January, this corresponding in part to the increased demands of cotton production at those times of the year.

The demands of cotton and corn production at Waverly would have reduced the time available to hunt, fish, and gather wild plants. This has also been noted at Sharpley's Bottom and is evidenced there in 1918 by an increased purchase of cornmeal and meat from April to October (Kern *et al.* 1982b:91). At Waverly, lead shot and black powder were purchased only during slower agricultural months: February, March, June, July, and September. Based upon oral history, the tenants supplemented their diets substantially with wild foods. Informants mentioned hunting raccoon, opossum, squirrel, rabbit, and turtle, fishing for brim, buffalo, catfish, and eel, and gathering berries and nuts. Fish were taken with hook and line, fish baskets, and net seines. Pigs were turned loose in the woods to forage and 100-pound shoats harvested by hunting. In 1888 hunting was with cap-and-ball rifles, as shown in the ledgers, but the archaeology revealed a much wider assortment: shot-

Table 14.5

MONTHLY CONSUMPTION OF SELECTED ITEMS

	J	F	M	A	M	J	J	A	S	O	N	D
Cotton seed[a]	—	—	—	1	—	—	—	—	—	—	—	—
Seeds, papers of[b]	—	—	15	—	—	—	—	—	—	—	—	—
Onion sets[a]	—	—	2	—	—	—	—	—	—	—	—	—
Seed corn[a]	—	—	1	—	—	—	—	—	—	—	—	—
Turning plow[b]	—	1	—	—	—	—	—	—	—	—	—	—
Plowpoint[b]	—	—	4	—	2	1	1	—	1	—	—	—
Sweep[b]	—	—	1	—	—	—	—	—	—	—	—	—
Bull tongue[b]	—	—	1	—	—	—	—	—	—	—	—	—
Hoe[b]	—	—	2	4	10	—	—	—	—	—	—	—
Powder[c]	—	.20	.30	—	—	.20	.10	—	.16	—	—	—
Shot[c]	—	.10	.40	—	—	.30	.10	—	.24	—	—	—
Oil[c]	—	.10	.55	.85	.05	.25	.50	.35	.05	.55	—	—
Nails in pounds	—	20	38	1	—	1	—	1	5	1	—	—

[a]Number of purchases.
[b]Number of units.
[c]Dollar amounts.

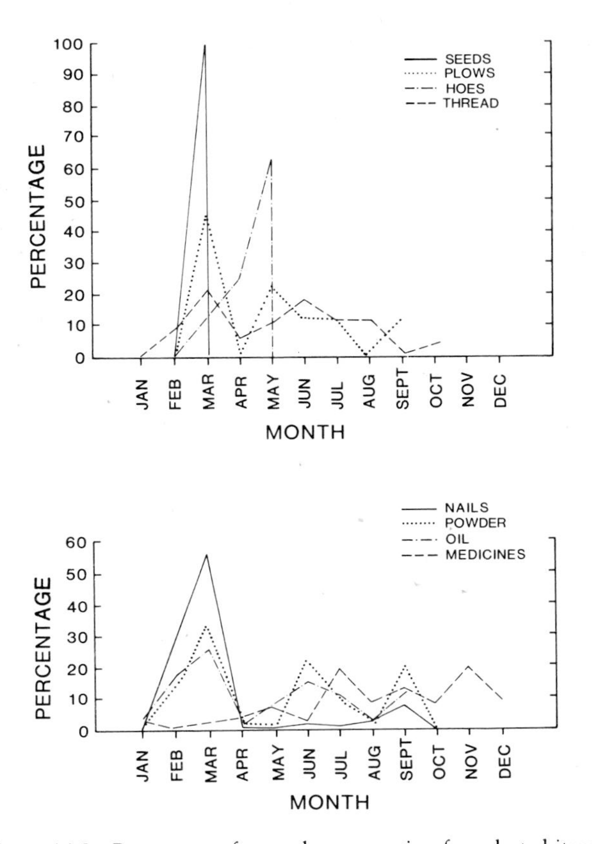

Figure 14.2 Percentage of annual consumption for selected items.

guns (10-, 12-, 16-, and 20-gauge; .410), rifles and pistols (.22, .32, .38, .44, and .45 calibers) but only one lead ball and no sprue.

William Richard Adams (1980) analyzed the zooarchaeological materials from Waverly tenant sites (1880s–1940s) and identified the following species: deer, opossum, raccoon, fox squirrel, gray squirrel, cottontail rabbit, swamp rabbit, groundhog, wood rat, partridge, prairie chicken, mallard, wood duck, scaup, soft-shell turtle, snapping turtle, channel catfish, bullhead catfish, brim, bowfin, buffalo, red horse, sauger, and river mussels; domesticated fauna like sheep, goat, pig, cow, chicken, duck, rabbit; and presumably nonfood fauna like horse, dog, cat, Norway rat, and box turtle. Deer and cow were harvested as older individuals.

Ledger data reveal that nearly all meat purchased was pork. While fish, chicken, and lamb were sold there, none of the tenants surveyed purchased any. In the ledger, hog meat was 32 times as common as beef by weight for tenants, but in the archaeological assemblage the two were about equal using two different means of calculating the meat weight (0.87:1, pork:beef using an average of several sources; 1.12:1, pork:beef using White 1953).

Comparison of Purchases

Purchases at the Long store were compared to examine the differences between expenditures by black tenant farmers, a black landowner, and two white planters (Table 14.6). Several problems must be recognized before interpretation begins. Did the tenants have enough money to make significant purchases at other stores? This can only be approached in terms of their production of the major cash crop, cotton. On the Armstead Plantation just west of Waverly, the 1880 tenant average was 4.8 bales of cotton. From the ginning records of Long we think the 12 tenants surveyed did not produce quite this much, certainly they were not credited with more than two or three bales above their rent, for all but one tenant finished the year in debt by the equivalent of one to five bales of cotton. The average amount of purchases for the 12 tenants was $112.18 and this figure does not include banking transactions like mule rental. Given a production of four bales, less one for rent, this would provide an annual income of only $120 to $130 or so. Thus, we see that the tenants had little, if any, ability to purchase items outside of Waverly except when they worked as day laborers during the slack periods in the agricultural calendar. We assume that the Long ledger data for the tenants closely approximates their total purchases for the years indicated. The same is true for the black landowner and probable ferryman, Hiram Finney. The storekeeper and the two planters certainly would have purchased many things not on the store ledger, so we must be careful in comparing their purchases with those of the tenants. However, on the basis of what they did purchase, we see the differences as largely economic, not social or racial as such.

Comparison of the various statuses does show some important differences. We would expect the greatest similarity to be between the black tenants and the black landowner since the latter had just purchased his property was still probably maintaining much of his tenant financial attributes. The storekeeper would support his own business, so we may expect whenever possible he made his purchases at his own store. But he would also be in an excellent position to order better items directly from companies and would have traveled to town more often to handle business matters. The planters must have made substantial purchases in town and directly from companies. The only perspective we have is on what they actually bought at Long's, not their total purchase patterns.

Of the 27 groups presented as percentage of purchases in Table 14.6, the tenant was the highest ranked in only four groups (clothing, alcohol, personal items, and construction materials); however, only the clothing group is of a size sufficient enough to be significant. The tenant spent 5 to 10 times what the others did for ready-made clothing, in terms of relative totals. The black landowner ranked the highest in eight groups (shoes, medicine, infant care, home business/entertainment, tools, agricultural equipment, feed/seed, and transportation), some of these likely reflecting the increased expenditures necessary for a new farmer to replace the goods formerly supplied to him as a tenant. Not included in this ranking was the purchase of a wagon ($28.75) because it would have skewed the other figures for items with substantially shorter lifespans. Of particular interest was Finney's subscription to the

Table 14.6
COMPARISON OF TENANT, LANDOWNER, STOREKEEPER, AND PLANTER

	Black tenants		Black landowner		Storekeeper		Planters	
Clothing	$31.61	28.18%	$4.54	4.95%	$4.50	3.85%	$4.28	2.84%
Shoes	7.88	7.02	9.42	10.26	1.50	1.28	4.88	3.24
Adornment	—	—	—	—	2.05	1.76	.31	.21
Grooming	.06	.05	—	—	.60	.51	.05	.03
Medicine	1.54	1.37	4.55	4.96	4.00	3.43	1.25	.83
Tobacco items	1.63	1.45	1.20	1.31	.20	.17	2.42	1.61
Alcohol	.12	.11	—	—	—	—	—	—
Personal	.36	.32	—	—	.30	.21	.25	.16
Infant care	—	—	.14	.15	—	—	—	—
Furnishings	—	—	—	—	—	—	6.25	4.15
Food	43.04	38.37	26.32	28.67	24.43	20.92	81.50	54.09
Culinary	.09	.08	.15	.16	1.00	.86	.12	.07
Gustatory	.22	.20	.05	.05	—	—	.94	.62
Cleaning	.22	.20	.60	.65	6.40	5.48	1.20	.79
Laundry	.24	.21	.88	.96	2.40	2.06	2.23	1.48
Sewing	10.11	9.01	11.98	13.05	37.31	31.95	11.50	7.63
Illumination	.60	.53	2.85	3.10	16.40	14.04	3.56	2.36
Entertain/business	.05	.04	2.42	2.64	2.88	2.47	1.35	.89
Construction material	.97	.86	.05	.05	.30	.17	.04	.03
Hardware	.52	.46	.78	.85	1.30	1.11	9.65	6.40
Tools	.17	.15	1.15	1.25	1.00	.86	.30	.20
Agricultural equipment	2.36	2.10	3.95	4.30	1.60	1.37	.99	.66
Feed/seeds	7.77	6.93	10.67	11.62	4.65	3.98	7.57	5.02
Fishing	—	—	—	—	—	—	.06	.04
Hunting	.22	.20	.82	.89	3.25	2.75	3.89	2.58
Transportation	1.86	1.66	7.17[a]	7.81	.50	.43	1.07	.71
Other	.54	.48	2.10	2.29	.30	.26	5.02	3.33
Total	$112.18	99.98%	$91.79	99.97%	$116.77	99.99%	$150.68	99.97%

[a]Does not include $28.75 for a wagon.

Chicago Times and his purchase of a "3rd and 5th Reader," probably McGuffy's Reader. The storekeeper was highest in seven groups (adornment, grooming, culinary, cleaning, sewing, illumination, and hunting). While one could argue a greater emphasis on appearance from these data, this would be inaccurate—the storekeeper could simply better afford those nonessential items. Surprisingly, one-third of Long's purchases were for cloth; obviously he was having clothing made. Not surprisingly, lamp oil, chimneys, and wicks were a substantial expenditure along with writing paper. The averages for the planters produced only six groups being the highest (tobacco, furnishings, food, hardware, fishing, and other). The planters' consumptions must have been greater, so we assume that we are seeing the local purchases, those less in value and more mundane.

Archaeological Visibility

The final area of study lay in the archaeological visibility of tenant farmers in the late 1880s. Archaeological visibility means the ability to see a past event or occupation at a site in terms of the physical changes there and, hence, record its observable attributes. Visibility as a factor of importance has been briefly examined by several authors (Baker 1980; Deetz 1977:14–15; Gould 1977:362–364). Visibility generally increases with:

1. intensity of occupation;
2. length of occupation;
3. higher economic and social status;
4. permanence of occupation;
5. access to and ability to purchase durable building materials;
6. time (correlated with increase in industrial production and hence availability of merchandise).

In order to quantify our observations the ledger data was compared with the archaeological data from two houses at the Goodall/Mathews site (22CL571). The Henry Goodall cabin (22CL571B) was a log dogtrot with a stick-and-mud chimney; it was located several hundred feet north of the main ferry road. The cabin was built probably in 1884 when Henry and Lou were married. On the basis of artifacts the site dates from the 1880s until the 1910s; informants remember the cabin standing in the 1910s but felt that the Goodalls had moved to the Cook Plantation prior to 1913. Thus, this site is particularly comparable to the ledger data; indeed, the items listed may have been recovered in the excavations. The Ellen Mathews house was described by informants and revealed by excavations to be a one-room frame house. Jimmy Witherspoon was the earliest known occupant, but little is known about him. He was born a slave and was a renter at Waverly in 1888—the year he appeared in the Long ledgers, he was still a renter in 1913 (Young 1913). It is assumed that this was his house during this time. A concrete headstone marks his grave on the hill above. Ellen and Jeff Mathews moved to Waverly in the late 1910s or early 1920s to be with their grown son and his family. They were old and supported themselves as day laborers—chopping and picking cotton, fishing in the Tombigbee, gardening, and perhaps renting a small patch for a cash crop. Jeff died in the early 1930s and Ellen stayed on there until the 1940s. Artifacts recovered from the site indicate the initial occupation occurred during the late 1880s or early 1890s and that relatively little material was deposited until the 1920s. Most of the artifacts from the site date to the period of the Mathews occupation, the ca. 1920–1950 period. Informants stated that only blacks lived at these two houses, so ethnicity is comparable to the ledger data.

With the store ledger we have the rare opportunity to study the kinds of items entering the cultural system at Waverly. At an archaeological site one studies the residue, the outflow from that cultural system. That residue is incomplete, however, because some items never leave the system and are curated sufficiently to be inherited by later people. Other items enter the archaeological record incompletely; for example, we find only a rim sherd from a plate or one blade from a pair of scissors. Some artifacts are lost, others discarded casually or purposefully—each is represented differently in the archaeological remains. Once the items leave the cultural system they are subjected to a host of natural factors of movement and decay. Time diminishes the artifacts of humanity and we are left with only bits and pieces. Let us examine the store inventory by using an archaeological eye (Eiseley 1971:81) to imagine those items as discarded and resting in the ground for a century. What would remain?

What would remain can be seen by examining the artifacts recovered from the excavated sites. What would not remain in any quantity would be the the organic materials like paper, cloth, leather, wood, and food products. Since most tenant purchases at the store were food and clothing, those groups are grossly underrepresented archaeologically when compared to the store ledger. Nothing would remain of the cloth itself; of the finished clothing, only buttons, corset stays, hooks, and suspender hardware would last much time. Shoes would leave their more durable fragments, like hooks, buttons, eyes, nails, screws, rubber soles, and heels. Food generally was sold in bulk packages wrapped in brown paper at the store.

Items like sugar, rice, and meal—frequent ledger items—would not have their archaeological correlates. Meat represented the bulk of the food purchases, so we might expect bones, but the extremely acid soils of Waverly must have destroyed many. (The bones that did survive are etched and lack the outer cell layers.) While Long did sell condiments like extracts in bottles, the tenants rarely purchased any. In brief, virtually everything the tenant bought would not have survived more than a few years in the ground. What we are viewing archaeologically are the 10% to 20% of the purchases having a durable nature. Items like dishes and pans would survive, but the tenants rarely purchased them at the store. Glass survives well, but in the average year only $1.54 was spent on medicines (4–6 bottles), and few other sources of glass were present: bluing bottles, snuff bottles, lamps, and lamp chimneys. Canning jars are never mentioned in the store inventory nor are stoneware vessels like jugs or crocks. Tin cans appear infrequently in the ledgers: snuff, salmon, sardines, and possibly turpentine and linseed oil containers. Construction hardware and tools would be found archaeologically as would agricultural equipment like hoes and harness hardware. By comparing the ledger data with the archaeological data, we can begin to appreciate how much of the cultural data is missing. We would never know that Hiram Finney read with interest the activities in Chicago. Even though we may learn much about tenant life from the archaeology, we must recognize that the ephemeral tenant is largely invisible from the material realm, as well as the historical one.

The results of our comparisons between tenant expenditures and the archaeological record are presented in Table 14.7. The ratio of the archaeological to the ledger data (A:L) provides a valuable perspective. In preliminary analysis, the results were heavily skewed by the architectural and construction data, like nails, where 10,137 nails were found at the sites but only $2.03 worth of nails were found in the

Table 14.7

COMPARISON OF ARCHAEOLOGICAL AND STORE LEDGER FREQUENCIES FOR TENANTS

	Store ledger		22CL571A&D		22CL571B		Combined		Difference	A:L ratio
Sewing	$10.11	9.18%	8	.58%	2	.51%	10	.56%	−8.62%	1:16.38
Agriculture	10.13	9.20	45	3.26	34	8.63	79	4.45	−4.75	1:2.07
Clothing/shoes	39.49	35.85	276	20.00	77	19.54	353	19.91	−15.95	1:1.80
Food	43.04	39.07	417	30.24	113	28.68	530	29.89	−9.18	1:1.3
Illumination and heat	.60	.55	15	1.09	3	.76	18	1.10	.46	1.84:1
Grooming	1.60	1.45	40	2.90	12	3.04	52	2.93	1.48	2.02:1
Transportation	1.86	1.69	68	4.93	19	4.82	87	4.91	3.21	2.90:1
Personal accoutrements	.36	.33	15	1.09	5	1.27	20	1.13	.80	3.42:1
Cleaning/laundry	.46	.42	24	1.74	2	.51	26	1.47	1.04	3.48:1
Indulgences	1.75	1.59	109	7.90	13	3.30	122	6.88	5.29	4.33:1
Tools	.17	.15	41	2.97	11	2.80	52	2.93	2.78	19.53:1
Hunting	.22	.20	66	4.78	13	3.30	79	4.45	4.25	22.25:1
Culinary	.09	.08	25	1.81	9	2.28	34	1.92	1.84	24:1
Entertainment	.05	.04	33	2.39	10	2.54	43	2.42	2.38	60.50:1
Gustatory	.22	.20	170	12.33	64	16.24	234	13.20	11.16	66:1
Adornment	—	—	8	.58	1	.25	9	.51	.51	—
Domestic furnishings	—	—	17	1.23	4	1.01	21	1.18	1.18	—
Fishing	—	—	2	.14	2	.51	4	.22	.22	—
Total	110.15	100.0%	1379	99.96%	394	99.99%	1773	99.96%		

ledger for the tenants surveyed. Hence, we subtracted these items from the expenditure and archaeological columns to provide a more balanced perspective.

Food items (mostly meat), agricultural equipment, clothing, and shoes occurred in greater frequency in the ledger than in the sites. This probably results from poor preservation of organic remains. For the agricultural category, this may result from many items having fairly long lifespans, as well as the domestic nature of the sites. Food and clothing represent the major expenditures for tenants and are also archaeologically the most visible categories, discounting architecture and construction. Food and clothing represent 74.92% of all ledger expenditure for tenants, while these categories make up 49.80% of the items seen in the archaeological record. A study of 1933 commissary purchases of 25 tenants in Arkansas revealed that 64.40% of purchases were for food and 14.20% for clothing (Woofter 1936:102), remarkably similar to the Waverly sample.

Not too surprisingly, the category of sewing (mostly cloth) was quite underrepresented archaeologically at a A:L ratio of 1:16.38, largely reflecting poor cloth preservation. Virtually all else was represented archaeologically at a higher frequency than observed in the purchase data. The ranking by category produces three extremes needing discussion. Tools were 19.53 times as frequent archaeologically than in the ledgers. This may indicate that tools were kept around the yard and house after they were broken and not discarded as "trash." Hunting items, like ammunition, appear 22.25 times as frequent archaeologically, but this probably results from a faulty comparison: ledgers list ammunition by the box, while the archaeological data is by cartridge count. Household business and entertainment items appear 60.50 times as frequently in the sites as in the ledgers; the most reasonable explanation appears to be in the manner these artifacts became incorporated in the archaeological site. Most of these items are children's toys, like marbles and broken dolls, items probably lost, not discarded. For most other artifacts from the site we are dealing with fragments swept out the door or kicked around the site; items having no further usage.

CONCLUSIONS

This essay presented a perspective on material culture for tenant farmers at Waverly plantation. We examined the pricing structure in the store ledgers and found that the storekeeper *did* price items differently, but the price variations were probably affected more by seasonality and payment mode (cash or credit) rather than social or racial status as such. Prices for certain staples like meat, meal, and molasses tended to rise during the period of peak demand, either due to that demand, a shortage of supply, or both. Because tenants bought nearly everything on credit, they paid 10% more than a stranger passing through Waverly would have paid in cash for the same items.

The reconstruction of the inventory reflects a wide assortment of goods available to the customers of Long's store. However, the tenants were only rarely able to afford much of the store's available stock; instead they concentrated their purchases mostly on food and clothing. The ledgers also reveal Long's importance to the community because the services he performed were as pivotal to the community as was the merchandise he sold. The ledgers provide a view, not otherwise obtained, of tenant farmer material culture, as well as a picture of the general store. General stores were a very important part of rural life; their ledgers exist in many archives and, in some cases, in the extant stores. A diachronic study of a general store ledger would provide a microcosm of the changes in a community's purchases and hence in their needs and values.

Comparing the purchases of four social status levels of individuals was not as fruitful as hoped. Purchases by the merchant and planter represent an unknown percentage of their total annual expenditures, while the tenant purchases were much more complete. It appears that tenants purchased more ready-made clothing than the other individuals and that planters may have purchased more food. A major problem inherent in this study is that virtually all the store customers were tenant farmers, all most likely with a set credit limit. The white planters and the storekeeper were sporadic customers and obviously relied on many other sources, therefore any comparisons of their purchases may be considered interesting but inconclusive.

The final analysis was to compare the store ledgers with the archaeological record. After deleting the categories of architecture and construction, it was possible to view the correlation between the two sets of data. Many of the initial expectations seemed to be confirmed: food was underrepresented archaeologically as was clothing; most incidentals were underrepresented in the ledgers. Still, it is obvious from both the historical and archaeological data that black tenant farmer material culture at Waverly was heavily oriented toward the necessities of existence—food and clothing. Although the archaeological and archival data provide valuable insights into the poverty of tenant farmers, that very poverty makes those tenants materially ephemeral and invisible.

The Waverly ledger study confirms the value of historical archaeologists using complementary data sets derived from archival, archaeological, and oral sources. No single source provided the past reality of Waverly or its tenant farmers. Only through the use of several data sources was it possible to reconstruct the Goodall family's life in the waning years of the past century. The artifacts and the ledger pages are like pages from a family scrapbook used for only a year or two and then relegated to an attic along with a few relics. The scrapbook's rediscovery years later evokes memories, yet fleeting, ephemeral ones. We can never reconstruct their past, but we can, by combining these many vantage points, see glimpses of their life in that hillside cabin of a century ago.

ACKNOWLEDGMENTS

The research on Waverly Plantation was conducted by many individuals. We especially thank David Barton and Betty Belanus for their oral data on the plantation, Howard Adkins and Jack Elliott Jr. for their archival research, and Timothy Riordan, who was field director. We thank David F. Barton, George L. Miller, Lee Minnerly, Timothy B. Riordan, Stephanie H. Rodeffer, Lester A. Ross, and Stanley South for reading the manuscript of this essay and commenting on various drafts. Mr. and Mrs. Robert Snow of Waverly provided the Long ledger for analysis, without their assistance this study would not have been possible. We also thank the many informants who shared their memories from the turn of the century. The Waverly Project was conducted under contract C-55026(79) with the Heritage Conservation and Recreation Service, with funding from the U.S. Army Corps of Engineers, Mobile District. Versions of this article were presented in the mitigation report and in a paper delivered to the Society for Historical Archaeology meeting in New Orleans, January 1981.

REFERENCES

Adams, William Hampton
1977 Silcott, Washington: Ethnoarchaeology of a rural American community. Laboratory of Anthropology, *Reports of Investigations* 54. Pullman: Washington State University.

Adams, William Hampton, ed.
1980 *Waverly Plantation: Ethnoarchaeology of a Tenant Farming Community.* Washington, D.C.: National Technical Information Service.

Adams, William Hampton, Steven D. Smith, David F. Barton, Timothy B. Riordan, and Stephen Poyser
1981 *Bay Springs Mill: Historical Archaeology of a Rural Mississippi Cotton Milling Community.* Washington, D.C.: National Technical Information Service.

Adams, William Richard
1980 Faunal remains from tenant farmer sites, Waverly Plantation, Mississippi. In *Waverly Plantation: Ethnoarchaeology of a Tenant Farming Community.* William H. Adams, ed. Washington, D.C.: National Technical Information Service. Pp. 437–451.

Agee, James, and Walker Evans
1960 *Let Us Now Praise Famous Men.* New York: Ballantine.

Ascher, Robert, and Charles H. Fairbanks
1971 Excavation of a slave cabin: Georgia, U.S.A. *Historical Archaeology* 5:3–17.

Baker, Vernon G.
1980 Archaeological visibility of Afro-American culture: an example from Black Lucy's garden, Andover, Massachusetts. In *Archaeological Perspectives on Ethnicity in America.* Robert L. Schuyler, ed. Farmingdale, N.Y.: Baywood. Pp. 29–37.

Blassingame, John W.
1972 *The Slave Community.* New York: Oxford University Press.

Branson, E. C.
1923a Social occasions and contacts in a rural county. *The Journal of Social Forces* 1:162–163.
1923b Farm tenancy in the cotton belt: How farm tenants live. *The Journal of Social Forces* 1:213–221.
1923c Farm tenancy in the cotton belt: The social estate of white farm tenants. *The Journal of Social Forces* 1:450–457.

Bridges, Sarah T., and Bert Salwen
1980 Weeksville: The archaeology of a black urban community. In *Archaeological Perspectives on Ethnicity in America.* Robert L. Schuyler, ed. Farmingdale, N.Y.: Baywood. Pp. 38–47.

Carson, Gerald
1965 *The Old Country Store.* New York: Dutton.

Cates, H. R.
1917 *Farm Practice in the Cultivation of Cotton.* U.S. Department of Agriculture Bulletin 551.

Clark, Thomas D.
1944 *Pills, Petticoats and Plows: The Southern Country Store.* Indianapolis: Bobbs-Merrill.

Deetz, James
1977 *In Small Things Forgotten.* Garden City, N.J.: Anchor.

Eiseley, Loren C.
1971 *The Night Country*. New York: Charles Scribner's Sons.
Fairbanks, Charles H.
1974 The Kingsley slave cabins in Duval County, Florida, 1968. *Conference on Historic Site Archaeology Papers, 1972*. 7:62–93.
Fogel, R., and S. Engerman
1974 *Time on the Cross: The Economics of American Negro Slavery*. Boston: Little, Brown.
Geismar, Joan H.
1980 Skunk Hollow: A preliminary statement on archaeological investigations at a 19th century black community. In *Archaeological Perspectives on Ethnicity in America*. Robert L. Schuyler, ed. Farmingdale, N.Y.: Baywood. Pp. 60–68.
Genovese, Eugene
1974 *Roll, Jordan, Roll*. New York: Pantheon Books.
Gould, Richard A.
1977 Some current problems in ethnoarchaeology. In *Experimental Archeology*. Daniel Ingersoll, John E. Yellen, and William MacDonald, eds. New York: Columbia University Press. Pp. 359–377.
Gutman, Herbert C.
1976 *The Black Family in Slavery and Freedom, 1750–1925*. New York: Pantheon Books.
Handler, Jerome S., and Frederick W. Lange
1978 *Plantation Slavery in Barbados: An Archaeological and Historical Investigation*. Cambridge: Harvard University Press.
Johnson, Charles S., Edwin R. Embree, and W. W. Alexander
1935 *The Collapse of Cotton Tenancy*. Chapel Hill: University of North Carolina Press.
Kern, John R.
1980 Interdisciplinary investigations at Sharpley's Bottom historic sites, Tombigbee River Multiple Resource District, Alabama and Mississippi: Interim draft report. Report submitted to the Heritage Conservation and Recreation Service—Atlanta. Jackson, Michigan: Commonwealth Associates.
Kern, John R., C. Stephan Demeter, E. Suzanne Carter, Judith D. Tordoff, C. Jason Dotson, Ira Berlin, Steven F. Miller, Joseph P. Reidy, and Leslie S. Rowland.
1982a Sharpley's Bottom historic sites: Phase I interdisciplinary investigations, Tombigbee River Multiresource District, Alabama and Mississippi. Report submitted to the Heritage Conservation and Recreation Service—Atlanta. Jackson, Michigan: Commonwealth Associates.
Kern, John R., Steven F. Miller, Ira Berlin, and Joseph P. Reidy
1982b Sharpley's Bottom historic sites: Phase II historical investigations, Tombigbee River Multiresource District, Alabama and Mississippi. Report submitted to the Heritage Conservation and Recreation Service—Atlanta. Jackson, Michigan: Commonwealth Associates.
Long, Henry C.
1885 Payment and Receipt Book, 1879–1885. Snow Collection, Waverly National Historic Landmark, Mississippi.
1889 Account Book, 1887–1889. Snow Collection, Waverly National Historic Landmark, Mississippi.
McDaniel, George W.
1979 Preserving a family's history: Black family life, 1770–1979, on the Bennehan-Cameron plantation. Paper presented at the American Anthropological Conference, Cincinnati, Ohio.
Maguire, Jane
1975 *On Shares: Ed Brown's Story*. New York: Norton.
Moore, Sue A. Mullins
1981 The antebellum Barrier Island Plantation: A search for an archaeological pattern. Ph.D. dissertation, Anthropology Department, University of Florida, Gainesville.

Nathans, Sydney
1979 Fortress without walls: A black community after slavery. Paper presented at the American Anthropological Conference, Cincinnati, Ohio.

Otto, John Solomon
1977 Artifacts and status differences: A comparison of ceramics from planter, overseer, and slave sites on an antebellum plantation. In *Research Strategies in Historical Archaeology*. Stanley South, ed. New York: Academic Press. Pp. 91–118.

Prunty, Merle, Jr.
1955 The renaissance of the southern plantation. *The Geographical Review* 45(4):459–491.

Ransom, Roger L., and Richard Sutch
1977 *One Kind of Freedom: The Economic Consequences of Emancipation*. Cambridge: Cambridge University Press.

Riordan, Timothy B.
1976 The Euroamerican occupation of Alpaweyma (45AS82). Master's thesis, Anthropology Department, Washington State University, Pullman.
1978 Relative economic status of black and white regiments in the pre-World War I army: An example from Fort Walla Walla. Paper presented at the 31st Annual Northwest Anthropological Conference, Pullman.

Rosengarten, Theodore
1974 *All God's Dangers*. New York: Knopf.

Schuyler, Robert L.
1974 Sandy ground: Archaeological sampling in a black community in metropolitan New York. *Conference on Historic Site Archaeology Papers* 10(2):99–120.
1980 Sandy ground: Archaeology of a 19th century oystering village. In *Archaeological Perspectives on Ethnicity in America*. Robert L. Schuyler, ed. Farmingdale, N.Y.: Baywood. Pp. 48–59.

Singleton, Theresa
1980 The archaeology of Afro-American slavery in coastal Georgia: A regional perception of slave household and community patterns. Ph.D. dissertation, Anthropology Department, University of Florida, Gainesville.

Smith, Steven D., William Hampton Adams, and Timothy B. Riordan
1980 The humanly touched thing. In *Waverly Plantation: Ethnoarchaeology of a Tenant Farming Community*. William H. Adams, ed. Washington, D.C.: National Technical Information Service. Pp. 263–284.

Smith, Steven D., David F. Barton, and Timothy B. Riordan
1982 *Ethnoarchaeology of the Bay Springs Farmsteads: A Study of Rural American Settlement*. Washington, D.C.: National Technical Information Service.

South, Stanley
1977 *Method and Theory in Historical Archaeology*. New York: Academic Press.

Sprague, Roderick
1981 A functional classification for artifacts from 19th and 20th century historical sites. *North American Archaeologist* 2(3):251–261.

Thomas, Norman
1934 *The Plight of the Share-Cropper*. New York: League for Industrial Democracy.

U.S. Census of Population
1900 Clay County, Mississippi. Department of Archives and History, Jackson.

White, Theodore E.
1953 A method of calcultating the dietary percentage of various food animals utilized by aboriginal peoples. *American Antiquity* 18:393–399.

Works Progress Administration
1941 *Slave Narratives: A Folk History in the United States from Interviews with Former Slaves*. Vol. 9 (Mississippi). Washington, D.C.: Works Progress Administration.

Woofter, Thomas J.
1936 *Landlord and Tenant on the Cotton Plantation*. Research Monograph 5. Washington, D.C.: Works Progress Administration.

Young, George Hampton
1848 Letters to James McDowell. Manuscript on file, Duke University Archives, Durham, North Carolina.

Young, William Lowndes
1913 Probate Court Estate #2365. Clay County Courthouse, West Point, Mississippi.

Index

A

B

C